LAND CLAIMS IN FLORIDA

1824

RECORDS FROM THE 18TH CONGRESS FIRST SESSION
HOUSE OF REPRESENTATIVES DOCUMENT NUMBER 412

U.S. CONGRESS

Heritage Books
2025

HERITAGE BOOKS

AN IMPRINT OF HERITAGE BOOKS, INC.

Books, CDs, and more—Worldwide

For our listing of thousands of titles see our website
at
www.HeritageBooks.com

A Facsimile Reprint
Published 2025 by
HERITAGE BOOKS, INC.
Publishing Division
5810 Ruatan Street
Berwyn Heights, MD 20740

Records from the 18th Congress First Session
House of Representatives Document Number 412
1824

Previously published:
Mountain Press
Signal Mountain, Tennessee
1999

International Standard Book Number
Paperbound: 978-0-7884-9886-2

LAND CLAIMS IN FLORIDA.

COMMUNICATED TO THE HOUSE OF REPRESENTATIVES, MAY 20, 1824.

TREASURY DEPARTMENT, *May* 20, 1824.

The Secretary of the Treasury, by direction of the President, has the honor to transmit, herewith, for the information of the Committee on Public Lands, copies of the following documents, viz:

No. 1. Report from Messrs. Floyd and Blair, commissioners for ascertaining land claims in East Florida, including the evidence taken in the case of John H. McIntosh, taken 21st February, 1824.
2. Decrees of the commissioners.
3. A joint letter from the above commissioners, dated 29th December, 1823.
4. A letter from W. W. Blair, dated 24th September, 1823, enclosing a memorial from the inhabitants of St. Augustine.
5. A letter from the Hon. R. M. Johnson, enclosing one from W. W. Blair, dated 21st February, 1824.
6. A letter from W. W. Blair, dated 7th August, 1823.
7. A letter from Alexander Hamilton, dated 14th July, 1823.
8. A letter from Alexander Hamilton, dated 12th January, 1824.
9. A letter from Alexander Hamilton, dated 22d January, 1824.
10. A letter from Alexander Hamilton, dated 23d January, 1824.
11. A letter from Alexander Hamilton, dated 31st March, 1824.
12. A letter from Alexander Hamilton, dated 1st May, 1824.

The minutes of the Board of Commissioners, and the evidence taken in the other cases acted upon by them, are too voluminous to be transcribed in season to be submitted to the committee during the present session of Congress.

Hon. CHRISTOPHER RANKIN, *Chairman Committee on Public Lands.*

No. 1.

Report of Davis Floyd and W. W. Blair, Land Commissioners in East Florida.

JOHN H. McINTOSH AND OTHERS, *vs.* UNITED STATES.

In conformity to the provision of an act of Congress, passed on the 8th of May, 1822, constituting a Board of Land Commissioners for Florida, and requiring of them, in certain cases, to report the testimony, with their opinions, to the Secretary of the Treasury, to be laid before Congress for their determination," we respectfully submit the following report:

" The laws and ordinances, heretofore existing, of the Governments making the grants, respectively," have, of necessity, been the first subject of inquiry with the commissioners, not only because they were pointed out by the statute as our peculiar guides, but because it was obviously impossible to do justice with exactitude without them; but we are not able to say that we have arrived at all the information that might have been possessed on that subject, owing to the careless manner in which the Spanish records have ever been kept; to the removal of all the British records upon the retrocession of the territory, and the subordination of the authorities here, subsequently to those at Havana. The rules by which we have been governed in our adjudications are drawn—
1st. From the code of Spanish law, entitled the Laws of the Indies.
2d. From royal orders made with particular reference to this Territory.
3d. The decrees and regulations appointed and published by the local Governors.
4th. The customs and usages which prevailed in the various offices in the Territorial Government.

As the general or local enactments and customs of the British Government are not drawn in question, by any of the claims now submitted and reported for the revision of Congress, that part of the subject will more properly constitute the matter of another report, when claims of that description shall be regularly before us.

The authority first referred to contains the following general provision, which, as far as we are able to understand it, applies to all the ultra-marine provinces of the Spanish empire:

Of the sale, adjustment, and distribution of lands, lots, and waters.*

In order that our subjects be encouraged to the discovery and settlement of the Indies, and may live with the comfort and convenience which we desire, it is our will that houses, lots, lands, knights' shares, and peasants' shares of land, may and shall be distributed to all those who go to settle new lands in townships and villages, which, by the Governor of the new settlement, shall be assigned them, making a distinction between gentlemen and peasants, and those of an inferior degree and merit, and increase and give them of better quality, according to the importance of their services; and that they may devote themselves to the culture and improvement of them, and, having made on them their residence and place of labor, and resided in those townships four years, we grant them the right, from thenceforward, to sell and dispose of them, at their will, freely, as of a thing their property.

Continuation of the same ordinance.

And, as it may happen that, in distributing the lands, there may be a doubt as to the measurements, we declare that a peasant's portion is a lot of fifty feet in breadth, and one hundred in depth, arable land, capable of producing one hundred fanegas of wheat and ten of Indian corn; as much land as two oxen can plough in a day, for the raising of esculent roots, and eight of woodland; pasture land for eight breeding sows, twenty cows, and five mares, one hundred sheep, and twenty goats. A *gentleman's portion* (caballeria) is a lot of one hundred feet in breadth and two hundred in depth, and all the remainder five times the *peasant's portion*, (peonia,) to wit: arable land capable of producing five hundred *fanegas* of wheat or barley, fifty of Indian corn, as much land as ten oxen can plough in a day for raising esculent roots, and eight of woodland; pasture land for fifty breeding sows, one hundred cows, twenty mares, five hundred sheep, and one hundred goats; and we direct that the distribution be made in such form as that all may participate in the good or middling, and of that kind of which there may not be any in that part which shall be pointed out to each.

This seems to have been the rule for the distribution of the public lands during the first administration of the Spanish Government within these provinces, and after the retrocession, up to the date of the 2d September, in the year 1790, when Governor Quesada published the following regulations, referring, for his authority, to a royal order, investing him with plenary powers, but which we have not been able to procure.

Internal regulations of police.

Don Juan Nepomuceno de Quesada, Colonel in the royal armies, Governor of this city of St. Augustine and province of East Florida, for His Majesty, &c.

Whereas I am commanded, by royal orders, agreeable to the public wants, to apply the most seasonable and quick remedies thereto: for the purpose, therefore, of accomplishing this in the edict commonly called "Internal regulations of police," I have taken the most conducive steps, notwithstanding much to my sorrow. There has been so much to amend and establish, that a voluminous code would scarcely be sufficient for me to comprise all, in proportion to the ardent desire which animates me for the prosperity of the province and the service of the sovereign; wherefore, merely for the present, and reserving, hereafter, when permitted by my other duties, the right of attending particularly to this important subject, I, therefore, make known and order the following:

1. I grant to all the inhabitants, permanently settled, and subjects of His Majesty, in his royal name, for their use, the quantity of land they may require, in proportion to their force, in any part of this desert province, without any exception. To this end, those desirous of obtaining the same will present themselves to me within twenty days, stating their circumstances by memorial; what lands they have obtained to the present period, and what quantity, and in what place they are desirous of locating them now, under the precise condition that it will be without injury to a third person. I will attend to their solicitude according to the examination I may make thereof; and, although the laws of the Indies authorize me to make an absolute distribution of the same, and being in the case of the first of title 12th, book 4th, I abstain therefrom from powerful motives. But, for the greater security of those interested, I will forward my ideas and representations on the subject to the King, persuaded that, in consequence thereof, those obtaining grants from me now will be confirmed in the possession of the same.

2. Relates to free blacks.

3. Relates to the raising of horned cattle near the city.

4. The King, our master, by a royal order of the 5th April, 1786, granted to all the foreigners, inhabitants of this province, during the British dominion, the liberty of remaining protected in the possession of their lands and property, under the following indispensable conditions: that they take the oath of allegiance; that they will not add to said lands, or transfer the same from one to another. Therefore, all those who are discontented, or will not conform with said conditions within thirty days, must remove from the above-mentioned province, presenting themselves in person, or by letter, manifesting their resolution on the subject, that I may proceed thereon as may be most expedient.

5. Relates to the rules to be observed by new subjects, as regards foreign commerce.

6. Declaring the port of St. Augustine open by the laws of the Indies.

7. Relates to bakers and the assize of bread.

8. Relates to the regulation of the market, the quality and weight of beef, &c.

9. Relates to the cleansing of chimneys.

10. Relates to the appointment of police officers for the city and country.

11. Not permitting persons to come into the province without knowing their object for so doing.

12. Prohibiting all women, under the age of forty, (whether widows or single,) from living otherwise than under the immediate protection of their parents or relations.

13. Prohibiting women from leading a dissolute life.

14. Recommending to the inhabitants to present their ideas as to the best method of repairing the roads, and making easy the water conveyance in the province.

15. Granting to persons vacant lands under article the first, that they may build houses at the distance of six miles apart for the accommodation of passengers going or returning from St. Johns.

* Book 4th, law 1st. chap. 12th, of the collection of the Laws of the Indies.

16. Appointing a patrol of six men, and a commander, for the purpose of going through the country to prevent disorders, robberies, &c.

17. Recommending the clearing of the woods through which the public roads pass.

18. Relative to the license on taverns.

19. Relates to the cleanliness of the streets.

20. Ordering that all filth and dirt collected in the yards and houses to be thrown in the marsh at the back of the town.

21. Ordering all owners of stone or wooden houses (should said houses be in a ruinous state) to have them repaired within six months.

22. Not permitting persons to build houses without the knowledge of the commandant of engineers.

23. Forbidding masters or supercargoes of vessels from selling their cargoes by wholesale, without first exposing the same for sale by retail, eight days previously, to the public.

24. Prohibiting that hogs and dogs should be allowed at large, except hounds and pointers.

25. Prohibiting persons from galloping horses through the streets.

26. Prohibiting horses from going at large.

27. Prohibiting persons from walking the streets after 9 o'clock at night, without a lantern with a light therein.

28. Prohibiting, at the same time, the use of fire-arms, sword canes, knives, dirks, &c.

29. Persons, with lawful arms, are not permitted to walk at night in groups of more than two persons; and, in no wise, with noisy and suspicious women.

30. Not permitting the sale of gunpowder by shop-keepers or tavern-keepers, to the boys, or other persons, except those known.

31. Prohibiting artificial fire-works, rockets, &c.

32. Prohibiting silversmiths, storekeepers, or other persons from purchasing any article whatsoever from soldiers, slaves, house servants, or children.

33. Relative to billiard tables, and prohibiting games of hazard.

34. Prohibiting gaming in private houses.

35. Expressly forbidding all games in hotels, taverns, wine stores, &c.

36. The owners of billiard tables expressly forbid from admitting tradesmen, laborers, domestics, and boys on working days.

37. As relates to the duties of the Catholics in the observance of their religion.

A certificate of Domingo Rodriguez de Leon, Government notary, as to the publication of the foregoing regulations; as also a note of the said notary, attesting that a copy of the said regulations was posted in the usual place pointed out.

St. Augustine, *September 2*, 1790.

A true and correct translation from a document in the Spanish language.

F. J. FATIO, *S. B. L. C.*

Although the authority vested in the Governor of this province by the Code of the Indies, is specifically disclaimed in practice by Governor Quesada, it is apparent that it did not cease to be the law: 1st, because the Governor was incompetent to repeal a law of the empire; and, 2d, because he professes only to abstain from its execution for the present, and until he could know the royal will in relation to that subject.

The precise extent to which these regulations interfered with the provisions of the general law, and the privileges of the emigrant or inhabitant, cannot be clearly understood, from its equivocal phraseology; nor is it eminently important to know if it be proper to construe the following letter and extract from a royal order in connexion with it, as, in that case, it will be seen that the following powers reserved to himself by the decree of the Governor are over-ruled, or regulated and restrained, by the order of the captain general of the Havana. The Governor seems to have written to the captain general of Cuba touching various subjects in connexion with the situation and police of this territory, but among them no notice is taken of the anterior act of distribution. An appeal seems to have been made in favor of admitting Irish emigrants upon a peculiarly favorable footing, and some allusion was evidently made to the custom which was supposed to have existed at some anterior period, of paying from the royal treasury for the transportation and temporary maintenance of emigrants. These subjects are put to rest, and a rule prescribed to the Governor for the disposition, in future, of the public domain to voluntary emigrants.

[TRANSLATION.]

Havana, *October* 29, 1790.

I acknowledge the information given me by your lordship, under date of the 16th of September last, relative to Don Thomas Wooster, whose conduct and transactions gave cause for his leaving that province by order of the Government, of which I will inform His Majesty.

Relative to the introduction of families from Ireland, which your lordship proposes, I cannot accede on other terms than strictly adhering to what the King has advised me on the subject, and herewith transcribe the same for your lordship's government.

"No settlers shall be admitted in Louisiana or Florida, should they pretend to have their transportation to those provinces, and maintenance there for some time, paid by the royal treasury. That those foreigners alone will be received who may, of their own free will, present themselves, and swear allegiance to His Majesty, to whom there shall be granted and measured lands gratis, in proportion to the working hands each family may have. That they shall not be molested in matters of religion, although there shall be no other public worship than the Catholic. That there shall be given them no other assistance or aid than lands, protection, and good treatment; each family having the right of taking with them their property, of any description, all free from duties; but in case of exporting the same to any other place, they shall pay the six per cent. as established, and obliging them only to take up arms in defence of the province, should an enemy invade the same."

To which rules your lordship must adhere in any solicitude that may occur under similar circumstances. God preserve your lordship many years.

LUIS DE LAS CASAS.

His Lordship Don Juan Nepomuceno de Quesada.

St. Augustine, Florida, *December* 12, 1790.

Take an account of the royal accountant's office.

[A flourish.]

St. Augustine, Florida, *December* 12, 1790.

An account was taken in the accountant's office under my charge.

GONZALO ZAMORANO.

A true and correct translation from a document in the Spanish language.

F. J. FATIO, *S. B. L. C.*

It is evident that the rule prescribed by the above order relates exclusively to emigrants, leaving the law as it stood before in relation to those who had already, or should have thereafter, the character of inhabitants or subjects.

It is worthy of notice, also, that, although it provides for giving lands in proportion to the laboring hands introduced, it has entirely failed to designate the quantity each laborer should receive, either leaving that part of the subject to the government of existing custom, or to the sound discretion of the Governor.

The provisions of this ordinance may be considered as having defined and rendered certain the bounty upon emigration, which seems to have been uncertain, or but little understood before.

The following order, issued by Governor Quesada, to carry into effect the preceding, must be construed to relate to emigrants in general, although it is evident that it was made to apply to those cases of residents who had not received their titles in consequence of the prevailing uncertainty as to the quantity they should receive. It assigns 100 acres to each father of a family, and 50 to each other person, white or black, composing it; and an additional quantity of 1,000 acres when it was probable it would be cultivated.

[TRANSLATION.]

St. Augustine, Florida, *November* 20, 1790.

Don Juan Nepomuceno de Quesada, colonel of the royal armies, and commander-in-chief of this city and province of St. Augustine, Florida, by His Majesty:

Whereas, by the last packet which arrived at this port, his excellency, the captain general of this province, encloses me, under date of the 29th of November, of the last year, the following royal order:

In virtue of which I order the same to be published for the present, that it may be made known to all, being understood that only those shall be admitted as resident settlers, who, besides their good conduct and honorable proceedings, are good farmers and mechanics, who are beneficial to the settlement and advancement of the province, for which purpose there shall be granted them the gifts set forth in the inserted royal order.

It is also made known to those who have obtained lands, in the mean time, from this Government, that they present themselves to the same within the space of two months, for the purpose of asking and obtaining the requisite title of property from the office of the Government Secretary, from whence the necessary orders will be issued after having registered the same in the notary's office.

And, that it may serve as an incitement to all, I order, according to the powers I am vested with, and make known for the present, that the grants be of 100 acres to each father of a family, and 50 to each white person, or of color, of which said family is composed; also, that if persons are desirous of obtaining a greater quantity of land, and there being a probability of their cultivating the same, they shall obtain an additional number of 1,000 acres; it being understood that, in all the concessions, the utility and not the quality of the lands shall be attended to, so that each person shall acquire a proportionate quantity of each; as, also, that the width of each of said concessions must be only the third part the length, and said length must not extend on the banks of the rivers and creeks, but towards the interior of the lands, resting always with the Government the care of rewarding or punishing with additional expenses or absolute privation, as time shall discover, the merit, application, and advantages of the agriculturists, or the contrary vices.

A copy from the original, I attest:

DOMINGO RODRIGUEZ DE LEON,
Notary of Government.

In conformity to the spirit of the above orders, the Governor appointed one Pedro Marrott to the office of the Surveyor General, in October, 1791; and, along with his commission, gave him sundry instructions as to the manner in which he should proceed in distributing to emigrants their respective portions of public territory, which are as follows:

[TRANSLATION.]

St. Augustine, Florida, *October* 24, 1791.

Instructions which are given to the Captain Don Pedro Marrott, of the third battalion of the infantry regiment of Cuba, which garrison the city of St. Augustine, Florida, appointed by the Government, with the assent of the council of ministers, to proceed to the survey and laying off of the lands, which is to be executed by order of His Majesty, for the benefit of the new settlers.

1st. He will take with him the public surveyor, and will take care that the measurements be made, adhering to the title, and to that ordered in the edict of which I transmit a copy, in the document No. 1, which will more fully instruct on the subject.

2d. He will likewise take with him a canoe, with two tents, two tarpaulings, four sailors, and two laborers, who will assist in the necessary work, with a pay of $4 the first, and $2 the latter; and in case of the sickness or abandonment, they can be replaced, informing the Government thereof, that those may be noted in a book formed for the purpose, of what may be owing them.

3d. There will also be formed another large book, in which will be placed the distribution which may be made of the lands, with the name of the whites of each family, and the number of slaves, with a distinction of the ages and sexes of each white or colored person.

4th. He will not consent that they pass off as fit persons to obtain lands, those who belong to other places, and, in general, to those who have not been admitted by the Government under the oath of allegiance, and therefore declared to be proper.

For the purpose of obviating frauds in this part, he will receive the oath from those wishing lands, according to the number of persons of their families, and they shall be informed that if, for the future, any fraud is committed they will remain liable to any deduction of lands the Government may think proper to make.

5th. The married sons of families can obtain the part belonging to them, acting conjointly with their fathers, but they shall be notified that it must be forever; and that in the book will be written the number of acres appertaining to each.

6th. He will inform, particularly all those obtaining these gifts, that certain conditions must be performed before they can consider themselves owners in absolute right, and lawful for them to dispose of what is now granted them.

7th. He must send them to the Government Secretary's office for their respective titles, where they will be informed of what is necessary.

8th. Those who obtain lands cannot change or alienate them without informing the Government, that it may take just measures to prevent confusion.

9th. When lands are to be surveyed, bounding those of individuals having them of their own, they will be cited to appear for the purpose of exhibiting their titles, permitting them to remain in possession, running the lines without injuring them, and the Government reserving the right of examining, at a proper time, the validity of their titles, and defects of their petitions.

10th. On the sides of rivers, creeks, and roads, there must not be left small vacant spaces between the lands which are distributed, and, for the purpose of avoiding it, cutting off a part of the depth, and adding the same quantity to the front, and by this method the line of division of one tract may serve for that of the adjoining. The front of all tracts must be, if possible, not more than a third part.

The 11th and 12th articles are obliterated, and treat of the buildings appertaining to the royal domain.

NOTE.—It will be made known to all those who are to obtain lands, that 100 English varas are equal to 3 Spanish caballerias, on which footing the measurement will be made.

The foregoing is a true and correct translation from a document in the Spanish language.

F. J. FATIO, S. B. L. C.

How far these regulations were observed in practice by Captain Marrott and his successors in office, will appear by the testimony of witnesses, whose examination makes a part of this report.

The next governmental act, in order of time, relates to the houses and lots in the city of St. Augustine.

Although time was allowed by the treaty of cession between Great Britain and Spain for the subjects of the former to sell their property in this province and remove, it was found impossible, in a great many cases, to get purchasers at any thing like fair prices; and the owners preferred, in all such cases, abandoning their property, which, immediately, by the laws of Spain, re-attached to the royal domain.

The following order from the King will show the manner in which that property was disposed of, and has become the property of individuals:

[TRANSLATION.]

The King to the Governor and Commander-in-chief of the province of St. Augustine, Florida.

In a letter dated November 20, 1791, your predecessor gave an account, with accompanying documents, of the steps he had taken; and, according to which, the sale of the lots and houses relinquished by the English, and becoming part of my royal domain, agreeably to the third article of the preliminary treaty of peace concluded with that Power; as also in regard to what had taken place relative to the estates owned by the widow Donna Isabel Perpall, purchased from the English in a suspicious manner; but she not only being a widow, but poor, a Spaniard, and very possibly having acted with the most honest intentions, which makes her deserving of my royal clemency; and a number of other inhabitants being nearly in the same case, suspected of having purchased houses, some after the time allowed the English to sell, and others without his consent and intervention; and although it was necessary to make a minute examination, he neglected doing the same, thinking it would be for the good of the service; and observing that said buildings were falling to decay, he ordered their sale at public auction, a valuation being first made by skilful persons, with the proviso that those taking said property should give security for the payment of the materials and lots when he thought it convenient, and repair said houses in the course of one year, paying, in the meantime, five per cent. annually, which was accordingly so done. After the purchasers had consented to pay him the principal amount, and having verified the sale, the total thereof amounted to 157,974 reals and a *quartilla,** including the value of the houses said to appertain to the above named Donna Isabel Perpall, to Mateo Martinez Fernandez, and to Manuel de Herrera, which were declared as belonging to my royal domain on account of their sale being false. And, lastly, in your letter of the 20th October, 1798, you stated, with proof, that some refused the payment of five per cent., founding their objections on the grants of lands made to the foreigners establishing themselves in that colony, and that the houses and lots in that city were not comprehended in those grants; and seeing the continued increase therein of taverns and shops, without any improvement whatever in agriculture and other staples of commerce, you gave an account, for my royal resolution, not only of this incident, but likewise of the other, pending from the time of your predecessor.

Having observed, in my council of the Indies, the opinion of my fiscal, with the information on that subject given by the accountant general's office, and consulting on the same the 17th April last, I have resolved to remit, in favor of those indebted to the finance, the payments of the capital and interests on the houses and lots they acquired, and approve the sale and other steps as taken by your said predecessor, giving to each a title of possession and property, that they may be secured hereafter in the possession of said estate, it being thus my will; and let an account of the present be taken in said accountant general's office.

Done at Aranjuez, the 17th June, 1801.

I, THE KING.
ANTONIO PORCELL.

By order of the King, our master:

OFFICIAL.

To the Governor of Florida, informing him of having remitted, in favor of those indebted to the finance in that city, the payment of the capital and interests on the houses and lots they acquired at the transfer of the country by the English, and so forth, as expressed therein.

COMMUNICATED.

MADRID, July 9, 1801.

Take an account thereof in the northern department of the accountant general's office of the Indies.

PEDRO APARICI.

* About $19,746 78.

ST. AUGUSTINE, FLORIDA, *February* 18, 1802.

Take an account of this royal letter patent in the accountant's office, and be it afterwards annexed to the proceedings on the subject, and it will be delivered to the Attorney General, that he may give his opinion thereon.

ENRIQUE WHITE.

ST. AUGUSTINE, FLORIDA, *February* 18, 1802.

An account of this royal letter patent was taken in the principal accountant's office under my charge.

GONZALO ZAMORANO.

The following decreé of Governor White seems to have had no other object than to carry into execution the will of his King, in relation to the debts due him for the sale of property in this city.

[TRANSLATION.]

Having seen ——————; let what His Majesty orders in his royal letter patent of the 17th June last be kept, complied with, and executed, posting the same by handbills in the customary places, and inserting particularly as relates to the royal donation and grant of the houses and lots, which, by appertaining to his royal domain, were sold here in the year 1791, with the yearly interest of five per cent., on the value of the property, to which the purchasers bound themselves. Let the royal approbation of said sale be likewise published; and, in consequence of the same royal gift, let the mortgages given them by the purchasers on said property be cancelled, and those which progressively have been made over to other proprietors, to whom said property was transferred by the original owners; at the same time, for the security of these last, let the conveyances of the royal donation be drawn out, to which, for the security and possession of the legitimate possessors, let the royal favor be also extended. And, in respect to the doubts which took place as to the legitimate ownership of the property in the possession of Donna Isabel Perpall, Mateo Martin Hernandez, and Don Manuel de Herrera, in the proceedings relative to the sale of said lots and houses, which were, notwithstanding, sold as the others, as belonging to the royal domain, inform them in particular, or their legitimate agents, of the royal patent, that it is also extended to the aforesaid property, that they may make use of all their rights; upon which, and in all incidents relative thereto, and which, in this general provision, cannot be taken into consideration, other provision will progressively be made, and as the cases and circumstances may require; of all which the fiscal representation shall be informed with respect to what concerns his duty.

WHITE.

LICIENTIATE ORTEGA.

Don Enrique White, colonel in the royal army, civil and military Governor of the city of St. Augustine and province of East Florida, for His Majesty, provided the foregoing, which he signed, after having consulted his lieutenant auditor of war and assessor general, on the 18th of March, 1802.

JOSE ZUBIZARETTA, *Government Notary.*

St. Augustine, same day, month, and year, I notified the foregoing act to Don Gonzalo Zamorana, accountant of the royal finance, to take cognizance of the same, which I attest.

ZUBIZARETTA, *Notary.*

A true translation from a document in the Spanish language.

F. J. FATIO, *S. B. L. C.*

The following order of Governor White brings us back to the subject of the public lands, and the terms on which they should thereafter be granted to individuals.

[TRANSLATION.]

ST. AUGUSTINE, *October* 12, 1803.

Don ENRIQUE WHITE, *colonel of the royal armies, civil and military Governor and chief of the royal finance of the city and province of St. Augustine, Florida, by His Majesty, &c.*

Whereas, it being necessary to vary and modify, in part, the rules and conditions which the Government had established for the concessions and divisions of lands to the new settlers, in consideration of the actual circumstances, on account of the great number of persons coming to enjoy the favors and privileges which His Majesty has granted to those who may come to establish themselves in this province, many abuses have arisen, on the part of those grantees, under the system and object which influenced the Government at that time in the prosecution of that plan; those, as well as other inconveniences, which experience has demonstrated, have plainly shown that they may tend to the hindrance of the advancement and prosperity of the province; for which reason, and to remedy the same, I have thought proper and ordered that the rules prescribed in the following articles be observed for the future:

1. That, whenever the new settlers shall take the customary oath of allegiance, they shall declare exactly the number of their children, their sexes and ages, and, in consideration of which, lands will be allotted them, excepting those under eight years of age.

2. That, to each head of a family there shall be granted fifty acres of land, and an equal quantity to a single person, widow or widower, and to the children or slaves of sixteen years, twenty-five acres each; but, from the age of eight to sixteen years, they shall be granted fifteen acres each.

3. That, to those employed in the town, of whatever class they may be, if lands be granted them, or to their slaves, it shall be with the express condition of their cultivating the same within one month of the concession; being understood that, if they fail in so doing, it shall be granted to whomsoever shall denounce and lawfully prove the same.

4. That all concessions, in which no time is specified, shall become extinct, and shall be considered as null, if the persons to whom they are made do not take possession and cultivate the same within the space of six months.

5. That, to none of those who cede or convey their lands to others, under pretence of selling the improvements, there shall be granted them more lands in future; nor shall these transfers or conveyances be admitted, if done without the consent of Government.

6. Notwithstanding what is stated in the foregoing article, if it should suit any settler to change his situation, if he desires it, granting him lands in the place he may choose, but, on consideration of giving up the improvements

of the land he left, for the benefit of the royal revenue; which will prevent the abuse of the transfers and sales, which are prohibited under any pretext whatever, until the proper time pointed out in the former plan or rules.

7. That, on the lands not fit for cultivation, but have timber, or that are only proper for pastures, for which purpose alone they have been solicited, the owner cannot prevent any person from cutting and appropriating the timber to his own use, who may present themselves with an order from the Government; but it is understood that it shall not injure the owner thereof.

8. That all those who shall, for the future, ask for lands, must indicate a fixed spot from whence the measurement must commence; which will be the cause of avoiding the mistakes and disputes which by that fault have been experienced, particularly a short time back.

9. That all persons who shall have abandoned or discontinued the cultivation, nor actually cultivates the lands, which at any period shall have been measured to them by the Surveyor General, although they have obtained the corresponding title of property from the notary's office, they shall lose their right to the same, and shall be given to any person not having lands for cultivation, who shall legally prove that said lands have been uncultivated at least two years following.

And for the punctual observance of what has been set forth, and that no person may plead ignorance, I order that copies be posted up in the public places of this city, as is customary, and that one be transmitted to the brevet captain of militia, commandant of the same, and commissioned judge of the rivers St. John's and St. Mary's, Don John McQueen, that he may cause it to be made known to those inhabitants.

ENRIQUE WHITE.

By order of His Excellency,

JOSE DE ZUBIZARETTA, Notary of Government.

It is worthy of remark, that this order refers to the abuses under the former regulations, and undertakes to correct them. It ought, therefore, to be confined to the same subject-matter; and as we have already construed *those* to relate exclusively to emigrants, *this* must receive the same interpretation. The use of the terms "*new settlers*," in the preamble and first section, the only parts descriptive of the persons to whom it should be applied, confirms the interpretation. The quantity of land to be given to each head of a family is reduced from one hundred to fifty; but the same quantity is allowed to each single person, widow, or widower; to each child or slave, of sixteen years, twenty-five acres; and to those over eight years, fifteen acres. The third, fourth, and ninth sections prescribe the manner in which lands shall be forfeited to the Crown for non-performance of conditions. The third and ninth require that legal proof shall be made, in the one case, of non-possession, within one month; in the other of abandonment for two years; and, in both, the estate is given to the prosecutor. The fourth declares that the grant or concession shall be null if the grantee fails to take possession within the space of six months, without requiring a legal investigation. Under the two former sections, it seems to the board that nothing could work a forfeiture but a decree of a competent tribunal, and a subsequent grant or concession to another individual; under the latter, it seems to be uncertain whether a subsequent grant alone would not be sufficient.

The following letter to the Captain General of the Island of Cuba, purports to have enclosed the preceding order of Governor White, and communicates the reasons upon which it was founded, for his intelligence and approbation.

It is worthy of being noticed, that the regulations are said to be for " the purpose of avoiding the abuses which have been experienced in the granting of lands to the new settlers." The former rule is recognised as a bounty upon emigration, and justified, at the time when "there were few strangers who came in solicitude of lands;" but subsequently changed because there were "many who came."

[TRANSLATION.]

St. Augustine, Florida, October 15, 1803.

For the purpose of avoiding the abuses which have been experienced in the granting of lands to new settlers, without certain restrictions that will oblige them to cultivate the same, I have thought it convenient to establish the rules in the accompanying document, which I forward your lordship for your intelligence and approval.

My predecessor has assigned one hundred acres of land to the fathers of families, and fifty to each child and slave, whether full grown or small; a quantity really excessive, and could only have taken place at that time, in which there were a few strangers who came in solicitude of lands; but at present there are many who come, and, consequently, there would result the greatest injury in the improvement of the province, unless said number of acres be diminished, on account of its being more than one individual can cultivate in a year, even divided in three parts, for the purpose of giving rest to the lands; which circumstance I have also had present, for the deduction which has been made. God preserve your lordship many years.

THE MARQUIS DE SOMERUELOS.

To the Captain General.

I certify the foregoing to be a true and correct translation from a document in the Spanish language.

F. J. FATIO, S. B. L. C.

The next order is dated April, 1805, and seems to have had no other object than to alter the provision of the 9th section of the previous, so as to appropriate the value of all forfeited buildings, in favor of the royal finance, instead of to the prosecutor.

It can be taken to relate only to such cases as fall within the meaning of the section referred to, and which it purports to alter. These, we have already seen, are cases of emigrants who have abandoned their possessions for two years.

[TRANSLATION.]

Don Enrique White, *Colonel of the royal armies, Civil and Military Governor of this city and province, and Superior Chief of the Royal Finance.*

St. Augustine, Florida, April 2, 1805.

Whereas, on the 12th of October, 1803, I thought proper to have published an edict in which were prescribed various rules to remedy the many abuses and disorders, as committed on the part of those obtaining lands; and ordering, in the ninth article of said edict, that all persons having abandoned, or that may not have continued cultivating, or do not actually cultivate the lands which may have been measured for them at any time by a surveyor, although the necessary title of possession should have been given them from the notary's office, they would lose their right to them, and would be given to any person who, not having lands to cultivate, would lawfully prove, in a summary manner, that the said lands were without cultivation for at least two years in succession; it is now made known that the improvements, or buildings, remaining on the lands thus abandoned or uncultivated, in the specified time, their value shall be appropriated in favor of the royal finance, as a deposite, until a new determination; and thus it may be made known to all persons, I order copies to be posted in the customary places, and that another be transmitted to the brevet captain of militia, and commandant of the same, and commissioned judge of the rivers St. John's and St. Mary's, Don Juan McQueen, that he may make the same known to the inhabitants thereof.

I certify that the foregoing is a true and correct translation from a document in the Spanish language.

F. J. FATIO, *S. B. L. C.*

Although Governor White was continued in office until the year 1811, we have not been able to obtain any subsequent official publication of his, relating to the disposal of public lands.

[*See White's edict of May* 31, 1805, *page* 749.]

Governor Estrada, who succeeded White in the administration, immediately upon his coming into office, issued the following commission, and, shortly afterwards, the following instructions to George J. F. Clarke, as Surveyor General of this province. The duties and responsibilities of that office can only be made to appear by parol evidence, as it was neither created nor regulated by any law of the empire, but depended alone upon the will of the acting Governor. The following commission demonstrates the existence of such an office, and the following instructions explain the manner in which the Governor was desirous its duties should be performed at that time; but parol evidence alone can explain what alterations were compelled by necessity, or permitted by the unwritten authorization of the Governor himself. These will appear by the annexed examinations.

[TRANSLATION.]

Don JUAN JOSE DE ESTRADA, &c.

Whereas, the appointment of public surveyor being vacant, on account of the absence of Don John Porcel, who exercised the same, and, wherefore, being in want of one for the measurement by the Government in the laying off of lands gratis to the new settlers, and those of each private individual, to fill up said appointment without prejudice to the person whom his Majesty may think proper to appoint; and there not being at the present period any person to practise the same, and having seen the memorial made by Don George Clarke, soliciting it, and having, at the same time, the qualities of capacity and aptness, according to the information given by the Commandant of Engineers, to whose examination he was made liable, as will be seen by the proceedings on that subject; using, therefore, the powers appertaining to me, I have thought proper to appoint the said Don George Clarke public surveyor in this province and its jurisdiction, receiving the emoluments per tariff, which, for that purpose, will be made by the said Commandant of Engineers, with the advice of the said Government, and under the terms and instructions they may think proper to make in the present circumstances, and other occurrences which may hereafter take place. And, that the above-mentioned Don George Clarke may be appointed and known as said public surveyor, and, that all rights appertaining to him may be observed, I have ordered that, he previously taking the accustomed oath, there be given him the present commission, signed by me, and countersigned by the undersigned secretary, in St. Augustine, &c. May 2, 1811.

JUAN JOSE DE ESTRADA,
THOMAS DE AGUILAR.

NOTE.—A copy was transmitted, with the same date, to the Commandant of Engineers. A correct translation from a document in the Spanish language.

F. J. FATIO, *S. B. L. C.*

[TRANSLATION.]

ST. AUGUSTINE OF FLORIDA, *June* 10, 1811.

Instructions to be observed by the acting surveyor, Don George Clarke, in partitioning land, and the fees to be paid by those who call on him for this purpose.

ART. 1. The possessors of lands in this province shall be considered under three classes: First, as proprietors; second, as grantees; and third, as grantees and proprietors. The first are those who hold lands by titles not obtained by grants from the Government; the second are they who, on compliance of certain conditions of time and labor, will get titles of property; and the third are those who have acquired those titles.

ART. 2. The surveyor having been called on by any person to measure and bound lands to him, he will require his title of property or grant from Government, that, on sight thereof, he may proceed to its measurement and demarcation.

ART. 3. For this purpose he will cite to appear those persons having lands adjoining, that, in the presence of them and their titles, all matters may be regulated in justice. This has reference to possessors of the second and third classes, and those who purchased under the following article:

ART. 4. On the side of rivers, creeks, and roads, spaces of *little* "consideration are not to be left vacant between lands distributed. In order to avoid this, he will endeavor to reduce the depth and augment the front, so as that the boundary line of one tract may serve for that of another. In the front of all lands he will endeavor not to exceed one-third part." This article, extracted from the instructions that, for the same purpose, were given by Government on the 24th October, 1791, will be considered as now in its full force and vigor. That part should be regarded as the front of the land which faces to the best side, namely, first, on rivers, second, on navigable creeks, and third, on roads; and the depth will be the longitudinal extension back. All lands that depend, or have depended, on the grant of Government, should have been, and must be, bounded in rectangular parallelograms, whose front line will be one-third of that of the depth, or as nearly so as possible, for the purpose of not leaving empty spaces of less than ten chains in front.

ART. 5. To each person whose lands have been measured a plat will be given, constructed in running lines of ink, marking, in the perimeter, the corners, by a small circle of a line in diameter; and, on the longitude of each line, note its magnetic direction and length in chains and links. When the perimeter should not have some of its lines straight, on account of its being bounded by a river, creek, or swamp, he will bound on them, and note the surface he considers sufficient to augment or diminish a rectilineal surface. In the centre of the plat he will place, in numbers, the acres of land which he has measured. The scale of these plats will invariably be of one inch to four chains. The plat being made, he will deliver it, with the following inscription:

Plat of the number of acres of land of A B, in such a place, measured and bounded by the public surveyor of this province, Don George Clarke, East Florida, the day of the year and month, on the same tract.

GEORGE CLARKE.

ART. 6. The surveyor will keep a book of large paper, and copy therein the plats he gives out, according to the foregoing article. These plats will be numbered. At the beginning of the book there will be an index, showing the page of each plat, its number, and the person to whom the land appertains. At the end of the book he will have a sheet of a sufficient size for a general plan, containing the surveys for individuals, with the number of each. This plan will be on a scale of eighty chains to one inch.

ART. 7. The book mentioned in the foregoing article will serve to show Government what lands are vacant, or not measured; he should form, in legal surveys, a journal of his operations, to satisfy the persons having lands adjoining.

ART. 8. That the boundaries should be permanent, he will cause to be drove down, at the corners, stakes of three feet long, and three inches thick at their heads, leaving them three inches above ground, informing the owners thereof, that they should encircle them with a deposite of oyster-shells, of two feet in diameter, and as much in depth, as a durable mark, that their boundaries may be known.

ART. 9. Those who employ the surveyor will pay him four dollars per day for his personal services, calculating from his departure from the mansion where he is found until he concludes the work performed for them.

ART. 10. For the measurement of lumber, which is likewise placed in charge of the surveyor, he will be paid by those who employ him at the rate of two and a half *reals* the thousand feet, superficial, of one inch thick, when the measurement is made on logs; and, when on sawed lumber, at four *reals*. It must be considered that this payment is to be made as well by the purchaser as by the seller.

MANUEL DE LA HITA.

I certify the foregoing to be a true and correct translation from a document in the Spanish language.

F. J. FATIO, *S. B. L. C.*

The following letter, from Governor Estrada to the Captain General of Cuba, is designed, principally, to obtain permission to sell, instead of giving away, the public lands; but it introduces to the notice of the Government a condition annexed by Governor White to his concessions of lands, to wit: the condition of ten years' occupancy, before the claimant should be entitled to a royal grant, or the privilege of disposing of his estate. We have not been able to find such an order in writing, but it is proved to have been practised during the greater part of White's administration.

[TRANSLATION.]

MOST EXCELLENT SIR:

The miserable situation, at present, of this city and province, and seeing that, of the one hundred and forty-one thousand thirty-one dollars and four reals, which are allowed annually for salaries, there are owing, to the end of April last, nine hundred and twenty-five thousand one hundred and thirty-three dollars one and a half reals, obliges me to seek for some adequate measure to relieve myself from the difficulties under which I labor for the want of funds: for most urgent wants, such as the purchase of provisions, the allowance and pay of the third battalion of Cuba, the annual presents of the Indians, and the payment of the large balance of accounts due the persons employed in the royal finance, invalids, Florida pensioners, and to the heads of families, settlers who receive a daily pension and charity, whose outcries are so continual that the most obdurate heart would melt at them with compassion.

The greatest part of the commerce of this province consists, at present, of British vessels, arriving at the port of Fernandina, in Amelia Island, for the purpose of loading with timber, to convey to their arsenals in England, leaving the small duty of seven and a half per cent., under moderate valuations, these inhabitants cutting the same on the most convenient places, without any restriction whatever; our neighbors, the Americans, also availing themselves of cutting the wood, clandestinely, without paying us any duty, adding the inconveniency of its not being in my power to put a stop thereto on account of the uninhabited situation of the places where the same takes place.

That the King may receive the benefit therefrom, I am of opinion that a very advantageous step may be taken for the advancement of this province, which is, that, for the purpose of aiding the royal treasury of West Florida, (which may not be in so deplorable a situation as this,) a determination was taken to sell to the natives and foreigners, without distinction, the public lands, according to their quality, the said system be established here, transferring to the new settlers admitted, or to be admitted, conformably to what His Majesty sets forth by royal orders.

The lands are granted, gratis, to those who, with the necessary requisites, come to settle; but, by the administratory arrangement, the title of ownership cannot be issued them until after ten years' possession and uninterrupted cultivation, which practice is injudicious, on account of its being too long a period for them to dispose of the land granted them according to the number of their families and slaves; and, should there occur in that time any diplomatic change, they could not prove their legitimate possession, being liable to lose all their improvements thereon.

The public lands being purchased by those, and, also, by the inhabitants already established here, which I do not doubt they would do if the prescribed time of ten years were not necessary, then this great difficulty would be obviated, and a greater number of new settlers would come, and receiving, of course, their title of possession, they would prize it, having cost them their money, and they would improve the land to procure some utility; the results would be the greatest advancement and prosperity of the country, income to the royal treasury, and would prevent, in some measure, the Americans from being benefited by what belongs to us; as each settler would take very good care that their property should not be taken away.

The measure which I propose to your excellency is not only for the utility of the country, or in regard to the unfortunate state of this royal treasury, but, likewise, the situation in which the nation is placed at present; as it is necessary to put into operation the most effectual ways and means to support and alleviate, in some manner, the immense burden and expense it is at, without opposing, in any wise, the will of the sovereign, who wishes the prosperity and increase of his royal interests by all possible means; and I therefore believe that his royal intentions would be fully realized by the settlement of this province, and alleviation of his royal finance. In virtue of which, should your excellency conceive that this measure will meet the approbation of His Majesty, I await that of your excellency to put it in execution.

God preserve your excellency many years. St. Augustine, Florida, June 19, 1811.

To His Excellency the MARQUIS OF SOMERUELOS.

I certify the foregoing to be a true and correct translation from a document in the Spanish language.

F. J. FATIO, *S. B. L. C.*

[TRANSLATION.]

I have seen your letters, Nos. 26 and 37, setting forth, in the present circumstances, the ability of alienating public lands to the new settlers of that province, on the terms expressed therein; and, in answer, inform you that the said alienation cannot take place, as the admission of citizens of the United States in the Floridas is expressly prohibited by a royal order of the 14th November, 1804, and by another of the 31st March, 1806, forbidding, on no pretext whatever, the sale of lands to foreigners coming into East Florida.

God preserve you many years.   Havana, September 14, 1811.

THE MARQUIS DE SOMERUELOS.

To the GOVERNOR OF EAST FLORIDA.

I hereby certify the foregoing to be a true and correct translation from a document in the Spanish language.

F. J. FATIO, S. B. L. C.

The reply of the captain general alludes to two royal orders, dated in 1804 and 1806, which we have not been able to obtain, nor do they seem to be important to the general objects of the commission.

[TRANSLATION.]

HAVANA.

Royal order communicated officially to his excellency the political chief and captain general of this city, superior chief of the province of the island of Cuba and the two Floridas, by the ultra marine department in the peninsula; that, for a compliance thereof, it be inserted in this gazette.

The Secretary of State, and of the office of Governor of the Peninsula, has communicated to me the following decree:

Don Fernando the Seventh, by the grace of God, and by the constitution of the Spanish monarchy, King of the Spains, and, in his absence and captivity, the regency of the kingdom, appointed by the General and Extraordinary Cortes, to all to whom these presents may come, greeting: Know ye that the Cortes have decreed the following:

The General and Extraordinary Cortes, considering that the conversion of public lands into private property is one of the measures which the welfare of the people, as well as the advancement of agriculture and industry, most imperiously demands, and desiring, at the same time, that this class of lands should serve as an aid to the public necessities, a reward to the deserving defenders of the country, and a support to the citizens who are not proprietors, do decree—

ART. 1. All the uncultivated or public lands, and those of the corporation of cities, with the timber thereon, or without it, both in the peninsula and adjacent islands, as well as in the ultra-marine provinces, except the commons necessary for the towns, shall be made private property, taking care that those of the corporations of cities give an annual rent by the most convenient means, which, at the proposal of the respective provincial deputations, shall be approved of by the Cortes.

ART. 2. In whatever manner these lands be distributed, it shall be in full property, and in the class of enclosures, that the owners thereof may fence them without injury to the pathways, roads, water-courses, and passage, and use them freely and exclusively, and apply them to the use or culture which best suits them; but they can never entail nor pass them at any time, or anywise, to a *mortmain*.

ART. 3. In the alienation of said lands, a preference shall be given to the inhabitants of the town within the limits of which they are, and to the proprietors who use the said uncultivated lands.

ART. 4. The provincial deputations shall propose to the Cortes, through the medium of the regency, the time and the terms when it will be most convenient to carry this disposition into effect in their respective provinces, according to the circumstances of the country, and the lands which it may be indispensable to preserve for the townships, in order that the Cortes determine upon what may be most convenient to each territory.

ART. 5. This business is recommended to the zeal of the regency of the kingdom, and to the two Secretaries of State, in order that they may bring forward and inform the Cortes, at all times, of the representations which the provincial deputations direct to them.

ART. 6. Without injury to what has been provided, half of the uncultivated and public lands of the monarchy, excepting the commons of towns, is reserved, that the entire, or any part which is deemed necessary, may serve as a pledge for the payment of the national debt; and with the preference for the credits which the inhabitants of the towns to which the lands appertain may have against the nation, the first place amongst those credits to be given to such as arise from supplies for the national armies, or loans which the said inhabitants may have made for the war since the 1st of May, 1808.

ART. 7. In the alienation for the public debt of this half of the uncultivated and public lands, or the part which it is deemed necessary to pledge, the inhabitants of the respective towns, and the occupiers who use the said lands, shall be preferred as purchasers; and the credits competently adjusted which either the one or the other may have on account of the said supplies and loans, shall be admitted in payment for the full value; and, in defect thereof, any other lawful national credit which they may have.

ART. 8. In the said half of the uncultivated and public lands there shall be comprehended and computed the part which may be justly and lawfully alienated, in some provinces, for the expense of the present war.

ART. 9. Of the remaining uncultivated and public lands, or of the arable lands belonging to corporations of towns, there shall be given, gratuitously, a quantity of those fittest for culture, to each captain, lieutenant, or sub-lieutenant, who, from advanced age, or being disabled in the military service, with due leave, without censure, and with a lawful document accrediting his good behaviour; and the same to each sergeant, corporal, soldier, trumpeter, and drummer, who, for the same causes, or having completed the time, obtain a final discharge, without censure, whether either the one or the other be natives or foreigners, wherever, in the districts in which they may fix their residence, there may be this class of lands.

ART. 10. The quantity which in each town is granted to officers or soldiers, shall be in equal proportion of value to the space and quality of the same, and more or less in some places than in others, according to their circumstances, and the greater or less extent of the lands, managing, if possible, that, at the least, each quantity shall be such as to be sufficient, regularly cultivated, for the maintenance of an individual.

ART. 11. The assignment of these quantities shall be made by the constitutional councils of the towns to which lands appertain, as soon as the interested present to them the documents which accredit their good services and resignation, the syndic being heard, as respects the whole, in a concise and lawful manner, and without exacting any costs or dues whatever. After which, the proceedings shall be sent to the provincial deputation, that they may approve it, and remedy any grievance.

ART. 12. The concession of these quantities of land, which shall be called *patriotic bounty*, shall not extend, at present, to other individuals but those who served, or have served in the present war, or in the pacification of the actual disturbances of any of the ultra-marine provinces; but includes the captains, lieutenants, sub-lieutenants, and troops, who, having served in one or the other, have retired without censure, and with lawful leave, from having been wounded and incapacitated to serve in action, and not in any other manner.

ART. 13. It also includes those individuals, not military, who, having served as partisans, or contributed in any other manner to the national defence in this war, or in the disturbances of America, have remained, or remain, wounded or disabled by the result of battle.

ART. 14. These favors shall be granted to the said individuals, although they should enjoy other rewards for their services and distinguished actions.

ART. 15. Out of the same remaining uncultivated and public lands, those fittest for culture shall be marked out and given gratuitously, by lot, to every inhabitant of the respective towns who asks for it, and has no other land of his own, and in a quantity proportioned to the extent of the land, so as that the whole of those divided, in any case, do not exceed the fourth part of the said uncultivated and public lands; and, if these should not be sufficient, the quantity shall be given in the arable land of the corporations of the town, directing, in such case, a redeemable fee, equivalent to the income of the same in the five years, up to the end of 1807, in order that the municipal funds should not decay.

ART. 16. If any of the grantees in the preceding article should, for two successive years, fail to pay the fee, the quantity of land belonging to the corporation, or to keep it employed usefully, it shall be granted to a more laborious inhabitant who has no land of his own.

ART. 17. The writings for these concessions shall be made also, without any expense, by the councils, and shall be approved by the provincial deputations.

ART. 18. All the quantities of land which are conceded conformably to articles 9, 10, 12, 13, and 15, shall be also in full property for the grantees and their successors, on the terms and with the privileges which the 2d article expresses; but the owners of these quantities cannot alienate them before four years from the time they were granted, nor ever subject them to entail, or pass them, at any time, or by any title to *mortmain*.

ART. 19. Whoever of the said grantees, or his successors, establishes his permanent residence on the same quantity of land, shall be exempt, for eight years, from every contribution or impost upon that land or its products.

ART. 20. This decree shall be circulated, not only in all the towns of the monarchy, but also in all the national armies, publishing it in them, so as that it may come to be known by all the individuals composing them.

The regency of the kingdom will take notice of the above, and will do what is necessary for its accomplishment, causing it to be printed, published, and circulated.

FRANCISCO CISCAR, President.

The deputy FLORENCIO CASTILLO, *Secretary.*
The deputy JUAN MARIA HERRERA, *Secretary.*
Given at Cadiz, the 4th of January, 1813.

To the Regency of the Kingdom:

Wherefore, we command all tribunals, judges, chiefs, Governors, and other authorities, as well civil as military and ecclesiastical, of whatever class or degree, that they keep and cause to be kept, comply with and execute, the present decree in all its parts: You will take notice of the same for its completion, and you will order that it be printed, published, and circulated.

J. MOSQUERA Y FIGUERA.
THE DUKE DEL INFANTADO.
JOHN VILLAVICENCIO.
IGN. RODRG. DE RIVAS.
JUAN PEREZ VILLAMIL.

Given in Cadiz, the 7th of January, 1813.

CADIZ, January 22, 1813.

By order of the regency of the kingdom, I communicate this to your excellency, in order that, transmitting it to the provincial deputation as soon as it be installed, you keep, and comply punctually with, the part which respects you, exciting the zeal of your excellency, to the end that agriculture and industry, aided by this powerful auxiliary, should be elevated to the point of grandeur of which it is susceptible; and that the beneficent views of the august national congress, and of their highnesses, in their incessant toils, may produce the happy results anticipated for the Spaniards of both hemispheres. Their highnesses also desire that the same provincial deputations give an account, through the medium of the ultra-marine department, provisionally in my charge, of the circulation of this decree, as soon as your excellency has communicated it, without preventing your excellency from doing so separately; and also from making the observations which, from the knowledge you have of the country, you judge proper, and conducive to the elucidation of the matter. God preserve your excellency many years.

JOSEPH DE LIMOTA.

To the CAPTAIN GENERAL *of the Island of Cuba, Political Chief of the Havana.*

The object of the preceding order of the Cortes seems to have been to encourage agriculture, to reward those who had served their country, and to support the poor. To this end it declares:

1st. That all public lands shall be made private; which was, in fact, an instruction to the Governors of provinces to use liberally, and without delay, the powers vested in them in relation to the disposal of public lands, and with a view to the purposes declared in the preamble.

2d. That they should be granted in fee simple.

3d. To those who resided in the adjacent towns.

4th. That the provincial deputations propose the best manner of carrying into execution.

5th. That the regency and two secretaries of state inform what the provincial deputations report on this subject.

6th. One-half of the public lands are reserved from the above decree, as a pledge for the public debt, and to pay the claims which the inhabitants of the nearest towns may have against the nation: first, for supplies furnished, during the war, to the army; second, for loans made to the Government, for that purpose, since 1808.

7th. In addition to the above, any other national credit shall be allowed which is lawful, and lands granted therefor.

8th. In the reserved half shall be computed those lands that shall be justly sold, in some of the provinces, to support the war.

9th. Of the lands remaining undisposed of, as above, there shall be given to each captain, lieutenant, or sub-lieutenant, who shall quit the service from advanced age, or wounds, without censure, an undefined quantity; and the same to each soldier or private who shall retire for the same causes, or who shall complete his times without censure.

10th. The quantity given to each shall, if possible, be sufficient to support a family.

11th. The assignment of quantities shall be made by the constitutional councils of the town.

12th. This provision includes the officers and soldiers, both of the Spanish army and troops employed in the provinces.

13th. It includes those who, though not in commission, acted in the national defence, and remained wounded or disabled.

14th. Having received other rewards shall not exclude them from these gifts.

15th. The public lands that remain uncultivated shall be divided off among the inhabitants who have no other lands.

16th. If the proprietors fail to cultivate for two years, it shall be given to a more industrious inhabitant.

17th. The grants or concessions shall be made without expense.

18th. These lands shall not be alienated in less than four years.

19th. Those who live upon their lands shall be exempt from impost or contribution for eight years.

20th. Directs the publication of this decree.

The following letter is the basis of the royal order of 1815. It sets out the merit of the militia of this province and asks for compensation for them for their services and sacrifices during the rebellion.

No. 203.   [TRANSLATION.]
MOST EXCELLENT SIR: ST. AUGUSTINE, FLORIDA, June 4, 1813.

The first of this month I discharged from the military service in which they were imployed, the three companies of white militia of this city, not only for want of provisions here, but for the urgent necessity there was that the inhabitants should be allowed to turn, once more, their attention to the care of their respective families and occupations, with the object of making as light as possible the injuries suffered by them in the insurrection of the province.

With this motive, I cannot but recommend to your excellency the fidelity manifested by the militia and third battalion of Cuba in the performance of their duty, from the first moment in which the rebellion broke out, and for which I consider them worthy the gifts to which the Supreme Government may think them entitled, taking the liberty of recommending the granting of some, which may be as follows: to each officer who has been in actual service in said militia, a royal commission for each grade he may obtain as provincial, and to the soldiers a certain quantity of land, as established by regulation in this province, agreeably to the number of persons composing each family, and which gift can also be made exclusively to the married officers and soldiers of the said third battalion of Cuba.

Men in general require to be excited by some stimulus, and it is not easy to find any who are indifferent to public approbation of their services. What I propose, without giving them in reality any thing, will be the means of contenting them, and produce henceforward the best effects; it being understood that this gift will be for those who occupy themselves in the defence. And for this end, and in case that these, my ideas, merit the approbation of your excellency, I enclose, as regards the officers of both corps, lists of those who ought, in that case, to be comprehended. God preserve your excellency many years.

His Excellency Don JUAN RUIZ DE APODACA.

The Governor of the city of St. Augustine, East Florida, gives notice of his having discharged from the military service the companies of white militia of said city; and recommends their merits, as well as the third battalion of Cuba, which they obtained on account of the insurrection of this province.

A true translation from a document in the Spanish language.

F. J. FATIO, S. B. L. C.

The following is an explanation, by the King, of the edict published by the Cortes, January 4, 1813.

MADRID, June 8, 1814.

The King, wishing to prevent the doubts which have begun to arise on account of the decree of the 4th of January of the year last past, relative to the distribution of lands, and that there disappear whatever competition that may have taken place by the forgetfulness, or little observance of the provisions of the laws of the Indians and ordinances of Intendants, with great injury to the royal exchequer, and of the owners, who, regulating themselves accordingly, had obtained the legal acquisition; he has, therefore, been pleased to order that the Intendants comply strictly with what has been ordered in the said ordinances relative to the distribution of lands; the proceeds of which, together with the rest appertaining to the royal finance, serve to support the expenses of the same; and, in the proceedings thereof, they adhere to what is prescribed in the laws of the Indies, and particularly in the royal instruction of the 15th of October, 1754; not admitting, in any wise, the least appeal of a corporation or town whatever, against those lands that are laid off or measured for the use of their owners, in virtue of a title of gift, agreement, or purchase; as His Majesty wishes, in no wise, that interpretations be given contrary to what has been ordered, to the prejudice of his royal interests or those of his royal subjects in those dominions: which I communicate to your lordship, by royal order, for your information, and that you may order the punctual compliance thereof. God preserve your lordship many years.

GONGORA.

The GOVERNOR of St. Augustine, Florida.

The following is an answer of the King to a letter of Governor Kindelan to the Captain General of Cuba, in June, 1813, approving the gifts and rewards proposed for the disbanded militia of this province.

HAVANA, July 7, 1815.

Under the date of the 29th of March last, his excellency the minister of Indies writes me the following:

I have informed the King of what your excellency sets forth in your letter, No. 236, of the year 1813, relative to the rewards which the Governor of East Florida considers the individuals of the companies of white militia, and married officers and soldiers of the third battalion of the regiment of Cuba entitled to for their meritorious conduct during the insurrection of the province; and at the same time that His Majesty approves said gifts he desires that your excellency will inform him as to the reward which the commandant of the third battalion of Cuba, Don Juan José de Estrada, who acted as Governor *pro tem.* at the commencement of the rebellion; the officers of artillery, Don Ygnacio Salens, and Don Manuel Poulin; and of dragoons, Don Juan Pucheman, are entitled to, as mentioned by the Governor in his official letter. By royal order, I communicate the same to his excellency for your information and compliance therewith, enclosing the royal commissions of local militia, according to the note forwarded by your excellency."

I forward you a copy of the same, enclosing also the documents above mentioned, that you may give them their correspondent direction, with the intention, by the first opportunity, of informing His Majesty of what I consider just, as to the remuneration before mentioned. God preserve you many years.

APODACA,
Governor pro tem. of East Florida.

A true translation from a document in the Spanish language.

F. J. FATIO, *S. B. L. C.*

The following royal order invests the superintendent of the island of Cuba with the superintendency of the two Floridas, and makes it his especial duty to advance the population and settlements of those provinces by all the means in their power.

Among them he has exercised the power of making grants of land, upon the condition of bringing an actual population upon them.

[TRANSLATION.]

HAVANA, *October* 10, 1823.

Don Juan Nepomuceno de Arocha, honorary comptroller of the army, and secretary of the intendancy of the army, superintendency of the public finance of this island and that of Puerto Rico.

I do hereby certify that, in compliance with the decree of the 7th of this month, of the superintendent Don Francisco Javier de Ambari, made at the petition of Don Fernando de la Maza Arredondo, of the 4th instant, and filed in the Secretary's office under my charge, exists the royal order of the following tenor: "His Majesty, understanding by the letters of your lordship of the 14th and 18th of August and 21st of October, of the year last past, No. 18, 28, and 107, of the resolutions concluded with the captain general of that island, to regulate all that appertains to the branch of the royal finance, and to attend to the protection and advancement of the two Floridas, and having conformed himself with the advice given by the supreme council of the Indies, in their deliberations held on the 11th of August last, His Majesty has been pleased to approve, for the present, all which has been done with respect to the regulations of said branch, as also the supplies administered by the board of royal finance for the payment of the regiment of Louisiana, and other indispensable expenditures for the fortifications and defence of the cities of St. Augustine and Pensacola, authorizing your lordship, in case of necessity, to aid or supply them. His Majesty likewise has determined, for the present, the superintendency of the two Floridas in favor of your lordship, as superintendent of the island of Cuba; and, lastly, His Majesty has been pleased to command me to inform your lordship, as I now do, that you facilitate the increase of the population of those provinces by all the means which your prudence or zeal can dictate; informing, as soon as possible, the motives for the absence of Don Juan Miguel de Losadas and Don Manuel Gonzalez Almirez from their offices.

All which I communicate to your lordship by royal order, for your intelligence and compliance thereof. God preserve your lordship many years.

GARAY.

MADRID, *September* 3, 1817. A true and correct translation.   F. J. FATIO, *S. B. L. C.*

To the Intendant of Havana, JUAN NEPOMUCENO DE AROCHA.

The concession to John H. McIntosh being the first case before us for final adjudication, we have deemed it proper to make a general inquest into the customs and usages of the different departments of the Spanish provincial Government in connexion with it, that we might be able to ascertain with more certainty how far the written rules prescribed by the Governors, from time to time, were carried into execution; and, further, that we might be able to fix upon certain principles, as corollaries from the whole, to serve as a general basis for future decisions. It was found necessary to mingle the testimony peculiar to Mr. McIntosh's case with our general examination. It, however, forms but an inconsiderable part of the following evidence, which is now reported precisely as written by the secretary of the board, who was instructed to give, as near as possible, the language of the witnesses.

We are conscious that some errors have crept into it; but we have not thought ourselves authorized to make any material alterations after the disappearance of the witnesses, and, therefore, report it as substantially the testimony of the most intelligent and respectable inhabitants within our reach, touching the customs and usages of the Spanish provincial Governments.

Evidence in the case of John H. McIntosh vs. *the United States.*

JOHN H. McINTOSH *vs.* THE UNITED STATES.

George Morrison, sworn and examined December 8, 1823, deposeth that Mr. McIntosh sent, in July, 1804, under his charge, two old negro men, and capable of working, and built one negro house. Recollects that Mr. McIntosh sent in his negroes, about two hundred, in the early part of the spring of 1804, time enough to make a crop, and settled them on Fort George, Pablo, and McGirt's creek, in February, on property belonging to Mr. McIntosh, and there made crops, one crop at Pablo, and planted at Fort George and McGirt's until 1812. That the lands at Fort George, Pablo, and McGirt's, are distinct from the lands claimed. That the two negroes remained on the lands at Indian river three years; the two last years they supported themselves. He went to the tract in May following, the year he took the negroes there. That the two negroes were left under the control of the neighbors. Mr. McIntosh never undertook to cultivate. Mr. McIntosh sent a vessel, in 1803, from Cumberland, loaded with lumber for building, which was lost in consequence of the vessel's stranding on the bar of Indian river. He never saw Mr. McIntosh or any of his family upon the land. Witness has never been on the land since, but says he knows the island called Marrott's, and has been on it; has also been on the tract called Stewart's swamp. Found out the tracts claimed by information from a Mr. Merritt. Visited these tracts by request of Mr. McIntosh. Says he does not know if Mr. McIntosh took possession of Marrott's island, Stewart's swamp, or Cabbage swamp. The negroes abandoned the 6,000 acre tract. Does not know whether Mr. McIntosh gave any security as required by the grant. Supposes that the negroes abandoned the 6,000 acre tract on account of the white people leaving that part of the country. The negroes had no stock. Mr. McIntosh never received any confirmatory title; the concession from Governor White required that the conditions should be performed within twelve months.

James Hull, being duly sworn and examined, says that he saw two negroes belonging to Mr. McIntosh, on the tract claimed at the head of Indian river, in 1805. The negroes remained there in 1806, and had about one acre cultivated. Says that Mr. McIntosh came into the province in 1804.

Where grants were made of several tracts, in order to make out the quantity he had a right to claim, was it necessary to occupy each tract?

Witness says he did not think it necessary, and the contrary was the custom; says that, in 1804, Governor White required that the grantee should take possession of his lands, and continue to occupy them; always understood that Mr. McIntosh had a large number of negroes. Witness resided about thirty miles from Mr. McIntosh's settlement at Fort George.

Testimony of George J. F. Clarke.

Witness has no recollection what year Mr. McIntosh came into the province; thinks that he came about 1801, or after; understands that Mr. McIntosh moved into the country, and brought a large number of negroes, and settled them in the northern part of the province. When a person takes up a quantity of land he could divide it in a number of parcels, and, by settling on a part, retain the whole. Subsequent to 1803, it was the rule, in memorializing for lands, that a concession was first given, but a royal title was never given until ten years' occupancy was proved. Should any person purchase a tract, and one was given him, and he should put his force upon the tract purchased, and but two negroes on the tract granted, he complies with the condition of the grant. The claimant was always obliged to prove to the Governor his having complied with the conditions of the grant before obtaining royal titles. Mr. McIntosh was excepted in the general pardon by the King, although the fact was not generally known. Mr. McIntosh sailed from St. Mary's, in 1818 or 1819, for St. Augustine. He was pardoned by special order in 1816 or 1817.

Testimony of Gabriel W. Perpall.

Witness states that, when lands were granted to any person for head-rights, under the royal order of 1790, although in several tracts, by his taking possession of one of said tracts he made good the whole, and that he could not dispose of said lands until the ten years were expired, except the improvements thereon, and that others could take possession of said lands by his abandoning them. A person (memorialist) petitioning for lands, should he bring into the country any number of head-rights, although he establish himself in any part of the province, and not on the lands granted him, he was *bona fide* entitled to them as having complied with the conditions. It was necessary that the person or persons having lands granted him or them, should come forward, and prove his locating the lands granted before the ten years had expired, when he got his fee simple thereof; and that, by placing on the property one or two head-rights, the land was considered as being taken possession of by the party. He does not know of any claim being approved of by the Governor knowing that the conditions were partly complied with. If a person comes into the province with a certain number of head-rights, by placing one or two on the lands granted, the Governor would confirm the title. When a party comes forward to prove the confirmation of his title to lands, it was necessary to do so by witnesses. The Governor told witness that Mr. McIntosh had applied for leave to come on shore, and that the Governor returned for answer that he could only be responsible for his safety as long as he, the said McIntosh, remained in his sight. Witness was here when Mr. McIntosh came into the then province, but does not recollect at what time. Does not know how many negroes he brought into the province, and does not know at what time; was never on any of the tracts alluded to.

Antonio Alvarez, sworn and examined. Witness says that possession was considered a survey, being on the land, or making improvements thereon. Witness was never on the tract on Indian river. Witness says that, when a person obtained a concession or grant of land on conditions, that he was obliged to prove the said conditions to have been fulfilled to the Governor, before he could obtain the royal title for the same. Witness says, in cases where lands were granted on conditions, and the lands abandoned previous to the performance of said conditions, the Governor would, nevertheless, consider himself authorized to exercise his discretion to grant confirmatory or royal titles. Does not recollect when Mr. McIntosh came to this country. Witness does not feel himself able to say as to the custom, whether the conditions would be considered as performed, should the claimant, instead of settling on the lands granted, settle elsewhere. Witness says he was a clerk in the escrivano's office in the year 1807, and continued such under the administrations of Governors White, Estrada, Kindelan, Estrada, and Coppinger. Witness, being cross-examined, states that it was also necessary that the party should prove his having complied with the conditions of the grant, before royal orders were given. Does not know if, in case of any persons bringing head-rights into the country, and locating them on other lands, and not on those granted, whether the concession would be confirmed or not. Witness says that Governor White was very particular as to the parties complying with the conditions of their grants. Witness states that he was in the Governor's office, which had nothing to do with the judiciary, but merely with the military and police.

Testimony of Joseph M. Hernandez.

Witness says it was necessary to represent in the memorial the number of head-rights, in order to ascertain the quantity of acres: it was necessary to settle the head-rights upon the lands conceded. In applying for royal titles it was necessary to prove that the conditions were performed. The Governors were generally reasonably rigid in requiring conditions to be performed. That placing one or two negroes on the lands granted, the grantee would have the right of possession as against third persons. The Government did not require that all the head-rights should be placed thereon immediately, and that a person was obliged to take *bona fide* possession of the land in the time specified in the memorial. Witness says, that where a person abandoned the land conceded to him, upon condition of occupying it a certain number of years, it was discretionary with Governor White, upon an application after two years' abandonment, to conform or reject his title. The other Governors required that the grantees should prove the cultivation, and uninterrupted possession, for ten years, of said lands. The Government considered it an abandonment when the party left the Territory, but not where the party removed from one tract to another. Witness says, that if several tracts of land were granted for head-rights, and mentioned in a concession, if the person take possession of one tract, and holds it for ten years, it gave him a right to the other tracts. Witness claims a tract of land formerly conceded to a person who left this Territory, and has returned for the purpose of claiming the same. Government, for the encouragement of emigration, required that grantees should settle on the lands granted them. Witness says, that if a person settled on a different tract of land with his head-rights, and not upon the one granted to him, the grantee, by placing a few persons on the tract so granted him, would be in possession thereof. Witness does not know that lands were granted to individuals for head-rights, without the conditions being complied with; he believes that one grant was made to a Mr. Huertas, by Governor Kindelan, without conditions. The Governors have uniformly re-granted land where the party has abandoned the same on any circumstance whatever. The consideration for giving lands in this Territory, was the removal of emigrants here; they received lands in proportion to the number of their families; they need not settle on more than one tract.

When the grant is for several, or many, and the sending any force, however small, upon one was considered as occupying the whole. Where the emigrant left the Territory with an intention to abandon his settlement, after two years absence, the Governors felt themselves at liberty to forfeit his right by granting to others. There was no other legal mode practised of declaring a forfeiture but by a subsequent grant to others.

George Morrison re-examined.

The witness did not see any object or mark to attract notice on the three hundred acre tract, Stewart's Swamp; was never round the tract, but had been on it; saw no lines; saw a small ancient improvement. Has been on the Cabbage swamp tract; does not know how many acres; never was round the tract; had been through it in one or two places; did not see any marked trees or lines; saw no improvement; saw nothing to attract notice. Has been on the six thousand acre tract at the head of Indian river; has been through it in several directions; passed on it three or four days; saw no marked lines or corners; did not see the beginning corner marked on the survey; supposed the two negroes were settled, and that the building was made for their accommodation; was about the middle of the tract, near the east line, called by the witness an improvement. The three hundred acre tract lies between the Indian river and the Musquito lagoon, about ten miles above the Haul Over. The Cabbage swamp lies between the river and the sea, near a place called the Narrows; made a small hole on the Cabbage swamp tract, about three or four feet deep, to procure water near the river; the river was salt; the witness was, at the time, a subject of the King of Spain; was born in Virginia, and was in the employ of claimant. Witness says he came for the first time into Florida, with Mr. McIntosh, in the spring of 1804, when Mr. McIntosh brought his negroes, in the month of February. Witness took the oath of allegiance in June or July; the claimant settled his negroes at Fort George, Pablo, and McGirt's creek. Witness repeats that the claimant sent a vessel loaded with lumber from Cumberland, for the purpose of making a settlement on Indian river, in the year 1803; says that the last time he, the witness, was upon the tract, was in May, 1805; continued in the employment of claimant until 1823, and still continues in his employ, but for the last year receives no wages; is paid by claimant when specially employed; does not know the particular time the two negroes returned to Fort George from the tract on Indian river; thinks the negroes did not return until the beginning of the year 1807; understood at the time, from the negroes, that they returned in consequence of the white population leaving that part of the country.

George J. F. Clarke, being re-examined, says that the survey signed by himself, as having surveyed a tract of six thousand acres, was not surveyed by him in person, but by his deputies, Robert McHardy and Charles Clarke. Says Charles Clarke told him that he had surveyed a part, and that Robert McHardy was employed by him to survey, who gave to witness a general description of the land. Witness believes that his deputies made, each, partial surveys. The deputies were competent to survey the land in question. Witness gave directions, in 1817, to Robert McHardy to survey the tract in question; and, in the latter part of 1818 or beginning of 1819, he instructed Charles Clark to survey. The witness does not recollect when he made the plat.

Question. Do you think the plat bearing your name was made at the time it bears date?

Answer. I do not know. I believe it was made before the winter of 1818 or 1819, but do not know whether it was made in 1817 or 1818.

Witness doubts whether he has the notes of the survey made by his deputies. Kept no regular book of surveys since June or July, 1817, but kept copies of surveys. Gave the plat to claimant in 1820 or 1821, in the town of St. Mary's. The claimant, witness thinks, called for it. Claimant did not call for the plat until the time it was handed to him; but he frequently informed claimant that the plat was ready. Witness had, generally, authority to survey lands as Surveyor General, and no special order was necessary for him. It was not customary for the Governor to issue an order of survey to witness; yet, when applications were ignorantly made to the Governor, orders were sometimes issued to him. In the case of the claimant there was no other survey. Claimant requested witness to survey his lands in 1817. Does not know whether he saw Robert McHardy in 1817 or 1818. McHardy was not a regular surveyor. He sent to witness his notes of survey in the summer of 1817. Witness was, for many years, surveyor; and, upon receiving field notes from his deputies, it was customary for him to make out his plats, which he dated with the date of the notes. This practice was not objected to by the Government. Does not think it was customary to apply to the Government for the appointment of a special surveyor, upon the ground of his being otherwise employed. While witness resided at St. Mary's he was acting as surveyor and Lieutenant Governor, that is, captain of a division over that part lying north and west of St. John's; also, Spanish consul residing at St. Mary's. When the land was not specially designated, the witness would locate wherever claimant pointed out, provided the place was vacant; and in cases where the land was specially located by the grant, he would, nevertheless, at the request of the grantee, locate in any other place.

Was such custom objected to by the Spanish Government?

Knows that several grants have, under similar circumstances, been confirmed, and without their having made any petition for the transfer; does not recollect any cases in particular, but where the claimant resided in one part of the country, he required of the claimant to procure an order to change the survey. In many instances he changed the location after actual possession, without special authority from the Governor; where the claimant lived on his survey the witness was not bound to respect the metes or bounds, but might give others. The plat and concession do not agree; witness does not know whether the survey includes the improvements made by Mr. McIntosh; says that he did not give any instructions to McHardy having reference to the metes and bounds mentioned in the concession. Did not consider himself under the necessity to conform to the order of Government contained in the grant or concession. Did not consider the metes and bounds contained in the concession as an order of Government. Might have surveyed the lands on St. John's river, or elsewhere, although by the concession directed to be located at Musquito. Does not think the Government required the petitioners to designate their lands. The Government, in the opinion of the witness, are not acquainted with the character of the lands in the different parts of the country. He was, from the commencement of his appointment, in the habit of changing the location. Has done it frequently, in large tracts as well as small. Has also divided entire tracts. Always was customary with him, and antecedent to the royal order of 1815. Had done so for Mr. Seton, Bethune, and Argotes. These grants were made under the royal order of 1790. The original practice pursued by foreigners to procure land under the order of 1790, was, first, the oath of allegiance; second, applied for the quantity of lands to the Surveyor General, who determined the quantity to be given, who had it surveyed and platted. The plat was then given to the claimant when called for. Claimant then presented his plat to the secretary for royal titles. This practice was continued until between the years 1801 and 1804, when Governor White changed the system into a direct application to himself. The grants under the first practice were absolute. The witness does not know whether Governor White had any royal authority for the change. The general impression was, at the time, that he had no authority. The former practice was not established by royal orders. Believes if there had been any royal order changing the mode of granting lands, it would have been published. Witness states the latter practice as changing the royal order of 1790. Witness has seen the royal order of 1790.

If any approbation had been made by royal order would it have been published?

The witness answers that he thinks it would.

George J. F. Clarke appeared before the board the 11th of December, and presented duplicates of surveys made by him as late Surveyor General. These plats were taken and kept for the purpose of satisfying Government what lands were vacant, and that they exhibit an account of all lands located and surveyed by witness under the Spanish Government. These acts were done in a country where we did not always do as we would, but as we could; that the situation of the country rendered the data very precarious in consequence of the Indian disturbance, and the various rebellions of the country; and witness considered it sufficient information to the inquiries of Government, and conceived himself answerable only to God Almighty and Governor Coppinger.

Question. Were you interrupted by the Indians in making your survey?

Answer. In no other way than the fear of losing my life by them.

Question. In what section of the country did this fear extend?

Answer. In the southern and western parts of the province.

Question. What do you mean by the southern?

Answer. All south of St. Augustine. Witness understood from his deputies that the Indians frequently destroyed the marks and trees pointing out the surveys.

Question. Did an apprehension of Indians, southerly, at all times, render it unsafe to survey in that direction?

Answer. The deputies reported that they did not go into particulars, as much as they wished, on account of the dread of Indians, but made such marks as would identify the land.

Question. Do you know of any instance where the survey was interrupted by the Indians?

Answer. I do not.

Question. During your surveyorship did the white population reside south of this place?

Answer. Very little—as much as at present. Witness was interrupted in his surveys in the rebellion of 1812, and the invasion of McGregor in 1817. The rebellion of 1812 lasted until 1816.

Question. Would you make plats of surveys without regular field notes?

Answer. I would for the purpose of identifying lands, to answer the inquiries of Government; for the purpose of knowing where a particular piece of land was located. Witness generally made out two surveys and plats, one for Government, the other for the grantee.

Question. Did Government entirely rely upon you for information respecting the location of lands?

Answer. Principally so: but there were instances where persons surveyed by special permission from the Government.

Question. Did Government keep any memorandum of the lands that were located?

Answer. No regular record. The surveys were generally handed into the Government office.

Question. How could you answer the questions of Government when other persons were employed to survey?

Answer. Only as far as the other surveys came to my knowledge; for they were not reported to me.

Question. As Surveyor General did you not consider the permission to others to survey irregular?

Answer. I did. I know of Government refusing to give permissions to persons to survey.

Question. How did you know this?

Answer. From the decrees sent me; a copy of a request was once sent to me, when an individual applied for a special survey, and the Governor stated that, if the Surveyor General could not survey, his deputies could.

Question. Did you ever remonstrate against the custom of granting special permission to survey?

Answer. Not officially; I mentioned it once or twice to Governor Coppinger.

Question. Upon what principle did you make this communication?

Answer. Anterior to my appointment there had been several permissions of this kind granted, and I was desirous of regulating things so as to prevent confusion, for which purpose I made a sketch of the rivers and streams.

Question. When this practice was stopped, did those persons specially appointed to survey report to you?

Answer. They did.

Question. How do you know that permission to survey was refused?

Answer. I was told that the Governor would give no further permission.

Question. What has become of your sketches?

Answer. They were generally lost when McGregor sacked Fernandina. I believe I have some few.

Question. Was there ever a regular field book kept of the surveys in this country?

Answer. There was not.

Question. When lands were granted for so many acres, upon a certain river, what rule was adopted in laying them off as to dimensions and figure?

Answer. I followed no rule, but governed myself by the localities.

Question. Do you know of any general rules?

Answer. I am not certain, but believe that, in the general instructions given me, there are rules.

Question. Were those general rules given you? Answer. They were not.

Question. When you were appointed surveyor did you know where the lands were located?

Answer. I did not.

Question. Did Mr. Marrott pursue any rules as to the survey, as far as conformable to the particular form of the grant?

Answer. None but the most general rules, and the survey was made in the manner the grantee pointed out.

Question. Have you any knowledge that Marrott kept a field book?

Answer. Does not know. Witness says Purcell had particular and rigid instructions as to survey.

Question. Was Mr. Purcell limited to any particular section to survey?

Answer. He *generally* surveyed on Halifax river; but he also surveyed in other parts of the country.

Question. How do you know that he was confined to Halifax river?

Answer. From conjecture and hearsay about the year 1801.

Question. Do you know that the lands surveyed then were according to particular form? Answer. I do not.

Question. Do you know the hand-writing of Purcell? Answer, I do.

Question. Did you ever see Governor White's instructions of the 12th of October, 1803, relative to the confiscation and granting of land, consisting of nine articles? Answer. I never did.

Question. Did you not consider it your duty to become acquainted with the rules and regulations relative to lands?

Answer. All those relative to lands I considered necessary.

Question. What regulations did you become acquainted with?

Answer. I know of no other than the quantity governing the grant, and without injury to a third person. I have never seen any other instructions than those contained in my commission.

Question. Have you those instructions?

Answer. I believe I have, and have not read them more than two or three times, as other instructions were given me afterwards, which were verbal.

Question. Did your verbal instructions differ essentially from those which were written?

Answer. The Government allowed me to pursue such a course as I thought proper.

Question. Were your first instructions limited?

Answer. I do not recollect whether they were limited or not; they referred to some general rules on surveying.

Question. Have you your instructions?

Answer. I am not certain, but think I have. I changed the location of the lands of Argote, and, in part, that of Seton and Bethune. Mr. Seton's was changed anterior to 1817, and the others after.

Question. Did these persons comply with the conditions upon which their lands were granted?

Answer. Mr. Seton did comply; Mr. Bethune did not.

Question. Were you well acquainted with Governor White? Answer. Intimately.

Question. Was he not a very strict and a very honest man? Answer. He bore that character.

Question. When a grant was made on conditions, and those conditions not complied with, was the land not confiscated by Governor White?

Answer. He would exercise his pleasure.

Question. Did he not require that persons applying for land should locate these lands?

Answer. He does not think that it was a requisition.

Question. If the location of lands was made known by the parties to Governor White, would he allow them to change the location?

Answer. Always, as I have been told.

Question. If the party did not apply to Governor White to change this location, would he allow them to do so?

Answer. I think not, unless he received an order from some one.

Question. When Captain Marrott made a survey, was it optional with him afterwards to change the location, without applying to Governor White?

Answer. It was not.

Question. Would Governor White allow any one to change their location without his permission?

Answer. He would not.

Question. Would you have changed the location of lands during the life of Governor White?

Answer. I was not in office during that period.

Question. Do you imagine that any other surveyor would have done it? Answer. I imagine not.

Question. Would you have done it under Estrada?

Answer. I would; I received my first instructions from him.

Question. Do you know of no particular reason that induced Estrada to pursue a different course from White?

Answer. I do not.

Question. How long did Estrada remain Governor?

Answer. From 1811 to 1812, when he was superseded by Kindelan.

Question. Who preceded you as surveyor?

Answer. Between Purcell and myself there was a considerable interval of time.

Question. How long? Answer. Two or three years.

Question. Was Purcell surveyor in Governor White's time? Answer. No; he was not in the country.

Question. Do you know if Purcell was an intelligent man? Answer. He was rather too much the contrary.

Question. Who appointed him? Answer. I believe Governor White appointed him.

Question. When did Marrott cease to be surveyor? Answer. In about 1800.

Question. Who superseded him? Answer. A young man by the name of John Travers.

Testimony of Mr. Turnbull.

Question. When grants were made upon condition, and the condition not complied with, were the lands not forfeited?

Answer. Certainly, according to the regulations of Governor White, which I got out of the office for my guide; and, finding them so very hard to comply with, that I did not return to this country after leaving it.

Question. When, in the petition of the grantee, he located his lands, was it optional for him to change his location?

Answer. It was not, without petitioning the Governor.

Question. Could the surveyor change the location of the lands granted?

Answer. I was informed by Mr. Purcell and Mr. Tate that he could not.

Question. Was Tate an intelligent man? Answer. He was: the office he held was that of practical surveyor.

Question. Was Purcell an intelligent man? Answer. He was not.

Question. Did you ever hear Purcell say that he was governed by any particular rules?

Answer. He told me he was; and the parties were generally given one-third in front and two-thirds in depth.

Question. When a particular description or outline was given in the grant, could the surveyors change the same?

Answer. I do not know whether the surveyor was bound to do so.

Question. Was Mr. Purcell considered as a general surveyor at that time? Answer. I believe he was.

Question. Did you understand that his powers were confined to a particular section of the country?

Answer. I did not.

Question. Do you know that, when Government granted lands upon conditions, she required the same to be fulfilled?

Answer. Yes.

Question. If lands were granted you would you conceive it a performance of the conditions by settling on any other land?

Answer. No.

Question. If you had settled your negroes on lands not granted, and cultivated the same, and had placed a few negroes on lands granted, would you consider it complying with the conditions?

Answer. No; I think I ought to place all my force on the lands granted.

Question. When you applied for lands, did you not take pains to find out what rules were to govern you, and did you do so?

Answer. Yes; and received the same from Mr. Tate, who obtained them from the record.

Question. Did you get any memorandum of lands that had been granted?

Answer. I did, from Mr. Tate; but I do not know whether they were taken from the record, as they had no signature.

Question. Was it necessary to present to the Government, when you applied for lands, a list of your property?

Answer. I did, and presented a schedule of all my property.

Question. Why did you not take possession of the lands granted you?

Answer. I employed a person to make camps, which cost me sixty dollars.

Question. Why did you not go on with the settlement?

Answer. Because I considered the conditions so difficult that I abandoned it. I have a British claim to Marrott's island, in the case now before the board.

Question. What was the general custom of the Governors as to the granting of lands?

Answer. I only know the practice at the time of the regulations.

Question. Do you know, of your own particular knowledge, what was the general custom of surveyors in laying off lands?

Answer. I know of no other custom than that of one-third front and two-thirds in depth.

Question. How long have you been in the province?

Answer. About four months in 1803, and one month in 1804.

Question. Where have you lived since that time?   Answer. In Georgia.

Question. Have you been in this country since?   Answer. Not under the Spanish Government.

Question. Who got you those regulations?

Answer. Mr. Tate, and translated by Bernardino Sanchez, as public interpreter.

Question. Was it the general opinion here, in 1803, that the regulations of Governor White were in force?

Answer. I presume so.

Question. Did you ascertain from Mr. Purcell that there were general regulations governing his survey?

Answer. He told me there were.

Mr. Clarke re-examined, the 12th of December, 1823, by Mr. Lancaster.

Question. Were you not authorized by the Government to appoint deputies under you to survey?

Answer. I was.

Question. As far as you know, was your work always received and approved by the Government?

Answer. It was.

Question. In all the plats which you have made out, did you not endeavor to date them as nearly as possible at the time when the survey was actually made?

Answer. Yes; before I was authorized to distribute lands, I frequently surveyed for individuals before they petitioned and had a concession; I then dated the survey so as to correspond with the concession, or an order I had to distribute lands.

Question. Was a survey actually necessary to a settler to enable him to obtain a royal title?

Answer. No; royal titles were made sometimes without a survey.

Examined by the United States' attorney.

Question. What was the taking possession, in the eye of the Spanish law?

Answer. Any work done by the parties on the premises.

Question. Was the digging of a well, or planting of a tree, taking possession?

Answer. Yes; the digging of a well, planting a post, or surveying, or any work costing him labor or money.

Question. Did it matter how trivial the labor or expense was?   Answer. There was no rule to go by.

Question. When a person obtained a concession of land on condition of improvement, as in the case of a mill-seat, what was necessary to be done?

Answer. I conceived there were two conditions; that of settling the land without injury to a third person, and building a mill.

Question. In such a condition as a mill-seat was it not necessary that the conditions be substantially complied with?

Answer. Yes.

Examined by Mr. Hamilton.

Question. Was your authority to appoint deputy surveyors in writing?

Answer. It was not. It was merely verbal.

Question. Were you ever authorized to appoint deputy surveyors to survey lands during your absence?

Answer. I was.

Question. In what manner were you authorized to make these appointments?

Answer. By the Governor; directing me to do, in all cases, for the best.

Question. Have you not made out many plats long subsequent to the 24th of January, 1818?

Answer. Yes, many.

Question. Can you tell to whom you have made these plats?   Answer. I do not recollect.

Question. Do you recollect making the plats of Mr. McIntosh's survey of Indian river tract after January 24, 1818?   Answer. I do not recollect.

Question. You mentioned that Mr. McHardy had run the river line, and one of the back lines, but that that survey was not sufficient, and that you sent Mr. Charles Clarke to complete the survey?

Answer. I said that I had received from Mr. McHardy data sufficient to satisfy the Government; and that the Government respected the survey made.

Question. Was McHardy an active and intelligent surveyor?   Answer. He was.

Question. When did you employ Mr. McHardy?   Answer. I think it was as early as 1815.

Question. Were his notes proofs of his capacity?   Answer. They were.

Question. Were they accurate?   Answer. I cannot say, as I never re-surveyed any of his surveys.

Question. Had not the field notes of McHardy an appearance of accuracy?

Answer. Sometimes his plats were handsomely and well made out, and his field notes had the appearance of accuracy.

Question. Do you not suppose, when he acted from your orders, he done so strictly? Answer. He did so.

Question. In what manner did you give your orders?

Answer. Sometimes in writing, sometimes verbally; when he was not present, always in writing.

Question. Was he a permanent deputy of yours? Answer. At times he was, and at others he was not.

Question. When was he a permanent deputy?

Answer. I cannot say as to date; he was so occasionally between the years 1815 and 1821. By a permanent deputy, I mean he could survey grants with my permission.

Question. Was he your deputy at the commencement of his employment? Answer. No, not until 1817.

Question. Where did you see him in the year 1817? Answer. I cannot recollect.

Question. Did you give him any verbal instructions in 1817? Answer. I do not recollect.

Question. Did you give him any written instructions in 1817?

Answer. We corresponded, but I do not recollect whether I gave him instructions or not.

Question. In what manner did you give him his appointment as deputy surveyor? Answer. I cannot say.

Question. When a grant was given him containing the metes and bounds, would he not go strictly by them? Answer. Not always.

Question. In the case of McIntosh, did you give him written or verbal instructions?

Answer. I do not recollect.

Question. Do you recollect of giving him any instructions?

Answer. I do not, but I recollect of calling on him for several surveys. I requested him to make various surveys for various persons, and at various times.

Question. Look at the grant of 6,000 acres, and the survey, and tell me if they agree in metes and bounds? Answer. They do not.

Question. Are they essentially different? Answer. They are.

Question. If McHardy was given that grant, would he not consider it his duty to go by the metes and bounds?

Answer. He would not. Mr. McIntosh, soon after his return to the province, requested me to survey the lands he had, unsurveyed, in the province, and placed in my hands the papers relative to the lands he got from Government.

Question. Did you retain possession of the papers?

Answer. I do not know that they were all in my possession.

Question. Are you the agent of Mr. McIntosh?

Answer. I was, and in one instance with power to make a conveyance of one tract of land which he had sold to Mr. Kingsley; which tract was Fort George.

Question. Had you authority to sell his lands?

Answer. I had a power to attend generally to his business, and a special power to sell said tract of Fort George.

Question. Did you leave with Mr. McHardy the papers of Mr. McIntosh relative to the Indian river tract? Answer. I did not.

Question. Who did? Answer. I believe that no one did.

Question. Who directed McHardy to make survey? Answer. I did.

Question. Are you sure that *you gave* the order to McHardy to survey McIntosh's lands? Answer. I did.

Question. How are you sure?

Answer. As he had not the papers, it was necessary he should have something from me to go by.

Question. Did Mr. McIntosh direct you where he wished the survey made?

Answer. When he showed me his papers, I saw that the land could not be surveyed to Mr. McIntosh's advantage, if it was surveyed as the grant directed: I, therefore, advised him to make the change.

Question. Did you advise him as surveyor or as agent?

Answer. I advised him as surveyor and not as agent; and I directed McHardy to make the survey, as appears by the plat.

Question. Did you give McHardy any reasons for the change from the grant? Answer. I did not.

Question. When did you give him these instructions? Answer. About the year 1817.

Question. Did you advise McHardy to make out the survey, and give McIntosh as much good land as possible?

Answer. I did. I do not recollect whether I told McHardy to survey for McIntosh or not.

Question. Do you believe that he made a memorandum at the time you gave him the directions?

Answer. I do not; the probability is that I gave him directions to survey a certain quantity of land, without telling him for whom.

Question. Did the field notes you received from McHardy designate the land as belonging to McIntosh?

Answer. I think not.

Question. At the time you gave him directions to survey, did you give him any other?

Answer. I cannot recollect.

Question. You are perfectly sure you gave directions to McHardy to survey Mr. McIntosh's land?

Answer. I am perfectly sure I gave McHardy directions to survey these lands.

Question. What is the reason you are sure you gave these directions?

Answer. Because I received field notes from him of the survey, and must, therefore, have given him directions.

Question. Did you make that plat of Marrott's island? Answer. I did.

Question. Who surveyed that?

Answer. I do not think it has been regularly surveyed, that is, regularly chained. McHardy gave me the field notes.

Question. Did you give McHardy orders to survey Marrott's island at the same time with the other tracts?

Answer. I did; though I cannot recollect the time.

Question. From whom did you receive the field notes of Marrott's island? Answer. From McHardy.

Question. What did you direct him to do in respect to these tracts?

Answer. I directed Charles Clarke to ascertain the front line of 6,000 acres, for the purpose of locating some other tracts. I also directed him to pass on the other tracts to see where they lay.

Question. Did he inform you of his being on these tracts?

Answer. He gave me a description of Marrott's island and the 6,000 acre tract.

Question. Whose lands were located by Clarke next to the 6,000 acre tract?

Answer. Argotes' tract, then Garvin's, and then he located his own land.

Question. Have you copies of Argotes' tract? Answer. I have.

Question. Do you suppose that the person who made those surveys was an accurate surveyor?

Answer. I have no reason to suppose otherwise.

Question. Did you receive the field notes of Argotes' tract from Clarke? Answer. No: from McHardy.

Question. Who surveyed Garvin's tract? Answer. McHardy.

Question. Who surveyed Charles Clarke's tract? Answer. Charles Clarke himself.

Question. When did he do it? Answer. I do not know whether it was in 1819 or 1820.

Question. Do you think it could be in 1818? Answer. I do not know. I think it was in 1819 or 1820.

Question. Do you recollect when Mr. McIntosh removed from Florida?

Answer. About 1813, when the United States' troops left the province.

Question. Did Mr. McIntosh remove all his negroes from Florida?

Answer. He did all those within his control.

Question. Where did he afterwards settle? Answer. In Georgia.

Question. Did he ever bring them back? Answer. Never.

Question. When did he take the benefit of the pardon?

Answer. He returned personally to take the pardon in 1816 or 1817, but I am not certain.

Question. Was it a special pardon? Answer. It was.

Question. Has Marrott's island, or any part of it, been granted to any other person?

Answer. I do not know whether it was ever surveyed or granted to any other person.

Question. In the case where lands are granted in one entire tract, and that tract be abandoned, would not a re-grant of a part of that tract be a forfeiture of the whole?

Answer. That depended on the inclination of the Governor.

Question. Would the Governor have re-granted that land if he considered it as appertaining to the royal domain? Answer. This I am unable to answer.

Question. Why do you suppose that it depended upon the will of the Governor to make this forfeiture?

Answer. Because, as he was arbitrary, there was no one to oppose him.

Question. Do you know what quantity of land Mr. McIntosh has in this country?

Answer. I do not know exactly, but believe about 20,000 acres. His lands are generally valuable. The certificates were kept in a field book, which I have not.

Question. Did the Government direct you to keep a field book? Answer. Yes.

Examined by Mr. Lancaster.

Question. What validity, under the Spanish Government, had British grants, where the grantees had removed from the province under the treaty of 1783?

Answer. If they had not recorded their grants, and got them recognised by the Spanish Government, they had no validity. Recorded and recognised are the same thing. All persons who claimed lands under British grants came forward, and had them recorded.

Question. Upon what conditions were these British grants recorded, and what has the grantee to conform to?

Answer. The grants were recorded upon condition of taking the oath of allegiance.

Question. Were they recorded upon any other condition? Answer. No, sir.

Question. Were those rules rigidly enforced, and the lands forfeited in consequence of their not being observed? Answer. Yes.

Question. What was the evidence of forfeiture? Answer. Their being granted to another person.

Question. Was the re-granting of lands the only mode of declaring them forfeited?

Answer. I know of no other.

SATURDAY, *December* 13, 1823.

Testimony of Mr. Segin. Examined by Mr. Macon.

Question. What is your age? Answer. Thirty-eight years.

Question. How long have you resided in the province? Answer. Ever since I was born.

Question. Were you a clerk in any office? Answer. I was a clerk in the escrivano's office.

Question. How old were you when you were first taken into that office?

Answer. About fourteen or fifteen years.

Question. How long did you write in that office? Answer. About ten or twelve years.

Question. Were the grants recorded in the office in which you wrote?

Answer. The royal titles were, but not the grants.

Question. Were you in the escrivano's office during Governor White's administration? Answer. I was.

Question. Up to what period did you remain in that office?

Answer. From 1800 to 1806 or 1807, and from 1809 to 1812 or '13.

Question. Did you continue in the office in any other capacity?

Answer. In 1812 or 1813 Mr. Entralgo and myself were appointed escrivanos *pro tem.* on account of the death of Zubizarreta.

Question. How long did you continue as acting escrivano?

Answer. Until some time in 1814, when Mr. Entralgo was appointed by the King as escrivano?

Question. After the period of 1814, had you any charge in the office? Answer. Not officially.

Question. Were you not very intimate, and frequently attending the office, after the period of 1814?

Answer. I was appointed escrivano at Fernandina, and continued in that appointment until 1817.

Question. When you were at Fernandina, was it your duty to record grants to lands in your office?

Answer. It was not, but merely deeds and conveyances.

Question. After your return from Fernandina in 1817, did you not frequent the escrivano's office?

Answer. When business called me there.

Question. As far as you were advised, did not the customs of the escrivano's office continue the same after you left it, as when you were in it? Answer. They did.

Question. Do you not suppose that, if the customs were changed, you would have known it?

Answer. I suppose I should.

Question. After your return from Fernandina, in the business you transacted with them, did you not find the same customs prevailing as before? Answer. I did.

Question. Were the concessions issued from the escrivano's office?

Answer. They were not; they were issued from the Secretary's office, and the royal titles from the escrivano's office.

Question. Had the escrivano any thing to do but the bare registering of the royal titles? Answer. He had not.

Question. What do you mean by recording?

Answer. The original was placed in the care of the escrivano, who gave certified copies of them when required of him.

Question. Whose duty was it to make out the royal title?

Answer. The escrivano's, by order of the Governor. The royal title was made out by the escrivano, and taken to the Governor to sign, after which it was returned to the escrivano, who filed it in his office. The escrivano made out the royal title when the Governor was satisfied that the party was entitled to it.

Question. Was it not usual to consult the escrivano previous to any application for royal titles?

Answer. It was not necessary, though it was sometimes done.

Question. When a party applying for confirmatory titles to the Governor, was it not necessary to satisfy him that the conditions were performed?

Answer. It was, and he would not issue them unless satisfied.

Question. In what manner did the parties satisfy the Governor that they had complied with the condition?

Answer. He directed the party to prove by witnesses before him, the escrivano, or judge, that they had done so.

Question. Was it always required that the party examined should be put on oath? Answer. Always.

Question. Was it not always necessary for the party to prove by witnesses, in addition to his own oath, the compliance with the conditions of the concession? Answer. It was.

Question. Were you ever present when the party claiming royal titles proved the compliance of the conditions of the concession? Answer. Several times,

Question. Were not the examination of those witnesses in these cases strict? Answer. Yes.

Question. Do you know of any royal title being refused by the Governor for a non-compliance of conditions?

Answer. None. The parties would not dare go before the Governor, if they had not complied with the conditions.

Question. Do you know of any person failing to apply for royal titles who had a concession, and had not complied with the conditions? Answer. I do not know of any person.

Question. Was it necessary to locate the lands granted in correspondence with the description of the concession? Answer. It was generally so.

Question. When a party obtained a concession which was occupied, was it not necessary to petition for a new location on vacant lands? Answer. Yes, it was.

Question. How was the legality of the previous possession ascertained?

Answer. By the previous occupant proving his possession by his certificate.

Question. Were not the original concessions found in the Secretary's office? Answer. They were.

Question. Where a person had a concession for a tract of land, adversely occupied, would the Governor allow him to locate it elsewhere? Answer. Yes.

Question. Do you think that when a person had obtained concession of lands for head-rights, and when it was shown to the Governor that he had removed his head-rights out of the Spanish dominion, that the concession would be confirmed by royal title? Answer. I cannot say, having never known such a case.

Question. When a person had a concession of land for head-rights, was it not necessary to settle them on the lands conceded before he applied for the royal title?

Answer. If his head-rights were one hundred, by placing one upon the land, it would be considered as complying with the conditions.

Question. Where a person applying for royal title in confirmation of his concession for head-rights, was it not necessary to prove to the Governor that he had the head-rights? Answer. I believe it was.

Question. When a party applied for a confirmation of a concession of head-rights, and it was shown to the court that the party had removed himself, his family, and negroes out of the Spanish dominion, that the Governor would have given a royal title? Answer. I think he would not.

Question. Was not Governor White very rigid in exacting a compliance of the conditions annexed to concessions of lands? Answer. I do not think that Governor White was more rigid than the other Governors.

Question. Do you think that the situation which you were in permitted you to know whether Governor White was more rigid than the other Governors. Answer. Yes, I could perceive that whilst I was in the office.

Question. Was not the public domain highly estimated by the Governors?

Answer. You must show services before you could obtain grants, and lands could not be purchased for money.

Question. When a person was injured by the Governor could he not appeal to a higher tribunal?

Answer. Yes.

Question. Was not a decree of the Governor considered the law of the land until it was reversed by a higher tribunal? Answer. Yes.

Question. During the Spanish Government did you not practise law here? Answer. Yes.

Question. How were the British titles of such claimants as removed from here under the treaty of 1783 regarded by the Spanish administration of this country since that time?

Answer. I do not know: I was not born until 1785.

By Judge Floyd.

Question. Could any other person have any thing to do with the public lands but the Governor?

Answer. No one.

Question. Was the Governor tenacious of this right? Answer. He was.

MONDAY MORNING, DECEMBER 15, 1823.

Mr. Perpall re-examined by Mr. Macon.

Question. Have you been a resident of this country since the year 1790?

Answer. No. I left this country in 1790, and returned in 1803.

Question. Have you resided since 1803 in St. Augustine? Answer. I have.

Question. What time of 1803 did you return? Answer. On the 29th June.

Question. Was Colonel White Governor of the province when you returned? Answer. He was.

Question. Were you well acquainted with Governor White? Answer. I was.

Question. Have you not also been well acquainted with all the Governors that succeeded him?

Answer. I have.

Question. Was not Governor White remarkably rigid in a compliance of his official duties? Answer. He was.

Question. Was he not also very particular in granting the public lands? Answer. He was.

Question. As far as you know, did not Governor White exact a rigid compliance with all the conditions annexed in the concessions of lands?

Answer. He did, as far as I know: he was the most rigid Governor we have had in that respect.

Question. As far as you know, were not Governor White's officers very much in awe of him?

Answer: They were.

Question. Did not persons, petitioning for lands from Governor White for their head-rights, find great difficulty in obtaining them? Answer. No difficulty, upon proving what they were entitled to.

Question. Was it not a principle of the Spanish Government, in granting land, to procure population or reward services? Answer. It was: but there were no grants for services until the year 1815—meaning military services.

By Mr. Lancaster.

Question. Had the Governors not discretionary powers, at all times, to grant lands? Answer. I do not know.

Question. Was it not always a custom with the Governor to grant lands for the erection of mills? Answer. It was.

Question. Was it not also the custom to grant lands for making tanyards?

Answer. Yes, or any other machinery that was beneficial to the country.

Question. Did they not also grant lands for cowpens? Answer. Yes.

Question. Was it not also customary to grant lands for turtle crawls?

Answer. A person fishing for turtle in Indian river applied for lands as head-rights, which were granted him.

Question. Were these various grants, as far as you know, under any particular order?

Answer. They were made pursuant to the order of 1790. Where lands were granted for the erection of mills, tanyards, and cowpens, they were never given in fee simple, and the lands reverted to the King when the parties thought proper to remove therefrom.

Question. When a tanyard had been erected, did you ever know a royal title to be given?

Answer. I do not know that it was ever given.

Question. Do you know what validity the Spanish Government gave to British grants, where the grantees moved out of the province under the treaty of 1783?

Answer. None, except they remained here and took the oath of allegiance.

By Mr. Hamilton.

Question. Do you believe that the Governors had the power to grant a definite quantity of lands?

Answer. I do not know.

Question. Have you seen the royal order of 1790? Answer. I have of 1790, 1791, 1792, 1793, and 1815.

Question. Have you these royal orders? Answer. I have.

Question. Will you produce them to the board? Answer. I will.

Question. How did you get them? Answer. From my brother-in-law, Mr. Arribas, at Havana.

Question. Have you seen the regulations made by Governor White?

Answer. I have: they were made on account of a difference existing with the settlers at Musquito.

Question. Were these rules adhered to by the other Governors?

Answer. They were, except the diminution of the quantity relative to head-rights.

Question. Have you seen any other rules by Governor White? Answer. No.

Question. Have you got a copy of the regulations by Governor White? Answer. I have not.

Question. Did you, at any time, apply for lands as head-rights? Answer. I have.

Question. What course did you pursue, considering yourself acting in pursuance to the regulations?

Answer. I presented my memorial asking for lands according to the number of head-rights, and they were granted to me on conditions of taking possession and cultivating the same for ten years.

Question. At the expiration of ten years, was it necessary to prove the possession and cultivation before you obtained royal titles? Answer. It was.

Question. Was your own oath necessary, with other evidence? Answer. It was.

Question. Was there much form and strictness in making this examination?

Answer. There was of form, but not of strictness.

Question. Was it not always necessary that proof should be given on a substantial compliance of the conditions? Answer. It was.

Question. Would it be a compliance of the conditions if the grantee should put but two negroes on the lands, and cultivate elsewhere? Answer. It would.

Question. How do you reconcile the present answer with a former one, that it would be necessary to prove that you had cultivated the lands, and placed your head-rights thereon to get royal titles?

Answer. I do not mean to be understood that it was necessary to have uninterrupted possession with the head-rights, and that the lands granted should be cultivated for ten years successively: possession and cultivation during the ten years were sufficient. A substantial performance was all that was necessary. In order to get a royal title, it was necessary to petition for the same; and, upon proof of the performance of the conditions in the concession, it was granted.

Question. If the lands were abandoned for two years, did he not grant those lands to others?

Answer. I believe not, if the parties were in the province, and had their head-rights with them.

Question. If a petitioner were in possession of the lands, and cultivated the same, would he grant him other land? Answer. He would grant him other lands for the surplus of his head-rights.

Question. If a person were to place his head-rights on lands at Musquito and move them on other lands, would he be entitled to a royal title for the first, provided his head-rights were in the territory.

Answer. If his head-rights were in the province he would be entitled to it.'

Question. Was it not necessary to obtain from the Governor an order of survey, in order to have lands surveyed. Answer. It was.

Question. Was there any other person to whom you could apply for an order to survey?

Answer. There was not.

Question. Was it not necessary to petition the Governor for permission to change the location of lands?

Answer. It was.

Question. Did you ever apply to the Governor for permission to change location?

Answer. I did make one application. It was commonly thought necessary, and it was granted where a person could show good cause for the same.

Question. Could you not obtain this change of location by applying to the Surveyor General?

Answer. No; to the Governor.

Question. Could you change metes and bounds of a tract without applying to the Governor? Answer. No.

Question. Do you think the surveyor, without presenting a petition to the Governor, [could] change the survey? Answer. I do not believe he could.

Question. When grants were made in one entire tract, had the surveyor, without permission of the Governor, power to divide it in various tracts? Answer. I believe not.

Question. Did you ever know of an instance of such a change? Answer. No.

Question. Did you ever know an application to the Governor to divide the location? Answer. Not in my knowledge.

Question. What was the nature of the lands granted for saw-mills? Answer. Pine barren, generally.

Question. If, in these lands for mill seats there should be plantable lands, would not the Governor grant them to persons applying for the same? Answer. I do not know.

Question. Was it, or was it not, necessary that the Surveyor General should survey himself, or could he do so by deputies?

Answer. He might appoint a deputy, but it was his, the Surveyor General's, duty, to certify the same.

Question. Was it not the duty of the Surveyor General to make a report of all the surveys made? Answer. I believe not.

Question. Was there at any time, to your knowledge, a Surveyor General's office kept in this city? Answer. Not to my knowledge.

Question. For the last twelve years where did the Surveyor General reside?

Answer. I do not know; but understood that Mr. Clarke was Surveyor General, and he resided at St. Mary's.

Question. Had you any doubts that Mr. Clarke was Surveyor General? Answer. None.

Question. Where did Mr. Clarke reside when Surveyor General?

Answer. Generally at St. Mary's, but visited St. Augustine now and then.

Question. When the Surveyor General was absent, how did persons get their lands surveyed?

Answer. By representing to the Governor that he was absent, and requesting a special surveyor should be appointed.

Question. Do you know whether the Governor gave Mr. Clarke verbal powers, independent of his written instructions, as to the division of lands?

Answer. I do not know. If any, it was Governor Coppinger; he had great confidence in Mr. Clarke.

Question. As you were intimate with Governor White, you know whether his acts in this province were approved of by the Captain General of Cuba?

Answer. I do not know: he was a cautious, discreet man, and never communicated his official concerns to any person.

Question. When Mr. Clarke visited this city did it cause any degree of interest among the inhabitants? Answer. No.

By Mr. Floyd.

Question. Do you know when there was a Surveyor General appointed? Answer. I do not.

Question. Did you ever see the instructions to the Surveyor General? Answer. No.

Question. If a person introduced a number of head-rights, obtained for them a concession, and afterwards, before the ten years had expired, by misfortune lost them or sold them, would his grant be confirmed? Answer. I think it would.

By Mr. Blair.

Question. Are those regulations before you the same published by Governor White in 1803? Answer. They are.

Question. Do you think the lands granted by other Governors governed by those regulations? Answer. I believe they were, except what appertains to head-rights.

Question. Was the regulation prescribing the shape of lands adhered to by Governor White and his successors? Answer. They were attended to by Governor White, but not by his successors.

Question. When two persons' lands interfered, had each not a right to call for a re-survey, according to the regulations of 1803? Yes.

Question. Did not the Governors subsequent to White, require the regulation laying off land one-third in front and two-thirds in rear, to be conformed to? Answer. Only where individuals required it.

Question. Were foreigners permitted to hold lands in Florida?

Answer. No, unless they took the oath of allegiance.

By Mr. Lancaster.

Question. When grants were located on lands previously occupied, was it not a matter of course to locate them elsewhere? Answer. It was.

By Judge Floyd.

Question. What was the rule where the land called for was discovered to be covered by water, or was not good? Answer. To locate elsewhere, upon application to the Governor.

TUESDAY, *December* 16, 1823.

Mr. Andrew Burgevin, by Mr. Hamilton.

Question. How long have you resided in this country? Answer. Since October, 1817.

Question. What has been your employment since your arrival?

Answer. I was appointed surveyor some months after my arrival.

Question. By whom were you appointed?

Answer. First by Mr. Clarke, as one of his deputies, and afterwards by the Governor; that is to say, when a person wished a survey, I got a license from the Governor.

Question. Did you make any surveys? Answer. Yes.

Question. When you received your license from the Governor, did you receive any instructions? Answer. No.

Question. Were you ordered to obey the instructions of George Clarke, by the Governor? Answer. I was not.

Question. To whom did you make returns? Answer. To the owners of the lands.

Question. Did you not consider yourself bound, when you were called on to survey, to give one-third front and two-thirds depth?

Answer. I never received any instructions on the subject.

Question. When have you seen George Clarke? Answer. I do not remember.

Question. Have you not conversed with him within the last week? Answer. I do not know whether I did or not.

Question. When you had an order of survey, were you accurate in the surveys?

Answer. I was; and always went on the lands to survey.

Question. Did you ever certify to plats of land which you never surveyed?

Answer. When I received an order of survey, I went on the lands.

Question. Did you make actual surveys in all cases where you have given certificates?

Answer. I went upon the land, but was sometimes prevented from making the survey, for fear of being murdered by the Indians.

Question. Do you know whether Mr. McHardy had an appointment from the Governor as surveyor?

Answer. Mr. McHardy surveyed as I did.

Question. Did Mr. Clarke direct you to make a survey for him?   Answer. He did.

Question. Did you ever survey lands belonging to Mr. Clarke?

Answer. I did, by an order from the Governor, obtained by petition.

Question. What tract did you survey for him?   Answer. A tract in Alachua.

Question. Did you go to that land in Alachua, and make the survey?

Answer. I did go to Alachua, but did not go round the land.   I have not been in the Hammock.

Question. Was Mr. Clarke aware as to the manner you surveyed the land?

Answer. I believe he was; and that Mr. Clarke knew, or was aware, that it could not be done otherwise.

Question. Did Mr. Clarke tell you it was unnecessary to go upon the land to be surveyed?   Answer. He did not.

Question. Did Mr. Clarke tell you it was unnecessary to make actual surveys?

Answer. Yes, provided the survey could not be made.

Question. Have you not made many surveys since 1818?

Answer. I have.   The original survey was given to the owner, who deposited it in Mr. Entralgo's office.

Question. Did Clarke give you any written instructions?   Answer. He did not.

WEDNESDAY MORNING, *December* 17, 1823.

Daniel Hurlbert, by Mr. Macon.

Question. What year did you settle in this country?

Answer. I became a Spanish subject in the latter part of 1801, or the first part of 1802.

Question. When you first came into this country did you apply for lands?

Answer. It was near two years after I came into the country that I applied for lands.

Question. When you applied for lands did you apply for your head-rights?   Answer. Yes.

Question. In what manner did you make this application?   Answer. By memorial to the Governor.

Question. Before you got a final title was it not necessary to prove to the Governor the number of head-rights stated in the memorial?

Answer. It was; the concession which I had was conditional.

Question. At the time you applied for your head-rights was it not necessary to produce them?   Answer. It was.

Question. As far as you know was this necessary?   Answer. Generally.

Question. Do you know of any instance where this was not done?   Answer. I do not.

Question. Do you not believe it was always necessary?   Answer. I do.

Question. Do you know in what manner orders of survey were procured?

Answer. Yes; by a memorial to the Governor.

Question. Was that order directed to any particular person?   Answer. It was directed to the surveyor.

Question. In order to change the location of lands was it not necessary to memorialize the Governor?

Answer. Certainly.

Question. Do you know of an instance where the Governor refused to change the location of lands?

Answer. Never, except with the interference of a third person.

Question. Where persons changed their location did you not know that they applied to Government?

Answer. Yes.

Question. As far as you know, was it not necessary that the conditions of grants should be substantially complied with?

Answer. Yes, it was.

By Mr. Hamilton.

Question. Was it necessary to take possession and cultivate the land?

Answer. According to the time of the grant.

Question. Where lands were granted to a person for head-rights, and the grantee should put one or two negroes on the grant, would it be considered as complying with the conditions?

Answer. It would be, if the head-rights remained in the province.

Question. Do you know any thing of the instructions of the Surveyor General?   Answer. I do not.

By Mr. Blair.

Question. Do you know what has been the custom in forfeiting lands?

Answer. In the time of Governor White they were much more strict than latterly.

Question. Do you know whether it was the custom of the country to require the person to put all his head-rights on the lands granted him?

Answer. It was not customary to put all the head-rights on the lands granted him.

Question. I case where a person came into the province, and procured lands in separate parcels, was he obliged to take possession of each separate tract?

Answer. It has not been the custom while the head-rights remained in the province.

Question. Where a person procured land for head-rights, and settled the head-rights on land purchased, would the person be entitled to the land conceded?

Answer. Yes; provided the head-rights remained in the Territory.

Question. What did you consider taking possession of the land?

Answer. Upon putting my head-rights upon the lands granted.   It was necessary, also, to cultivate the land to take possession.   Government granted land for the purpose of populating the country.

Examined by Judge Floyd.

Question. Was it customary for the order of survey to be contained in the concession?

Answer. No; you were obliged to petition Government.

Question. Do you know when the Surveyor General was appointed?   Answer. I do not.

Question. Do you know what were the rules and regulations in the Surveyor General's office?   Answer. No.

Question. Were there regulations? Answer. There were.
Question. Do you know if George Clarke was appointed Surveyor General? Answer. I understood so.
Question. Do you know by whom he was appointed?
Answer. By Governor Coppinger or Kindelan; but I do not know by which.

Farquhar Bethune sworn and examined on behalf of the United States.

Witness says, I have been a resident in the Territory since 1803; and in and about 1805 I saw Mr. McIntosh at Fort George, with a large number of negroes, which, I believe, he informed me he had introduced from Georgia. I also know that Mr. McIntosh did, in 1812 or 1813, carry back a large number of negroes into Georgia, and that they were never brought back under the Spanish Government. I presume that Mr. McIntosh brought as many as one hundred and fifty negroes into the province. I have understood, from what source I cannot recollect, that Mr. McIntosh purchased some of Mr. McQueen's negroes. I heard of the regulations of Governor White, I think, in the year 1805 or 1806. I have seen them: I considered them as official acts, and binding while he was Governor. We obtained land under him by memorial setting forth our head-rights; upon which the concession was issued, corresponding to the representation of those head-rights; they were granted on condition of locating by a certain time, but the concession was not considered forfeited by a non-compliance in the stated time; royal titles would not be given unless the parties would show they had complied with the conditions: I allude now to the royal order of 1790. Previous to the appointment of Surveyor General it was necessary, when a tract of land was granted, and found to be in possession of another, to apply by memorial to the Governor for permission to change the location; but if not in possession, and after the appointment of a Surveyor General, it was unnecessary. I have lands, the location of which was made without application to the Governor. I claim one small tract, the location of which was changed by a decision of the tribunal, there being a difficulty as to the concession or grant, there having been a grant or concession made previously to another person, who came forward and made a representation of the case; upon which the judge ordered that I should be allowed to change the location. I also claim one large tract, a mill seat, for sixteen thousand acres: the change of location of this claim was made in 1817 or 1818. The general regulations for surveying lands under the royal order of 1790, granted for head-rights, were, that, when upon rivers, they should be one-third front, and two-thirds back. The same regulations were not pursued in the location of lands under the royal order of 1815. My lands are in the interior, upon a creek partly navigable. I understood from the Surveyor General, and from no other public officer, that it was not necessary to apply for permission to change location of land. I applied to Mr. Clarke to know what was necessary to be done to insure a change of location. I was induced to this, by knowing changes of the kind made by particular surveyors, and I supposed that the Surveyor General had better authority for so doing than the private surveyors had.

Question. Did you ever understand from Mr. Clarke that he was vested by the Government with the discretionary power of changing the location of lands?
Answer. Mr. Clarke informed me that he had that power by virtue of his office.
Question. Did you ever know this to be done by any other person than George J. F. Clarke?
Answer. There was no other surveyor here.
Question. In case a grant was made, and the land granted was found vacant, and that it had been so for more than two years, although granted to another, would not the first grantee lose his right to it?
Answer. In such cases the Government required the first grantee to be cited, and, in case he could not show good reasons for his not complying with the conditions of his grant, he lost all title to the same.
Question. Would not it be considered as *prima-facie* evidence in case the land had been vacant for two years in succession; and would not the first grantee be then obliged, in defence of his claim, to come forward and show cause why he had not complied with the conditions of the grant?
Answer. When the first claimant resisted the grant to the second was then cited by the first.
Question. When a tract of land was granted to a second person, and found to be in legal possession of the first grantee, what was the course pursued?
Answer. It was a requisite, previous to the appointment of a Surveyor General, for the second grantee to present a memorial to the Governor stating the case, and petition for a change of location. Those persons in the neighborhood of St. Augustine, after the appointment of Surveyor General, applied to Government. The Surveyor General resided, previous to 1817, at St. Mary's, (Georgia.) The regulation of Governor White was, that any lands which had been vacant for more than two years reverted to the Government, and were liable to be disposed of. This regulation, however, was not enforced. It referred, I believe, to persons in general, without regard to their being in or out of the Territory. I was a judge under the Spanish Government for two years, in 1813 and 1814. My jurisdiction was unlimited as to object and amount: the parties could appeal for any amount above one hundred dollars. It was necessary that I should make myself acquainted with the orders and regulations of the Governors. In deciding differences relating to lands I considered myself as bound to conform to the orders and regulations of the Governor. Disputes concerning lands were settled or adjudicated upon by the judge and Governor, (constituting what was called the tribunal,) instituted either originally or by appeal. The regulations of the Governors were considered as the laws of the land, subject to be changed by the Governor who promulgated them, or his successors. That the permission to change the location of concessions was a matter of course, and the memorial requesting this permission was equally a matter of form. A concession was always considered as a good title against the Government, subject, alone, when the land was previously granted and in possession, to a change of location.
Question. Did you ever know of a refusal of permission to change the location upon reasonable grounds?
Answer. Never.
Question. In order to divide a concession in two parts was it not necessary to apply to the Governor for permission?
Answer. It was before the appointment of a Surveyor General.
Question. Have you any grant or concession which was divided by the Surveyor General?
Answer. Yes, the mill grant was so divided; this was in 1818.
Question. What was the fate of lands which had been granted by the British Government by the operation of the treaty with Great Britain in 1783?
Answer. Those persons who remained and took the oath of allegiance were confirmed in their titles; but those who left the country lost their claims, and the land reverted to the Spanish Government.
Question. Could any person, having lands granted to him for head-rights, obtain other lands without showing that he had fulfilled the conditions of the first, and introducing additional negroes?
Answer. He could not, unless he could show that the first lands were not sufficient for his hands.
Question. What was the character of Governor White?
Answer. He was a man of strict integrity, and was distinguished for the scrupulous performance of the duties of his office.

Question. Was he considered as lavish of the public lands?   Answer. Quite the contrary.

Question. At what time did he come into office?   Answer. In about 1794 or 1795.

Question. When did he die?   Answer. In 1811.

Question. What was the character of Governor Kindelan?

Answer. A respectable man, and a man of integrity.

Question. Was he strict in the discharge of his duty?

Answer. Very much so: as much so as White, but a more polished man than White: he was quite an intelligent man.   During the time of White and Kindelan there was no Surveyor General: persons were sometimes appointed to survey a particular district.

Question. Had either of those persons appointed power to change the location within their district?

Answer. I fancy they had not.

Question. When persons applied for lands to Governor White or Governor Kindelan, did they not require that proof should be made of the performance of the conditions?

Answer. Yes.

Question. Was not this proof made before the tribunal?   Answer. Yes.

Question. Would either of those Governors issue royal titles unless they were satisfied that the grantees had acted in good faith?

Answer. They would not.

Question. When permission or grants were given for cowpens, did not the Government reserve to itself the right of granting away all the plantable lands included in it?

Answer. I do not know.

Question. What was the estate conveyed by permission to pasture?

Answer. I believe an absolute one to the applicant and his heirs.

Question. Upon a disuse it reverted to the Government?   Answer. I am unable to say.

Question. Did you not always understand that the Government of Cuba approved of the conduct of Governor White?

Answer. I have always understood so.

Question. By whom were the Governors of this province appointed?   Answer. By the King.

Question. White and Kindelan were both appointed by the King?

Answer. Kindelan was a brigadier general, and White a colonel, at the time of their appointments.

Question. Who appointed Coppinger?   Answer. The captain general of Cuba.

Question. Did he come from Cuba here?   Answer. Yes, sir.

Question. What rank had he?   Answer. He was a colonel.

Question. What was his character?

Answer. In my opinion much less respectable than either of the others.

Question. Was he not considered as negligent of the duties of his office?

Answer. I considered him lax.

Question. Was he considered as an honest man?

Answer. I do not think that, in point of integrity, he stood so high as White or Kindelan.

Question. Was it not supposed that, by a proper application to Governor Coppinger, improper favors might be obtained?   Answer. A suspicion was entertained, by many, of his honesty: I know not how correctly.

The commissioners have found it difficult to elicit many general principles from the uncertain and conflicting evidence before us.   It will be perceived, by the examinations of the most intelligent and respectable inhabitants of the Territory, that the royal orders, addressed to the Governors of this province, did nothing more than announce the royal will, leaving it to the local authorities to adopt and arrange all the means necessary to carry it into execution.   These administrative arrangements seem, in some cases, to enlarge, and sometimes to narrow, the operations of the order.   They were sometimes in writing, and published to the community, but were often adopted in practice without any written authority.   None of the written rules seem to have been uniformly adhered to by all the Governors; and the practice changed, not only with the change of officers, but, also, with every alteration in the circumstances and condition of the country.

Under these circumstances, we have felt ourselves bound to regard the actual practice of the Government, by its various functionaries, rather than adhere to the neglected rules published by the local authorities, particularly where they seemed to be in opposition.   This rule we felt ourselves bound to adopt in justice to the community, first, because the will of the Governor, whether written or unwritten, was the rule of conduct to all the other functionaries, and equally authoritative when it was equally well ascertained; second, because the people were bound to conform to existing customs, as there was no tribunal to which they could appeal to enforce the execution of any written law or regulation.   We also felt ourselves bound to confirm, or recommend for confirmation, all cases consummated by royal title, without condition, and when no evidence of fraud, either against the Government of Spain or the United States was produced before us, because such grants would evidently be valid against the Spanish Government—a rule prescribed by the treaty itself, and repeated in the act of Congress passed on the 8th of May, 1822.   Besides which, it would evidently be attended by the most unjust consequences to the grantees, in such cases, to go back beyond the grant, and, after years have elapsed, and a considerable portion of the population have left the country, to require proof of conditions performed or services rendered.   But, although we receive an unconditional royal grant, as *prima facie* evidence of right, we do not preclude ourselves from inquiring into the verity of the grant itself, or whether it may not have been antedated.

In relation to conditions we have, in general, required proof of a substantial compliance, according to the actual practice of the Government; but it will be perceived they were of various kinds, and the consequences of non-performance still more various, and, withal, entirely uncertain, depending on the discretion of the Governors.   Under these circumstances it has been found difficult to digest any set of rules to embrace so great a variety of cases.   We have exercised our best discretion in doing substantial justice between the United States and all such claimants.

St. Augustine, *February* 21, 1824.

DAVIS FLOYD.
W. W. BLAIR.

No. 2.

We send herewith the following cases, which have been before us for final adjudication, together with the evidence where the cases are beyond the final jurisdiction of the commission.

LIST OF CASES.

Ramon de Fuentes, - - -	House and lot,	-	Confirmed.
James Bosley, - - -	500 acres,	-	Confirmed.
John H. McIntosh, - - -	6,000 acres,	-	Advised for the confirmation of Congress.
John H. McIntosh, - - -	300 acres,	-	Advised for the confirmation of Congress.
John H. McIntosh, - - -	1,000 acres,	-	Advised for the confirmation of Congress.
Pedro Miranda, - - -	1,000 acres,	-	Confirmed.
Bernardo Segui, - - -	7,000 acres,	-	Advised for the confirmation of Congress.
Mary Ann Davis, - - -	500 acres,	-	Confirmed.
Samuel Fairbanks, - - -	Lot in St. Augustine,		Confirmed.
Samuel Fairbanks, - - -	240 acres,	-	Confirmed; 80 of which confirmed to Wm. Beardon and wife.
Moses Elias Levy, - - -	36,000 acres,	-	Advised for confirmation.
Antelm Gay, No. 1, - - -	160 acres,	-	Confirmed.
Antelm Gay, No. 6, - - -	400 acres,	-	Confirmed.
Antelm Gay, No. 7, - - -	5,000 acres,	-	Advised for confirmation.
Antelm Gay, No. 8, - - -	300 acres,	-	Confirmed.
Belton A. Copp, - - -	1,200 acres,	-	Recommended for confirmation.
William Berrie, - - -	350 acres,	-	Confirmed.
John Huertas, - - -	15,009 acres,	-	Recommended for confirmation.
Eliza Robinson, - - -	105 acres,	-	Confirmed.
S. Fairbanks and others, -	2,000 acres,	-	Confirmed.
Peter Bagley, - - -	200 acres,	-	Confirmed.
Charles Hogan, - - -	200 acres,	-	Confirmed.
Samuel Fairbanks, - - -	500 acres,	-	Confirmed.
Reuben Hogan, - - -	385 acres,	-	Confirmed.
Francis R. Sanchez, - - -	4,000 acres,	-	Recommended for confirmation.
Joseph Delespine, - - -	560 acres,	-	Confirmed.
Joseph Delespine, - - -	600 acres,	-	Confirmed.
Eusebio Bushnell, - - -	600 acres,	-	Confirmed.
Sarah Tate, - - -	450 acres,	-	Confirmed.
Moses E. Levy, - - -	14,500 acres,	-	Recommended for confirmation.
Antelm Gay, - - -	400 acres,	-	Confirmed.
Antelm Gay, - - -	700 acres,	-	Confirmed.
Antelm Gay, - - -	500 acres,	-	Ordered to be reported to Congress for consideration.
Avice and Viel, - - -	1,000 acres,	-	Ordered to be reported to Congress with the facts attending it, and opinion that the same should be confirmed.
Peter Fouchard, - - -	1,500 acres,	-	Confirmed.

The following cases, which are reported on minutes of the board to have been confirmed or recommended for confirmation, have since been discovered to be interfered with by British grants, and, therefore, are not reported.

William's heirs, -	-	-	-	-	-	2,020 acres.
William's heirs, -	-	-	-	-	-	180 acres.
James and Emanuel Ormond,	-	-	-	-	-	2,000 acres.
Ant. Gay and Francis J. Avice, -	-	-	-	-	-	2,000 acres.
Michael Crosby's heirs,	-	-	-	-	-	2,000 acres.
Michael Crosby's heirs,	-	-	-	-	-	500 acres.

DAVIS FLOYD.
W. W. BLAIR.

COPIES OF DECREES.

Ramon de Fuentes vs. the United States.

This is a claim for a house and lot in the city of St. Augustine, known and designated in the schedule of the buildings and lots in said city as lot No. 203, in square 28, measuring upon its front from east to west fifteen Spanish yards, and in depth, from north to south, sixty Spanish yards, with its improvements and appurtenances. Upon this day this cause came on to be heard, and upon exhibits therein filed, and the testimony of Peter Miranda, Charles W. Clarke, Nicholas Rodriguez, Francis Medicis, being therein taken, and the board being sufficiently advised of and concerning the premises, do order and decree that all claim of the United States of and to said lot be released to said claimant; which decree was ordered to be recorded.

JANUARY 16, 1824.

James Bosley vs. the United States. *Claim to five hundred acres of land at Moultrie.*

In this case James Bosley claims five hundred acres of land at Bella Vista, or Moultrie, in virtue of a deed of bargain and sale from William G. D. Worthington, dated 8th of October, 1822, who derived title from Charles Gobert and others, dated 26th February, 1822, who derived title in virtue of a public sale of property of José Maria de la Torre, who, by a memorial and decree of the Governor of East Florida, dated 30th July, 1806, claimed the same. It also appeared in evidence that the said Charles Gobert, who received the lands subject to the same conditions on which they were granted to José Maria de la Torre, took possession, and held uninterrupted possession of the same up to the end of the year 1820. This being all the evidence in the case which was submitted to the board, and they being fully advised of and concerning the premises, give the following opinion, to wit: The claimant, James Bosley, having produced a regular claim of title from the competent Spanish authorities, to himself, the only question which could arise, (the power of the Governor being admitted to grant lands,) is whether the conditions contained in the original concession have been complied with, and whether the transfers have been such as were conformable to the regulations and laws of the Spanish provinces. From all the researches which we have been able to make, we find no difficulty in deciding that, in the year 1806, lands were granted under the royal order of 1790, to such settlers as, of their own free will, presented themselves and swore allegiance; and in proportion to the number of their families, and grants made from 1790 to 1803, (29th October,) were regulated by certain edicts of the King—vide 1791. To remedy certain evils, and which had become manifest, the acting Governor adopted certain rules and regulations to be observed in granting lands—vide regulations 29th October, 1803. We find another regulation, that no title of absolute property would be given until the grantee had occupied or held possession ten years. This regulation we have received incidentally from other documents and oral testimony, there being no such written documents within our reach. Those regulations of 1803, had sundry other conditions applicable to ordinary cases, which it is unnecessary here to examine. As the then Governor ordered this five hundred acres of land to be sold for the payment of the debts of the original grantee, we feel bound to presume that he possessed the power, and that no failure had taken place previous to the sale; and, as no other condition could, with propriety, apply to the purchaser than the holding possession, cultivating, &c., we feel no hesitation, from the evidence in the case, and orders and regulations of the Spanish authorities, in ordering and adjudging, and we do hereby order and adjudge, that the claim which the United States may have to the land in question, be relinquished in favor of said James Bosley, and that he be confirmed in his title to the same, so far as the United States have an interest, and no further.

John H. McIntosh vs. the United States.

The claimant applied, by a memorial, to the Spanish Governor, on the 18th May, 1803, for a concession of land, under the royal order of 1790, allowing head-rights to new settlers, and obtained a grant for ten thousand nine hundred acres, it being the amount he was entitled to by the number of his family, but upon the condition, in substance, that he would take possession of said lands in twelve months from the date of the grant.

Whether he had performed this condition, or had afterwards forfeited the right acquired by its performance, were the questions before us which gave rise to the voluminous examination of facts attached to our report. We think it was sufficiently proved that Mr. McIntosh came into the province, with all his head-rights, within or about the time limited in the concession; that this was a substantial compliance with the views of the Government, but that custom made it necessary that he should settle a part on the lands conceded; that he did settle a small part of his force on one of the tracts; and that this was taking possession, according to the custom of the country, of the whole concession. We also think it is proved that he remained in the province, and employed his head-rights in planting, until the year 1812, when he removed them to the State of Georgia, where he has ever since remained. We do not think there is any evidence of a forfeiture under the written regulations, or the practice of the local Government, both of which required the fact of abandonment to be ascertained by a legal tribunal, and a subsequent grant to another person, to divest a right already vested by possession. We also find that Mr. McIntosh was pardoned by a special act of the King, in the year 1816 or 1817, which restored him, in general, to the privileges of a subject. We do therefore advise, that the claim of the United States in and to the aforesaid concession of land, ought to be relinquished to the said McIntosh.

Pedro Miranda vs. the United States. Memorial for 1,000 acres of land.

The claimant, in support of his title, produced, in evidence, a memorial and decree for a thousand acres of land, without conditions, dated January 2, 1816, to Don José Simeon Sanchez; also a deed of bargain and sale from José Simeon Sanchez, for the said one thousand acres of land, dated April 15, 1823. This case being submitted, and the board being fully advised of and concerning the premises, do order and adjudge, that the claim of the said Pedro Miranda be confirmed to him and his heirs, so far as the United States may have any interest to the one thousand acres of land aforesaid, and no further.

Bernardo Segui vs. the United States. Memorial for 7,000 acres of land.

The claimant in this case produced, in evidence, a memorial and decree of absolute property from the Governor, dated December 20, 1815, for seven thousand acres of land; as also a plat and certificate of survey, by which it appears that, in virtue of the decrees of the Cortes of January 22, 1813, and the royal order of 1815, there was granted to the claimant, in absolute property, the seven thousand acres of land, at the place set out in the memorial and certificate of survey; and as we conceive that, by the decrees and order aforesaid, the quantity to be apportioned, according to the merit of the applicant and the number of his family, was left alone to the discretion of the Governor for the time being, that title of the claimant would have been confirmed to him under the Spanish Government, we recommend the case to Congress for their confirmation.

Mary Ann Davis vs. the United States. Memorial for 500 acres of land.

The claimant, in support of her title, introduced sundry depositions, which went to prove that John Barker, the original grantee, made application to the Governor, in 1815 or 1816, for permission to settle on the King's road, at a place called Davis's creek, and occupy five hundred acres of land, and obtained permission from the Governor to settle there, with a promise to give a title at some future period; that the said Barker did settle on the land, and, after he had been on it for some time, the Governor offered to have the grant made out to him for the five hundred acres of land, but that he, Barker, was not able to pay the fees; that the family of Barker consisted of eight or nine, white and black; that the said Barker lived on the land from the year 1815 or 1816 till the year 1822; also a deed of bargain and sale from John Barker to claimant, Mary Ann Davis, dated September 12, 1822; that the said Barker enjoyed quiet and peaceable possession under the Spanish Government during the time aforesaid. The case being submitted, and the board being fully advised of and concerning the premises, do order and adjudge that the claim of the said claimant, Mary Ann Davis, to the five hundred acres of land as described in her said memorial, be confirmed to her and her heirs, so far as the United States may have any interest to the same, and no further.

Samuel Fairbanks vs. the United States. Memorial for 240 acres of land.

The claimant, Samuel Fairbanks, claims one hundred and sixty acres of land as tenant in common with Polly Beardon, wife of William Beardon, who was Polly Gilbert, daughter of Robert Gilbert, deceased. The said Samuel Fairbanks claims title in virtue of a deed of bargain and sale, dated March 16, 1822, from Absalom Beardon and Hannah his wife, who was Hannah Gilbert, daughter of Robert Gilbert, deceased, for the quantity of eighty acres of land; and one other deed of bargain and sale, dated October 28, 1823, from Robert Gilbert, son and heir of Robert Gilbert, deceased, and Elizabeth his wife, for eighty acres of land. And the claimants, in support of their respective rights, produce an absolute title from the Government of Spain to Robert Gilbert, in which royal title is recapitulated the original memorial, decree, and order of survey, as far back as 1791, signed by the Governor of the province in 1815; and also the deposition of one witness, who proves that the said Robert Gilbert is the only son, and Polly Beardon and Hannah Beardon the only daughters, of Robert Gilbert, deceased; and, furthermore, that the said Robert Gilbert lived on and cultivated the land in question until his death in 1820; that the claimants are still in possession of the same. The case being submitted, and the board being fully advised of and concerning the premises, order and adjudge as follows: that is, that the title of the said Samuel Fairbanks, for the quantity of one hundred and sixty acres, be confirmed to him and his heirs; and that the quantity of eighty acres of the aforesaid tract of two hundred and forty be confirmed to Polly Beardon, wife of William Beardon, and her heirs, so far as the United States may have any claim to the same, and no further.

Moses E. Levy vs. the United States.

This is a claim for thirty-six thousand acres of land lying in Alachua. The claimant produced, in evidence, a certified copy of a concession or grant made to Fernando de la Maza Arredondo and son, by the sub-delegate general, superintendent of the island of Cuba and the two Floridas, Alexander Ramirez, bearing date December 22, 1817, for four leagues of land to each wind, reckoned from a point, or the settlement of Alachua, to lay in rectilineal figure, with the conditions imposed, that the grantee shall settle upon said lands two hundred Spanish families; and that, also, they should begin the said establishment in three years from the date of the grant; which proceeding occurred with the advice of the fiscal of the royal domain and the Surveyor General, under a royal order to the said superintendent, &c., dated September 3, 1817, requiring him to use all the means in his power to augment the population in Florida. The claimant also produced a deed of conveyance for thirty-six thousand acres of land, executed by F. M. Arredondo, agent and attorney in fact for F. M. Arredondo and son, bearing date January 2, 1822, in exchange for another tract on Alligator creek, for which it is in proof claimant paid twenty-five thousand dollars. Claimant also produced, in evidence, a decree of the said sub-delegate general, superintendent of the island of Cuba, &c., dated December 2, 1820, allowing one year prolongation. It, however, appears, from the testimony of William T. Hall, (see exhibit F,) that the settlement did actually begin on the 12th of November, 1820, he, the deponent, being a Spanish subject employed to commence said settlement. Although, from much of the testimony taken in this cause, it appears that the hostile disposition of the Indians rendered a settlement difficult and precarious sooner than that period, and even then, yet, since that time (the testimony is abundant to show) a continuation of the settlement, the establishment of several families there, and a great expenditure of labor and money by the proprietors. It is in proof (see the depositions of F. P. Sanchez and Frederick Warburg) that Levy, the claimant, has expended, in the settlement of families, building houses, clearing lands, furnishing provisions, clothing, &c., upwards of $18,000; and that he has been making arrangements with many families in Europe, for several years past, to bring them to this country and settle them, for which purpose he purchased this tract of land. It is further in proof that there are settled on said grant fifty or more persons, of which about thirty have been introduced by Levy, the claimant, and that, amongst those he has introduced, there are five or six heads of families. Under all these circumstances, although it cannot be pretended that the condition of the grant to Arredondo has been complied with, we cannot but see a degree of merit in the claim of Mr. Levy for a part proportionate to his compliance, which entitles it to the peculiar consideration of Government. Whether the commissioners are bound to regard the merits of the original grant alone, or may decide upon the claims subsequently carved out of it, is a question upon which we have had some difficulty, and a difference of opinion; but, whatever may be the true construction of our powers, we have no difficulty in deciding in favor of the equity of Mr. Levy to have his claim confirmed to a quantity proportionate to the merit and extent of his compliance.

Antelm Gay vs. the United States.   Memorial for 160 acres of land.

The claimant produced, in evidence, the memorial and decree of absolute property, for one hundred and sixty acres of land, to Juan Leonardy, dated 15th February, 1816; also, a plat and certificate of survey, dated 28th April, 1819, of the same; and also, a deed of sale from grantee to the claimant, for the land in question. And the case being submitted, and the board, fully advised of and concerning the premises, do order and adjudge that the title of the claimant be confirmed to him and his heirs, so far as the United States have any interest, and no further.

Antelm Gay vs. the United States.   Memorial for 400 acres of land.

The claimant produced, in evidence, a memorial and concession for four hundred acres of land, in the name of John Andrew, dated 8th October, 1801; also, a memorial, and certain evidence adduced, which prove that the grantee took possession of the land granted him, and cultivated it for some time; that, in consequence of the revolution in 1812, he had been compelled to leave it; also, a conveyance from grantee to claimant, dated 24th day of April, 1820; also, a plat and certificate of survey, dated the 18th August, 1818. This case having been submitted, and the board, being fully advised of and concerning the premises, do order and adjudge that the title of claimant to the four hundred acres of land, as set out in his memorial, be confirmed to him, so far as the United States have interest, and no further.

Antelm Gay vs. the United States.   Memorial for 5,000 acres of land.

The claimant produced, in evidence, a memorial and decree of the acting Governor for fifteen thousand acres of land, with authority to locate five thousand acres of it at Tocoy, five miles above Picolata, dated 24th December, 1817, to Juan Huertas; also, a plat and certificate of survey of the same, dated 9th of September, 1818; and also, a deed from the grantee to the claimant, for the five thousand acres of land set out in the memorial, dated 7th July, 1821. This case being submitted, and the board, being fully advised of and concerning the premises, do order that the same be reported to Congress for their confirmation, with our opinion that (no fraud having been suggested) the claim ought to be confirmed.

Antelm Gay vs. the United States.   Memorial for 300 acres of land.

The claimant produced, in evidence, a memorial and decree for three hundred acres of land, in the name of Lewis Mattier, dated 3d February, 1801; also, an order of survey, dated the 26th April, 1821; also, a plat and certificate of survey of the same, dated 29th May, 1809; also, the certificate of R. McHardy and others, showing that the grantee had occupied the land in question, and cultivated it, for several years; and also, a deed from grantee to the claimant, dated 20th January, 1822. This case being submitted, and the board, fully advised of and concerning the premises, do order and adjudge that the title of the claimant be confirmed to him and his heirs, so far as the United States have any interest, and no further.

Belton A. Copp vs. the United States.   Memorial for 1,200 acres of land.

The claimant produced, in evidence, a memorial of Don Bernardo Segui, and a decree of the Governor accompanying the same, for twelve hundred acres of land, without condition, dated 22d January, 1818; also, a plat and certificate of survey of the lands in question, dated 1st August, 1818; also, a deed from the grantee to Don George

95   A

Fleming, dated the 18th January, 1819; also, a bill (or deed) of sale, from George Fleming to claimant, dated 23d day of August, 1821. This case being submitted, and it appearing that the claimant was not a resident in the province at the time of the cession, and the quantity claimed being over one thousand acres, we order and adjudge that the memorial, with all the evidence and documents, be forwarded to Congress for their determination, with our opinion that the claim ought to be confirmed.

William Berrie vs. the United States. Memorial for 350 acres of land.

The claimant produced, in evidence, an absolute grant from the Government for 350 acres of land, dated 12th February, 1817. This case being submitted, and the board, fully advised of and concerning the premises, do order and adjudge that the title of claimant to the land in question be confirmed to him and his heirs, so far as the United States have any interest, and no further.

Antelm Gay vs. the United States. Memorial for 600 acres of land.

The claimant produced, in evidence, a memorial and decree of the Governor for a tract of land, dated 27th May, 1799, in the name of John Granoply, the quantity undefined; also, certain depositions taken, by which it is proved that the grantee had taken possession, and improved the lands in question, by erecting buildings on it, clearing a small piece of the land, and establishing a cowpen; that possession was uninterrupted till 1819, December 29, when the grantee conveyed the land in question to the claimant, by deed of that date; also, a plat and certificate of survey of six hundred acres of land, pursuant to the memorial and decree aforesaid; also, the deposition of Don Bartolemé de Castro y Ferrer and others, proving that the grantee was a subject of the King of Spain, and resident in this province, at the change of flags. This case being submitted, and the board, being advised of and concerning the premises, do order and adjudge that the memorial, and evidence accompanying the same, be forwarded to Congress for their determination. The quantity being undefined, we conceive that, notwithstanding the claimant has made out a good equitable right to the land in question against the United States, yet, from the provisions of the act organizing this board, approved 8th May, 1822, the board are prohibited from confirming any claim, or part thereof, where the amount claimed is undefined.

Antelm Gay vs. the United States. Memorial for 2,000 acres of land.

The claimant produced, in evidence, a memorial and decree of the Governor, without condition, for the two thousand acres of land mentioned in his memorial, in the name of Pablo Rosette, dated 14th October, 1817; also, a plat and certificate of the same, of 25th July, 1818; as also, a deed of sale from grantee to claimant, dated 24th November, 1819; all of which we find to have been regularly executed according to the forms of the Governments under which they respectively took place.

The commissioners then referred to the parol examinations of Peter Miranda, &c., who were duly sworn in other cases of Mr. Gay, and who stated, in substance, that the said A. Gay had been a resident in the Territory of East Florida for a number of years, and was so at the exchange of flags. Wherefore, we do confirm unto the said A. Gay his right and title to the said claim of two thousand acres, as far as the United States have any interest, and no further.

John Huertas vs. the United States. Memorial for 15,000 acres of land.

The claimant produced, in evidence, an absolute title from the Governor for the 15,000 acres of land; that is to say, five thousand at Tocoy, and the remaining ten thousand on the St. John's river, dated the 24th December, 1817. Also, an order of survey, together with two plats and certificates of surveys, dated 4th June, 1822. This case being submitted, and the board fully advised of and concerning the premises, do order and adjudge that this case, with the memorial, documents, and other evidence, be forwarded to Congress, with our opinion that the same ought to be confirmed.

Eliza Robinson vs. the United States. Memorial for 105 acres of land.

The claimant produced, in evidence, a memorial in the name of Pedro Capo, and a decree of the Governor, dated the 5th of March, 1803; also, a deed of sale from the grantee to the claimant for the land in question, dated November 9, 1821; also, a plat and certificate of survey of the same. It was proved by Fran. J. Fatio that the original grantee, many years ago, cultivated the lands in question, and that he was a man of family. This case being submitted, and the board fully advised of and concerning the premises, do order and adjudge that the title of claimant to the one hundred and five acres of land in question be confirmed to her and her heirs, so far as the United States have any claim, and no further.

Samuel Fairbanks, &c. vs. the United States. Memorial for 2,000 acres of land.

The claimants produced, in evidence, a memorial of Joseph S. Sanchez, and the decree of the Governor thereon, granting two thousand acres of land at the place mentioned, without condition; also, a deed from Joseph S. Sanchez and wife, and Antonio Alvarez and wife, for one undivided half of the land in question, to the claimant, Samuel Fairbanks. It further appeared, in evidence, that the claimants were both resident in the province at the cession. This case being submitted, and the board being fully advised of and concerning the premises, do order and adjudge that the title of the claimants be confirmed to them and their heirs, as tenants in common, so far as the United States have any interest in the same, and no further.

Samuel Fairbanks vs. the United States. Memorial for 500 acres of land.

The claimant produced, in evidence, a memorial in the name of Rafael D. Fontaine, and the decree of the Governor granting him five hundred acres of land as petitioned for, without condition, dated 10th December, 1815; also, a plat and certificate of the survey of the same, dated 25th September, 1819; also, a deed from grantee to Samuel Fairbanks, dated 10th April, 1823. This case being submitted, and the board being fully advised of and concerning the premises, do order and adjudge that the title of the claimant to the five hundred acres of land, as set out in his memorial, be confirmed to him, so far as the United States have any interest in the same, and no further.

Peter Bagley vs. the United States. Memorial for 200 acres of land.

The claimant produced in evidence a memorial of Reuben Hogan, dated 19th December, 1799, and the decree of the Governor, dated 20th December, 1799; also, relinquishment from grantee to claimant, dated the 4th day of March, 1823. This case being submitted, and the board being fully advised of and concerning the premises, do order and adjudge that the title of the claimant to the two hundred acres of land, as set out in his memorial, be confirmed to him and his heirs so far as the United States have any interest in the same, and no further.

Charles Hogan vs. the United States. *Memorial for 200 acres of land.*

The claimant produced, in evidence, a title of absolute property to him for two hundred acres of land, dated 12th January, 1818. The case being submitted, and the board fully advised of and concerning the premises, do order and adjudge that the title of the claimant to the two hundred acres of land as described in his title, be confirmed to him and his heirs so far as the United States have any interest in the same, and no further.

Reuben Hogan vs. the United States. *Memorial for 385 acres of land.*

The claimant produced, in evidence, a royal title in absolute property to him and his heirs, dated 14th October, 1801, for three hundred and eighty-five acres of land, as set out in his memorial. This case being submitted, and the board fully advised of and concerning the premises, do order and adjudge that the title of the said claimant to the land aforesaid be confirmed to him and his heirs, so far as the United States have any interest in the same, and no further.

Francis R. Sanchez vs. the United States. *Memorial for 4,000 acres of land.*

The claimant produced, in evidence, his memorial to the Governor of Florida, dated 18th December, 1815; also, the Governor's decree granting him the land in his memorial of four thousand acres. This case being submitted, and there being an absolute title of property in the memorialist from the law and usages of this province, we have no doubt but, had the claimant applied to that Government, that his title would have been recognised as a sufficient one. We, therefore, recommend the same to Congress for their confirmation.

Joseph Delespine vs. the United States. *Memorial for 560 acres of land.*

The claimant produced, in evidence, the memorial of Antonio Huertas to the Governor of the province, dated the 3d of October, 1800, and the Governor's decree of the 7th same month, granting the same without condition; also, a plat and a certificate of survey of the same, dated 6th August, 1821; also a deed from grantee to claimant for the five hundred and sixty acres of land, as set out in his memorial, dated 9th July, 1821. It also appeared, in evidence, that the grantee has occupied the land for many years before, and within one year of the cession, as a pasture, and had cabins built for his slaves, who took care of his cattle. This case being submitted, and the board being fully advised of and concerning the premises, do order and adjudge that the title of the claimant to the five hundred and sixty acres of land, as set out in his memorial, be confirmed to him and his heirs, so far as the United States have any interest in the same, and no further.

Sarah Tate vs. the United States. *Memorial for 450 acres of land.*

The claimant produced, in evidence, the memorial of John E. Tate to the Governor, dated 18th September, 1811; also, the decree of the Governor, dated 20th of same month, granting the land solicited on conditions set out in the decree; also, an official document by which the applicant agreed to take the land upon the condition named in the decree, dated 23d September, 1811; also, a plat and certificate of the survey of the four hundred and fifty acres of land named in the memorial, dated 21st April, 1821. It also appeared, in evidence, that the grantee, shortly after the grant, made an attempt to establish himself on the land, but was prevented by the revolution of 1812; that, previous to the revolution, he had got out timber to build on the land, which afterwards decayed; that he died in the year 1822; and that the claimant is his only child. This case being submitted, and the board being fully advised of and concerning the premises, do order and adjudge that the title of the claimant to the four hundred and fifty acres of land set out in her memorial, be confirmed to her, and her heirs, so far as the United States have any interest in the same, and no further.

Peter Fouchard vs. the United States. *Memorial for 1,500 acres of land.*

The claimant produced, in evidence, his memorial to the Governor, dated the 16th November, 1815; also, the Governor's decree of absolute title, dated 20th November, 1815, for fifteen hundred acres of land at the place set out in his memorial. It also appeared, by the deposition filed, that the claimant was resident in the province at the cession, and is still so; and that, from the continued hostilities of the Indians, it was unsafe to take possession, and survey lands. This case being submitted, and the board being fully advised of and concerning the premises, do order and adjudge that the title of the claimant to the fifteen hundred acres of land, as set out in his memorial, be confirmed to him and his heirs so far as the United States have any interest in the same, and no further.

Eusebius Bushnell vs. the United States. *Memorial for 600 acres of land.*

The claimant produced, in evidence, his memorial dated March 17, 1799, for six hundred acres of land; also, the decree of the Governor for the same, dated 13th March, 1799. It appeared, in evidence, that the claimant was in possession of the land in question in the year 1803; that his son was killed in 1800 or 1801. The claimant died in the year 1812. This case being submitted, and the board fully advised of and concerning the premises, do order and adjudge that the claim to the six hundred acres of land in the memorial be confirmed to the unknown heirs of Eusebius Bushnell, deceased, and their heirs, as far as the United States have any interest in the same, and no further.

Antelm Gay vs. the United States. *Memorial for 400 acres of land.*

The claimant produced, in evidence, a royal title from the Government to Don Bartoleme de Castro y Ferrer, for four hundred acres of land, without condition, dated July 15, 1815; also, a plat and certificate of survey, dated 1809; also, a deed from grantee to claimant, dated 21st February, 1821. This case being submitted, and the board fully advised of and concerning the premises, do order and adjudge that the title of the claimant be confirmed to him and his heirs, so far as the United States have any interest, and no further.

Antelm Gay vs. the United States. *Memorial for 700 acres of land.*

The claimant produced, in evidence, a memorial and decree of the Governor for seven hundred acres of land, in absolute property, to Lewis Mattier, dated 19th August, 1814; also, a plat and certificate of survey of the same, dated 4th September, 1818; as, also, a deed of sale from grantee to claimant, for the land in question, dated 4th September, 1818. This case being submitted, and the board being fully advised of and concerning the premises, do order and adjudge that the title of the claimant to the seven hundred acres of land, as described in his memorial, be confirmed to him and his heirs, so far as the United States have any interest, and no further.

Avice & Viel vs. the United States. *Memorial for 1,000 acres of land.*

In this case the claimants produced, in evidence, the memorial of Francisco and John Triay, dated 19th August, 1794, together with the decree of the Governor for the same, dated the 26th of the same month; also, the memorial of the grantees and Don José Peso de Burgos to the Governor, praying liberty to exchange lands, dated 11th September, 1798, together with the decree of the Governor, permitting the exchange, dated the same day. It was proved, by depositions, that Mr. Burgos occupied the land twenty years; that Messrs. Triay occupied it before, knows not how long; that his family consisted of fifteen blacks and six whites; also, a deed of bargain and sale, from Maria M. de Burgos and others, widow and heirs of José Carlos Peso de Burgos, deceased, to claimants, for the land in question. This case being submitted, and the board conceiving that, as the claim is undefined in quantity, they have no jurisdiction of final confirmation; they, therefore, order and adjudge that the same, with the evidence and other documents, be forwarded on to Congress, with their opinion that it ought to be confirmed, inasmuch as, by the rules and regulations of the Spanish authorities at that time, the claimants prove that, from the number of their family, they were entitled, at the least, to one thousand acres.

Joseph Delespine vs. the United States.   Memorial for 600 acres of land.

The claimant produced, in evidence, the memorial of Don Juan Huertas, dated 3d May, 1811; also, the decree of the Governor, granting him the six hundred acres of land he solicits, without condition, dated 3d May, 1811; also, a plat and certificate of survey of the same, dated 18th March, 1821; also, a deed from grantee to the claimant, dated the 10th day of February, 1821. It also appeared, in evidence, that both the grantee and claimant were resident in the province at the time of the cession, and were Spanish subjects, and that grantee had been in possession of the land for upwards of three years before the cession. This case being submitted, and the board being fully advised of and concerning the premises, do order and adjudge that the title of claimant to the six hundred acres of land set forth in his memorial, be confirmed to him, so far as the United States have any interest in the same, and no further.

Samuel Fairbanks vs. the United States.   Memorial for lot in St. Augustine.

The claimant, in support of his title, produced, in evidence, the original grant from the Governor to Donna. Maria Ventura Rodriguez, dated 18th August, 1796, to the lot set out in the memorial; also, a power of attorney from the said Donna Maria Ventura Rodriguez to John A. Cavedo, authorizing and empowering him to sell and convey the lot aforesaid; and, also, the deed of John A. Cavedo, as attorney in fact for the said Donna Maria Ventura Rodriguez, to the claimant, Samuel Fairbanks, for the lot mentioned in the memorial. This case being submitted, and the board, fully advised of and concerning the premises, do order and adjudge that the claim of the said Samuel Fairbanks be confirmed to him and his heirs, to the lot in question, so far as the United States have any interest, and no further.

Heirs of Lorenzo Capo vs. the United States.   Memorial for 157 acres of land.

The claimants produced, in evidence, a plat and certificate from John Murphey, deputy surveyor, dated 3d January, 1783, for the quantity of fifty acres, surveyed for James Bradshaw; also, a receipt of John Murphey, for the surveyor's fees, with an endorsement on the back of the same, transferring it to Lorenzo Capo; also, a receipt of William Price, for the sum of fifty-seven dollars, the consideration of a tract of one hundred and seven acres, opposite the aforesaid tract. It also appeared, by the deposition of Anthony Hindman, that he has resided upwards of thirty years near the land in question; that he was well acquainted with James Bradshaw during the time the British had possession of this province; that he, Bradshaw, held possession of the island of fifty acres of land, and that he occupied and cultivated the land for from seven to nine years, uninterrupted; also, that he was well acquainted with William Price; that, after the death of Bradshaw, his whole property went into the possession of said Price, who was his administrator; and that, as such, he settled the business of the estate; and that, as a part of the property of said decedent, was sold the said island of fifty acres of land, to Laurence Capo, of this city, which contract was made and ratified in presence of this witness, in this city, in the year 1784. At the same time another contract was made between the said William Price and Laurence Capo, for the purchase of another tract of land containing about one hundred and seven acres, nearly adjoining the island aforesaid, for the sum of fifty-seven dollars; and that the last mentioned tract of land belonged solely to said William Price. It also appeared that the said Capo took possession of the two tracts of land aforesaid, and rented them out, for some time, under the Spanish Government; that the tenant of Capo planted the land in corn and other provisions. This case having been submitted, and the board fully advised of and concerning the premises, do order and adjudge that the title to the one hundred and fifty-seven acres of land, in the claimants' memorial, be confirmed to them as the legal heirs and representatives of Lorenzo, alias Laurence Capo, deceased, so far as the United States have any interest in the same, and no further.

Antelm Gay vs. the United States.   Memorial for 500 acres of land.

The claimant produced, in evidence, an absolute title from Government to Don George Fleming, for twenty thousand acres of land, for services performed under the royal orders of 1813 and 1815, dated 24th September, 1816; also, a plat and certificate of survey of the five hundred acres, part of the aforesaid grant, dated 2d February, 1820; also, a deed from Don George Fleming to Don Andres Burgevin, dated 21st February, 1820; also, a deed from said Don Andres Burgevin to claimant, Don Antelm Gay, 22d February, 1820, for the land aforesaid. This case being submitted, and the board dividing in opinion on this point, "whether the board have power to confirm to a claimant any part of a grant, where the quantity in the original is such as to take from them their power to decide finally," it is ordered that the memorial, and evidence accompanying the same, be forwarded to Congress for their decision.

Moses E. Levy vs. the United States.   Memorial for 14,500 acres of land.

The claimant produced, in evidence, the memorial of Don Fernando de la Maza Arredondo, by his son, to the Governor, dated 1st March, 1817, together with the decree of the Governor, dated 24th March, 1817, by which is granted to Don Fernando de la Maza Arredondo, the senior, thirty thousand acres of land, at the places named in his memorial; also, the memorial of Arredondo, Jun., dated 8th June, 1819, praying that the lands in the aforesaid memorial may be surveyed, &c.; also, the decree of the Governor, appointing Don Andres Burgevin, the surveyor, to perform the said surveys, same date; also, the plat and certificate of survey of fourteen thousand five hundred acres, dated 15th August, 1819; also, a royal title for the fourteen thousand five hundred acres of land, in favor of the said F. Arredondo, in absolute property, dated 9th August, 1819; also, a deed from grantee to Hernandez and Chauviteau, dated 3d August, 1820; also, a power of attorney from said Hernandez and Chauviteau to Moses E. Levy, authorizing him to convey the land in question, dated 2d November, 1820; also, a deed from said Moses E. Levy, attorney for Hernandez and Chaviteau, to Abraham M. Cohen, for the land aforesaid, dated 8th June, 1821; also, a deed from said A. M. Cohen to the claimant, dated 8th June, 1821; all which appear to have been regularly executed, according to the laws of the Government under which they were made. Although the royal title and survey bear date subsequent to the 24th day of January, 1818, yet the original concession, made at the time that the Governor was legally authorized to make it, and it being without condition, and there having been no suggestion of fraud in the transaction, we deem the concession obligatory on us. Therefore, we recommend the same for confirmation.

No. 3.

DEAR SIR: ST. AUGUSTINE, *December* 29, 1823.

We beg leave to lay before you, for your consideration, and the information of others who may feel interested in the subject, the following account of the proceedings of the Board of Land Commissioners constituted for East Florida, together with the difficulties which lay in the road to a successful termination of the duties of the commission; and, as far as we are able, to advise the measures most likely to facilitate the objects of the Government.

Immediately after the organization of the board, the question arose, what part of the claimants' exhibits are required to be recorded? A majority of the commissioners were of opinion that, according to the fourth section of the act, passed in May, 1822, the entire deraignment of title, when it could be produced, including all the papers to be read in evidence, should be recorded at the cost of the claimant. This decision gave rise to complaints among the people that they were loaded with unnecessary expenses, either by the Government or the commissioners. Although we believe the public mind is at present satisfied, at least in a great degree, in relation to that subject, in consequence of ascertaining that the expense is far short of what was apprehended, we still beg leave to say that the operation of this provision is severely felt by the poorer class of people in the Territory; and if it be possible to relieve them in any manner compatible with the views of the Government, it would not only be felt by them as a happy exemption, but would greatly facilitate the future operations of the board. In consequence of the necessity for translating and recording all the voluminous documents comprising Spanish titles to real estate, at the very time, also, that the law made it necessary that the secretary should record the memorials of the claimants and the proceedings of the board, more time has been consumed in preparation for final adjudication than comported with the expectations and wishes of this country, or, perhaps, with the views of the Government. This difficulty was the more sensibly felt, in consequence of the improvidence of the law in allowing but one secretary, and failing entirely to furnish him with the means of collecting his recording fees, which have not been paid, but in a very few instances, and are scattered, in small sums, through the United States and the Spanish islands. The law requires the services to be done unconditionally, and creates a simple debt against the claimant, which, in a great majority of cases, would not be worth collecting by the ordinary process of law. Under these circumstances we required the secretary to employ one assistant, which reduces his regular salary to a mere pittance, out of which it would be ungenerous and unjust to ask of him to employ another. The two secretaries, thus employed, placed the record in sufficient forwardness to authorize a notification to the public that we would begin to adjudicate on the second Monday of the present month. But it soon became apparent that the whole time of our principal secretary would be taken up in attendance on and recording the minutes of the board; so that translations having ceased to progress, would soon be overtaken, and claimants subjected to uncertain, and, therefore, harassing delays, while our clerks would be preparing their cases. To obviate this difficulty, and supply ourselves with the means of continually progressing, we have employed, upon our individual responsibility, another clerk to take and record the proceedings of the board, at the rate of four hundred dollars per annum, relying upon the justice or munificence of the Government to make an appropriation for that object. One clerk is now continually employed in translating; another, in recording the evidence of titles; and the third, in attendance on the board, which holds its sessions every day.

To return from this detail, we beg leave to advert to the petition of the inhabitants of this city in relation to a subject which was presented to our consideration at a very early period of the session.

Those who owned property in the city, or within the town of Fernandina, desired the board would exempt them from the trouble and expense of exhibiting their titles, or would give them time to appeal to the Government on that subject. A majority of the board agreed to wait the advice of your Department in answer to the petition of the people; and, also, to communicate such information in relation to the public property as they possessed, under an impression that an answer would be received in time to allow an exhibition of their titles, if it should be unfavorable, before the time limited by law shall have expired. The answer, however, has not been received, nor have any of those claims been exhibited.

We would respectfully submit that, by the second article of the treaty with Spain, "all public lots and squares, public edifices, fortifications, barracks, and other buildings, which are not private property," are transferred to the United States; and that, subsequently, this article was at least partially executed, by the Spanish authorities delivering to the agent of our Government a schedule, purporting to be of all such property, together with the actual possession of such as could be occupied. The Spanish inhabitants here look to the act of receiving that document as being a recognition, on the part of the United States, of their private rights to all other lots and houses.

In addition to this view of the subject they consider it rigorous policy in the Government to require of them to spread on record, at a considerable expense, (which, indeed, many of them are ill able to bear,) deraignments of titles to more than three hundred lots, for no other purpose than to show the Government its small modicum of ground. They think it would better comport with the views of a just and liberal sovereignty, to employ its executive and legal officers in ferreting out a few illegal claims, than to tax with extreme rigor the whole of a very poor community for that purpose.

In recapitulating these views we do but wish to show the grounds on which we suspended, as we then supposed temporarily, the reception of these claims. But, as this subject may be a matter of inquiry with other departments of the Government, we take the liberty of communicating the information we possess, in relation to the property said to belong to the United States within this city, besides that contained in the schedule before alluded to.

1. A row of water lots extending from the fort to the mouth of the St. Sebastian, the whole length of the town, and of various depths, from one to two hundred feet. Some of these, a few in number, are claimed as private property; but the majority, we believe, are acknowledged to belong to the public. A few years ago they were above high water mark, and were covered by orange groves; but the water has gradually encroached, until almost the whole area is subject to the ordinary flood. It is, however, said that the water is again retiring, and some of the inhabitants believe that some of these lots may hereafter be of value.

2. A swamp of about sixty yards in breadth, running parallel with the bay, and nearly through the centre of chartered limits of the city, containing from fifty to sixty or seventy acres; all of which is covered by a thin sheet of water at every flood tide, but with a slight embankment, of little more than one hundred yards, would entirely protect.

3. On the south and west the city is bounded by the river St. Sebastian, which forms, by its diurnal floods, an extensive march or swamp, which contains several hundred acres, but its value will depend upon the practicability of excluding the water.

4. An extensive esplanade, reaching fifteen hundred yards northward from the Castle, and from the St. Sebastian's on the west, to the North river on the east, a distance nearly as great; the whole commanded by the guns of the fort, and being the only approach to the town, has been kept by the Spanish authorities free from the least obstruction. A few grants have been made within it, and we at first believed, from casual information, that they were grants of temporary use, and made without authority; but we are since informed that the proprietors claim a higher degree of title, which they intend applying to the Government to affirm, and we must, therefore, decline expressing, because we have not had an opportunity of forming, an opinion upon the subject.

5. It has been said that some of the houses nearest the fort are built on public ground, perhaps by parol permission of a Governor, but contrary to an ordinance reserving a certain distance from the fort in every direction. Of this we do not speak with certainty, nor have we the means of certain information. Indeed, in relation to all these details, we beg leave to say we do not make them upon the assurance of any official investigation, but as bare suggestions growing out of the inquiries made of the inhabitants; of course, not to be taken as conclusive, but are merely intended to guide the inquiries of the Government in case it should think proper to relieve the inhabitants from the necessity of exhibiting their titles, and should take upon itself to separate the public from the private property by legal investigation.

Besides the above specifications we have no reason to suspect that any property in the city, claimed to be private, is not held by fair and equitable titles. Mr. Smith, the marshal of the district, and formerly mayor of the city, has been engaged in similar inquiries, without being able to trace any claim of the Spanish Government to property held as private.

The board has experienced some difficulty upon the subject of procuring transcripts of titles when they are not in possession of the claimant, and cannot be obtained but by an application to the keeper of the public archives. We first adopted a rule requiring claimants to file with our secretary their original papers, or attested copies; but, as the customs of the Spanish Government required all originals to be left in the public office, and but few copies were given out, the expense of transcripts was sensibly felt and complained of by the people, which, added to a serious doubt entertained by the board as to the legality of the requisition, induced us to discontinue the demand, and, finally, to rescind it.

In the mean time, however, a communication was received from the Department of State advising us of, and enclosing a letter to the keeper of the archives, directing him to deliver to our order the papers and records which had been turned over to his office by the Spanish authorities. This order, the officer to whom it was directed was unwilling to obey; and we did not feel ourselves authorized to make or enforce a peremptory demand. If it embraced any, it embraced all the public records of the Territory, and virtually abolished the office of the keeper of the archives, which had been established by an act of the Legislative Council, and approved by Congress. Besides which, the same act had deposited these records with that officer exclusively, and had made copies, certified by him alone, evidence in all the courts of the Territory. If they should be taken from his possession the object of the law would be defeated, as it is clear that a copy, certified by the secretary of the board, would not be legal evidence; nor could he ever receive them back, for the purpose of certifying copies, without the authority of a legislative act; because they are not bound in books that could be identified, but contained upon loose sheets of paper, which might be taken away or misplaced without the possibility of detection. They are even without a complete index, and the keeper is obliged to rely on his memory to facilitate his researches.

This will also suggest the great inconvenience of having such a mass of indigested record thrown in upon our secretary, who, if constantly employed, would not be able to meet the demand of the public for transcripts, for which the law would not allow him fees, and yet which he could not deny without the grossest outrage against the public.

In addition to these difficulties, in the way of making such a demand, the act of Congress under which we are acting, seems to confine us to the privilege of inspecting and taking transcripts of the public record within the Territory.

Finding ourselves unable to compel any other or better arrangement, our translating secretary is now obliged to take from the public records all such documents as are required to be produced in evidence before us. It is, however, but justice to the keeper of the archives to say that he has furnished every possible facility in the discharge of this troublesome duty.

Since our adjudications commenced we have been somewhat embarrassed by the presentation of cases not contemplated by any express provision of the statute, but apparently within its equity.

1st. Consists of cases in which the grantee has not made an entire, but has made a partial performance of the conditions of his grant.

2d. Cases in which purchasers from grantees of a part interest in such grants have made a compliance with the conditions in proportion to their interest.

We do not doubt that, in all cases, the Government intends to secure to the settler what he had a right to expect from the well-established customs and usages of the Spanish authorities; but the rigid limitations contained in the statute under which we are constituted leave the subject involved in embarrassment. In some instances within our knowledge, individuals have made heavy expenditures in improvements, extensive clearings, and numerous buildings, towards a compliance, but have stopped short of a fufilment. We feel confident that it is not the interest or desire of the Government to reduce these persons to poverty by taking from them, in some instances, all they possess, and the more especially as they received their property upon conditions which, by the usages of the Spanish Government, they had an unlimited time to perform. But, in all such cases, we would beg leave to suggest the propriety of directing such proportions to be surveyed in a given mathematical figure around their dwellings or improvements.

The last remark introduces a subject of greater difficulty. Owing to the fear of Indian hostilities which universally prevailed, many of the claims before us are without surveys or other means of location; and in many others the plats and certificates filed with the claim were made by the surveyors without their ever having been on or near the premises. The objects called for, which are generally a stake or a pine tree, were at first supplied by imagination, and, being without a mark or other designation, leave the location as uncertain as in former cases. Many of the concessions and grants thus vague and uncertain, will, no doubt, be affirmed; and the difficulty will be felt by the public surveyor when he is called on to re-survey these claims under the direction of the statute. He will be obliged to survey them, in many instances, wherever the party shall direct, or not survey at all, unless the Government will devise some means of avoiding the inconvenience.

We beg leave, also, to inform the Government that, as far as we are informed and believe, the country between the Suwannee and Appalachicola is unembarrassed by any other claim than that of Forbes & Co. We make this statement under the impression that it would comport with the wishes of the people of this country, and the views of the Government, to have that part of the public territory brought into market at as early a period as practicable. Mr. George J. F. Clarke, who officiated for many years as Surveyor General of this province under the Spanish authorities, and kept a record of all public surveys executed by himself or his deputies, upon examination before us, deposed that he knew of no location within the country bounded by these two rivers, except the one before alluded to; nor has any such claim been filed before us..

Under an impression that it is our duty to do so, we communicate that about the number of six hundred claims have been presented to the board, of which we hope to be able to report to Government from one to two hundred within the time limited by the act of Congress; and, also, that a greater number is believed to be still unpresented, some of which have been deposited in the office since the time allowed for filing them elapsed, under the impression that Government would renew the permission.

We remain, with sentiments of sincere respect, your obedient servants,

DAVIS FLOYD,
W. W. BLAIR.

Hon. WM. H. CRAWFORD, *Secretary of the Treasury.*

No. 4.

DEAR SIR: ST. AUGUSTINE, *September* 24, 1823.

Herewith you will receive a memorial from the inhabitants of this place, upon the subject of titles to lots of ground within the chartered limits of the town.

Many of the most respectable inhabitants regard the transfer stipulated in the second article of the treaty, of " all public lots and squares, public edifices, fortifications, barracks, and other buildings, which are not private property," as having been perfectly executed when the Spanish authorities here delivered to Colonel Butler a schedule of all such property, together with actual possession of all such as could be occupied, and they look to the act of receiving that document as containing a recognition on the part of the United States of their private rights to all other lots and houses.

In addition to this view of the subject, they consider it rigorous policy in the Government to require of them to spread on record, at considerable expense, which, indeed, many of them are ill able to bear, deraignments of titles to more than 300 lots, for no other purpose than to show the Government its small modicum of ground. They think it would better comport with the views of a just and liberal sovereignty to employ its executive and legal officers in ferreting out a few illegal claims, than to tax with extreme rigor the whole of a very poor community for that purpose.

With these views they are unwilling to believe that the several acts of Congress, subjecting land titles to the investigation of commissioners, were intended to embrace their claims to lots and houses; or they are flattered with the hope that an appeal to Government will procure them exemption from what they regard as a peculiar hardship. With a view to giving an opportunity for such an appeal, as well as to obtain information for ourselves, Judge Floyd and myself, previous to his leaving here for Kentucky, whither he has gone for his family, concurred in the propriety of asking the instruction of your Department on this subject, which was not then executed, only because of the judge's hasty departure without signing a letter that had been submitted to the board, and assented to.

Since that time, however, I have been occasionally engaged in making inquiries, which have resulted in ascertaining that several parcels of ground within the city, and not embraced by the schedule before alluded to, are public property.

1st. A row of water lots extending from the fort to the mouth of the Sr. Sebastian, the whole length of the town, and of various depths, from one to two hundred feet. Some of these lots, a few in number, are claimed as private property, but the great majority are acknowledged to belong to the public. A few years ago they were above high water mark, and were covered by groves of oranges, but the water has gradually encroached until almost the whole area is subjected to the ordinary flood. It is, however, said that the water is again retiring, and some of the inhabitants believe that these lots may hereafter be of value.

2d. A swamp of about sixty yards in width, running parallel with the bay and nearly through the centre of the chartered limits of the city, containing about fifty acres, which is covered by a thin sheet of water at every flood tide, but which a slight embankment of little more than a hundred yards would entirely exclude.

3d. On the south and west the city is bounded by the river St. Sebastian, which forms, by its diurnal floods, an extensive marsh or swamp, which contains from two to three hundred acres, but its value will depend on the practicability of excluding the water.

4th. An extensive espalanade reaching fifteen hundred yards northward from the castle, and from the St. Sebastian to the North river, a distance nearly as great, the whole commanded by the guns of the fort, and being the only approach to the town, has been kept by the Spanish authorities free from the least possible obstruction. A few grants have been of late made within it, but they are grants of merely temporary use, and even these seem to have been without authority.

5th. It is said that some of the houses nearest the fort are built on public ground, perhaps, by parol permission of a Governor, but contrary to an ordinance reserving a certain distance from the fort in every direction. Of this I do not speak with certainty, nor have I the means of certain information; and beside this, I have no reason to believe that any property in the city, claimed to be private, is rightfully the property of the public. Mr. Smith, the marshal of the district, and also the mayor of the city, has been employed, at my request, in similar inquiries, without being able to trace any claim of the Spanish Government to the property claimed as private within the city.

This information may not be of any importance to the Government, but I have thought it right to possess them of it while the memorial of the inhabitants is before them. And, in the mean time, beg leave to subscribe myself, with sentiments of cordial esteem,

Yours, &c.,   W. W. BLAIR.

Hon. WM. H. CRAWFORD.

To the Hon. William H. Crawford, Secretary of the Treasury. The memorial of the subscribers, lot-holders of the city of St. Augustine, humbly showeth:

That your memorialists, in common with the holders of land in the country, have been suffering great difficulties, hardships, and embarrassments, for two years, in consequence of the protracted and undetermined condition of the claims of the United States to lands in this Territory.

Thus situated, your memorialists trust it will not be deemed unreasonable that they represent to your Department their full conviction that neither the interest nor the policy of the United States require a determination of the land claims in any other mode than such as is consistent with equity, economy, simplicity, and despatch.

Of the lots in St. Augustine to which this memorial has exclusive reference, that part belonging to the United States was officially designated, and a schedule thereof delivered by the Spanish authorities to those of the United States; and, to this schedule your memorialists humbly beg your reference, as being ample and sufficient evidence of the extent of public property within the limits of this city.

The lots of private property are upwards of three hundred in number, and have passed through chains of title; some commencing in the seventeenth century, and the greater part early in the eighteenth century; and these chains or deraignments of title are not only on record, but the facts of descent, conveyance, and occupancy, are matter of great public notoriety.

Your memorialists further represent, that they are fearful that the late act of Congress prescribing the mode of ascertaining land claims may be so construed as to make it necessary that the lot-holders of St. Augustine should furnish the commissioners with copies of the deraignment of title, and your memorialists beg leave to urge on you the inexpediency of such a construction, from the following considerations:

First. Copies of all the titles to lots in St. Augustine would appear to be unnecessary, because they are already on record in the public archives.

Secondly. The lot-holders would not only be put to great inconvenience from delay, but, many of them, are absolutely unable to pay the expense attendant on the copying of such voluminous documents.

Thirdly. Such a construction of the law would have the effect of retarding the public business, and operating to the ruin of many individuals who have already suffered so severely from delay.

And, lastly. If, by inadvertence or otherwise, the official schedule referred to should be defective in omitting any public property, such defects your memorialists humbly submit to be of comparative insignificance, and can be remedied either by the personal knowledge of the land commissioners, or by a few hours' inquiry.

Under these considerations, your memorialists pray that you will be pleased to instruct the land commissioners, or otherwise act in the premises so that the lot-holders of St. Augustine may be relieved from the expense and inconvenience, and the public from the delay attendant on such a construction of the law.

PETRONA VALDEZ,

For myself, and as attorney for Joseph M. Hernandez, and by 124 other persons.

No. 5.

Sir: SENATE CHAMBER, *March* 11, 1824.

I send you a letter from Mr. Blair, of St. Augustine, explaining the conduct of that commission. I was requested to place it before you. Sincerely yours,

RD. M. JOHNSON.

Col. JAMES MONROE, *President.*

My Dear Sir: St. Augustine, *February* 21, 1824.

A letter received from General Call informs us that difficulties existed in the Senate, arising out of information received by a member of that body from a gentleman of this Territory relative to our proceedings, but particularly in relation to our decisions under the second section of the second law under which we were acting. Our decision was under the second clause of that section, and related exclusively to the extent of our jurisdiction. We decided that an "actual settler," within the meaning of the clause, was any person actually settled within the province at the exchange of flags. If the Senate have no other objection to our proceedings, we may deem ourselves peculiarly fortunate, for, among the almost innumerable questions we have been called on to decide growing out of the most inexplicable statute I remember to have seen, to have erred but once would be, of itself, a source of great consolation; but, to have erred only on a question that cannot, by possibility, injure the rights of the United States, is peculiarly so. But I deny that there is error in the decision rendered.

By the first act of Congress we have confirmatory jurisdiction to the amount of one thousand acres, unconditionally. By the second our jurisdiction is extended to three thousand five hundred acres, but only in favor of actual settlers. This latter provision is contained in the second section, which may be thus translated:

Actual settlers shall not be required to produce in evidence a deraignment of title where it cannot be obtained, but their claims shall be confirmed where they do not exceed three thousand five hundred acres, provided, they have been recognised by the Spanish Government, and provided the claimants shall produce satisfactory evidence of right to the land claimed.

The commissioners shall have jurisdiction over all claims of actual settlers to the amount of three thousand five hundred acres.

The first clause enables us to decide on cases without a deraignment of title, provided the claimants are actual settlers. Under this clause it has never become necessary to decide upon what was meant by actual settlers, because there is not a single claim filed before us that does not rely on a deraignment of title or actual possession of the premises claimed. A naked right without either has never been set up before us, nor is there a single case, in a list of nearly one thousand now before us, without a deraignment of title, when the claim is over one thousand acres.

The reason why a title or possession is always set up is very obvious. The law requires, in the absence of a title, that the party shall prove a recognition by the Spanish Government, and, therefore, a right to the property. If there is any written evidence of the claimant's right it is a muniment of title, and must be produced whether it amount to a complete title or not; but where there is no such writing, how can the claimant show a right or recognition without actual possession? A right could not be obtained by purchase, nor in any way known to the Spanish law, but by an actual settlement. I mean a naked right, independent of the Governor's discretionary power to bestow titles. For it is worthy of particular notice, that, although the Governors claimed the right to distribute lands at their discretion, for the promotion of laudable public objects, it was also understood that the royal order of 1790 was imperative, and invested the actual settler with a right to demand of the Governor his proportion of the public lands. We do not mean to say that every actual settlement gave an abstract right, but that it was the only basis for a right, separate from a title.

It is, besides, the basis of the only mode of recognition that this board can regard. Wherever the Spanish Government has recognised a claim in writing, if done in proper time and by competent authorities, it would amount to a title, as they had no settled form for conveyances, and a title means nothing more than an expression of the Governor's will in favor of the claim. But where there is no such expression in writing, could I rely on any proof that a Governor had said A B was entitled to a given quantity of land? I think not, because the Governors were incompetent to convey by any mode, except that established in the country, and because of the general insecurity of such testimony, against which most nations have provided in the form of statutes of frauds and perjury. But an uninterrupted possession of the premises under the Spanish Government, and with its knowledge and consent, although it might not amount to a sufficient recognition in all cases, would in all be the only safe basis for such proof. Although an actual and continued possession under the Spanish Government does not in all cases prove either a right or recognition of itself, yet we cannot see how either a right or recognition can be proved without it. This has been so well understood that not a single claim has been presented without either a deraignment, or an allegation of actual possession.

As far as the clause under consideration purports to extend our jurisdiction over one thousand acres, it is useless, because there is no case filed before us over that amount without a deraignment of title; and, in relation to all the cases without a deraignment, the words "actual settlers" are useless, because they all set out an actual possession.

Thus much for the first clause under consideration. The second extends our jurisdiction, not only to cases in which there is no deraignment of title, but to all cases under three thousand five hundred acres in favor of actual settlers. The question to which I allude arose under this clause in a case of Mr. Gay for two thousand acres, in which he produced a deraignment of title, and proved that he was a settler in Florida, but not on the land at the exchange of flags. The question then arose, what is meant by an actual settlement in the clause under consideration?—whether it meant a settlement in the Territory or on the land claimed. We discussed and considered it as a question of jurisdiction only, the discussion of which either way could enlarge or lessen the rights of any man in the Territory; the utmost effect it could have would be to confine our jurisdiction to the cases of those who occupied their lands, or extend it to those who lived on other lands in the province.

We decided upon taking jurisdiction in all cases of actual settlers within the Territory, for the following reasons:

1st. The words *actual settlers* are entirely vague and indefinite, the sentence in which they are found not containing any indication of place, or any means of ascertaining whether *actual settlers in the Territory*, or *actual settlers* on the land, were meant; for one is certainly as much an actual settler as the other. Beside which, it would have been so easy and natural, if the latter was meant, to have added " on the land," or to have used the plain English and legal word " occupants," instead of a word which has no precise meaning in the English language. As Congress choose to use the word without giving it any specific application, we thought it our duty to give the most general application. The word "*actual*," alone, qualifies the unmeaning word settler, and greatly strengthens our construction of it, because if settler means only those who were living on the land, the word " actual" seems to be unnecessary, as the fact of cultivating a plantation or not, can scarcely ever be dubious, nor is it a matter about which false pretences are ever used; but, if the other construction is adopted, it is often difficult to tell whether a person is a settler or a transient resident, and it is common to practise deceits to get the advantages of the former, without forfeiting citizenship elsewhere. This view seemed also to unlock the policy of the Government in this enactment. It seemed evidently to make a distinction between those who were permanently interested, and itinerant speculators who came for the purpose of obtaining lands upon a speculation, and removed elsewhere, or had their families in other places. Here we saw the basis of a proper distinction, but we own we have not been able to see the policy of making the distinction between the *town* and *country*. It is well known to the Government that the Americans who settled in the province lived on plantations, while the Spaniards all lived in the towns. To give the clause such a construction as would give us jurisdiction over American claims to the amount of three thousand five hundred acres, and confine it in cases of Spaniards to one thousand, seemed to us an invidious and unnecessary distinction.

How strange, too, that the Government should invest us with power to decide, finally, on claims of a difficult and doubtful character, to the amount of three thousand five hundred acres, and, in plain cases of a deraignment, jealously confine us to one thousand.

We have deemed it right to look at the operation as well as the letter of the act, and adapt it to practical purposes. It is the only way by which any set of commissioners will ever be able to do justice to the people or the Government. We have, in substance, construed the act to give us jurisdiction to the increased amount in favor of all actual inhabitants in this Territory; but, to avoid the ill consequences of an error, if it should be one, we have directed that all such cases over one thousand acres shall be reported with the evidence entire, so that the committee, if they think we have overreached our jurisdiction, may consider the cases as recommended instead of confirmed. Every possible inconvenience is thus avoided.

But, until it is altered by the Government, I must continue to place the distinction where it now is; but, to avoid inconvenience, we will also continue to report the evidence in cases over one thousand acres.

With sentiments of high respect, I remain your most obedient servant,

W. W. BLAIR.

Hon. Rd. M. Johnson.

No. 6.

Dear Sir: St. Augustine, *August* 7, 1823.

The Board of Commissioners have this day decided that it is necessary, under the fourth section of the act of the 8th of May, 1822, to have all written evidence of title presented to the board recorded by its secretary.

This decision, rendered unavoidable by the language of the act alluded to, and by the proceedings of several previous boards constituted for similar purposes, is likely to operate severely upon the poorer class of people in the Territory. If it be possible to relieve them, in any manner compatible with duty, it would afford me pleasure; and, as the views of the Government may be somewhat different, I solicit your exposition of the clause before alluded to.

In the mean time I remain your obedient servant,

W. W. BLAIR.

Hon. Wm. H. Crawford.

No. 7.

Sir: St. Augustine, *July* 14, 1823.

I enclose a translation of what is commonly called the royal order of 1815, together with a copy and translation of a letter supposed to have been written by Governor Kindelan, the apparent inducement to the order.

In the letter there has evidently been an erasure, and the word " extensiva" introduced in the place of " exclusiva." As the most numerous and extensive grants have been made in virtue of the above order, it is very important that correct copies of all the correspondence that may have passed between the captain general of the island of Cuba and the Governor of East Florida, should be procured for the consideration of the commissioners.

96   A

If a copy of the royal order could be obtained *in extenso* it would afford the commissioners a better opportunity to adjudicate upon many of these grants. The magnitude of the grants requires that the authority through which they are created should be scrupulously examined, the more especially as most of them are made to persons not enumerated in the military rolls, and generally as late as 1817, 1818.

The regulations issued under the Intendancy of Morales, forwarded for our Government, are expressly named for Louisiana and West Florida, and the concessions in this province have most certainly not been governed by those instructions. If the titles be genuine, there has been a most extraordinary latitude in the discretionary powers, or at least in the exercise of the powers of the Governors.

To a pilot named Miranda, three hundred and sixty thousand acres were granted by Governor White, and, by the same person, several from five to fifty thousand. Coppinger's grants do not exceed one hundred thousand, but there are very many from one thousand to seventy thousand.

The public archives, as placed in possession of the American commissioners at the cession, together with the contents of the six boxes of papers claimed by Governor Coppinger, ought to be put under our charge. The latter contain correspondence of much importance, connected with the disposition of public lands, and ought to be examined, and subject to more restraint than they are at present.

As the commissioners will require some accommodation for offices, ought we not to be authorized to hire, or would it not be advisable to appropriate, the " Treasurer's house" to this use?

It is rumored that Judge Blair has resigned. If so, permit me to suggest the propriety of appointing some person in this neighborhood, and particularly to recommend Dr. Richard B. Furman, of Charleston, now residing in this place, as every way qualified.

I have the honor to remain, your obedient servant,

ALEXANDER HAMILTON.

Hon. WILLIAM H. CRAWFORD.

No. 203.

MOST EXCELLENT SENOR: ST. AUGUSTINE, *June* 4, 1813.

On the 1st of the present month I discharged from the service the three companies of whites who were under arms in this place; and this I did, as well on account of the scarcity of provisions, which rendered it urgent, as their own necessity to devote themselves to the care of their respective families, and to their labors, after an insurrection from which both they and the province had suffered so much.

I cannot avoid recommending to your excellency the good order and fidelity that animated this militia, and, also, the third battalion of the regiment of Cuba, since the first moments of the insurrection, for all which I think them all worthy of the favors to which the supreme Government may deem them entitled; and I make bold to recommend that some favors, and such as I shall recommend, be granted unto them: that a commission be granted by the King to every officer of the militia who had been under arms, corresponding to the grade which he held under the denomination of provincial; and that a portion of lands be granted to each soldier, which, by the regulations established in this province, corresponds with the number of persons composing each family, and the same favors might also be extended to the married officers and soldiers of said third battalion of Cuba.

Men, in general, must be excited by something that will stimulate them, and it is not easy to find one who is indifferent as to the public estimation of his services. With what I propose, without giving them in reality any thing, they will receive a satisfaction which ultimately must be productive of beneficial effects, particularly if that favor be granted to those only who were at the defence. To that end, and in case your excellency should approve my proposal, I transmit, respecting the officers of both these corps, a list of those who, under that conception, ought to be comprised.

His Excellency Don JUAN RUIZ DE APODACA.

ST. AUGUSTINE, *June* 29, 1823.

I hereby certify the foregoing to be a true and correct copy of a document on file in my office.
WILLIAM REYNOLDS, *Keeper of the Public Archives.*

ST. AUGUSTINE, *June* 30, 1823.

I hereby certify that the foregoing translation is faithfully made, and that the copy of certificate is correct.
P. LYNCH.

HAVANA, *July* 7, 1815.

Under date of the 29th of March, ult., his excellency the Minister for the General Department of the Indies, writes me as follows:

" I have rendered an account to the King of the contents of the letter of your excellency, No. 236, of the year 1813, with respect to the rewards which you considered the Governor of East Florida ought to grant to the individuals composing the white local militia, and, also, to the married officers and soldiers of the third battalion of the regiment of Cuba, for the zeal they manifested during the insurrection of the province; and His Majesty, while he thus assents to said favors, desires that your excellency may state the recompense which you think due to the commandant of the third battalion of Cuba, Don Juan Jose de Estrada, who acted as Governor *pro tem.* during the first moments of the insurrection; to the officers of artillery, Don Ignacio Saleres and Don Manuel Paulin; and to the officer of dragoons, Don Juan Purcheman, whom the Governor mentions in his official despatch. By the desire of the King I communicate this information for the government of your excellency, including the royal despatches of the local militia, according to the note transmitted by your excellency."

And I transmit the same to you, including the documents therein mentioned, that you may act as directed, and report to His Majesty, by the first opportunity, whatever you may deem just with respect to the recompenses in question.   APODACA.

His Excellency the GOVERNOR *pro tem. of* East Florida.

ST. AUGUSTINE, *June* 19, 1823.

I hereby certify the foregoing to be a true and correct copy of a document on file in my office.
WILLIAM REYNOLDS, *Keeper of the Public Archives.*

ST. AUGUSTINE, *June* 29, 1823.

I hereby certify that the foregoing translation is faithfully made, and that the copy of certificate is correct.
P. LYNCH.

No. 8.

Sir: St. Augustine, *January* 12, 1824.

I take the liberty to request that the enclosed letter addressed to Davis Floyd, Esq., and recorded on the minutes of the commission, with the note to which it is an answer, may be presented to the consideration of the Committee on Public Lands, to which I deem it proper to subjoin the following extraordinary doubts of the *majority* of the commissioners, with a copy of the regulations of the 1st of August, submitted by me, and unanimously adopted by the commission.

The majority of the commission entertain, and have, at their sittings, expressed doubts whether the claimants to city property are required to present their claims to the adjudication of the commissioners.

The law makes no distinction. In my opinion the commissioners ought to possess a discretionary power to call on those only where there exists any suspicion of public interest. I make this suggestion with great deference, but with a perfect knowledge of all the circumstances.

The majority of the commission entertain, and have, at their sittings, expressed doubts whether they be not authorized to adjudicate finally on claims, a part of a grant, the whole amount of which exceeds our jurisdiction.

That Congress might be informed on this subject, previous to any future legislation, and to prevent the extravagant speculation that would result from such a decision, a motion was made to ascertain the sense of the commission, which the majority declined to consider, notwithstanding there were cases before it immediately involving the question.

There are other sources of objection to the proceedings of the commission, which were intended to be communicated by the *minority*, had the commission made an official report; and, as such, would necessarily have been subject to the inspection of Congress.*

The circumstances connected with the appointment of our secretary and assistant secretary, are, perhaps, within the knowledge of your Department.

In consequence, I recommend to the consideration of Congress, whether it would not be advisable to fix the salary of the secretary at fifteen hundred dollars, and authorize the appointment of an assistant, with a compensation of one thousand dollars; *and both should possess a knowledge of the Spanish language.* As yet there have been no fees paid for recording; and such is the poverty of the country, that it would be almost impossible to collect them. If Congress should not see fit to relieve the claimants from this charge, *incident to an investigation instituted for the purpose of ascertaining public lands, and, in many instances, charging claimants whose titles have been acknowledged for centuries,* I earnestly recommend that the compensation of the secretary shall have no contingent reference to this source of payment. If I be not misinformed, the Attorney General has given it as his opinion, and such is the construction of my colleagues, that the compensation to the secretary may amount to two thousand five hundred dollars. This may be a correct legal conclusion: it certainly is not a fair inference, and never was intended by Congress. The fees imposed on the claimants were meant to be appropriated in payment of the salary and the contingent expenses of the commission, and not to the amount of one thousand two hundred and fifty dollars, to be reserved by the secretary as an addition to his salary.

The important and procrastinated situation of the business of the commission renders it necessary that there should be an extension of its session, and the interests of the United States require that time should be allowed for a thorough investigation of the claims.

I have the honor to remain, with much respect, your obedient humble servant,

                                                                ALEXANDER HAMILTON.

William H. Crawford,
        Secretary of the Treasury.

Sir: St. Augustine, *January* 8, 1824.

It is with much pleasure I reply to your note of this morning, in the hope that a full explanation of our respective views of the course most advisable for the commission to pursue, may lead to the adoption of such regulations as will tend to facilitate the discharge of the important and delicate responsibilities with which we are entrusted.

It is for this purpose I submit the following propositions and regulations:

1st. That the secretary be directed to translate and record the royal orders, the official correspondence, the regulations of the Governors, and the instructions and calculations controlling the surveyors.

2d. That the commission ascertain whether the Governors of East Florida possessed any authority to dispose of the public lands independent of the royal orders, and whether their regulations are to be considered the acts of the Spanish Government, and, as such, to be respected in our adjudications.

3d. That the commission determine whether the royal order of the 29th March, 1815, authorizing grants for military services, be not controlled by that of the 29th October, 1790, and what are the conditions referred to in the latter order.

4th. That the commission ascertain whether the surveyors were authorized to change the location of concessions at discretion, and in the same manner to divide grants and locate the several parts; and whether they were not subject to certain regulations, and the table of Purcell explanatory of the same.

5th. That the commission determine whether they can inquire into the validity of the circumstances of a grant antecedent to the issuing of the royal titles, where the concessions have been made within the authority of the royal orders.

6th. That the commission decide whether the abandonment of the province by the British subjects, after its cession to Spain in 1783, did not, by operation of the treaty of cession, re-attach their lands to the royal domain.

7th. That the commission inquire whether grants containing the customary clause, "without injury to third persons," were valid against the Spanish Government, if it should appear that the lands petitioned for had been previously granted, without a subsequent decree and order to change the location.

8th. That the commission ascertain whether decrees for pasturage and mill-seats conveyed more than a permission to use the pasture and timber, and whether the Government did not reserve the right to concede to others all the plantable lands contained therein.

9th. That the commission determine whether lands abandoned for more than two years in succession were not considered vacant lands, reverting to the royal domain—the grantee continuing to reside in the province; and whether, if so, the effect of such an abandonment can accrue to the benefit of the United States when the absence of the claimant was an incidental consequence of the rebellion of 1812.

The propriety of establishing these preliminary principles will, I am confident, appear to you necessary upon mature reflection. Without settling some general law it will be impossible for the commission to do justice to the

* Mr. Lloyd, of the Senate, is fully informed.

claimants, and perform their duty to the United States.   The means of deciding are in the possession of the commissioners, for which the United States are principally indebted to the detention of the public documents from Governor Coppinger by the order of General Andrew Jackson.

I again offer for the consideration of the commission, regulations, the utility of which, if candidly examined, cannot fail to meet its concurrence, the more especially as the embarrassment of our present proceedings practically teaches the necessity of resorting to some change.

First regulation.—That the secretary be directed to prepare a descriptive list of the claims, according to the form presented by me, and adopted by the commission.

Second regulation.—That the secretary be directed to class the claims under the respective royal orders on which they are predicated, and that the commission proceed to the examination and adjudication of the claims in classes.

First class.—Those predicated on the royal order of the 29th March, 1790, separating those with, from those without, royal titles.

1st specification, those not exceeding 1,000 acres.
2d   do.   those not exceeding 3,500 do.
3d   do,   those exceeding   3,500 do.

Second class.—Those predicated on the royal schedule of the 17th June, 1801, granting the houses and lots, and remitting the principal and interest to the purchasers.

Third class.—Those under the royal order of 29th of March, 1815, authorizing bounties for military services, divisions, and specifications, as in the first class.

Fourth class.—Those under the royal order of September 3, 1817, directing the Intendant of Cuba to dispose of lands in East Florida.

Fifth class.—Those emanating from the British Government.

Sixth class.—Those grants for services, and not predicated in either of the royal orders.
(See Miranda's for 24 miles, and Arredondo's for 20 miles square, and Buyck's for 50,000 acres.)
Divisions and specifications as in first class.

Seventh class.—Those dated after the 24th January, 1818, and by the treaty declared null and void.

Third regulation.—That the commission commence, as soon as the papers are in readiness, to adjudicate upon the claims under the order of 1790, and, in the mean time, that they collect the evidence in the large grants to be transmitted to Congress during the present session.

Fourth regulation.—That in all those cases within the final jurisdiction of the commissioners, that the memorial of the claimant, or an abstract of the same made by one of the commissioners, together with the original grant, concession, or order of survey, be alone recorded, with a memorandum exhibiting the deraignment of title, as follows:

That C claims from B, by deed bearing date the ———— day of ————, in the year ————, who derived title from A, the grantee, on, &c.   Wills, deeds, bills of sale, or other mesne conveyances, not to be recorded, except by reference, as exhibits A, B, C.

Fifth regulation.—That in all cases beyond the final jurisdiction of the commissioners, that the memorial of the claimant, with the documents incident to the grant, the memorial, decree, order of survey, survey and confirmation, or royal titles, (if there be any,) be recorded, together with an abstract of the documentary evidence; but that the deraignment of title be only recorded by reference, as in the preceding regulations.

Seventh regulation.—That the commission will retain, through the whole course of the examination of witnesses, a supervisory control, that immaterial and illegal evidence be not recorded.

Eighth regulation.—That it will no longer be the duty of the secretary to make out memorials or prepare commissions for the examinations of witnesses.

Ninth regulation.—That the secretary will hereafter confine his written translations to material parts of Spanish documents, and, in all cases within the final jurisdiction of the commission, having royal titles, the attendance of the secretary will only be required to give parol translations.

Tenth regulation.—That, in all cases where there are royal titles, the fees for recording will only be charged on the memorial and royal title; but in all cases, on condition, seeking confirmation, fees will be charged on such records as the commission shall determine essential for the establishment of the claim when directed to be recorded.

I have been thus particular, to avoid the usual misunderstandings incident to the irregular manner in which our proceedings have been minuted, and more illegally kept, in loose sheets; and I anticipate that you will no longer indulge in so disingenuous an interpretation of my motives as to imagine that I would attempt to expose the regulations of the commission by the introduction, in a disguised form, of a practical illustration of their injurious inexpediency.   It is impossible that the commission can investigate the claims with advantage, if they are to be taken into consideration without any other system than the order in which they have been entered.   I am confident when you have deliberated upon these propositions and regulations, you will be convinced of the propriety of their adoption, the more especially if you reflect upon the embarrassments that now procrastinate our examination, and that, for all useful purposes, the business of the commission is now essentially suspended.   I appeal to your candor to acknowledge whether I have not repeatedly anticipated our present difficulties, as the necessary consequences of the decisions of the commission, and whether your recent anxiety to have perfected the descriptive list submitted by me might not be considered as conclusive evidence?

I am aware, in some instances arising from the unfortunate indulgence of the commission in permitting claims to be filed not corresponding with our regulations of the 1st August last, that the memorials present but an imperfect statement of the claim, which may, however, be supplied by a little extra attention on the part of the commissioners in collating from the testimony a brief analysis, or by directing the claimants to file supplementary memorials.

It is with much pleasure I avail myself of your admission, that " the time when we must make report to Congress will shortly elapse," to renew the proposition to report immediately to the Secretary of the Treasury the acts and proceedings of the commissioners; and, inasmuch as we have done little more than to order the claims to be filed, (none of which have been recorded,) that we suggest the propriety of an indefinite extension of our session, if our secretary is to translate and record all the testimony, and that further time be allowed for the admission of the numerous claims that remain to be presented.

I am perfectly willing " to take all the claims now in readiness into consideration," which state of preparation, according to the decisions of a majority of the commission, will place under our consideration only thirty-seven claims, of which eleven are not within our final jurisdiction, notwithstanding we have a secretary authorized by law, and two assistants appointed by the commission.

The following decisions I have uniformly opposed, and, in my estimation, they ought to be reported to Congress:

The majority of the commission have decided that all documents presented shall be recorded *in extenso,* and those in Spanish be translated by the secretary: thus giving an employment to the secretary of an indefinite termination; and, inasmuch as the mesne conveyances are of indifference to the United States, and as Congress has reserved no right to revise our proceedings within our final powers, there can be no necessity to record the evidence in cases of confirmation, as our decisions will undoubtedly be made upon the force and authenticity of the originals.

The majority of the commission have decided to adjudicate upon claims where the grants have issued subsequent to the 24th of January, 1818, and without giving any reasons for so doing, notwithstanding the treaty declares all such grants null and void.

The majority of the commission have decided that the authorization to confirm to actual settlers to the amount of three thousand five hundred acres, must be understood to include all persons *resident* in the Territory at the time of the cession, and not to be limited to those who were at that period in the actual possession and occupancy of the lands claimed.

The majority of the commission have decided that they will adjudicate on claims without examining the original documents, while they are aware that the public records, in the possession of the keeper of the public archives, have been much exposed, and are still kept in loose sheets, without schedule or descriptive list, and that the letter from Governor Kindelan, the foundation of the royal order of 1815, has been essentially altered, and that transcripts of different import have been furnished. The advertisement of the keeper of the public archives also makes known to the commission that a small grant has been withdrawn from the office, and one of 16,000 acres substituted.

The majority of the commission have repeatedly refused to report its proceedings, while they have unofficially communicated with the Secretary of the Treasury, without giving any intimation of the time, manner, or substance of their communication. The delicacy and propriety of such conduct I do not understand, and abstain from comment.

I have the honor to remain, with much respect and regard, your obedient servant,
ALEXANDER HAMILTON.

DAVIS FLOYD, Esq.

Note referred to, from David Floyd, Esq., to Alexander Hamilton.

" Inasmuch as the commissioners will be able to make final decisions of but few claims, and as much time will be necessary to investigate and report sundry rules, regulations, and customs, prevalent in the province relative to granting lands, and as the time when we must make report to Congress will shortly elapse, I would propose for consideration, whether it would not be proper to take all the claims now in a state of readiness into consideration, have them recorded, and finally decided; and whether we would be able to devote more of our time, and our secretary, to the investigation of new cases; or whether, probably, the whole time may not be necessary to the preparation of those before us. Yours," &c.

NOTICE.

Whereas, on or about the 27th November there was introduced into the office of the subscriber, in a clandestine and dishonorable manner, a document purporting to be a memorial and concession for 16,000 acres of land, to an inhabitant of this province, (whose name is, from motives of delicacy, withheld from the public, as he could not have been privy to the transaction,) this is, therefore, to give notice to those interested, but more particularly to him who was *mean* enough to take advantage of the confidence placed in him while in my office, that the imposition has been detected, and that the document now bears upon it my certificate of the circumstances, and the fact of its having been illegally introduced into the office. As I have reason to believe that the person who introduced the said document into my office *stole* therefrom another of a similar description, although not so valuable, I hereby offer a reward of $100 to any person who, knowing the facts, will give information, to enable me to prosecute the *thief* to conviction.

WILLIAM REYNOLDS, *Keeper of the public archives.*

NOTICE.

The following regulations have been adopted by the commissioners appointed to ascertain claims and titles to lands in that part of the Territory of Florida known as East Florida.

All persons claiming title to lands under any patent, grant, concession, or order of survey, will make a brief statement, by memorial, setting forth the situation, boundaries, and, if possible, the deraignment of title, to the lands claimed, together with the number of acres, when and by whom granted, and by what authority; and whether the same be the whole or part of the original grant.

All cases where grants have been made on conditions, it will be necessary to show the nature of the conditions; whether they have been performed; and, if not, the reasons why they have not been complied with.

Where lands are claimed by actual settlers, without grants, concessions, patents, or order of survey, the same must be declared, and the circumstances of possession and occupancy stated distinctly, together with the nature of the evidence in support of the claim; and whether the said possession ever was, and in what manner, acknowledged or sanctioned by the Spanish Government.

In all instances where claims are made in virtue of British patents, grants, &c., the claimants must describe in what manner they claim, whether as original patentees or grantees, or by assignment; also, whether they are in actual possession; and, if out of possession, that they claim, *bona fide*, as American citizens.

All original documents, if in the possession of the claimants, must be exhibited; and, in all other cases, certified copies, the memorial, order of survey, survey and confirmation, together with translations of the same.

Claimants will show whether they were actual residents at the time of the cession, and where they now reside.

The office of the commissioners will be at the Government house until further notice.
A. HAMILTON,
W. W. BLAIR,
DAVIS FLOYD,
Land Commissioners.

ST AUGUSTINE, *August* 1, 1823.

On the 8th of August a resolution was adopted by the commissioners, requiring only so much of the papers to be transmitted as were material, at suggestion.
A. HAMILTON.

No. 9.

SIR: ST. AUGUSTINE, *January* 22, 1824.

As the course I have pursued as a member of the Board of Land Commissioners may induce those who are interested to attempt to create prejudices, I take the liberty to request that no unfavorable impressions may be made until the proceedings of the board are subject to your inspection. I feel that all the invidious responsibilities of the commissions have devolved on me; and, whatever may be the result, I shall support the part I have taken with firmness. The board have commenced the adjudication of claims without settling the preliminary principles that are to govern their decisions. I have come to the determination, as the board will not ascertain the law, nor examine the original documents, to be present without taking any part in the adjudication, and to report to the Treasury Department, our proceedings for the consideration of Congress.

The act creating the commission terminates on the second Monday in February.

I am aware that, in writing to you, I ought not to ask to be excused; but such are the circumstances, that I must either communicate in haste, or lose an unexpected favorable opportunity.

I am, with much respect,

ALEXANDER HAMILTON.

JAMES MONROE, Esq.

No. 10.

SIR: ST. AUGUSTINE, *January* 23, 1824.

As a member of the commission appointed to ascertain claims and titles to land in East Florida, I have the honor to request that you will lay before the President of the United States the enclosed letter for his consideration.

With sentiments of the highest respect, I remain, sir, your obedient servant,

ALEXANDER HAMILTON.

Hon. W. H. CRAWFORD, *Secretary of the Treasury.*

SIR: ST. AUGUSTINE, *January* 23, 1824.

It is with extreme regret I have to inform you that I have considered it my duty to the interest of the United States to decline any participation in the final adjudication of claims to land, and to recommend that the proceedings of this commission be suspended until Congress shall have an opportunity to investigate its acts. I have also to advise, that the records in the possession of the keeper of the public archives, and those papers specially detained from Governor Coppinger by the order of General Jackson, be transferred to a different charge.

In assuming the responsibility I am aware that I have undertaken an invidious, embarrassing, and unthankful office, and I anticipate the corresponding sacrifice of reputation and respectability, if I be not justified by the result; and, were I to consult personal interest, I should be induced to resign, the more especially as there cannot accrue the slightest advantage to my character.

The act of Congress, in virtue of which we have been appointed, expires on the second Monday in February, when it is my intention to proceed to Charleston to anticipate any order that may be sent requiring my attendance in Washington, if such a requisition should be deemed necessary.

In partial explanation of the differences in the commission, I take the liberty to refer to my letter of the 10th instant, addressed to the Secretary of the Treasury, enclosing one from me to Davis Floyd, Esq., of the 8th of January, in answer to his note of the same date.

I have the honor to remain, with great respect, your obedient servant,

ALEXANDER HAMILTON.

JAMES MONROE, *President.*

I should recommend, as safe depositories of the public records, Edward R. Gibson and William Simmons.

No. 11.

SIR: WASHINGTON, *March* 31, 1824.

The remarkable differences of opinion that have characterized the proceedings of the Board of Commissioners appointed to ascertain claims and titles to land in East Florida, induce me to tender my resignation, notwithstanding I have had the satisfaction to observe that the act of the present session of Congress affirmatively supports the positions I have uniformly advocated.

In electing to pursue this course I desire to avoid the invidious task of being constrained, through the force of official duty, to arraign the conduct of those with whom I have been associated, when, perhaps, the pride of an avowed opinion may have created an injudicious pertinacity in its adherence, and caused the dictates, possibly, of the purest intentions, to become the subjects of serious reprehension, from the deleterious influence of their arbitrary practice. I allude to the extraordinary indisposition, constantly manifested, to adopt any measures that might tend to facilitate the progress of the duties with which we were charged; and, unaccountable as it may appear, the unexplained refusal to settle general principles as preliminary to correct adjudication, necessarily operating injurious to the rights of the United States, by embarrassing and paralyzing the influence of the minority of the commission, and to the claimants productive of endless inconvenience, expense, and trouble; the frequent decisions of important questions, in reference to the powers of the commission, without the certainty and responsibility of written opinions, and consequent invariable misconceptions of what was determined; the illegal and improper manner in which the minutes were kept on loose and imperfect sheets, and the still more extraordinary procedure, the refusal to secure and examine the original papers and records, trusting to their genuineness upon the certified transcripts of a territorial officer, whose assistant was one of the secretaries of Governor Coppinger, notwithstanding they were officially informed that a fraudulent erasure had been made in an important document in that office, corroborated by a tacit admission of the propriety of the charge, by the issue of subsequent transcripts, without persisting in the alteration, and while it was a subject of public notoriety that records had disappeared, and, in one instance, a grant of 16,000 acres discovered to have been introduced in place of another for less than as many hundreds. These papers and records are publicly exposed, and are without schedule, neither numbered nor lettered, and in loose sheets.

I must, however painful may be the reflection, notice, as inconsistent with the performance of a confidential trust, unsusceptible, from its peculiar nature of control through legislative provisions, and vitally dependant on the integrity with which it is administered, to answer the objects of its creation, the fact of practising the law in actions of real estate involving questions and conflicting interests which are the immediate subjects of their adjudication. In the first case involving any doubt, the claim of John H. McIntosh, my associates were both engaged as counsel.

In reference to this case I must remark that, in consequence of a determination to decide upon the validity of claims before any general principles were settled, I declined joining in the adjudication. The correspondence I had the honor to transmit to you from Charleston, and my communication of the 10th of January last, enclosing my answer to Davis Floyd, of the 8th of January, in reply to his note of the same date, will fully explain the arrangements and principles proposed by me to be adopted by the commissioners, together with which I take the liberty to refer to a copy of a tabular descriptive list* prepared by me for the use of the commission, exhibiting the circumstances of each and all the grants.

I cannot avoid mentioning that I have observed with regret the imperfections of the official report forwarded to your Department, and especially in the omissions of an adjudicated case connected with circumstances of peculiar delicacy; together with the suppression of the first regulations, and all the correspondence alluded to in the preceding paragraph.

To express my dissent from the conclusions of the report, I must remark, with all due deference, that the argument seems to be drawn from an extraordinary bias, indicative of an impulse corresponding with the feelings of counsel employed and interested in the cause of their clients. The report decides in favor of the unlimited powers of the Governors to dispose of the public lands; and commences in support of this position, with an extract from the Codes of India, 12th title, book 4th. In my estimation, the contrary is the just conclusion to be drawn from an examination of the whole documentary and respectable parol testimony. It is evident, from the extract taken from the Codes of India, through all the royal orders and official correspondence, to the change of the Intendancy of Florida, in 1817, to the Intendant of the island of Cuba, that the Governors possessed a very circumscribed and limited authority.

In answer to Zespedez, the first Governor after the recession of the Floridas to the King of Spain, by the Government of Great Britain, communicating the embarrassed state of the country, and asking permission to make grants of lands, the Count de Galvez, on the 4th July, 1785, Mexico, remarks, that he approves of the police arrangements contained in his letter of the 8th May, 1785, but, with respect to his request for instructions, for the purpose of granting lands " to the old Floridians, as well as any other Spaniards or foreigners, he will inform his excellency the Minister of the Indies, that, by his superior prudence, measures may be taken as are agreeable to him, or may merit the approbation of the King." It also is represented by Zespedez, that the houses abandoned by the English were rapidly decaying, and recommends that they should be sold; to which subject there appears no reference, until the royal order of the 17th June, 1801, is communicated to Governor White. In this order, Quesada, successor to Zespedez, is represented as having made sale of the houses and lots, for the benefit of the treasury, the payment of which is remitted, in consequence of information communicated by Governor White, in 1798, that the purchasers refused to comply with their promises, *founding their objections on the grants of land made gratis to foreigners*, after a consultation with the council of Indies, by the King. The next evidence is Quesada's edict, the copy of which in my possession is without date, but must have been antecedent to 1796, at which time he ceased to be Governor, announcing " that the grants to all the inhabitants, permanently settled, and subjects of His Majesty, in his royal name, and for their use, the quantity of land they may require, *in proportion to their force*, without any exception;" and predicates this authority on the 12th title, 4th book, of the Codes of India, but declines, until he receives instructions from his Government, " *to make absolute distributions for powerful motives*." On the 12th October, 1803, Governor White informs the Captain General of Cuba, that he had reduced the quantity of lands to be granted to new settlers, from one hundred acres, to heads of families, to fifty, and to laborers, from fifty acres to twenty-five, for the approbation of his Government. In the year 1813, Governor Kindelan recommends the services of the militia, and the married officers and soldiers of the Cuba battalion, as entitled to the royal favor, to which an answer is sent, in 1815, by the Captain General, communicating the royal disposition, and authorizes grants of land to be made to the privates of the militia, and exclusively to the married officers and soldiers of the Cuba battalion, giving to the *officers* of the militia royal commissions corresponding with their respective militia grades. On the 21st October, 1817, the powers of the Intendant of Cuba seem to be limited; for, by royal order of that date, the liberal policy authorized for the settlement of the island of Puerto Rico is extended to that of Cuba; and, in December, 1817, the same authority is given to the Intendant, in relation to the lands in Florida, and the Intendancy transferred to his direction.

The order of the regency of the 22d of January, 1813, provides for the division of the public lands into two equal parts, appropriating the one to the payment of the public responsibilities, and the other is declared for the use of private individuals; and makes provision for the disabled officers and soldiers honorably discharged. The tenth article of this ordinance is as follows: " The quantity which, in each town, is granted to officers or soldiers, shall be in equal proportion of value to the space and quality of the same, and more or less for some places than in others, according to their circumstances, and the greater or less extent of the lands; managing, if possible, *that, at the least, each quantity shall be such as to be sufficient, regularly cultivated, for the maintenance of an individual*."

In this statement we have a tacit admission, at least, of the first Governor, that his powers did not authorize him to grant lands, notwithstanding he considered the circumstances of the country, requiring the exercise of such a power. And, again, we find Governor Quesada, as late as 1793, practically construing his instructions imperfect, and predicating his sole authority on the limitations contained in the Code of India. It should also be remarked, that the Governors had their council, with whom they were directed to consult and advise; and, consequently, we may fairly conclude that, whatever doubts may have been entertained, when disposed in favor of the Territory, must have received their sanction. We have, in addition to this, the regulations of the regency in 1813, providing for the disposal of public lands, and for *military* services. Then, I ask, how can it be pretended that the Governor possessed an unlimited authority, and how the royal order of 1815, authorizing remuneration in lands for *military* services, could be construed as undefined? *This last royal order has not only been carried into effect by excessive grants, but has been made the excuse for repeated extravagant gifts to the same individual, for the same services.*

It is worthy of observation, that none of the grants, made in opposition to the regularly established custom, were in the possession of *actual settlers* at the time of the cession; and that, until the agrarian prodigal, Coppinger, issued absolute titles for mill-seats, cow-pens, &c., they were only considered and occupied as privileges to use the timber and pasture, the Government reserving the right to dispose of all the plantable lands within their customary limits of sixteen thousand acres.

The report is certainly in error in declaring, or even intimating, that no established rule, governing the surveyors, was legally in force. It was in evidence, that the written instructions to Marrott, and these in principle corresponding with the universal Spanish custom, direct that the front line shall not exceed one-third of the depth, and that they were uniformly pursued until the general jubilee distribution commenced upon the prospect of the

---

* In possession of Mr. Barton, of the Senate.

cession to the United States; and, even during the absence of all integrity and regulation, no written evidence could be produced of an authorized departure. In all differences about boundaries, references were always made, and conclusively, to these regulations.

To this will be opposed the evidence of George J. F. Clarke and his pretended deputy, Burgevin. In mentioning the name of the latter I ought to apologize to Mr. Clarke, as I considered him too contemptible for serious examination, and too trifling to support or injure any other.

The extravagant pretensions and inconsistent representations of Mr. Clarke, with a memory on some subjects singularly tenacious, and on others peculiarly forgetful, to my mind created such unfavorable impressions as to destroy all confidence in his accuracy. It is possible this gentleman may have mistaken his instructions. I certainly entertained much respect for him antecedent to his examination, and regretted his evidently painful situation afterwards. It was, however, *my* duty to make the examination without respect to his feelings. Several of his tracts, and those of his immediate friends, were involved in the successful establishment of the powers he advocated, and that of Mr. McIntosh, even further than my colleagues were aware. Mr. Clarke was an interested witness to the amount of forty thousand, and Burgevin exceeding twenty thousand acres.

I must here take the liberty to remark, that the conduct pursued by my colleagues gave to my examinations an invidious inquisitorial character, and, what was more unfortunate, it created an indirect sanction to witnesses to attempt to impose improper testimony.

I regret that the discrepancies of the report prevent my referring to Purcell's table of calculations, in connexion with Marrot's and Clarke's instructions. The whole would show a perfect system, and, notwithstanding the Governors may have exhibited occasional favoritism, there existed a most respectable degree of regularity while there was any expectation of responsibility to the Spanish Government.

The amount of acres of land included in the exceptionable grants cannot be estimated at less than one million five hundred thousand; and, as they are pretended to be surveyed, extending along the shores and spreading over the hammocks, giving to many tracts fronts greatly exceeding the depth; the public interests involved must bear almost a duplicate value to the numerical computation.

To those acquainted with the peculiarities of our southern countries, and who reflect that the extension of the front line gives a greater proportional advantage than the mere additional front, this estimate will not appear excessive. In a parallelogram composed of three successive square miles, receding from the river or front, the hammock, as in most cases, not extending in the same direction to exceed half a mile, the tract will have but one-sixth of what is appreciated the most valuable lands; when, if the relative position of the figure be reversed, the amount of hammock lands in the triple front will be one-half of the tract, and the whole brought within an average distance of the water of less than two-thirds of a mile, leaving to the United States, in the rear, the entire pine lands.

It is certainly material to the interest of the United States, and especially to the honest claimants, that the proceedings should be speedily examined. If the decision of the commission be correct, the business ought to be concluded in less than six months, and, if not, the sooner it is terminated the better.

It may not be improbable that, with some, the course I have pursued may be condemned as erroneous in not submitting, as the minority, to the judgment of the commission expressed by the majority. I am, nevertheless, conscious that, although this may in general, and in minor points, be correct, there are occasions when silent acquiescence would be censurable, and an independent opposition imperiously required.

It is my matured opinion that Congress will not sanction many of the claims recommended for confirmation as authorized by the Spanish Government, but will consider them as fraudulently made in anticipation of the cession of the Floridas to the United States.

I have the honor to remain, with much respect, your obedient humble servant,

                                                                    ALEXANDER HAMILTON.

Hon. WM. H. CRAWFORD, *Secretary of the Treasury.*

NOTE.—I am inclined to believe that all the papers I have referred to have not been embodied in the report of my colleagues.

No. 12.

SIR: NEW YORK, *May* 1, 1824.

I had the honor this morning, in reply to Mr. Jones's note received by to-day's mail, to inform the Government that I was not in possession of any draught of my letter written from Charleston, and that I should be under the necessity, with the exception of the copies of the letters contained therein, to give my communication from memory, which I now do, treating the subjects thereof more at large, affording the President a better opportunity to understand the bearings of the transactions to which it relates, with the request that this may be considered as its substitute.

I have dated the enclosed from Charleston to preserve the order of the correspondence, and to answer the reference in my letter of the 31st March, written the day after my arrival in Washington.

I am, respectfully, your most obedient servant,

                                                                    ALEXANDER HAMILTON.

Hon. W. H. CRAWFORD, *Secretary of the Treasury.*

SIR: CHARLESTON, *February* 25, 1824.

I had the honor, from St. Augustine, under date of the 10th of January, to transmit to you, for the inspection of the President, my correspondence with Davis Floyd, Esq., of the 8th of the same month, to which I have now to add the last communications that passed between myself and colleagues.

The majority of the commission having refused to settle any general principles, or to adopt any organization of our business that would facilitate or render it intelligible, I considered it my duty to assume the responsibility of withdrawing from the adjudication; at the same time I continued a constant attendant, noting in written memoranda whatever transpired.

I have come to this place in anticipation of some communication from the chairman of the Committee on Public Lands, requesting my attendance in Washington previous to the passage of any act of Congress extending the term of the commission.

With much respect, I remain, &c.,

                                                                    ALEXANDER HAMILTON.

Hon. W. H. CRAWFORD.

Sir:　　　　　　　　　　　　　　　　　　　　　　　　　St. Augustine, *January* 27, 1824.

We shall commence this morning making out a report of the proceedings of the board to send on to the Secretary of the Treasury. We would be sorry that a difference of opinion amongst the commissioners should deprive the people and the Government of the aid of any one member of the board, and hope therefore, that, notwithstanding we may have differed in opinion on an important question, whether the majority were right or wrong, it affords no good reason why we should not all unite in making up the report of the board; and, also, in rendering the reasons for the confirmation or rejection of such claims as have been decided. We, therefore, hope that you will change your previous determination, and unite with us in making out the report and decisions aforesaid.

We are, respectfully, &c.,

DAVIS FLOYD.
W. W. BLAIR.

Col. Alex. Hamilton.

As I had declined joining in the adjudication I conceived it a matter of delicacy to absent myself from all private meetings; and, having absolutely disapproved of the conduct of my colleagues, I returned the following answer to their letter, immediately upon its receipt. The board being in session, I wrote immediately, to prevent delay.

Gentlemen:　　　　　　　　　　　　　　　　　　　　St. Augustine, *January* 27, 1824.

If my attendance were not mere matter of form, I should regret that my absence would " deprive the people and the Government" of my assistance in making up the report of the commission; but as I have uniformly disapproved of the course that has been pursued, and since there has been no difference of opinion in the few cases that have been the subjects of your adjudication, I can perceive no other consequence in my interference than to occasion delay and embarrassment. As I have not heard, notwithstanding my constant attendance, the principles which have governed the commission in its decisions, it would be impossible for me to show their propriety; and to attempt to illustrate their inaccuracy by the assumption of what has been your interpretation of the rules, regulations, and royal orders, that have been in force, and governed the disposition of the lands in this Territory, while under the jurisdiction of the Spanish Government, would be a preposterous and most idle task.

When the report shall be made I presume the commission will terminate its session, to prevent further inconvenience resulting from my refusal to participate in its proceedings.

It is with great regret that I have considered it my duty to the public interest, and not less so to the claimants, who were deeply concerned in the propriety and strictness of our examinations, to decline your invitation to change my determination.

I have the honor to remain, with much respect, your obedient servant,

ALEXANDER HAMILTON.

Hons. Davis Floyd, and
　　Wm. W. Blair.

Gentlemen:　　　　　　　　　　　　　　　　　　　　St. Augustine, *January* 30, 1824.

It may be proper to inform you that, in my opinion, the document upon which Fernando de la Maza Arredondo, Jun., claims title to fifty thousand acres of land, is not authentic; and I have to request, in consideration of the interest of the United States, that the records of title in the office of the keeper of the public archives may be deposited in a trunk, and secured with separate locks—one for the use of the commissioners, and the other for the keeper of the public archives.

I am, with much respect, your obedient servant,

ALEXANDER HAMILTON.

Hons. Davis Floyd, and
　　W. W. Blair.

P. S. I shall be obliged to you to inform me what is your determination in relation to the records of title.

To the above no answer was given; but, on the succeeding day, while I was directing transcripts to be made from the minutes, Mr. Floyd joined me, when I directed his attention to my note in reference to the public records. It was our united opinion that these papers were insecurely kept; and mine, that it was our duty to direct the marshal to take forcible possession, if the proposition I had submitted should not be complied with. To this course Mr. Floyd objected, and alleged, as his reason, that he would not do any act that might compromise his communications to Washington. We then ordered the marshal to call upon the keeper of the public archives, and request him to concur with the proposed arrangement. The following is the answer, and such as I had anticipated. I had made repeated unsuccessful attempts to secure these papers, aware that I ought not in prudence, and in the exercise of a sound discretion, commence an investigation into their validity while they were subject to intrusions, and under an irresponsible control. The President had directed these documents to be transferred to the charge of the commissioners, which was not complied with, under an evasion sanctioned by the majority of the board. This order from the President was issued in consequence of a communication made by Mr. Floyd and myself, the day after his arrival in St. Augustine, at my suggestion.

The treaty declares that the public records shall be transferred to the American commissioners at the cession of the Territory. The communication of the President advises that the public records, transferred by Governor Coppinger (the Spanish) to General Jackson, (the American commissioner,) should be placed in charge of the land commission. The majority of the commissioners, with the keeper of the public archives, decide that, as there was no other than a constructive transfer, there was not such a delivery as to embrace the documents alluded to within the order of the President. It was also contended that, as the Florida Legislative Council had placed a certain portion of these papers in charge of the keeper of the public archives, he was bound to retain possession of them. To which it was objected that, inasmuch as Congress had limited the powers of the Legislative Council, and especially prohibiting them from interfering with the landed rights of the United States, they had no power to dispose of the original titles to lands that were, with the Territory, transferred as public property; in which character they had always been held under the Spanish Government. It being also a well established principle of law, that the muniments of title ought always to attend the highest right to the land, they were, in fact, the only evidences of the acts of the Government, to illustrate under what conditions and circumstances the public lands were appropriated. These records were the representatives of the allodial right of the King; and no sales could be made without the sanction of the Government, obtained by regular petition; and, in all cases where lands remained vacant for two successive years, they were considered reannexed to the " royal domain;" and were frequently, under such circumstances, conveyed to others by subsequent grants, and the improvements sold for the benefit of the public treasury. [See Governor White's regulations, published in 1803 and 1805.] The original grants were never given to the grantees—transcripts were alone issued.

The annexed report was made by the marshal on the 2d February, 1824.

To the honorable the commissioners appointed to ascertain claims and titles to land in East Florida:

GENTLEMEN: In obedience to your order of the 31st ultimo, I called at the office of the keeper of the public archives, and proposed to Antonio Alvarez, Esq., [*late secretary to Governor Coppinger,*] that all the original titles to lands in that office should be deposited in a chest to be provided for that purpose, on which should be placed two locks; the chest and key of one of the locks to remain in charge of the keeper of the public archives, the key of the other lock to remain in charge of the land commissioners; that, when any papers should be required, some person authorized by the commissioners would attend with their key at the office of the keeper of the public archives; that he might have free access to the papers, at the same time protecting them from improper exposure. Mr. Alvarez declined acceding to the arrangement proposed.

With much respect I remain your obedient servant,

WATERS SMITH, *Marshal E. F.*

NOTE.—The words within brackets by myself.   A. H.

Perceiving that my colleagues were determined not to take any steps that would coerce the production or tend to secure the public records, which became the more necessary after transcripts had been issued, with the official certificate that they were copies of the originals in his possession, I resolved to expose the proceedings of the commission, and, if possible, cause it to be suspended. Under the impression *that, as we ceased to be in commission* on the 7th February instant, the expiration of the act of Congress in virtue of which we had been appointed, it would be necessary to re-nominate us to the Senate, I had intended to have made a formal protest.

The majority of the commission having decided that, as Congress had, by the act of 3d of March, 1823, extended the final jurisdiction of the commissioners in favor of " actual settlers" to three thousand five hundred acres, this extension was not to be considered as confined to those only who were in the cultivation or occupation of the land claimed, but that it embraced the claims of all those who were merely residents within the Territory at its cession, the period referred to in the act. It was not alone on the ground that this interpretation was not authorized by fair construction, and the reasons apparent why Congress should be more confiding to the commission in a class of claimants so peculiarly advantageously situated, that I was opposed to their decision, but because I considered the public interests essentially jeopardized by the admission of claims that, in my opinion, *had been made in fraud of the United States, and in direct violation of the provisions of the royal order of* 1815, *in virtue of which they were avowedly made.* Of these grants few, if any, were in actual possession at the time of the cession, and of those which had been located since the surveys had not corresponded with the regulations of the Spanish Government, but in such a manner as, at least, to duplicate the injury to the public interest.

If the view I had taken of this subject was correct, and of which I entertain no doubt, it was of importance to the community, and every individual desirous to make purchases in Florida, that no act of the commission should facilitate the imposition intended to be practised upon those who might be induced to speculate under the sanction of the decisions of the commissioners. I consequently sent the subjoined note to the presiding commissioner:

SIR: ST. AUGUSTINE, *February* 4, 1824.

In order to guard against any unfortunate speculations that might arise from the decisions of the majority of the commissioners, permit me to recommend that no evidence of confirmation issue in those cases exceeding one thousand acres, where the claimants are not actually settled on the lands claimed, until Congress shall have an opportunity to examine our proceedings.

I am, with much respect, your obedient servant,

ALEXANDER HAMILTON.

To DAVIS FLOYD, Esq.

To the above no answer was made, and, on the following day, I departed for Charleston.

All which is respectfully submitted.

ALEXANDER HAMILTON.

MINUTES OF THE BOARD OF FLORIDA LAND COMMISSIONERS.

Board of Land Commissioners, city of St. Augustine, district of East Florida.

Agreeable to an act of Congress, entitled " An act for ascertaining claims and titles to land within the Territory of Florida," approved the 8th of May, 1822; also, an act of Congress entitled " An act amending and supplementary to the act for ascertaining claims and titles to land in the Territory of Florida, and to provide for the survey and disposal of the public lands in Florida," approved the 3d of March, 1823. Present: the Hons. Davis Floyd, William W. Blair, and Alexander Hamilton, appointed and commissioned for the purpose of ascertaining the claims and titles to lands within the district of East Florida: The said commissioners met at the Government house, in the city aforesaid, on Monday the 4th day of August, 1823, agreeably to previous notice published in the East Florida Herald, and proceeded to open their session for the performance of the duties assigned to their office. Whereupon, on motion,

Resolved, That the Hon. Davis Floyd be appointed presiding member of the board.

Ordered, That Francis J. Fatio be appointed secretary to this board. Whereupon, the said Francis J. Fatio took and subscribed the oath of office prescribed by the acts of Congress in that case made and provided.

Ordered, That John Lowe be appointed messenger to the Board of Commissioners.

Waters Smith presented to the board the following documents, with an accompanying memorial from James Bosley, of the city of Baltimore, to wit:

A deed from William G. D. Worthington to James Bosley, marked A, for five hundred acres of land;

A deed from Charles Gobert, and others, to said Worthington, marked B;

A certificate of Mr. Arredondo relative to Moultrie plantation;

Which documents were ordered to be filed by the secretary of the board.

RULES.

Ordered, In all cases where, in the deraignment of title, the documents may be very voluminous, the commissioners will require only so much of their contents as they may deem essential to a fair understanding of the claims.

Ordered, That the secretary of this board do apply to Patrick Lynch for all papers heretofore filed with said Lynch, relating to land titles in the district of East Florida, by virtue of an appointment as provisional secretary of this board made by the Hon. Alexander Hamilton; and that the accounts of said Lynch, for his services, be audited.

Ordered, That all claimants may be permitted, in the time of adjournment of the commissioners, to file their memorials and documents with the secretary, who shall produce them before the board at its next meeting for examination.

Ordered, That the board be adjourned until to-morrow morning at 10 o'clock.

TUESDAY, *August 5, 1823.*

The Board of Commissioners met according to adjournment. Present, all the members.

The following rules were then adopted:

Resolved, That claimants be not required to produce their title papers translated into the English language, but, in all cases, be permitted to file the original documents. The honorable Alexander Hamilton dissenting.

Ordered, That all the papers heretofore filed before the meeting of the board be returned to their respective owners, and that they be permitted to present the same in proper order.

Upon the motion of Francis J. Fatio, secretary of this board, Joseph B. Lancaster is admitted and sworn his deputy, well and truly and faithfully to perform the duties required of him by the Board of Commissioners.

Resolved, That the district attorney, the keeper of the public archives, nor the secretary to this board are not authorized to represent as attorneys or agents, any claims to lands before the commissioners. Honorable Davis Floyd dissenting.

The Board then adjourned until to-morrow morning, at 10 o'clock.

WEDNESDAY, *August 6, 1823.*

The board met according to adjournment. Present, all the members.

John H. McIntosh presented to the board his memorial for sundry tracts of land, with the following documents:

A memorial and certificate of four tracts of lands, with surveys of each. The first, a tract of land at the head of Indian river, containing six thousand acres, and bounded by Indian river and vacant lands; second, a tract called Stony Point, on Marrott's island, lying in Indian river; the number of acres not specified; third, a tract of land of 300 acres, situated on the north side of Marrott's island, and lies between the lagoon of Indian river, bordering on the said island and the Musquito lagoon; fourth, a tract of land of one thousand acres, called Cabbage swamp, situated on the east of Indian river, opposite the Narrows.

Also, a copy of the royal title to John McQueen for 98 caballerias and 8 acres, or about 3,254½ acres of land, upon St. John's river and McGirt's creek, together with a copy of the bill of sale for third tract; and another called Fort George, executed by said McQueen in favor of said McIntosh.

A conveyance from Timothy Hollingsworth to said McIntosh, of a tract of land containing eight hundred acres upon St. John's river, called Mulberry Grove.

An obligation from John McQueen to said McIntosh to make title to a tract of land upon Miami river, with a receipt acknowledging payment for said tract; also, a receipt from said McQueen to said McIntosh for the sum of $28,000, expressed to be the full consideration for three tracts of land.

Also, a title from said McQueen to said McIntosh for a tract of land on Miami river, containing 2,000 acres; also, an official copy of the concession to McQueen of said tract.

John B. Strong, Esq. moved the Board of Commissioners upon the following interrogatory, to wit: "Will the board require of the claimant to file with the secretary his memorial only for record, or will he be compelled to file therewith the documentary evidence of his title; and does the law require such document to be recorded, and fees paid to the secretary therefor?"

On which motion and interrogatory the board resolved that they will hear argument upon to-morrow.

The board then adjourned until to morrow morning, 10 o'clock.

THURSDAY, *August 7, 1823.*

The board met according to adjournment. Present, all the members.

John Love, by his agent, William R. Gibson, presented his memorial to the board, praying confirmation to three hundred acres of land, situate about fifteen miles south of St. Augustine; also, a document marked A, purporting to be a copy of Benjamin Lord's receipt for surveying the same, and a copy of an appraisement thereof by William Moss and George Gressall, all of which are ordered to be filed; also, an exhibit marked B, purporting to be a copy of a certificate of naturalization of said Love, obtained from the clerk's office of the federal district court, held in the city of Charleston, South Carolina.

Leave is given to John B. Strong, Esq., to withdraw his motion made on yesterday, and set down for argument for to-day.

Samuel Fairbanks, by John B. Strong, his attorney, presented his memorial, claiming title to a lot of ground in St. Augustine, on St. George street, containing near one acre of land, without any document accompanying the same; which is ordered to be filed.

The board adjourned until to-morrow morning, at 10 o'clock.

FRIDAY, *August 8, 1823.*

The board met according to adjournment. Present, all the members.

Patrick Lynch presented his account against the United States as provisional secretary to this board, appointed by the honorable Alexander Hamilton, one of the members of this board, from the 7th of June to the 5th of August, sixty days, at $1,250 per annum, $208 33; which is ordered to be certified to the Treasurer of the United States.

Duncan L. Clinch presented his memorial to this board, praying confirmation to a tract of land of five hundred acres, situated in the Twelve-mile swamp, near Joseph Thomas's land, and about seven miles northwest from St. Augustine; also, filed an original grant for the same, as spoken of in his memorial, to William Penn; a conveyance from said Penn to William Frazer and John Richardson, and a conveyance from Thomas Stone and William Wilson to Thomas Clarke; also a conveyance from C. W. and J. F. Clarke to said memorialist; also, a plat of survey of the same. All of which papers are ordered to be filed.

The board then adjourned until Monday morning, the 11th instant, at 10 o'clock.

MONDAY, *August* 11, 1823.

The board met according to adjournment.   Present, all the members.

No business occurring,

Ordered, That the board be adjourned until Wednesday, the 13th instant, at 10 o'clock in the morning.

WEDNESDAY, *August* 13, 1823.

The board met according to adjournment.   Present, all the members.

Samuel Fairbanks presented his memorial for eighty acres of land, lying in St. Antonio's bend, on the margin of St. John's river, being the one-third part of an undivided tract containing two hundred and forty acres, granted to Robert Gilbert, which grant, and a conveyance to the memorialist from Absalom Beardon and Hannah Beardon, his wife, one of the heirs of Robert Gilbert, the grantee, accompanies said memorial, and together therewith is ordered to be filed.

Fifteen sheets of royal orders, in the Spanish language, filed and ordered to be translated into the English language by the secretary of this board.

Resolved, That, hereafter, whenever a claimant of land shall present his evidence of title to the secretary of this board, desiring to bring the same before the commissioners, it shall be the duty of the said Secretary, without any fee therefor, to put the same in the form of a memorial, containing, in substance, what has already been required by the resolution of this board; and that the said secretary be authorized to obtain from the printer in this city one thousand blank copies of said form, and to authorize said printer to present his account therefor before this board, who will direct the said account to be paid out of the moneys which may come into their hands for appropriation; or, in case of none such, will certify said document to the Treasurer of the United States.

And be it further ordered, That the secretary be required to deliver one of those printed forms to any person or persons applying for the same.

Ordered, That the board be adjourned until to-morrow morning, 7 o'clock.

THURSDAY, *August* 14, 1823.

The board met according to adjournment.   Present, all the members.

A memorial from the citizens of St. Augustine, holders of lots in said city, received by this board.   After due consideration thereof, the board formed an address which, together with said memorial, is forwarded to the Secretary of the Treasury of the United States for information as to the subject-matter thereof; and the board postpone delivering any opinion upon said memorial until their address shall be answered.

Memorial of Peter Miranda for a tract of land of one thousand acres upon North river, to include Blide's Old Field, together with a grant to Joseph S. Sanchez for the same, and deed of conveyance from the grantee to memorialist, presented to the board, and ordered to be filed.

The board then adjourned until Monday morning, the 18th instant, at 11 o'clock.

MONDAY, *August* 18, 1823.

The board met according to adjournment. Present, the Hons. Alexander Hamilton and William W. Blair.

Memorial of Mary Ann Davis for 500 acres of land upon Davis's creek, upon the road from St. Augustine to St. John's river, about twenty-five miles from the former place, together with a conveyance for the same from John Barker and William G. Davis to memorialist, received, and ordered to be filed.

The memorial of Bernardo Segui for seven thousand acres of land at Buffalo bluff upon St. John's river, together with a survey and grant of the same, received and ordered to be filed.

The memorial of Moses E. Levy for thirty-six thousand acres of land upon Alachua, together with the exhibits thereto appended, and referred to in said memorial, marked A, B, C, D, E, F, G, H, and I, received and ordered to be filed.

The board then adjourned until Wednesday morning, the 20th instant, at 11 o'clock.

WEDNESDAY, *August* 20, 1823.

The board met according to adjournment.   Present, the Hons. Alexander Hamilton and William W. Blair.

Ordered, That the secretary of this board do call upon William Reynolds, Esq., keeper of the public archives for the district of East Florida, and require of him the original documents in the schedule marked A, and numbered from 1 to 35, inclusive, to be filed in the office of the secretary to this board, for the use of said board, and that the said secretary do forthwith observe this order, and report to this board upon to-morrow.

The board then adjourned until to-morrow morning, 11 o'clock.

THURSDAY, *August* 21, 1823.

The board met according to adjournment.   Present, the Hons. Alexander Hamilton and William W. Blair.

A copy of a letter from the secretary of this board to William Reynolds, Esq., keeper of the public archives, dated upon the 20th of August, 1823, and an answer thereto from said Reynolds, dated the 21st August, 1823, read before this board.

It is ordered by the board, that a *subpœna duces tecum* do issue against William Reynolds and Antonio Alvarez, on behalf of the United States; that they, as commissioners appointed for examining the archives of the district of East Florida, do appear here upon the 22d instant, with the original documents in their department contained in a schedule marked A, and numbered from 1 to 35, inclusive.

Mr. Hamilton moved the board that transcripts, in the Spanish language, of the documentary evidence of title to claims exceeding 3,500 acres, should be recorded by the secretary of this board in his record book, without charge to the claimants; upon which motion the board were divided.

The board then adjourned until to-morrow morning, 11 o'clock.

FRIDAY, *August* 22, 1823.

The board met according to adjournment.   Present, the Hons. Alexander Hamilton and William W. Blair.

William Reynolds and Antonio Alvarez appeared here under a *subpœna duces tecum*, with the documents referred to and required by said subpœna, and delivered said documents to the Board of Commissioners for their inspection.

Mr. Blair moved the board that the documents contained in the schedule marked A, and numbered 1 to 35, inclusive, which had been delivered to this board by Mr. Reynolds and Mr. Alvarez, the commissioners appointed by the Secretary of State of the United States, under and by virtue of his letter to them, dated upon the 5th of April, 1823, a copy of which letter is marked B, and filed with the secretary of this board, should be re-delivered to said commissioners; upon which motion the board were divided, and the documents retained.

Mr. Reynolds and Mr. Alvarez were discharged from any further attendance upon this board under a *subpœna duces tecum* awarded against them, on behalf of the United States, upon the 21st August, 1823.

The board then adjourned until Monday, the 25th instant, at 11 o'clock in the morning.

MONDAY, *August 25*, 1823.

The board met according to adjournment. Present, the Hons. Alexander Hamilton and William W. Blair.

The memorial of Antelm Gay, for 160 acres of land, in Twelve-mile swamp, with exhibits Nos. 1, 2, and 3, were laid before the board, and ordered to be filed.

The second memorial of Antelm Gay, for 400 acres of land, in Twelve-mile swamp, with the accompanying exhibits Nos. 1, 2, and 3, were laid before the board, and ordered to be filed.

The third memorial of Antelm Gay, for 700 acres of land, in Twelve-mile swamp, with exhibits Nos. 1, 2, and 3, were laid before the board, and ordered to be filed.

The fourth memorial of Antelm Gay, for 500 acres of land, eighteen miles north of St. Augustine, with Nos. 1, 2, and 3, were laid before the board, and excluded from the consideration of the board, because the grant bears date after the 24th of January, 1818.

The fifth memorial of Antelm Gay, for 600 acres of land, in Wilson's swamp, with exhibits Nos. 1, 2, and 3, were laid before the board, and ordered to be filed.

The sixth memorial of Antelm Gay, for 400 acres of land, at St. Vincente Ferrer, near the bluff on St. John's river, with exhibits Nos. 1, 2, and 3, were laid before the board, and ordered to be filed.

The seventh memorial of Antelm Gay, for 5,000 acres of land, at Tocoy, on the St. John's river, with exhibits Nos. 1, 2, and 3, were laid before the board, and ordered to be filed.

The eighth memorial of Antelm Gay, for 300 acres of land, at Mosquito, to include an old English settlement called Ross plantation, with exhibits Nos. 1, 2, 3, 4, and 5, were laid before the board, and ordered to be filed.

The ninth memorial of Antelm Gay and Francis J. Avice, for 2,000 acres of land, at Mosquito river, with exhibits Nos. 1, 2, and 3, were laid before the board, and ordered to be filed.

The tenth memorial of Antelm Gay, for 500 acres of land, upon Indian river, with exhibits Nos. 1, 2, 3, 4, and 5, were laid before the board, and ordered to be filed.

The eleventh memorial of Antelm Gay, for 500 acres of land, upon Indian river, with exhibits Nos. 1, 2, and 3, therein referred to, were laid before the board, and were excluded by the board from their consideration, because the grant bears date after the 24th of January, 1818.

The twelfth memorial of Antelm Gay, for two lots of land, in the city of St. Augustine, with exhibit No. 1, therein referred to, ordered to be filed; No. 2 not produced.

The thirteenth memorial of Antelm Gay, for a lot of land in Fernandina, with exhibits Nos. 1 and 2, were laid before the board, and ordered to be filed; No. 3, therein referred to, not produced.

Patrick Lynch and Lewis Huguon are appointed to transcribe the documents brought before this board by Messrs. Reynolds and Alvarez, upon the 22d instant.

No further business occurring, the board then adjourned until Thursday, the 28th instant, at 11 o'clock in the morning.

THURSDAY, *August 28*, 1823.

The board met according to adjournment. Present, the Hons. Alexander Hamilton and William W. Blair.

Ordered, That John Lowe, messenger to this board, do inform Edgar Macon, Esq., United States' attorney for the district of East Florida, that his presence is required before this board.

Edgar Macon, Esq., United States' attorney for the district of East Florida, is this day in attendance upon this board.

John Rodman, Esq., attorney-at-law for Antelm Gay, moved that the board do reconsider the cases Nos. 4 and 11, of said Gay, in which they have excluded the documents from consideration of the board, as appeared in their minutes of the 25th instant; and that they do hear an argument of said motion by parol; upon which motion the board were divided, Mr. Hamilton being unwilling to hear any argument, unless in writing.

No further business occurring, the board adjourned until Monday morning, the 1st of September, 1823, at 11 o'clock.

MONDAY, *September 1*, 1823.

The board met according to adjournment. Present, the Hons. Alexander Hamilton and William W. Blair.

Robert Miller and wife, by Belton A. Copp, present their memorial for 60 acres of land, in Martin's island, with a grant of the same to David Garvin, which is ordered to be filed.

Elizabeth Tucker, widow and administratrix of Andrew Tucker, deceased, by Belton A. Copp, presents her memorial for 300 acres of land, in Duval county, opposite Amelia island, with a survey of the same, marked B; and a certificate of the concession to Andrew Tucker of the same, marked A, which are ordered to be filed.

John Underwood, by Belton A. Copp, presents his memorial for 600 acres of land, upon Black creek, three-fourths of a mile south of St. Mary's river, with a memorial to Governor Coppinger, and his decree upon the same; also, a grant for the same; all of which are ordered to be filed.

John B. Richard's heirs, by Belton A. Copp, their agent, present their memorial for 230 acres of land, lying on the south side of St. John's river, in St. John's county, with a certificate of a grant of the same to the said John B. Richards, marked A; which are ordered to be filed.

Belton A. Copp presents a memorial for 1,200 acres of land, opposite New Buena Vista, called Gray's place or Pelitka, with a memorial of Bernardo Segui to Governor Coppinger for the same, and his decree, marked A; and, also, a title to the said Segui for the same, with a survey and bill of sale from the said Segui to George Flemming, and a bill of sale from said Flemming to the memorialist, all marked B; which are ordered to be filed.

Ordered, That the account of Patrick Lynch for sixteen dollars and eighty-two cents, this day presented to this board, for transcribing certain documents, under an appointment of this board made upon the 25th of August, be certified to the Treasurer of the United States for payment.

Ordered, That the account of Lewis Huguon for eight dollars and sixty-nine cents, this day presented to this board, for transcribing certain documents under an appointment of this board made upon the 25th of August, be certified to the Treasurer of the United States for payment.

The board then adjourned until Thursday morning the 4th instant, at 11 o'clock in the morning.

THURSDAY, *September 4*, 1823.

The Board of Commissioners met. Present, the Hons. Alexander Hamilton and William W. Blair, and adjourned until Monday the 8th of September, 1823, at 11 o'clock, A. M.

MONDAY, *September 8*, 1823.

Present, the Hon. Alexander Hamilton. William Berry presented his memorial to this board for three hundred and fifty acres of land at the Cowpen branch, and a grant for the same, marked A; which are ordered to be filed.

Juan Huertas presented his memorial to this board for fifteen thousand acres of land at Tocoy and Buena Vista, on St. John's river, with a grant for the same, marked A, and surveys of the same, in two parts, marked B and C, and order of survey, marked D; which are ordered to be filed.

Francis J. Avice presented to this board his memorial for five hundred acres of land at Little Lake George, with exhibit E, a title for the same to F. M. Arredondo, and a conveyance from said Arredondo to Andrew Burgevin, marked G, and a conveyance from said Burgevin to the memorialist, marked H; all of which are ordered to be filed.

Francis J. Avice and Prosper Viel presented to this board their memorial for one thousand acres of land on the river St. Sebastian, with title to the same, in the name of Jose Peso de Borgos, marked M, and survey of the same, marked N, and a conveyance from the widow and heirs of said Borgos to memorialists, marked Q; all of which are ordered to be filed.

Francis J. Avice presented to this board his memorial for six thousand acres of land upon the river St. John's, with a copy of a grant for the same to Juan Huertas, marked B; survey of the same, marked D; conveyance of the same from said Huertas to the memorialist, marked E.

Francis J. Avice presented his memorial to this board for one hundred and fifteen acres of land, situated on the river Matanzas, with a title for the same to Aysick Travers, a free black, marked A; a survey of the same, marked C; a conveyance of the same from said Travers to Andrew Burgevin, marked P; and a conveyance from Luis Solomon to memorialist, marked Q; all of which are ordered to be filed.

Eliza Robinson presented her memorial to this board for one hundred and five acres of land lying one and a half miles north of the city of St. Augustine, with a concession of the same to Pedro Capo, marked A; with a survey of the same, marked C; and a power of attorney from said Pedro Capo to Pedro Miranda, marked B; all of which are ordered to be filed.

Bernardo Segui presented his memorial to this board for three hundred acres of land on the river Halifax, near Pelican island, with a concession of the same to Estevan Arnau, marked A; survey of the same, marked B; and a conveyance from said Arnau to memorialist, marked C; all of which are ordered to be filed.

Bernardo Segui presented his memorial to this board for sixteen thousand acres of land, lying on the Ys or Indian river, with a concession of the same to memorialist, marked A, and a survey of the same, marked B; all of which are ordered to be filed.

Isaac Hendricks presented his memorial to this board for two hundred and sixteen acres of land, lying at the Cow-ford, on the river St. John's, with a concession of the same made to father of memorialist, and a survey of the same; and royal title, dated May 8, 1817, made to memorialist; all of which are ordered to be filed.

John Houston presented to this board his memorial for two hundred and seventy acres of land, called Pine island, on the river Nassau, with a title of the same to the memorialist; which are ordered to be filed.

John Houston presented to this board his memorial for one hundred and sixty acres of land lying at Cain's Swamp, on the river Nassau, with a title for the same to memorialist; which are ordered to be filed.

John Houston presented to this board his memorial for one hundred and fifty-five acres of land, lying at the Half-moon Bluff, on the river Nassau, with a title for the same to memorialist; all of which are ordered to be filed.

John Houston presented to this board his memorial for one hundred and twenty acres of land, lying on Mill Branch, or Dunn's creek, of the river Nassau, with a title for the same to memorialist; which are ordered to be filed.

Daniel C. Hart presented to this board his memorial for one hundred and fifty acres of land, lying at the Nine-mile Point, about six miles distant from Buena Vista, on the river St. John's, with a concession of the same to the memorialist; which are ordered to be filed.

The heirs of James Baird, by Robert Miller and wife, presented their memorial to this board for six hundred and twenty acres of land, lying upon an island, name unknown, between the mouths of the river Ys, or Indian river, and Jupiter river; with a petition of Guillermo Lawrence, and Governor Estrada's decree thereon; and a petition of Robert Miller to Governor Coppinger, and his decree upon the same; all of which are ordered to be filed.

Sarah Fish presented her memorial to this board for about ten thousand acres of land, lying on St. Anastasia Island, with a copy of the decree of the court, affirmed by the Governor, ordering said land to be sold; and an instrument purporting to affirm said sale, and vest said land in Josef Fish; also, a receipt for the purchase money to said Josef Fish; all of which are ordered to be filed.

Sarah Fish presented her memorial to this board for five hundred acres of land, lying in Graham's Swamp, at the head of the river Matanzas, with a title for the same, dated 24th of April, 1819, in favor of the heirs of Jesse Fish; which are ordered to be filed.

Edgar Macon, Esq., United States' attorney for the district of East Florida, attended here under the order of this board.

The board then adjourned until Thursday morning the 11th, at 11 o'clock.

THURSDAY, *September* 11, 1823.

The Board of Commissioners met this day. Present, the Hons. Alexander Hamilton and William W. Blair.

Sundry resolutions, in the words and figures following, to wit, (eight in number:)

Resolved, That the commissioners will, on the 15th day of September, commence the examination of the evidence of all claims, and conditionally adjudicate upon those arising under the royal order of 1790, commonly known as the order regulating *head-rights,* and such as may be founded on the general law of India.

Resolved, That as, by the proviso of the fourth section of the act of Congress, approved the 8th of May, 1822, the commissioners are not authorized to decide upon claims emanating both from the British and Spanish Governments, they will suspend forming any final decisions until the 1st of December, the ultimate period established by Congress for the admission of claims.

Resolved, That, in the opinion of the commissioners, in the acts of Congress, in virtue of which they are authorized to ascertain claims and titles to land, *no exception or distinction* is made between city and county property; but that, in consideration of the interests of the United States not requiring that the commissioners should be vested other than with discretionary power to examine claims to city lands, where the same, by common report, may appear to the commissioners questionable, they do recommend to the inhabitants of St. Augustine and Fernandina to memorialize Congress to relieve them from the necessity of exhibiting their claims to city lots, and the consequent expense and embarrassment incident thereto.

Resolved, That the secretary to the Board of Commissioners be authorized to demand the recording fees, established by law, upon all *memorials of claims* ordered to be recorded; but that, upon all other documents, no fees shall be demanded until the termination of the next session of Congress.

Resolved, That all memorials presented to the consideration of the commission shall be subscribed by the proper signature of the claimant, or by his agent.

Resolved, That the public papers received by the commissioners, in virtue of a *subpœna duces tecum,* and by them ordered to be transcribed, be returned to the keeper of the public archives by the secretary of the board, and that the transcripts of the same be immediately translated.

Resolved, That claimants desiring to obtain the testimony of any witnesses residing without the Territory of Florida, shall file, with the secretary, their interrogatories; and, that the district attorney, under direction of the board, shall, if required, annex cross-interrogatories on behalf of the United States; and, that in all cases where the witnesses are resident within the Territory, the claimants may file depositions taken *ex parte,* as the said witnesses are subject to the jurisdiction of the commissioners, leaving it optional with the claimants to proceed by filing interrogatories, were presented to the board by Mr. Hamilton; which were ordered to be laid over for further consideration.

Edgar Macon, Esq., attended here under the order of this board.

No further business occurring, the board adjourned until Saturday morning, September 13, 1823, at 11 o'clock.

SATURDAY, *September* 13, 1823.

The Board of Commissioners met this day. Present, the Hons. Alexander Hamilton and William W. Blair.

The Board of Commissioners adopted a resolution in the words and figures following, to wit:

" *Resolved,* That the public papers received by the commissioners in virtue of a *subpœna duces tecum,* and by them ordered to be transcribed, be returned to the keeper of the public archives by the secretary of the board, and that the transcripts of the same be immediately translated."

William Thomas Jones, a minor, by his father and natural guardian, presented his memorial to this board for two thousand acres of land, lying on the neck of land between St. John's river and Maxton's creek, known as Maxton's creek island, with a patent from the British Governor, James Grant, Esq., for the said lands, bearing date upon the 12th of January, 1790, in favor of Abraham Jones; also a conveyance for said lands from the heirs of said Abraham Jones, bearing date, as to the widow and a part of the heirs, upon the first of May, 1783, and as to the residue of said heirs, upon the 20th of February, 1820, in favor of William Jones; and a conveyance from the heirs of said William Jones to memorialist, bearing date upon the 19th of March, 1822; all of which are ordered to be filed.

John F. Brown presented his memorial to this board for ninety-five acres of land lying in a place called Clapboard creek, on the north side of the river St. John's, consisting of a small island called Pilots, and a pine barren near it, with a royal title made to Josiah Gray, on the 8th of February, 1819, with a conveyance from said Gray to George Fleming, dated 8th March, 1819, and a conveyance from said Fleming to John F. Brown, dated 22d November, 1820; also a memorial and certified copy of plat of said lands, bearing date 8th of May, 1816; also the grant for said land, bearing date the 16th of February, 1816; all of which are ordered to be filed.

John F. Brown presented to this board his memorial for fifty-one acres of land lying on the north side of St. John's river, and known by the name of Dames's point, comprising two islands, divided by a neck of land and marsh in front of said river, with a concession of the same, bearing date 16th February, 1816, to Josiah Gray; a memorial and certificate of survey, bearing date the 6th of May, 1816, and royal title dated 8th February, 1819; also a conveyance from said Gray to George Fleming, bearing date 8th of March, 1819, and a conveyance from said Fleming to John F. Brown, dated the 22d of November, 1820; which are ordered to be filed.

Mariano A. Berta presented his memorial to this board for one hundred and eighty-six acres of land lying in St. John's county, on Cartel point neck, with a royal title made to Andres Pacity, bearing date the 16th of October, 1815, for two hundred acres; and a conveyance from Maria del Castel, late widow of Andres Pacity, deceased, to Mariano A. Berta, of two hundred acres, more or less, dated upon the 13th day of June, 1822; which are ordered to be filed.

George Atkinson presented to this board his memorial for three hundred and fifty acres of land lying on the east side of the river St. John's, and known by the name of Colonel Castle, with a royal title to William Hart for the same, dated upon the 4th October, 1811; a power of attorney from said Hart to Doctor Thomas de Aguilar, dated the 9th of April, 1808; and conveyance from Aguilar to George Atkinson, dated 17th October, 1811; also memorial and plat of survey of said lands to said Atkinson, dated 25th of February, 1812; which are ordered to be filed.

Elihu Woodruff, Sidney P. Haines, and James Mavor, present their memorial to this board for three hundred and fifty acres of land lying near a place called Rolles' town, on the river St. John's, about six miles from the port of Buena Vista, with a royal title for the same to John Moore, dated the 9th of November, 1805, and a conveyance from said Moore to memorialist, dated upon the 3d day of May, 1823; which are ordered to be filed.

Jose Bernardo Reyes presented his memorial to this board for two hundred acres of land upon Moultrie creek, with a royal title to Bartolome de Castro y Ferrer, dated upon the 6th of July, 1818, exhibited and marked A; also a conveyance from said Ferrer to memorialist, dated upon the 21st of July, 1818, exhibited and marked B; which are ordered to be filed.

Samuel Worthington presented his memorial to this board for one hundred acres of land lying on river St. Mary's, near Pigeon creek, with a concession of the same to memorialist, dated the 18th of March, 1817; also a plat and certificate of survey of said lands, dated 9th of May, 1818; which are ordered to be filed.

Isaac Hendricks presented his memorial to this board for three hundred and fifty acres of land lying on the north side of the river St. John's, on McCoy's creek, with a royal title in favor of memorialist, dated upon the 28th of September, 1816, marked A; also a plat and certificate of survey of same, dated upon the 14th of February, 1817; which are ordered to be filed.

Robert Hutchinson presented his memorial to this board for one hundred and fifty acres of land lying on the west side of St. John's river, two miles north of McGirt's creek, with a concession to memorialist of said lands, dated December 12, 1815; also a plat and certificate of survey of the same, dated 12th January, 1817, marked C; which are ordered to be filed.

Nathaniel Wilds presented his memorial to this board for three hundred and thirty-three and one-third acres of land lying on the river St. Mary's, one mile below the junction of the Little and Big St. Mary's, with a royal title to Reuben Hogan, dated upon the 26th of May, 1815, and a conveyance of same from said Hogan to Nathaniel Wilds, dated the 26th of December, 1822; which are ordered to be filed.

Nathaniel Wilds presented his memorial to this board for three hundred acres of land lying on Lofton's creek, a branch of Nassau, with a survey of the same, dated the 4th of December, 1817, exhibited and marked B; which are ordered to be filed.

William Hart presented his memorial to this board for two hundred acres of land lying on San Pablo, with a concession of the same to memorialist, dated 19th of June, 1816; also a plat and certificate of survey of the same, dated the 1st of August, 1819, marked D; which are ordered to be filed.

The following resolution was introduced by Mr. Hamilton, in the words and figures following, to wit:

" *Resolved,* That the resolution of this board directing the secretary to prepare memorials be repealed, and that, henceforth, it shall be the duty of the secretary to examine all memorials, and endorse on the back of the same the particulars set forth, and in what, if at all, defective."

Upon a motion to adopt said resolution, the board were divided.

Ordered, That the marshal of the district of East Florida do pay the account of Lewis Huguon, $8 69, which was allowed by this board at a former day of their session.

Edgar Macon, Esq., United States' attorney for the district of East Florida, was this day in attendance under the order of this board.

The board then adjourned until Monday morning, the 15th instant, 11 o'clock.

MONDAY, *September* 15, 1823.

The board met according to adjournment. Present, the Hons. Alexander Hamilton and William W. Blair.

Mary Smith presented her memorial to this board for three hundred and fifty acres of land lying on Chica creek, with a royal grant for the same to Maria Tharp, dated upon the 23d of February, 1809; which are ordered to be filed.

Mary Smith presented her memorial to this board for four hundred and fifty acres of land lying at a place called Plantage Rico, on Nassau river, with a royal title in favor of Maria Tharp, dated 23d of February, 1809; which are ordered to be filed.

Archibald Clarke and Elihu Atwater presented their memorial to this board for two hundred and fifty acres of land lying on St. John's river, at or near a place called the Cow-ford; concession of the same to James William Lee by Governor Quesada, dated 11th of November, 1794; a conveyance from said Lee to Samuel Betts, dated 5th of September, 1803; also a conveyance from said Betts to James Hall, dated 20th of June, 1806, and a conveyance from said Hall to memorialists, dated the 11th of September, 1823; which are ordered to be filed.

Levin Gunby presented his memorial to this board for four hundred acres of land lying on the west side of St. John's river, at a place called Dames's point, with a concession to memorialist from Governor White, dated the 16th of August, 1803; which are ordered to be filed.

Edgar Macon, Esq., United States' Attorney for the district of East Florida, attended here this day under the order of this board.

George W. Martin presented his memorial to this board for three hundred acres of land lying in a place called the Big swamp, on the river St. John's, with a royal title made by Governor Coppinger in favor of Charles Clarke for the same, dated the 10th of April, 1817; a conveyance from said Clarke to memorialist, dated the 23d of April, 1822; and a conveyance from George J. F. Clarke to memorialist, dated 23d of April, 1822; also, a plat and certificate of survey, dated the 30th of May, 1820; all of which are ordered to be filed.

A resolution, in the words and figures following, was this day offered for the consideration of this board, to wit: " *Resolved*, That claimants desiring to obtain the testimony of any witnesses residing without the Territory of Florida, shall file with the secretary their interrogatories; and that the district attorney, under direction of the board, shall, if required, annex cross-interrogatories on behalf of the United States; and that, in all cases where the witnesses are resident within the Territory, the claimants may file depositions taken *ex parte*, as the said witnesses are subject to the jurisdiction of the commissioners, leaving it optional with the claimants to proceed by filing interrogatories; and that a commission, with the interrogatories so annexed, shall be directed to any person authorized to administer oaths, sealed by the secretary, and delivered to the party so making application; and it shall be the duty of said person to take the answers of said witnesses to all such interrogatories, and none other, and to certify the same, and whether the said commission was sealed when delivered." Which resolution was adopted by the board.

The board then adjourned until Thurday morning the 18th instant, at 11 o'clock.

THURSDAY, *September* 18, 1823.

The board met according to adjournment. Present, the Hons. Alexander Hamilton and William W. Blair.

Shadrach Standly presented his memorial to this board for three hundred acres of land lying on St. Mary's river, with a plat and certificate of survey to said Standly, dated the 10th of December, 1817; which are ordered to be filed.

Zachariah Hogan presented his memorial to this board for two hundred acres of land lying at Jacksonville, on the north side of the river St. John's, with a royal title made by Governor Coppinger in favor of Maria Suarez, widow of Turnel Taylor, dated upon the 13th of September, 1816; also, a plat and certificate of survey of the same, dated 21st of February, 1817; which are ordered to be filed.

Frederick McMunen presented his memorial to this board for four hundred and fifty acres of land lying at Wilder's plantation, about eight miles south of Trader's hill, on St. Mary's river, with a concession by Governor Coppinger for the same to said McMunen, dated 30th of January, 1816; also, a plat and certificate of the same, dated the 10th of February, 1816, all of which are ordered to be filed.

Robert Hutchinson presented his memorial to this board for three hundred and fifty acres of land lying on the west side of the river St. John's, near Girt's creek, with a concession of the same to said Hutchinson by Governor Coppinger, dated 9th of January, 1819, and a plat and certificate of survey of same, dated 15th of May, 1821; which are ordered to be filed.

Charles Love presented his memorial to this board for three hundred acres of land lying on the river St. Mary's, with a plat and certificate of survey of the same, dated upon the 10th of December, 1817; which are ordered to be filed.

John Houston presented his memorial to this board for three hundred and fifty-eight and one-half acres of land lying on a plantation called San Carlos, on the north side, and near the river St. John's, with a royal title for the same in favor of Spicer Christopher, made by Governor White upon the 8th of April, 1809; which are ordered to be filed.

Abraham Bellamy, Sen., presented his memorial to this board for three hundred and fifty acres of land lying on Funk Savannah branch, a branch of Nassau, with a concession of the same by Governor Estrada to Samuel Sands, dated the 10th of October, 1815; also, plat and certificate of survey of the same, dated the 10th of March, 1819; which are ordered to be filed.

Lewis Matteir presented his memorial to this board for one hundred and fifty acres of land lying at the head of Pablo creek, with a royal title made by Governor White to the heirs of Josefa Espinosa, dated the 25th of January, 1811; also, a conveyance from said heirs to said Matteir, bearing date 18th of January, 1819, and marked B; also, a plat and certificate of survey, dated the 4th of November, 1819; which are ordered to be filed.

Lewis Matteir presented his memorial to this board for three hundred acres of land lying on the south side of the river St. John's, at a place called Bori's branch, with a concession of the same to memorialist by Governor Estrada, dated the 24th October, 1815, marked (A;) also, a plat and certificate of survey, dated 3d of August, 1817, marked (B;) which are ordered to be filed.

Moses E. Levy presented his memorial to this board for two hundred and seventy-five acres of land, lying on the plains of San Diego, with a royal title in favor of Antonio Mier, made by Governor Coppinger the 16th of February, 1816; also, a conveyance from said Mier to memorialist, dated upon the 6th day of July, 1822; which are ordered to be filed.

Edgar Macon, Esq., United States' Attorney for the district of East Florida, attended here this day under the order of the board.

The board then adjourned until Thursday morning the 25th instant, at 11 o'clock.

THURSDAY, *September 25, 1823.*

The board met according to adjournment. Present, the Hons. Alexander Hamilton and William W. Blair.

A letter from the Department of State, addressed to the commissioners for ascertaining claims to lands in East Florida, dated upon the 4th of September, 1823, and subscribed by Daniel Brent, was this day received by this board, covering another letter addressed to William Reynolds, keeper of the public archives at St. Augustine. The letter from the Department of State to this board is ordered to be filed; and it is further ordered that the Secretary of this board do deliver to William Reynolds, Esq., the letter enclosed, addressed to him; and, also, open a communication with said Reynolds to know when, and in what manner, he will be willing and ready to deliver over to this board the documents referred to, and named in said letter.

Resolved, That the United States' marshal for the district of East Florida be directed to attend the sittings of this board upon this day, and that he be required to procure a house for the commissioners, and an office for their secretary.

Bartolome de Castro y Ferrer presented his memorial to this board for thirty-five acres of land, lying on San Pablo, in the county of St. John's, with a royal title for the same made by Governor Coppinger, and bearing date the 10th of April, 1817; which are ordered to be filed.

Bartolome de Castro y Ferrer presented his memorial to this board for one thousand acres of land, lying at a place called the Three Runs or Little creek, with a royal title for the same made by Governor Estrada, and dated 15th of July, 1815; also, a plat and certificate of survey, dated April 3, 1821; which are ordered to be filed.

Samuel Fairbanks and Joseph S. Sanchez presented their memorial to this board for two thousand acres of land lying on the river Santa Fé, with a concession to Joseph Simeon Sanchez of said land, dated the 12th of January, 1818, and made by Governor Coppinger; also, a conveyance for one thousand acres of land made to said Fairbanks upon the 28th of July, 1823, by Antonio Alvarez and wife, and Joseph S. Sanchez and wife; which are ordered to be filed.

William and John Lofton presented their memorial to this board for fifty acres of land, lying on Amelia island, at a place called *Cabbage Spot*, with a concession of the same to John Lofton, made by Governor Morales, and dated 18th September, 1800; which are ordered to be filed.

William and John Lofton presented their memorial to this board for two hundred acres of land lying on the north branch of the river Nassau, with a seal and a few words of a British grant, purporting to have been made in the year 1768; also, a conveyance from Cornelius Rain to John Lofton, bearing date 10th of November, 1769, for two hundred acres of land; which are ordered to be filed.

John Jones presented his memorial to this board for one hundred acres of land, lying on Trout creek, with a concession for the same made by Governor White upon the 26th of August, 1803; which are ordered to be filed.

Sarah Petty presented her memorial to this board for eight caballerias (about two hundred and sixty-five acres) of land, lying on Julinton creek, with a plat and certificate of survey of the same, dated the 9th of April, 1793, to George Long; also, a conveyance from Christina Long, Matthew Long, Joseph Long, and Jane Long, to memorialist, dated the 26th of November, one thousand eight hundred and twenty-one; which are ordered to be filed.

Sarah Petty presented her memorial to this board for six caballerias (about two hundred acres) of land, lying on the river St. Mary's, with a plat and certificate of the same, dated 30th of March, 1792, and made for John Houston; which are ordered to be filed.

Sarah Petty presented her memorial to this board for one hundred and fifty acres of land, lying on St. John's river, near Buena Vista, with a concession to Thomas Rodgers for fifty acres of land above Buena Vista, made by Governor White, and dated 5th of September, 1804; also, a receipt upon the concession, made by said Rodgers in favor of Mrs. Houston, for sundry commodities as a payment for said land, and dated the 4th of November, 1805; which are ordered to be filed.

Pedro Tropé presented his memorial to this board for one hundred and fifty acres of land, lying at Mosquitos, with a concession to Marie Ortega for the same by Governor White, and dated 15th of March, 1803; which are ordered to be filed.

William and John Lofton presented their memorial to this board for three hundred and fifty acres of land, lying between St. Mary's and Nassau rivers, with a plat and certificate of survey of the same to John Lofton, dated the —— day of February, 1792; which are ordered to be filed.

Joseph Summerall presented his memorial to this board for three hundred acres of land, lying on St. John's river, with a plat and certificate of survey made for Diego Clatworthy, dated the 11th of November, 1791; also, the will of Mary Ann Clatworthy, and a deposition of Edward M. Wanton, attached thereto; which, together with the certificates thereon, are ordered to be filed.

Joseph Summerall presented his memorial to this board for four hundred acres of land, lying on Willis's creek, near Julinton creek, with a concession of the same made by Governor Estrada, upon the 26th of June, 1815; also, a plat and certificate of survey, dated the 15th of May, 1821; which are ordered to be filed.

Joseph Summerall presented his memorial to this board for two hundred acres of land, lying at Long Bluff, on St. Mary's river, with a concession in favor of said Summerall for the same, dated the 28th of April, 1792, made by Governor Quesada; which are ordered to be filed.

Joseph Summerall presented his memorial to this board for one hundred and fifty acres of land, lying on Cormorant branch, with a concession of the same by Governor Coppinger, dated upon the 7th of May, 1817; also, a plat and certificate of survey, dated the 6th of June, 1819; which are ordered to be filed.

Joseph Summerall presented his memorial to this board for one hundred and fifty acres of land, lying five miles from Nassau river, on the head of the river or creek called *Williams*, with a plat and certificate of survey, dated upon the 11th of March, 1792; which are ordered to be filed.

Sarah Tate presented her memorial to this board for four hundred and fifty acres of land on the river St. John's, with a concession to John E. Tate for the same, made by Governor Estrada, and dated the 20th of September, 1811; also, said Tate's acceptance of the terms of the concession, marked No. 3, and dated 23d September, 1811, and decree of Governor Estrada thereon, dated upon the same day; also, a plat and certificate of the survey of same, dated 21st April, 1821; which are ordered to be filed.

98   A

Samuel Fairbanks presented his memorial to this board for five hundred acres of land, lying at a place called Derbin Swamp, with a concession to Rafael Dionisio Fontané, made by Governor Estrada, the 11th of December, 1815, marked No. 1; also, a plat and certificate of the same, dated the 25th of September, 1819, marked No. 2; also, a conveyance from grantee to memorialist, dated 10th of April, 1823, marked No. 3; which are ordered to be filed.

Peter Bagley presented his memorial to this board for two hundred acres of land on Pottsburgh creek, with a concession to Reuben Hogan for the same by Governor White, dated the 20th of December, 1799; also, a royal title to Reuben Hogan, dated 27th March, 1818, made by Governor Coppinger; also, a relinquishment by said Hogan to memorialist, dated the 4th of March, 1823; which are ordered to be filed.

Charles Hogan presented his memorial to this board for two hundred acres of land, lying on Hendricks's creek, on the river St. John's, with a royal title by Governor Coppinger for the same, dated the 12th of January, 1818.

Reuben Hogan presented his memorial to this board for three hundred and eighty-five acres of land, lying on Goldsburgh creek, with a royal title for the same, made by Governor Estrada, and dated 14th of October, 1811; which are ordered to be filed.

William and John Lofton presented their memorial to this board for three hundred and fifty acres of land, lying between St. Mary's and Nassau rivers, with a plat and certificate of survey of the same, dated 24th February, 1792; which are ordered to be filed.

Francis R. Sanchez presented his memorial to this board for four thousand acres of land, lying on the south side of the river Santa Fé, with a concession of the same to memorialist by Governor Estrada, dated the 18th of December, 1815; which are ordered to be filed.

Antonio Proctor presented his memorial to this board for one hundred and eighty-five acres of land, lying about five miles from St. Augustine, westward of a grove called Orange Grove, with a royal title for the same made by Governor Coppinger, and dated the 8th of March, 1816; also, a plat and certificate of survey of the same, dated the 18th of December, 1818; which are ordered to be filed.

Joseph Delespine presented his memorial to this board for forty-three thousand acres of land, lying on the west side of the river Ys or Indian river, opposite an island called Merritt's island, with a concession of the same to memorialist, dated the 9th of April, 1817, and made by Governor Coppinger; also, a certificate of said Delespine on the back of said concession, bearing date the 16th of November, 1820, marked B; also, plat and certificate of survey of the same, dated the 20th of February, 1820, marked A; which are ordered to be filed.

Joseph Delespine presented his memorial to this board for five hundred and sixty acres of land, lying at a place called Deep creek, about six miles north of St. Augustine, with a concession to Antonio Huertas, made by Governor Morales, and dated 17th of October, 1800, and a conveyance from said Huertas to memorialist, dated upon the 9th of July, 1821; also, a memorial and order of survey, dated the 31st March, 1820, and a plat and certificate of survey, dated 6th of April, 1821; which are ordered to be filed.

Ramon Sanchez presented his memorial to this board for two hundred acres of land, lying on the south side of the river St. John's, at a place known by the name of the Ship Yard, with a royal title for the same made by Governor Coppinger, and dated the 19th of April, 1816, marked B; which are ordered to be filed.

Peter Fouchard presented his memorial to this board for fifteen hundred acres of land, lying on the west side of Indian river, with a concession to said Fouchard of the same by Governor Estrada, and dated upon the 20th of November, 1815, marked A; also, a memorial and order of survey, dated 29th of December, 1815, marked B; which are ordered to be filed.

Joseph Delespine presented his memorial to this board for six hundred acres of land, lying about two miles north of St. Augustine, with a concession of the same to John Huertas, made by Governor Estrada, and dated 3d of May, 1811; also, memorial by said Huertas for leave to sell the said lands to said Delespine, dated the 10th of February, 1821, decree thereon, bearing date the same day, and conveyance from said Huertas to Joseph Delespine, dated upon the 10th of February, 1821, marked A; also, a plat and certificate of survey of the same, dated the 18th of March, 1821, marked B; which are ordered to be filed.

Edgar Macon, Esq., United States' attorney for the district of East Florida, attended here this day under the order of this board.

The board then adjourned until Monday, the 29th instant, at 11 o'clock in the morning.

MONDAY, *September* 29, 1823.

The board met according to adjournment. Present, the Hons. Alexander Hamilton and William W. Blair.

Francis P. Sanchez presented his memorial to this board for one hundred acres of land, lying at the head of North river, at a place called Qui Qui, in Diego plains, with a plat and certificate of survey, (exhibit A,) dated the 30th of June, 1818, made for Pablo Fontané; a royal title to José Fernandez, dated the 19th of June, 1816, and made by Governor Coppinger, (exhibit B;) a conveyance from José Fernandez to José Simeon Sanchez, dated 4th of September, 1816, (marked exhibit C;) a conveyance from José Simeon Sanchez to Pablo Fontané, dated the 16th of July, 1818, (marked exhibit D;) a conveyance from Pablo Fontané to Francisco P. Sanchez, dated the 18th of July, 1818, with an order of survey attached thereto, dated 31st October, 1818, (marked exhibit E;) which are ordered to be filed.

Francisco P. Sanchez presented his memorial to this board for nine hundred acres of land, lying on the west side of the river St. Sebastian, and made of what was two tracts, with a copy of a royal title made to John Geiger by Governor Coppinger, for six hundred acres, dated the 29th of July, 1817, and a memorandum of a purchase of three hundred acres, adjoining said tract, bought by said Geiger from William Travers, dated 6th October, 1820, marked exhibit A; plat and certificate of survey of nine hundred acres by Andres Burgevin, dated the 16th of September, 1820, marked exhibit B; and a certified copy of a conveyance from John Geiger to Francisco Pasqual Sanchez, dated the 16th of October, 1820, marked exhibit C; which are ordered to be filed.

Francis P. Sanchez presented his memorial to this board for two thousand acres of land, lying at a place called the Big Hammock, about forty miles westward from Buena Vista, on a creek, with a plat and certificate of survey of 2,000 acres, made for Thomas de Aguilar, by Andres Burgevin, upon the 9th of September, 1819, marked exhibit A; a certified copy of a royal title made to said Aguilar by Governor Coppinger for 2,000 acres, dated the 7th of December, 1817, marked exhibit B; a conveyance from Pedro Miranda, in fact for Thomas Aguilar to Francisco P. Sanchez and José M. Hernandez, dated the 22d day of February, 1822, and marked C; which are ordered to be filed.

Francis P. Sanchez presented his memorial to this board for two hundred and twenty acres of land, lying on the St. Mary's river, at a place called McIntosh's causeway, with a plat and certificate of survey of the same for Domingo Estacholy, by George J. F. Clarke, dated the 15th of May, 1817, marked exhibit A; a certified copy of a royal grant to Domingo Estacholy by Governor Coppinger, and dated the 5th of December, 1816, marked and referred to as exhibit B; a conveyance from Ursula Llafico, widow of the late Domingo Estacholy, to Francis P. Sanchez, dated the 29th of July, 1822, and marked and referred to as exhibit C; which are ordered to be filed.

Francis P. Sanchez presented his memorial to this board for three hundred and eighty acres of land, lying to the north of Diego plains, with a plat and certificate of survey of the same for memorialist by Roberto McHardy, dated the 1st of May, 1819, marked and referred to as exhibit A; a certified copy of a royal title in favor of José Simeon Sanchez made by Governor Coppinger, and dated 26th of June, 1816, marked and referred to as exhibit B; a certified copy of a conveyance from José Simeon Sanchez to Francisco de Paula Sanchez, dated the 26th of January, 1818, and marked and referred to as exhibit C; which are ordered to be filed.

Francis P. Sanchez presented his memorial to this board for three hundred and forty-five acres of land, lying on the river St. John's, at a place called the Ship Yard, distance about half a mile from San Vincente Ferrer, with a plat and certificate of survey of the same made for heirs of Juan Rafo, by George J. F. Clarke, and dated the 4th of September, 1820, marked and referred to as exhibit A; a certified copy of a royal title in favor of Juan Rafo, by Governor Coppinger, dated the 8th of May, 1816, marked and referred to as exhibit B; a certified copy of a conveyance from Pedro Miranda, on behalf of the heirs of Juan Rafo, deceased, to Thomas de Aguilar, dated the 2d of July, 1820, marked and referred to as exhibit C; a certified copy of a conveyance from Thomas de Aguilar to Francisco Pasqual Sanchez, dated the 11th of January, 1811, marked and referred to as exhibit D; which are ordered to be filed.

Francis P. Sanchez presented his memorial to this board for eight hundred acres of land in two tracts, the one of four hundred and fifty acres, lying at a place called Funk's Savannah, which runs to the waters of Nassau river, with a plat and certificate of survey of the same made by Andrew Burgevin for José Maria Ugarté, dated the 15th of February, 1821, marked and referred to as exhibit A; the other tract of three hundred and fifty acres, situated at a creek called Alligator creek, with a plat and certificate of survey of same made by Andrew Burgevin for José Maria Ugarte dated 15th February, 1821, marked and referred to as exhibit B; a certified copy of a concession to José Maria Ugarté, of eight hundred acres of land, made by Governor Coppinger, and dated the 17th of December, 1817, marked and referred to as exhibit C; a certified copy of a royal title to said José Maria Ugarté for four hundred and fifty acres, made by Governor Coppinger, and dated the 5th of February, 1818, marked and referred to as exhibit D; a certified copy of a royal title to José Maria Ugarté for three hundred and fifty acres of land made by Governor Coppinger, dated the 5th of February, 1818, and marked and referred to as exhibit E; a conveyance from José Maria Ugarté to Francis P. Sanchez for four hundred and fifty acres of land, dated 25th of September, 1821, marked and referred to as exhibit F; and a conveyance from Joseph Maria Ugarté to Francis P. Sanchez for three hundred and fifty acres of land, dated 25th of September, 1821, marked and referred to as exhibit G; all of which are ordered to be filed.

Francis P. Sanchez presented his memorial to this board for two thousand seven hundred acres of land on St. John's river, at a place known by the name of Dunn's lake when the British occupied this Territory, with a plat and certificate of survey of the same made for Fernando de la Maza Arredondo, Sen., by George J. F. Clarke, and dated the 2d of April, 1818, marked and referred to as exhibit A; a certified copy of a royal title to Fernando de la Maza Arredondo, Sen., made by Governor Coppinger, and dated 13th of December, 1817, marked and referred to as exhibit B; a certified copy of a conveyance from Fernando de la Maza Arredondo, Jun., as attorney in fact of his father, of the same name, to Pedro Miranda, dated 15th of December, 1817, marked and referred to as exhibit C; a certified copy of a conveyance from Pedro Miranda to Francisco Pasqual Sanchez, dated the 11th of January, 1821, marked and referred to as exhibit D; which are ordered to be filed.

Philip R. Yonge presented his memorial to this board for two thousand acres of land, lying in the Twelve mile swamp, with a plat and certificate of survey made for memorialist by George J. F. Clarke, and dated 4th of November, 1815, marked and referred to as exhibit A; a certified copy of a concession to memorialist by Governor Kindelan, of two thousand acres, dated 23d of February, 1815; a certified copy of a royal title, made to said Philip R. Yonge by Governor Coppinger, dated 26th of January, 1816, referred to, and marked B; which are ordered to filed.

George Atkinson, executor of Lindsey Todd, presented his memorial to this board for three hundred and ninety acres of land, lying on Cedar creek, on the St. John's river, with a plat and certificate of survey to Lindsey Todd made by George J. F. Clarke, and dated 21st of April, 1817, referred to, and marked A; a copy of concession, and a copy of a royal title, to Lindsey Todd made by Governor Coppinger, and dated the 11th of February, 1817; which are ordered to be filed.

George Atkinson, executor of Lindsey Todd, presented his memorial to this board for six hundred acres of land, lying at New Smyrna, with a certified copy of a plat and certificate of survey of the same made for Lindsey Todd by John Purcell, and dated 19th of December, 1803, referred to, and marked A; a copy of concession for the same to said Todd by Governor White, dated the 21st of July, 1803; also, a certified copy of a royal title made by Governor Estrada to Lindsey Todd, dated July 1, 1815; which are ordered to be filed.

George Atkinson presented his memorial to this board for two hundred and twenty acres of land, lying between North river and Guana creek, with a plat and certificate of survey of the same for Andres Burgevin by Pedro Marrot, upon the 27th of May, 1793, referred to and marked A; a certified copy of concession by Governor Quesada to Andres Atkinson, dated 29th of April, 1793, referred to, and marked B; which are ordered to be filed.

George Atkinson presented his memorial to this board for one thousand and sixty acres of land, lying on the north side of the river Nassau, at a place known by the name of Spell's Swamp, with a plat and certificate of survey made for George Atkinson by George J. F. Clarke, upon the 30th day of October, 1816, referred to and marked A; a certified copy of a royal title made by Governor Coppinger to George Atkinson, and dated 8th March, 1816, referred to and marked B; also, a concession to said George Atkinson made by Governor Coppinger, and dated 16th of February, 1816; which are ordered to be filed.

George Atkinson presented his memorial to this board for five hundred and fifty acres of land, lying on the west of the river St. John's, with a certified copy of a plat and certificate of survey to memorialist, made by George J. F. Clarke, and dated August the 1st, 1815, referred to and marked A; a certified copy of a royal title to memorialist made by Governor Coppinger, and dated 22d of February, 1816, referred to, and marked B; also, a certified copy of concession of said land to memorialist made by Governor White, and dated the 9th of August, 1803; which are ordered to be filed.

George Atkinson presented his memorial to this board for one thousand acres of land, lying on the west side of the river St. John's, at the mouth of a creek called Muy, with a plat and certificate of survey of the same for memorialist, made by George J. F. Clarke, upon the 10th of March, 1821, referred to, and marked C; a certified copy of a concession of said lands made by Governor Coppinger to memorialist, dated 21st of April, 1817, referred to, and marked D; which are ordered to be filed.

Antonio Hindsman presented his memorial to this board for two hundred and forty acres of land, lying on the west side of North river, at a place called Araguey, with a certified copy of a royal title for the same made by Governor Coppinger to the memorialist, 1st September, 1819, referred to, and marked A; which are ordered to be filed.

Philip·Weadman presented his memorial to this board for one hundred and fifty acres of land, lying on the road to Picolata, twelve miles north of the city of St. Augustine, with a certified copy of a royal title made to the memorialist by Governor Coppinger, dated 3d July, 1819, referred to, and marked A; which are ordered to be filed.

Edgar Macon, Esq. attended here this day, under the order of this board.

The board then adjourned until Monday the 6th of October, 1823, at 11 o'clock in the morning.

MONDAY, *October* 6, 1823.

The board met according to adjournment. Present, the Hons. Alexander Hamilton and William W. Blair.

James Hall presented his memorial to this board for seven hundred and seventy-five acres of land, lying near Julinton creek, on St. John's river, between Dauyen and Durbin creeks, with a plat and certificate of survey made by George J. F. Clarke, bearing date 21st July, 1819, marked and referred to as exhibit A; also, a concession of the same number of acres, bearing date the 8th day of January, 1818, made by Governor Coppinger, marked and referred to as exhibit B; which are ordered to be filed.

Robert Prichard's heirs presented their memorial to this board for seven hundred acres of land, lying on Goodby's lake, on the river St. John's, with a plat and certificate of survey of the same made by George J. F. Clarke, and dated upon the 18th of July, 1819, referred to, and marked as exhibit A; and also, a certified copy of concession for same number of acres made to Robert Prichard by Governor White, dated upon the 22d of March, 1800, referred to, and marked as exhibit B; which are ordered to be filed.

John Lacount presented his memorial to this board for three hundred acres of land, lying at the east side of Dunn's lake, or George's lake, on the river St. John's, with a plat and certificate of survey made by George J. F. Clarke for memorialist, for the same number of acres, dated upon the 26th of April, 1821, marked and referred to as exhibit A; a certified copy of concession made to memorialist for same number of acres by Governor Estrada, dated the 11th of August, 1815, marked and referred to as exhibit B; which are ordered to be filed.

Agueda Segui presented her memorial to this board for twelve hundred acres of land, lying at a place known by the name of the Three Runs, on the road to San Vincente Ferrer, on the St. John's river, with a plat and certificate of survey of the same made by Andres Burgevin for the memorialist, dated 8th of January, 1819, marked and referred to as exhibit A; also, a certified copy of a royal title made to Bernardo Segui by Governor Coppinger for the same land, dated upon the 20th July, 1816, marked and referred to as exhibit B; which are ordered to be filed.

Edgar Macon, Esq., United States' attorney for the district of East Florida, attended this day, under the order of this board.

The board then adjourned until Thursday the 9th day of this present month, at 11 o'clock in the morning.

THURSDAY, *October* 9, 1823.

The board met according to adjournment. Present, the Hons. Alexander Hamilton and William W. Blair.

Edgar Macon, Esq., United States' attorney for the district of East Florida, attended this day upon the sitting of this board, under their order.

Henry Eckford presented his memorial to this board for an undivided moiety of two thousand acres of land, lying on Musquito river, and to the westward of where stood the village of New Smyrna, with a certified copy of a concession to Samuel Betts for two thousand acres, made by Governor White, and dated 8th of July, 1803, marked C; a conveyance from Samuel Betts to Joseph F. White of two undivided third parts of said tract, bearing date the 13th of April, 1816, marked and referred to as exhibit A; a conveyance from said Joseph F. White to Henry Eckford of the one equal undivided moiety, or half part, of the grant to Samuel Betts of two thousand acres, bearing date the 22d day of January, 1823, marked and referred to as exhibit B; which are ordered to be filed.

Matthias B. Edgar presented his memorial to this board for five thousand acres of land, lying in St. John's county, on the west side of the Oklawaha river, being the half of a ten thousand acre survey conveyed by Richard S. Hackley to Ezbon Slossen, with a copy of a conveyance from said Hackley to said Ezbon Slossen for ten thousand acres, made 12th February, 1823, and a copy of conveyance from said Ezbon Slossen to Matthias B. Edgar for five thousand acres, dated 21st of February, 1823; and it is ordered by the board that the consideration of said papers be postponed until after they shall have decided upon the question now before them upon the claims of Antelm Gay.

Anthony Dey presented his memorial to this board for fifty thousand acres of land, lying in the county of St. John's, on the left bank or westerly side of the Ocklawaha, at the old Indian crossing place, with an original conveyance; and, also, a copy thereof made by Richard S. Hackley, and Harriet his wife, to said Dey for the said fifty thousand acres of land, bearing date the 14th day of December, 1822. And it is ordered by the board that all consideration of said papers be postponed until they shall have decided upon the question now before them upon the claims of Antelm Gay.

The board then adjourned until Monday the 13th instant, at 11 o'clock in the morning.

MONDAY, *October* 13, 1823.

The board met according to adjournment. Present, the Hons. Alexander Hamilton and William W. Blair.

Eleazer Waterman's heirs, by Sarah Waterman, widow of said Eleazer Waterman, deceased, presented their memorial to this board, praying confirmation of title to one hundred and seventy-five acres of land, lying on the south side of Bell's river, with a plat and certificate of survey of the same made by George J. F. Clarke, dated 4th of February, 1815, marked and referred to as exhibit A; and a certified copy of a royal title made to Eleazer Waterman for one hundred and seventy-five acres, by Governor Coppinger, dated February 22, 1816, marked and referred to as exhibit B; which are ordered to be filed.

Eleazer Waterman's heirs, by Sarah Waterman, widow of said Eleazer Waterman, presented their memorial to this board for five thousand four hundred and sixty acres of land, lying at McQueen's swamp near St. Mary's river, with a plat and certificate of survey of the same bearing date 21st of March, 1821, made by George J. F. Clarke, and marked and referred to as exhibit A; and a copy of a concession for six miles square made to said Eleazer Waterman, dated upon the 15th of February, 1816, marked and referred to as exhibit B; also, a certificate of George J. F. Clarke that the terms of said grant were complied with, dated 20th of May, 1820, marked and referred to as exhibit C; which were ordered to be filed.

Eleazer Waterman's heirs, by Sarah Waterman, widow of said Eleazer Waterman, deceased, presented their memorial to this board, praying confirmation of title to two hundred and sixty acres of land, lying on Bell's river, with a plat and certificate of survey of the same made by George J. F. Clarke, and dated the 5th of February,

1816, marked A; a copy of a royal title made to Joseph Howell by Governor Coppinger, who afterwards sold the same to Eleazer Waterman, as is recognised by said title, which bears date 22d of February, 1816, marked and referred to as exhibit B; which are ordered to be filed.

Eleazer Waterman's heirs, by Sarah Waterman, widow of said Eleazer Waterman, deceased, presented their memorial to this board for confirmation of title to two hundred and seventy acres of land, lying on McQueen's swamp, near the river St. Mary's, with a plat and certificate of survey of the same made by George J. F. Clarke, and dated the 20th of March, 1816, marked A; and a copy of concession of the same made to said Eleazer Waterman by Governor Coppinger, dated 17th of February, 1816, marked and referred to as exhibit B; which are ordered to be filed.

Andrew Burgevin presented his memorial to this board for sixteen thousand acres of land, lying on Pallisur's creek, at the crossing place on the road leading to Chocohati, with a certified copy of a concession to said Burgevin, of five miles square, made by Governor Coppinger, and bearing date January 13, 1818; which are ordered to be filed.

John Gianopoly presented his memorial to this board, praying confirmation of title to five hundred acres of land, lying at the place west of the head of the lagoon of St. Marcos, distance twelve miles from St. Augustine, with a plat and certificate of survey of the same made by Andres Burgevin, and dated 29th of October, 1819; also, a certified copy of a concession to said Gianopoly made by Governor White, and dated upon the 6th of July, 1799; which are ordered to be filed.

John Gianopoly presented his memorial to this board, praying confirmation of title to fifteen acres of land, lying without the Gates fifteen hundred yards, with a plat and certificate of survey of same amount, made for said Gianopoly by G. Darling, and dated October 7th, 1823, with a certified copy of a concession to Domingo Segui, Jun., for ten acres of land made by Governor White, the 19th of January, 1805, and a conveyance from said Segui to said Gianopoly, dated 25th of June, 1821; which are ordered to be filed.

John Gianopoly presented his memorial to this board, praying confirmation of title to ten acres of land, lying without the Gates fifteen hundred yards, with a plat and certificate of survey of the same, made for said Gianopoly, by G. Darling, and bearing date October 3, 1823; also a copy of concession of ten acres to John Gianopoly, made by Governor White, and dated June 1, 1807; which are ordered to be filed.

Antonio Montero's heirs presented their memorial to this board, praying confirmation of title to twenty-five acres of land, lying on the road to Capuaca, and adjoining the lands of John Gianopoly, with a plat and certificate of survey of the same, made by G. Darling, and dated upon the 3d ———— , 1823; also a certified copy of concession of the same amount of lands to Antonio Montero, made by Governor White, and dated January 23, 1808; which are ordered to be filed.

William Williams's heirs presented their memorial to this board, praying confirmation of title to two thousand and twenty acres of land, lying at Spring Garden, on the St. John's river, with a plat and certificate of survey of the same, bearing date the 20th of December, 1822, made by Andrew Burgevin for said heirs; also a certified copy of concession to William Williams for the same, made by Governor White, and bearing date upon the 1st day of September, 1804; which are ordered to be filed.

William Williams's heirs presented their memorial to this board, praying confirmation of title to two thousand two hundred acres of land, lying at New Smyrna, at a place on the Mosquitos, with a certified copy of a concession to William Williams for two thousand two hundred acres, made by Governor White, and dated 21st of July, 1803; which are ordered to be filed.

Lorenzo Capo's heirs presented their memorial to this board, praying confirmation of title to fifty acres of land, lying on an island in the North river, and to one hundred and seven acres of land adjoining the fifty acre tract, except being divided by a creek, with a deposition of Anthony Hindsman, taken before William Robertson, upon the 10th day of September, 1822; a receipt from William Price to Lorenzo Capo, dated 21st of January, 1784; a receipt of John Murphy to William Price for surveyor's fees, dated 21st of January, 1784; and a plat and certificate of survey of fifty acres, made for James Breedshaw by John Murphy, dated January 3, 1783; which are ordered to be filed.

Lorenzo Capo's heirs presented their memorial to this board, praying confirmation of title to one hundred and sixty acres of land, lying in the Twelve-mile swamp, adjoining the lands of Lewis Schofield, with a copy of concession of one hundred and seventy-five acres to Lorenzo Capo, made by Governor White, dated the 24th of February, 1808; also a memorial and order of survey for the same, bearing date the 18th of June, 1819; which are ordered to be filed.

Bartholome Mestre presented his memorial to this board, praying confirmation of title to three hundred acres of land, lying on Thompson's branch, on the opposite side of the Matanzas river, from the Little bar, with a certified copy of concession of lands to said Mestre, made by Governor White, and bearing date the 28th of June, 1796; which are ordered to be filed.

Augustin Buyck presented his memorial to this board, praying confirmation of title to two hundred acres of land, lying at the Mosquitos, adjoining the lands of Josiah Dupont, with a copy of concession to said Buyck of the same amount of lands, made by Governor White, upon the 3d of May, 1799; which are ordered to be filed.

Josiah Dupont's heirs presented their memorial to this board, praying confirmation of title to five hundred acres of land, lying in Graham's swamp, adjoining the lands of Charles and George Clarke, with a certified copy of concession to Josiah Dupont of five hundred acres, made by Governor White, upon the 29th of July, 1801; which are ordered to be filed.

Josiah Dupont's heirs presented their memorial to this board, praying confirmation of title to five hundred acres of land, lying at the Mosquitos, between the lands of Travers, Carter, Pallisier, and Madam Clarke, with a certified copy of a concession of the same to Josiah Dupont, made by Governor Quesada, and dated the 18th day of October, 1794; which are ordered to be filed.

Gideon Dupont's heirs presented their memorial to this board, praying confirmation of title to one thousand four hundred acres of land, lying in Graham's swamp, next to the lands of Josiah Dupont, deceased, with a certified copy of concession to Gideon Dupont for seven hundred acres, with seven hundred acres intervening space, made by Governor White, and dated June 3, 1802; which are ordered to be filed.

Augustin Buyck presented his memorial to this board, praying confirmation of title to one thousand five hundred acres of land, lying in the vicinity of the old town of St. Peter's, at the Mosquitos, in the place called Spruce Pair creek, with a copy of concession made by Governor White to said Buyck for one thousand five hundred acres, bearing date the 18th of July, 1801; which are ordered to be filed.

Augustin Buyck and the heirs of Josiah Dupont presented their memorial to this board, praying confirmation of title to an island of about thirty acres of land, lying between the two bars of the Matanzas, with a certified copy of concession of the same to Augustin Buyck and Josiah Dupont, made by Governor Quesada, and dated 9th of August, 1794; which are ordered to be filed.

Augustin Buyck presented his memorial to this board, praying confirmation of title to one thousand five hundred acres of land, lying in the vicinity of the old town of St. Peter's, north of the town, in the swamp of hammock, opposite Mount Oswald, towards the beach, with a copy of concession of the same to said Buyck, made by Governor White, and dated upon the 18th of July, 1801; which are ordered to be filed.

Andrew Plyme's heirs presented their memorial to this board, praying confirmation of title to five hundred acres of land, lying at the place called Doctor's lake, on the St. John's river, occupied by Christopher Nelly in the time of the British, with a copy of concession to said Andrew Plyme for the same, made by Governor Quesada, and dated the 10th of February, 1791; which are ordered to be filed.

Eusebius Bushnell's heirs presented their memorial to this board, praying confirmation of title to six hundred acres of land lying, in the Twelve-mile swamp, adjoining Cowan's land, with a certified copy of concession of the same to Eusebius Bushnell, made by Governor White, and dated the 13th of March, 1799; which are ordered to be filed.

Edgar Macon, Esquire, United States' attorney for the district of East Florida, attended here this day under the order of this board.

Samuel A. Laurence presented his memorial to this board for confirmation of title to twenty-three thousand and forty acres of land, lying in St. John's county, commencing on the left or western bank of the Ocklawaha creek or river, at the upper crossing place, where the path from St. John's river to Chicuchaty traverses the said river, running back southwestwardly, in a course perpendicular to the general direction of the river at that place, six hundred and eighty chains; thence, northwardly, for quantity, with a duplicate copy of a deed of conveyance from Richard S. Hackley and Harriet, his wife, to said Samuel A. Laurence, dated upon the 24th day of December, 1822; and it is ordered by the board that all consideration of said memorial be postponed until after they shall have decided upon a question now before them in relation to some claims of Antelm Gay.

Samuel Sterry Laurence presented his memorial to this board for confirmation of title of ninety-two thousand one hundred and sixty acres of land, lying in St. John's county, on the east side of the Ocklawaha river, with a duplicate copy of a deed of conveyance for said lands made by Richard S. Hackley and Harriet, his wife, to said Samuel Sterry Laurence, bearing date the 24th day of December, 1822; and it is ordered by the board that all consideration of said memorial be postponed until after they shall have decided upon a question now before them in relation to some claims of Antelm Gay.

The board then adjourned until Thursday, the 16th instant, at eleven o'clock in the morning.

THURSDAY, *October* 16, 1823.

The Board of Commissioners met upon this day, pursuant to adjournment. Present, the Hons. Alexander Hamilton and William W. Blair.

John D. Vaughn presented his memorial to this board, praying confirmation of title to two hundred and fifty acres of land, lying in Amelia island, together with a royal title for the same made by Governor Coppinger, and bearing date upon the 18th of June, 1821, marked and referred to as exhibit A; which are ordered to be filed.

John D. Vaughn presented his memorial to this board, praying confirmation of title to nine hundred and fifty acres of land, lying on Lofton's creek, near Nassau river, with a plat and certificate of survey of the same made by George J. F. Clarke, and dated upon the 8th day of December, 1816, marked and referred to as exhibit B; and a deposition of George J. F. Clarke, sworn to before Thomas H. Miller, a justice of the peace at the town of St. Mary's, in Georgia, upon the 15th day of September, 1821, marked and referred to as exhibit C; which are ordered to be filed.

Edgar Macon, Esquire, United States' attorney for the district of East Florida, attended the session of the board this day under their order.

The board then adjourned until Monday the 20th day of this month, at 11 o'clock in the morning.

MONDAY, *October* 20, 1823.

The board met pursuant to adjournment: Present, the Hons. Alexander Hamilton and William W. Blair.

Philip Embara presented his memorial to this board, praying confirmation of title to one hundred acres of land, lying about three miles west from the ferry, at a place called Pevit, with a plat and certificate of survey of the same made by Robert McHardy, dated the 11th of March, 1817, referred to, and marked exhibit C; also, a certified copy of concession to said Philip Embara for said lands, made by Governor White, and dated 5th of January, 1807, referred to, and marked A; also, a memorial and order of survey, dated March 3, 1817, referred to, and marked exhibit B; which are ordered to be filed.

Juana Paredes presented her memorial to this board, praying confirmation of title to one hundred and ten acres of land, lying at a place on the North river, known by the name of Marshall's plantation, with a plat and certificate of survey of the same, made by G. Darling, dated 16th of September, 1823, exhibit marked A; a certified copy of a concession made to the father of memorialist, John Paredes, by Governor White, dated 17th of April, 1807, referred to, and marked B; also, a memorial and order of survey, dated June 2, 1818, referred to, and marked as exhibit C; which are ordered to be filed.

John Underwood presented his memorial to this board, praying confirmation of title to eight thousand four hundred and seventy-six acres of land lying on Little St. Mary's river, bounded on the west by lands of John Forbes, with a plat and certificate of survey made by George J. F. Clarke, dated 17th of July, 1819, referred to, and marked exhibit A; a certified copy of concession of said lands made by Governor Coppinger, dated 15th of July, 1816, exhibited, and marked B; a petition of said Underwood, marked C; and a petition of sundry people on behalf of said Underwood, marked D; which are ordered to be filed.

Edgar Macon, Esq., United States' attorney for the district of East Florida, attended the sitting of the board this day under their order.

The board then adjourned until Thursday the 23d of this month, at 11 o'clock in the morning.

THURSDAY, *October* 23, 1823.

The Hon. W. W. Blair, pursuant to adjournment, was present, and adjourned the board until Monday the 27th instant, at 11 o'clock in the morning.

MONDAY, *October* 27, 1823.

The board met pursuant to adjournment: Present, the Hons. Alexander Hamilton and William W. Blair.

Andrew McDowell and Alexander Black presented their memorial to this board, praying confirmation of title to four hundred and ninety acres of land, lying on a creek to the east of the river St. John's, at a place called Little Orange Grove, in East Florida, with a certified copy of concession to Andrew Burgevin made by Governor Coppinger, dated the 11th of December, 1817, referred to, and marked exhibit A; memorial dated the 2d January,

1818, and order of survey dated the 5th of January, 1818, referred to, and marked exhibit B; plat and certificate of survey made by Robert McHardy, dated 27th of March, 1818, referred to, and marked exhibit C; certified copy of royal title made by Governor Coppinger to Andrew Burgevin, and dated 24th April, 1818, referred to, and marked exhibit D; a certified copy of conveyance from said Burgevin to Francis P. Sanchez, dated 12th of June, 1820, referred to, and marked exhibit E; and conveyance from said Sanchez to memorialist, dated 10th of June, 1823, referred to, and marked exhibit F; which are ordered to be filed.

Samuel Clarke and George F. Brown presented their memorial to this board, praying confirmation of title to three thousand acres of land, lying on Pigeon creek, a creek of St. Mary's river, in East Florida, with a plat and certificate of survey of same, made by George J. F. Clarke, and dated 15th of November, 1819, referred to, and marked exhibit A; a certified copy of concession to Thomas Travers made by Governor White, and dated 30th of April, 1799, referred to, and marked exhibit B; a certified copy of Royal title by Governor Coppinger to heirs of Thomas Travers, deceased, dated 15th of February, 1819, referred to, and marked exhibit C; a certified copy of conveyance from William Travers, for himself and on behalf of the other heirs of Thomas Travers, deceased, to Francis P. Sanchez, in trust, dated 20th of December, 1819, referred to, and marked exhibit D; which are ordered to be filed.

Joseph Delespine presented his memorial, praying confirmation of title to ninety-two thousand one hundred and sixty acres of land, lying on the north of the river De los Maimies, which lies on the northwest of Cayo Viscayo, with proceedings had before the Captain General of Cuba, granting said lands to Juan Xavier de Arambide, dated in Havana, 14th December, 1813, and a certified copy of proceedings had before the corporation of St. Augustine in relation to said claim, dated 22d March, 1814, all referred to, and marked exhibit A; a certified copy of conveyance from John B. Strong, attorney for Juan Xavier de Arambide Goicochea, to George Clarke, dated 29th April, 1820; also, power of attorney from said Arambide to John B. Strong, dated Puerto Principe, 20th of January, 1820, referred to, and marked exhibit B; memorial and order of survey dated 7th of May, 1821, referred to, and marked exhibit C; conveyance from George J. F. Clarke to J. B. Strong, dated 4th January, 1823, referred to, and marked D; a conveyance from John B. Strong to Joseph Delespine, dated 25th February, 1822, referred to, and marked E; which are ordered to be filed.

Joseph Delespine presented his memorial to this board, praying confirmation of title to ten thousand two hundred and forty acres of land, lying on a creek on the northwest side of Indian river, towards the north end, running northwest, with a certified copy of concession of said lands to Pablo F. Fontaine, made by Governor Coppinger, and dated 10th of November, 1817, referred to, and marked exhibit A; an order of survey dated 21st of August, 1820, and plat and certificate made by Andres Burgevin, dated 18th of September, 1820, referred to, and marked exhibit B; a conveyance from Pablo F. Fontaine to Joseph Delespine, dated 6th of March, 1822, referred to, and marked exhibit C; which are ordered to be filed.

Andrew McDowell and Alexander Black presented their memorial to this board, praying confirmation of title to five hundred acres of land, lying on the creek or lagoon of Spring Garden, about half a league, in a northeastwardly direction from a place called Little Orange Grove, with a certified copy of concession made to Andres Burgevin by Governor Coppinger, dated 24th of January, 1818, referred to, and marked A; a memorial for, and order of survey, dated 26th of January, 1818, referred to, and marked exhibit B; a plat and certificate of survey made by Robert McHardy, dated 27th of March, 1818, referred to, and marked exhibit C; a certified copy of royal title to Andres Burgevin made by Governor Coppinger, and dated 24th of April, 1819, referred to, and marked exhibit D; a certified copy of conveyance from Andres Burgevin to Francis P. Sanchez, dated 12th of June, 1820, referred to, and marked exhibit E; conveyance from said Sanchez to memorialist, dated 10th of June, 1823, referred to, and marked exhibit F; which are ordered to be filed.

Andrew McDowell and Alexander Black presented their memorial to this board, praying confirmation of title to nine hundred acres of land, lying in East Florida, between the Halifax and Matanzas rivers, and is a part of Graham's swamp, with a certified copy of royal title to said lands, made upon the 20th of June, 1815, by Governor Estrada, in favor of Jose de la Maza Arredondo, referred to, and marked exhibit A; a plat and certificate of survey made by Robert McHardy, and dated 12th of March, 1818, referred to, and marked exhibit B; a conveyance from Fernando de la Maza Arredondo, Jun., attorney in fact for Jose de la Maza Arredondo, to Francis P. Sanchez, dated 12th of June, 1820, referred to, and marked exhibit C; a copy of conveyance from Francis P. Sanchez to memorialist, dated 10th of June, 1823, referred to, and marked exhibit D; which are ordered to be filed.

Francis P. Sanchez presented his memorial to this board, praying confirmation of title to two hundred and fifty acres of land, lying in East Florida, on the south side of the river St. John's, at a place called Wills's swamp, about nine miles south of the late military post of St. Nicholas, with a plat and certificate of survey made by George J. F. Clarke for David S. H. Miller, dated 3d of May, 1817, referred to, and marked exhibit A; a certified copy of concession of said lands to David S. Miller, made by Governor Coppinger, and dated 18th of March, 1817, referred to, and marked B; a conveyance from said Miller to Francis P. Sanchez, dated 25th of January, 1822, referred to, and marked exhibit C; which are ordered to be filed.

Francis P. Sanchez presented his memorial to this board praying confirmation of title to five hundred acres of land, lying in East Florida, being part of a grant of ten thousand acres of land made to F. M. Arredondo, about five miles to the eastward of a place called Spring Garden, with a certified copy of concession to F. M. Arredondo, Jun. of ten thousand acres, by Governor Coppinger, dated 20th of March, 1817, referred to as exhibit A; a copy of royal title to said F. M. Arredondo, Jun. for five hundred acres, part of ten thousand acres, conceded as aforesaid, made by Governor Coppinger, and dated 9th of August, 1820, referred to, and marked exhibit B; a copy of conveyance from said F. M. Arredondo, Jun. to Julia Guillet, wife of Andres Burgevin, of said five hundred acres, dated 18th of December, 1820, referred to, and marked exhibit C; a certified copy of conveyance from Julia Guillet, wife of Andres Burgevin, to Francis P. Sanchez, dated 8th of January, 1821, referred to, and marked exhibit D; a memorial and order of survey dated 20th of August, 1819, referred to, and marked exhibit E; and a plat and certificate of survey made by Andres Burgevin, dated 9th of August, 1820, referred to, and marked as exhibit F; which are ordered to be filed.

Francis P. Sanchez presented his memorial to this board, praying confirmation of title to six hundred acres of land, lying in East Florida, on the North river, about sixteen miles from the city of St. Augustine, between the road to San Vincente Ferrer and lands of John Andreo, with a copy of three concessions to Roque Leonardy of two thousand acres, one dated the 11th of April, 1793, made by Governor Quesada; another, dated 24th of December, 1792, made by Governor Quesada; another 3d of January, 1799, made by Governor White; all of which are referred to, and marked exhibit A; memorial for resurvey, dated 3d April, 1819, and order thereon, dated 5th of April, 1819, referred to, and marked exhibit B; a certified copy of plats and certificates of surveys for fourteen hundred acres and six hundred acres, both dated 28th of April, 1819, made by Andres Burgevin for the heirs of Roque Leonardy and Aguida Coll, referred to, and marked exhibits C and D; a certified copy of royal title made o the heirs of Roque Leonardy, of six hundred acres of land, by Governor Coppinger, dated upon the 25th of

May, 1821, referred to, and marked exhibit E; and a conveyance from the heirs of Roque Leonardy, deceased, to Francis P. Sanchez, dated 21st of March, 1822, referred to, and marked exhibit F; which are ordered to be filed.

Raymond Sanchez, for himself and the other heirs of Sebastian Espinosa, deceased, presented his memorial to this board, praying confirmation of title to five hundred acres of land, lying in East Florida, at a place called Ulridge, in Diego plains, with a certified copy of concession made to Bernardino Sanchez, on behalf of Sebastian Espinosa, by Governor White, dated the 5th of September, 1801, referred to, and marked exhibit A; a certified copy of royal title in favor of Sebastian Espinosa, made by Governor Coppinger, dated 31st of March, 1818, referred to, and marked exhibit B; which are ordered to be filed.

Magdelina Juaneda, widow of Nicholas Sanchez, deceased, for herself and the heirs of Nicholas Sanchez, deceased, presented her memorial to this board, praying confirmation of title to three hundred and eighty-five acres of land, lying in East Florida, in Diego Plains, on the south side of the land of Sebastian Espinosa, with a certified copy of royal title made to Nicholas Sanchez by Governor Coppinger, dated upon the 4th of April, 1816, for said lands referred to, and marked exhibit A; which are ordered to be filed.

Teresa Marshall's heirs, by Eliza Burnell, one of said heirs, presented their memorial to this board, praying confirmation of title to five hundred and thirty-three and one-third acres of land, lying in East Florida, on the North river, on the west side thereof, about nine miles from the city of St. Augustine, and is known by the name of Santa Teresa, with a certified copy of concession to Teresa Gill made by Governor Quesada, and dated upon the 10th of October, 1791, referred to, and marked exhibit A; and, also, a memorial from Teresa Marshall to Governor Coppinger, dated 6th of May, 1819, for permission to obtain from G. J. F. Clarke a certified copy of the survey of said lands made by Josiah Dupont, with certificate of Pedro Marrot, together with said copy and certificate of said Clarke, dated same date, referred to, and marked exhibit B; which are ordered to be filed.

Reuben Charles presented his memorial to this board, praying confirmation of title to one hundred acres of land, lying at the Nine-mile spring, on the King's road, adjoining the lands of Marshall and Hindsman, with a certified copy of concession to Lewis Scofield, made by Governor White, dated the 16th of June, 1796; also, a conveyance from Margaret Scofield to Reuben Charles, dated 2d day of May, 1823; which are ordered to be filed.

Josiah Dupont's heirs presented their memorial to this board, praying confirmation of title to nine hundred and twenty acres of land, lying at the Matanzas, on the head of the last water stream, ten miles south of the fort at Matanzas; also, nine hundred and twenty-five acres of land in Graham's swamp, on Graham's creek, with a certified copy of concession made to Josiah Dupont by Governor Quesada, dated 31st of August, 1792; which are ordered to be filed.

John Kershaw, trustee for the children of John and Margaret Du Bose, presented his memorial to this board, praying confirmation of title to one hundred acres of land lying at a place called Governor grand, upon the North river, with a certified copy of royal title to José and Miguel Andre, made by Governor Estrada, dated 24th of November, 1815, No. 1; a certified copy of concession of said lands to said José and Miguel Andrew, dated 24th of November, 1815, and made by Governor Estrada, No. 2; a petition of José and Miguel Andrew, dated 29th of August, 1815, and decree of Governor Estrada thereon, dated 13th of December, 1815, No. 3; a memorial and order of survey, dated 29th of January, 1819, No. 4; and, also, a certified copy of plat and certificate of survey made by Andres Burgevin, dated February 1, 1819, No. 5; which are ordered to be filed.

John Floyd's heirs, alias José Juaneda's heirs, by John Rodman, their attorney, presented their memorial to this board, praying confirmation of title to two hundred acres of land, lying on the North river, about twenty miles from St. Augustine, with a certified copy of concession made to Augustin Buyck by Governor Quesada, of three hundred acres, dated upon the 1st of February, 1793, No. 1; a certified copy of transfer of two hundred acres of land to José Juaneda by Governor White, dated the 30th of April, 1799, No. 2; also, a plat and certificate of survey made by Pedro Marrot, dated the 15th of May, 1793, for Augustin Buyck, No. 3; which are ordered to be filed.

Robert Prichard's heirs presented their memorial to this board, praying confirmation of title to four hundred and fifty acres of land, lying in Jacksonville, comprising the town of Jacksonville, on the west side of the river St. John's, in Duval county, with a certified copy of concession to Robert Prichard made by Governor Quesada, and dated January 3, 1791; which are ordered to be filed.

Prudence Plummer presented her memorial to this board, praying confirmation of title to three hundred and fifty acres and one-half acre of land lying on east side of the river St. John's, known by the name of Montpelier, with a certified copy of plat and certificate of survey made by Pedro Marrot, and dated 6th of January, 1792, for Samuel Eastlake; and, also, a decree of the Attorney General of East Florida, Joseph Ortega, dated 17th September, 1800, in favor of Prudence Plummer; which are ordered to be filed.

Caroline Eliza McHardy's heirs presented, by their guardians, their memorial to this board, praying confirmation of title to eleven hundred acres of land in two tracts: one tract of five hundred acres lying in McDougal's swamp, in the district of Mosquito; the other tract of six hundred acres lies in Bisset's swamp, in the district of Mosquito, with the following documents: a certified copy of concession to Caroline Isabel Williams, of eleven hundred acres of land, made by Governor Estrada, and dated upon the 20th of August, 1815, numbered 1; a memorial and order of survey for the same, 2d of September, 1818, numbered 2; plat and certificate of survey of five hundred acres made by Andres Burgevin, and dated 8th of September, 1818, numbered 3; a plat and certificate of survey of six hundred acres made by Andres Burgevin, and dated 8th September, 1818, numbered 4; petition for absolute title, dated 20th of March, 1819, numbered 5; and a certificate of improvements made upon the land, dated 27th of May, 1819, numbered 6; which are ordered to be filed.

John Rodman, trustee for the benefit of the creditors of Robert McHardy, deceased, presented his memorial, praying confirmation of title to one thousand acres of land, lying and situate at Tomoka, with a copy of royal title to Robert McHardy for the same, made by Governor Estrada, and dated 3d of July, 1815; which are ordered to be filed.

John Rodman, trustee for the benefit of the creditors of Robert McHardy, deceased, presented his memorial to this board, praying confirmation of title to sixteen thousand acres of land lying on the west side of the river St. John's, in a district where there is a spring and stream of fresh water, formerly known by the name of *Old Stores*, with a certified copy of concession of said lands to Robert McHardy by Governor Kindelan, dated upon the 8th of November, 1814; also, a memorial and order of survey, dated 7th of February, 1815, and a plat and certificate of survey made by Andres Burgevin, dated the 10th of May, 1819; which are ordered to be filed.

John Rodman, trustee for the benefit of the creditors of Robert McHardy, deceased, presented his memorial to this board, praying confirmation of title to three thousand acres of land, lying at a place called Turkey branch, on the west side of St. John's river, and distant therefrom about forty-five miles, with a certified copy of concession of said lands to Robert McHardy by Governor Estrada, and dated upon the 29th of September, 1811; also, a plat and certificate of survey made by George J. F. Clarke, dated 8th of May, 1819; which are ordered to be filed.

John Rodman, trustee for the benefit of the creditors of Robert McHardy, deceased, presented his memorial to this board, praying confirmation of title to six hundred acres of land in two tracts of three hundred acres each; the one situated in a place called McDougall's swamp, in the district of Mosquito; the other on the west side of the river St. John's, with a grant or concession of six hundred acres in two tracts of three hundred acres each, made to Robert McHardy by Governor Coppinger, and dated upon the 4th day of July, 1815; also, a petition for, and order of survey thereon, dated September 2, 1818; and a plat and certificate of survey made for said McHardy, of three hundred acres in McDougall's swamp, by Andres Burgevin, and dated the 24th of September, 1818; which are ordered to be filed.

Philip R. Young presented his memorial to this board, praying confirmation of title to twenty-five thousand acres of land in two tracts; one of thirteen thousand acres, lying on the west side of Long lake, about forty miles south of lake George; the other of twelve thousand acres, lying on the west side of a lake called Second lake, with the following documents: a plat and certificate of survey of thirteen thousand acres made by Andres Burgevin, dated 2d of August, 1819, and marked A; the other a copy of a plat and certificate of survey of twelve thousand acres made by Andres Burgevin, and dated 2d of August, 1819, marked B; copy of a petition of Philip R. Young for twenty-five thousand acres of land, dated 5th of December, 1816, and a decree of Governor Coppinger thereon, dated 11th of February, 1817, marked C; and a copy of a royal title made to Philip R. Young by Governor Coppinger, dated the 22d of February, 1816, marked D; which are ordered to be filed.

George Atkinson presented his memorial to this board, praying confirmation of title to four thousand acres of land, lying about twenty miles west of the river Ocklawaha, and on the northeast side of the road that goes from Joe Gray's to the town of Alachua, with a plat and certificate of survey made by George J. F. Clarke, and dated 15th of December, 1817, marked A; also, a copy of conveyance from Pedro Miranda to George Atkinson, dated 20th of June, 1821, marked B; also, a copy of concession to Pedro Miranda made by Governor White, and dated 22d of February, 1810; which are ordered to be filed.

Edgar Macon, Esq., United States' attorney for the district of East Florida, attended the session of the board, this day, under their order.

The board then adjourned until Thursday, 30th of this month, at 11 o'clock in the morning.

THURSDAY, *October* 30, 1823.

The board met according to adjournment. Present, the Hons. Alexander Hamilton and William W. Blair.

Edward Macon, Esq., United States' attorney for the district of East Florida, attended the session of the board this day, under their order.

Samuel Clarke and George S. Brown, mortgagees, presented their memorial to this board, praying confirmation of title to four hundred acres of land lying in East Florida, in the county of St. John's, near Picolata, and is distant about two and a half miles south of the plantation of Manuel Solano, together with a certified copy of concession of seven hundred and fifty acres of land, in two tracts, made by Governor White, in favor of Edward Wanton, upon the 23d of November, 1801, referred to, and marked exhibit A. A certified copy of royal title for four hundred acres in favor of said Wanton, referred to, and marked exhibit B; a certified copy of conveyance from Edward Wanton to Louis Guibert, of four hundred acres of land, dated upon the 18th of May, 1820, referred to, and marked exhibit C; a deed of mortgage from Louis Guibert to memorialists, dated the 29th of April, 1823, together with a copy of plat and certificate of survey made by George Clarke, dated 17th of November, 1819, referred to, and marked exhibit D; which are ordered to be filed.

Samuel Clark presented his memorial to this board, praying confirmation of title to a lot of ground in Fernandina, in Amelia island, with a certified copy of certificate of survey made by George J. F. Clarke, dated 6th of May, 1817, marked exhibit A; a certified copy of royal title made by Governor Coppinger to Teresa Marshall, and dated 21st of May, 1819, marked exhibit B; and an indenture of conveyance made by Teresa Marshall to Samuel Clarke, dated November 9, 1818, marked exhibit C; which are ordered to be filed.

Christina Hill, widow of Joseph Sanchez, deceased, on behalf of herself and his children, presented her memorial to this board, praying confirmation of title to four hundred and five acres of land, fifty-five acres thereof lying at a place called *Casina Loca*, and the residue in *Diego plains*, bounded on the north by lands granted Sebastian Espinosa, with a certified copy of concession made by Governor Estrada, dated 17th November, 1815, for the amount of four hundred and five acres of land in favor of Christina Hill, widow of Joseph Sanchez, marked exhibit A; and a certified copy of royal title in favor of the widow and heirs of José Sanchez, made by Governor Coppinger, and dated the 16th of April, 1818, marked exhibit B; which are ordered to be filed.

Francis P. Sanchez presented his memorial to this board, praying confirmation of title to fourteen hundred acres of land, part of a concession to José M. Hernandez of twenty thousand acres, lying in two tracts; the one tract being of seven hundred acres, part of a ten thousand acre survey under said concession, which lies upon the west bank of lake George, and is situated at the northeast corner of said ten thousand acre survey; the other tract is seven hundred acres, part of a survey of five thousand acres under said concession, situated on the east side of the river St. John's, between a place called Buffalo bluff, and another place called Mount Tucker, with a certified copy of concession of twenty thousand acres to Joseph M. Hernandez, made by Governor Coppinger, dated 18th of November, 1817, marked exhibit A; a certified copy of royal title for ten thousand acres to José M. Hernandez, made by Governor Coppinger, and dated the 9th of April, 1821, exhibit B; a plat and certificate of survey of ten thousand acres made for Joseph M. Hernandez by Andres Burgevin, and dated the 4th of April, 1821, marked exhibit C; a plat and certificate of survey of seven hundred acres in favor of Francis P. Sanchez, by Andrew Burgevin, dated 22d of May, 1823, marked exhibit D; a certified copy of royal title to Joseph M. Hernandez of ten thousand acres, in two tracts, or one tract on both sides of St. John's river, made by Governor Coppinger, and dated 9th of April, 1821, marked exhibit E; a plat and certificate of survey of five thousand acres made by Andres Burgevin, dated 4th of April, 1821, marked exhibit F; a plat of seven hundred acres of land, parcel of said five thousand acre survey, and is marked exhibit G; a conveyance from José M. Hernandez to Andres Burgevin of fourteen hundred acres, in two tracts, dated 30th July, 1821, marked exhibit H; and a conveyance from Andres Burgevin to Francisco P. Sanchez, of fourteen hundred acres aforesaid, dated 15th of February, 1822, marked exhibit I; which are ordered to be filed.

The board then adjourned their sittings from this house to the house of Joseph Sanchez, upon the corner of the public square in this city, to meet again upon Monday the 3d day of November, 1823, at 11 o'clock in the morning.

MONDAY, *November* 3, 1823.

The board met according to adjournment. Present, all the members.

Edgar Macon, Esq., United States' attorney for the district of East Florida, was in attendance before the board this day, under their order.

99   A

Joseph Arnau presented his memorial to this board, praying confirmation of title to two hundred and nine acres of land on the North river, a part thereof being an island, with a certified copy of concession to memorialist made by Governor White, and dated 31st of August, 1799; which are ordered to be filed.

William Ladd presented his memorial to this board, praying confirmation of title to fifteen hundred and twenty-five acres of land lying on Hillsborough river, Mosquito, and beginning at the entrance of Fresh Water brook, adjoining a tract originally granted to James Ormond, with a certified copy of concession to memorialist made by Governor White, and dated 3d of January, 1804; which are ordered to be filed.

John Christopher presented his memorial to this board, praying confirmation of title to fifty acres of land lying on the river Nassau, adjoining other lands of memorialist, with a certified copy of concession to John Tucker, dated 24th of May, 1804, and made by Governor White, and marked A; a copy of certificate of exchange of lands between John Tucker and Gilbert Mann, dated 22d of January, 1807, marked B; and a copy of certificate of relinquishment of said plantation to John Christopher, dated 31st of October, 1807, marked C; which are ordered to be filed.

John Christopher presented his memorial to this board, praying confirmation of title to five hundred acres of land lying on the river Nassau, with a certified copy of royal title to Spicer Christopher, made by Governor White, and dated the 8th of April, 1809; a certified copy of plat and certificate of survey made by Pedro Marrot, and dated 5th of February, 1792; which are ordered to be filed.

Farquhar Bethune presented his memorial to this board, praying confirmation of title to eleven hundred acres of land, lying on the Halifax river, Mosquito, and is bounded on the north by lands of Samuel Williams, with a certified copy of royal title to memorialist, made by Governor Kindelan, dated the 4th of March, 1814; a certified copy of plat and certificate of survey, made by Juan Purcell, and dated the 18th of May, 1806; which are ordered to be filed.

John Middleton presented his memorial to this board, praying confirmation of title to two hundred acres of land, lying on Cedar branch, on the west side of the river St. John's, with a certified copy of royal title to William Garvin, made by Governor Coppinger, dated 29th of March, 1817, marked A; a conveyance from William Garvin to John Middleton, for said lands, dated the 3d of December, 1821, marked B; a plat and certificate of survey, made by George J. F. Clarke, dated 6th April, 1817, marked C; which are ordered to be filed.

John Middleton presented his memorial to this board, praying confirmation of title to a lot of ground in the town of Fernandina, designated, in the plan of said town, as No. 8, in square 21, with a certificate of survey by George J. F. Clarke, for Benjamin Ayres, for half lot No. 8, in said plan, marked A; a conveyance from William P. Yonge to John Middleton, for a lot, dated, 10th of July, 1818, marked B; which are ordered to be filed.

John Middleton presented his memorial to this board, praying confirmation of title to two half lots in the town of Fernandina, designated, in the plan of said town, by the numbers 3 and 4, in square 14, with a concession of a lot to Anna Wiggins, made by Governor Kindelan, the 21st of May, 1814, and marked A; a conveyance from Henry A. Yonge to memorialist, dated 25th of August, 1819, marked B; a concession, to Guillermo Buason, of a lot No. 6, in square 14, by Governor Kindelan, dated 4th of March, 1814; which are ordered to be filed.

José Sanchez presented his memorial to this board, praying confirmation of title to two hundred and ten acres of land, lying upon the west bank of the river Hillsborough, or South Mosquito, to the southward of the town of Smyrna, with a royal title to Rafael Andreo, dated June 2, 1817, made by Governor Coppinger, with a conveyance from Fernando de la Maza Arredondo, Jun., to memorialist, dated 25th of March, 1822, marked A; and a certified copy of plat and certificate, made by Robert McHardy, and dated the 22d of January, 1818, marked Z; which are ordered to be filed.

John Larcey presented his memorial to this board, praying confirmation of title to three hundred acres of land, lying in three tracts: one of one hundred and fifty acres, on Front creek, between the lands of Joseph Fenwick and the river St. John's; also, one tract of fifty acres, on Cedar creek; and one other tract, of one hundred acres, on a branch of Six-mile creek, with a copy of concession to memorialist, of three hundred acres, made by Governor Estrada, and dated the 21st of August, 1815, and marked A; a certificate of survey and two plats, the one of fifty and the other of one hundred acres of land, made by George J. F. Clarke, and dated the 28th of May, 1821, marked B; which are ordered to be filed.

The board then adjourned until Thursday, the 6th instant, at 11 o'clock in the morning.

THURSDAY, *November* 6, 1823.

The Hon. Davis Floyd was present, and adjourned the board until Monday, the 10th instant, at 11 o'clock in the morning.

MONDAY, *November* 10, 1823.

The board met pursuant to adjournment. Present, the Hons. Davis Floyd and William W. Blair; and adjourned until three o'clock, at which time they again met. Present, the Hons. Davis Floyd and Alexander Hamilton.

Charles Seton presented his memorial to this board, praying confirmation of title to fourteen hundred acres of land, lying on the river Nassau, and beginning on said river, below the junction of Thomas creek therewith, together with a certified copy of concession of said land, made by Governor Kindelan upon the 1st of March, 1815; a plat and certificate of survey, of twelve hundred and fifty-one acres, made by George J. F. Clarke, and dated the 16th of May, 1816; also, a plat and certificate of survey, of five hundred and twenty acres, made upon the same day, by same surveyor; which are ordered to be filed.

Charles Seton presented his memorial to this board, praying confirmation of title to sixteen thousand acres of land, lying on the Nassau river: the first line commencing at a pine a little below the entrance to Plummer's swamp, with a conditional concession made to memorialist, by Governor Coppinger, and dated upon the 8th day of May, 1816; a plat and certificate of survey, made by George J. F. Clarke, of fifteen thousand six hundred and thirty acres, dated upon the 1st of November, 1816; a certificate of George J. F. Clarke, dated 28th of August, 1817; an agreement made upon the 1st of March, 1817, between Samuel Kingsley, master millwright, Calvin Waterman, and Benjamin Waterman, of the one part, and Charles Seton, of the other, together with an inventory of expenditures in mill building, dated from the 31st of December, 1816, to 7th of January, 1822; which are ordered to be filed.

Charles Seton presented his memorial to this board, praying confirmation of title to six hundred acres of land, lying in Sample swamp, on the river Nassau, with a royal title of said land to memorialist, made by Governor Coppinger the 13th of September, 1816; and a plat and certificate of survey of the same, made by George J. F. Clarke, and dated the 18th May, 1816; which are ordered to be filed.

Charles Seton presented his memorial to this board, praying confirmation of title to seven hundred acres of land, lying on the river St. Mary's, joining the old township formerly belonging to Thomas Cryer, with a certificate of Pedro Marrot, showing a grant, by Governor White, for the same to George Anons, dated 14th of April, 1792; a royal title, to William Carney, of said land, made by Governor Coppinger, and dated 26th of August, 1818; and a conveyance from said Carney to memorialist, dated 28th of April, 1818; and a relinquishment of dower, subscribed by Mary Carney, as wife to said William Carney, in favor of memorialist, dated 10th of April, 1819; which are ordered to be filed.

Charles Seton presented his memorial to this board, praying confirmation of title to forty acres of land, lying on Pelot's island, in the river St. John's, with a concession thereof, made by Governor White, in favor of Thomas Holland, and dated 30th of December, 1807; also, a plat and certificate of survey, made by George J. F. Clarke, and dated 6th of January, 1815; which are ordered to be filed.

The inhabitants of the town of Fernandina presented their memorial to this board, praying confirmation of title, to the use of the inhabitants of said town, of fifteen hundred varras, commencing at the flag-staff of said town, and forming a circle; which is ordered to be filed.

Francis Kinloch presented his memorial to this board, praying confirmation of title to two thousand three hundred and fifty acres of land, lying in East Florida, on the east side of the river St. John's, at a place called Periwinkle bluff, about twenty-nine miles southwest, one-half south, from the town of St. Augustine, with a copy, certified from the original record in England, of a grant to Francis Kinloch, Esq., for the said tract, bearing date upon the 3d day of June, 1816, marked A No. 1, and executed by James Grant, Esq., Governor and commander of the said province, under the jurisdiction of Great Britain; also, a precept from the said James Grant, Esq., to the Surveyor General, to survey said tract to the said Francis Kinloch, Esq., dated the 7th of May, 1766, marked A No. 2, with a plat and certificate of survey of the said tract, certified the 30th May, 1766, marked A No. 3; which are ordered to be filed.

Francis Kinloch, Esq., presented his memorial to this board, praying confirmation of title to five hundred acres of land, lying in East Florida, on the east side of the river St. John's, about twenty-nine miles southwest, one-half south, from St. Augustine, adjoining his tract of two thousand three hundred and fifty acres, and lying on the north side thereof, and adjoining the river, with a certified copy, from the original record in England, of a grant for said five hundred acres, made to Francis Kinloch, Esq., by James Grant, Esq., Governor and commander of said province, under the jurisdiction of the Government of Great Britain, dated upon the 3d day of June, 1766, marked B No. 1; a precept or order of survey, by said James Grant, Esq., dated 9th of May, 1766, marked B No. 2; and a plat and certificate of survey, marked B No. 3, certified by John Funk, deputy surveyor, upon the 30th of May, 1766; also, the affidavit of Francis Kinloch, and the affidavit of Cleland Kinloch, sworn to upon the —— day of June, 1823; also, an authentication of the papers filed in both his claims, dated Consulate of the United States of America, London, upon the 27th of September, 1822, and signed by Thomas Aspinwall; which are ordered to be filed.

Edgar Macon, Esq., United States' attorney for the district of East Florida, attended the sitting of the board, during this day, under their order.

The board then adjourned until Saturday, the 13th instant, at three o'clock, P. M.

SATURDAY, *November* 13, 1823.

The board met pursuant to adjournment. Present, all the members.

Ramon de Fuentes presented his memorial to this board, by his agent, praying confirmation of title to a square of ground in the city of St. Augustine, designated as square 28, and lots Nos. 202 and 203; which is ordered to be filed.

Robert Hutchinson, by his attorney, presented his memorial to this board, praying confirmation of title to one hundred and fifty acres of land, lying on little St. Mary's swamp, about seven miles from its junction with St. Mary's river, with a concession to memorialist for four hundred and fifty acres made by Governor Coppinger, and dated the 8th of May, 1816; which are ordered to be filed.

David S. H. Miller presented his memorial to this board, by his attorney, praying confirmation of title to three hundred acres of land, lying on the south side of the river St. John's, with a royal title in favor of Anna Hogan for the same amount, made by Governor Coppinger, and dated 24th December, 1817; also, a plat and certificate of survey of three hundred acres made by George J. F. Clarke, and dated 24th of June, 1818; which are ordered to be filed.

William Fitzpatrick, by his attorney, presented his memorial to this board, praying confirmation of title to five hundred and forty acres of land, lying on the north side of the river St. John's, at the mouth of said river, at a place called Cedar point, with a copy of concession dated 2d of November, 1795, made by Governor Quesada; and a plat and certificate of survey, made by John Purcell, dated 24th of January, 1800; which are ordered to be filed.

Zachariah Hogan presented his memorial to this board, by his attorney, praying confirmation of title to fifty acres of land, lying on the north side of the river St. John's, on or near Front creek, with a royal title to said Hogan made by Governor Coppinger, and dated 22d of July, 1818; which are ordered to be filed.

John Houston presented, by his attorney, his memorial to this board, praying confirmation of title to one hundred acres of land, lying on Talbot island, with a royal title made to Spicer Christopher by Governor White, and dated 12th of April, 1809; which are ordered to be filed.

John Houston presented, by his attorney, his memorial to this board, praying confirmation of title to one hundred acres of land, lying on Talbot island, with a royal title for the same, made to Spicer Christopher by Governor White, and dated 12th of April, 1809; which are ordered to be filed.

John D. Edwards presented, by his attorney, his memorial to this board, praying confirmation of title to three hundred and fifty acres of land, lying on a branch on Nassau river, at a place called Lardin, with a certified copy of a royal title, made to Isaac Carter by Governor White, and dated 4th of June, 1806; which are ordered to be filed.

John Dixon, by his attorney, presented his memorial to this board, praying confirmation of title to one hundred acres of land, lying on St. Mary's river, at a place called Fack's swamp, with a concession to memorialist made by Governor White, and dated 31st of May, 1805; which are ordered to be filed.

Isaac Hendricks presented his memorial to this board, by his attorney, praying confirmation of title to two hundred acres of land, lying on Pottsburg creek, five miles from the river St. John's, on the south side of said river, with an order of survey, and plat and certificate of survey, by Pedro Marrot, dated the 22d of January, 1792; which are ordered to be filed.

William Gardiner, by his attorney, presented his memorial to this board, praying confirmation of title to one hundred and fifty acres of land, lying on the south side of St. John's river, with a concession to said William Gardiner of said land, made by Governor Kindelan, and dated the 6th of April, 1815; which are ordered to be filed.

Uriah Bowden presented, by his attorney, his memorial to this board, praying confirmation of title to two hundred acres of land, lying on the south side of the river St. John's, adjoining lands granted to Gilbert, with a royal title for the same in favor of memorialist, made by Governor Kindelan, and dated 17th of April, 1815; which are ordered to be filed.

Moses Bowden, by his attorney, presented his memorial to this board, praying confirmation of title to two hundred and fifty acres of land, lying on the south side of the river St. John's, with a concession of the same to memorialist by Governor Kindelan, dated 5th of April, 1815; which are ordered to be filed.

David Turner, by his attorney, presented his memorial to this board, praying confirmation of title to three hundred and ninety acres of land, lying on the north side of the St. John's river, with a concession to memorialist of three hundred and ninety acres, made by Governor White, and dated 3d of February, 1809; which are ordered to be filed.

John Uptegrove, by his attorney, presented his memorial to this board, praying confirmation of title to two hundred and fifty acres of land, lying on the north side of the river Nassau, at a place called Peach Orchard, with a concession to memorialist, made by Governor White, and dated 27th of July, 1803; which are ordered to be filed.

William Lain presented, by his attorney, his memorial to this board, praying confirmation of title to two hundred and ten acres of land, lying on Front creek, a branch of St. John's river, with a plat and certificate of survey, dated 10th of February, 1793, made by Pedro Marrot for memorialist; which are ordered to be filed.

Isaac Hendricks, by his attorney, presented his memorial to this board, praying confirmation of title to two hundred acres of land, lying on the south side of the river St. John's, near the Cow ford, with a concession to William Hendricks by Governor White, dated the 6th of December, 1796; which are ordered to be filed.

Edgar Macon, Esq., United States' attorney for the district of East Florida, was present at the sitting of the board this day, under their order.

A resolution was adopted by this board in the words and figures following, to wit:

"*Resolved*, That the marshal apply to the keeper of the public archives, and that he present him with a copy of the letter addressed to the board by the Department of State, and know from him what and how many papers of the kind referred to in that letter are in his possession; and that he request the keeper of the public archives to deliver them to him, or show cause, if any he can, why he does not do so."

The board then adjourned until to-morrow evening at three o'clock.

FRIDAY, *November* 14, 1823.

The board met pursuant to adjournment. Present, Davis Floyd and Alexander Hamilton, Esquires.

Waters Smith, marshal for the district of East Florida, made his return here upon the resolution adopted by the board yesterday, in the words and figures following, to wit:

"Served William Reynolds, Esq., keeper of the public archives, with a copy of this resolution, and with a copy of the letter addressed to the board by the Department of State. Said Reynolds stated that he would personally appear before the Land Commissioners this day, at three o'clock P. M.

"WATERS SMITH, *Marshal.*"

"ST. AUGUSTINE, *November* 14, 1823."

William Reynolds, Esq., attended here before the board, and made a parol answer to the resolution adopted by this board upon yesterday. Whereupon the board discharged the said William Reynolds from further attendance upon the board at this time, and discharged the rule for him to show cause.

The board then adjourned until Monday, 17th instant, at three o'clock P. M.

SATURDAY, *November* 15, 1823.

The board having met by special arrangement upon this day, at 4 o'clock P. M.: (Present, all the members:) to take into consideration a letter addressed to them by Edgar Macon, Esq., chairman of a committee of a public meeting, dated 15th of November, 1823, do answer as follows, to the first question, to wit:

1st. Whether the regulations published in the newspapers are still in force, and are required to be observed by the claimants to land in this district?

Answer. One of the regulations adopted by the board at its first meeting, and published, requiring claimants to present translations of their title papers, has been rescinded. Some other regulations, to wit: those requiring the claimants to say whether the claim presented be the whole or part of the original grant, and to present certified copies of their title papers have not been exacted of claimants, though these regulations have not been formally annulled. Claimants have generally conformed to the last regulation as written, but not always: neither have any memorials been rejected for the non-production of such papers, where they have been referred to as on record in the public archives, or in the clerk's office of the superior or county courts. With those exceptions the regulations, as published, are in force as far as we now remember.

Question 2d. Whether any other rules and regulations on the subject have been adopted by the board; and particularly, first, whether all the documents presented with the memorial to the board must be translated by the secretary of the board before the claim can be taken into consideration?

Answer. The board have adopted some other resolutions, but we presume that answers to the specifications to this question are all that is required. We answer to the first specification, to wit: that the board has not adopted any resolution upon the subject, but they believe it necessary that all the papers produced and filed as evidence in each case should be translated by the secretary before it is finally decided on by the board.

Second specification, to wit: Whether all the documents in each case, together with the memorial, must be recorded? We answer, that we require the memorial, and all the documents produced by the parties, and filed as evidence, to be recorded.

Third specification, to wit: Whether any claim will be taken into consideration before it be recorded with the accompanying documents?

Answer. We do not require the memorial or evidence of title in any case to be recorded before we take it into consideration.

Fourth specification. If the documents are to be recorded, is the record to be in the original Spanish, or the translation, or both?

Answer. The translations are alone to be recorded.

Fifth specification. Are the claimants required to pay for the recording of the documents; or only for the recording of the memorial or claim?

Answer. The claimants are required to pay for all the papers they require to be recorded, and for no more.

Sixth specification. Have any of the claims presented yet been recorded in any manner whatever?

Answer. None of the claims have yet been recorded.

Ordered, That the secretary do make out a copy of the proceedings of the board upon this day, and furnish Mr. Macon therewith.

The board then adjourned.

MONDAY, *November* 17, 1823.

The board met pursuant to adjournment. Present, the Hons. Davis Floyd and Alexander Hamilton.

Edgar Macon, Esq., United States' attorney, attended the board, this day, under their order.

James Hutchinson's heirs, by their attorney, George Murray, presented their memorial to this board, praying confirmation of title to two thousand acres of land, lying on an island in the lagoon which runs south from the mouth of Indian river to Jupiter inlet, with a certified copy of concession in favor of James Hutchinson, made by Governor White, and dated 14th of April, 1807, marked A. The affidavit of Joseph Hutchinson, subscribed and sworn to 24th April, 1823, marked B; also, another statement of Joseph Hutchinson, of same date, with the certificate and seal of John G. Cowling, notary public in the city of Augusta, in the State of Georgia, attached thereto, marked C; which are ordered to be filed.

Francis Dalcour, executor of John Forbes, by his attorney, George Murray, presented his memorial to this board, praying confirmation of title to seven thousand acres of land lying on little St. Mary's river, with a concession of ten thousand acres to said John Forbes, dated 28th of July, 1814, made by Governor Kindelan, marked A; also, a plat and certificate of survey of the same, made by George J. F. Clarke, and dated 23d of October, 1816; which are ordered to be filed.

Francis Dalcour, executor of the last will and testament of John Forbes, deceased, by George Murray, his attorney, presented his memorial to this board, praying confirmation of title to three thousand acres of land, lying in Cabbage Swamp, on or near an arm of the little St. Mary's river, being part of a ten thousand acre grant in bundle No. 1; and, also, a plat and certificate of survey of three thousand acres, made by George J. F. Clarke, and dated 20th of October, 1816; which are ordered to be filed.

John Bunch, by George Murray, his attorney, presented his memorial to this board, praying confirmation of title to two thousand one hundred and seventy acres of land, lying on the waters of the Mosquito, or Halifax river, with a concession made to him by Governor White, and dated 11th day of August, 1804, marked A; and a copy of plat and certificate of survey of same, marked B, made by Andrew Burgevin, and dated June 5, 1823; which are ordered to be filed.

John Bunch, by George Murray, his attorney, presented his memorial to this board, praying confirmation of title to nine hundred and ninety-five acres of land, lying on Mosquito, or Halifax river, near and fronting Pelican Island, with a royal title for the same made to the heirs of Patrick Dean, made by Governor Coppinger, and dated 4th of June, 1819; which are ordered to be filed.

Juan Blas Entralgo, by his attorney, George Murray, presented his memorial to this board, praying confirmation of title to four thousand acres of land, lying about five miles east of Spring Garden, with a certified copy of conveyance from F. M. Arredondo, Jun., to memorialist, dated 5th of January, 1821, marked A, and a royal title to F. M. Arredondo, Jun., made by Governor Coppinger, and dated 9th of August, 1820, marked B; which are ordered to be filed.

Juan Blas Entralgo, by his attorney, George Murray, presented his memorial to this board, praying confirmation of title to two thousand acres of land, lying on the western bank of St. John's river, with a royal title for the same, dated 15th of November, 1817, made by Governor Coppinger; and a plat and certificate of survey, made by George J. F. Clarke, dated 10th of April, 1818; which are ordered to be filed.

Catalina de Tenis Hipulos, by her attorney, George Murray, presented her memorial to this board, praying confirmation of title to two thousand acres of land, lying about forty miles west from Buena Vista, in the part called the Big Grove, with a royal title to memorialist, made by Governor Coppinger, and dated 7th of December, 1817, marked A; and a plat and certificate of survey, made by Andres Burgevin, and dated 9th of September, 1819, marked B; which are ordered to be filed.

Bartolome de Castro y Ferrer, executor of Manuel Solano, deceased, by George Murray, his attorney, presented his memorial to this board, praying confirmation of title to one hundred acres of land, lying on the west side of St. Sebastian creek, at the place called Solano's ferry, with a certified copy of concession to Manuel Solano, made by Governor Quesada, and dated 11th of June, 1791, marked A; which are ordered to be filed.

William Travers, by George Murray, his attorney, presented his memorial to this board, praying confirmation of title to four hundred and fifty acres of land, lying at a place called Santa Lucia, with a certified copy of concession made by Governor White to Lazaro Ortega, dated 4th of June, 1798, marked A; a certified copy of royal title to Lazaro Ortega for four hundred and fifty acres, made by Governor Coppinger, dated 9th of April, 1821, marked B; a certified copy of conveyance from Lorenzo Ortega to William Travers, dated 11th of May, 1821, marked C; and a memorial, order of survey, and plat and certificate, made by Andras Burgevin for said Ortega, and dated 15th March, 1821, marked D; which are ordered to be filed.

Ferdinand Falany's executor, on behalf of his heirs, by his attorney, George Murray, presented his memorial to this board, praying confirmation of title to twelve hundred acres of land, lying on Moultrie creek, with a certified copy of royal title made to said Falany by Governor Coppinger, and dated 18th of May, 1819; which are ordered to be filed.

Peter Cose Fatio, by his attorney, George Murray, presented his memorial to this board, praying confirmation of title to five hundred acres of land, lying on the river Guana, with a certified copy of royal title to memorialist, made by Governor Estrada, and dated the 12th of October, 1815; which are ordered to be filed.

Thomas Forbes, by George Murray, attorney for William Travers, agent for said Forbes, presented his memorial to this board, praying confirmation of title to five hundred acres of land, lying on the lower part of Cedar Swamp, near the river St. John's, with a certified copy of a British grant made by Governor Tonyn, and dated 16th of June, 1782, with a plat and certificate thereof appendant to said copy; which are ordered to be filed.

William Panton, by his attorney, George Murray, presented his memorial to this board, praying confirmation of title to five hundred acres of land, lying on the landing of Cedar Swamp, bounded on the southwest by lands of Peter Edwards and vacant lands, and on all other sides by vacant lands, with a certified copy of a British grant made by Governor Tonyn, dated the 9th of September, 1782, with a plat and certificate thereof appendant to said copy; which are ordered to be filed.

Juan Blas Entralgo, by his attorney, George Murray, presented his memorial to this board for twenty thousand acres of land, lying at Chachala, in the district of Alachua, and forty-five miles west of St. John's river, with a certified copy of royal title made to George Clarke by Governor Coppinger, and dated 17th of December, 1817, marked A; a certified copy of conveyance from George Clarke to memorialist, dated 7th of February, 1820, marked B; and a plat and certificate of survey of two surveys, one of two thousand acres, the other of twenty thousand acres, made by Andres Burgevin; the first dated 10th of June, 1819, the last dated 2d of August, 1819, which are appendant to a concession of twenty-six thousand acres made to George J. F. Clarke by Governor Coppinger, and dated 17th of December, 1817; which are ordered to be filed.

James Smith's representatives, by Archibald Clarke, their attorney, presented their memorial to this board, praying confirmation of title to two hundred and fifty acres of land, lying between the river Little St. Mary's and head of Nassau river, with a certified copy of concession to Henry Giebel, made by Governor White, and dated the 17th of March, 1806, with a certificate of the Government secretary *pro tem.* of an exchange of lands by the said Henry Giebel, and a conveyance from said Henry Giebel to John Thorp; which are ordered to be filed.

John K. S. Holzendorf, on behalf of his wife, late, &c., by Archibald Clarke, his attorney, presented his memorial to this board, praying confirmation of title to four hundred acres of land, lying on Graham's swamp, (Matanzas river,) with a certified copy of concession by Governor White to Valentine Fitzpatrick, dated 27th of July, 1803; which are ordered to be filed.

Sarah Waterman, on behalf of herself and the other heirs of Eleazer Waterman, deceased, by Archibald Clarke, her attorney, presented her memorial to this board, praying confirmation of title to two hundred and sixty acres of land, lying on Mills's swamp, in Duval county, with a certified copy of concession to Eleazer Waterman, made by Governor Coppinger, and dated the 18th of March, 1816; also a plat and certificate of survey made by George J. F. Clarke, and dated 9th of April, 1821.

Augustin Buyck, by John B. Strong, his attorney, presented his memorial to this board for fifty thousand acres of land, lying on the north and south of the Mosquitos, and has not been surveyed, with a certified copy of concession for same amount to memorialist, made by Governor White, and dated 29th of July, 1802, and a receipt of Bernardo Segui for taxes, dated 12th of October, 1803; which are ordered to be filed.

Gideon Dupont's heirs, by John B. Strong, their attorney, presented their memorial to this board, praying confirmation of title to four hundred and fifty acres of land, lying at a place called Moultrie, and is about five miles south of the city of St. Augustine, on the Matanzas river, with a certified copy of concession to Antonio Uzina, made by Governor Zespedes, for thirty acres, dated 4th of May, 1787, and a confirmation thereof by Governor Quesada, dated 15th of November, 1792; memorial of Antonio Uzina and John Holzendorf to Spanish Governor, dated December 15, 1794, and decree of Governor Quesada thereon of same date; a certificate of the Government secretary, that John Holzendorf had leave to sell his lands on a place called Moultrie to Richard Ryan, dated 15th of April, 1796; a permission from Governor White to said Richard Ryan to sell to Gideon Dupont, dated 20th November, 1797; a conveyance from Richardson Ryan to Gideon Dupont of four hundred acres of land at Moultrie, dated 9th of December, 1797; which are ordered to be filed.

Bartolome de Castro y Ferrer presented his memorial to this board, praying confirmation of title to two thousand two hundred and sixty-six and two-thirds acres of land, at San Pablo, on a creek by the same name, near the mouth of the river St. John's, about forty miles to the north of St. Augustine, with a royal title made to John McQueen by Governor White, dated February 27, 1804; a certified copy of conveyance from said McQueen to memorialist, dated 9th of February, 1809, marked exhibit B; and a plat and certificate of survey made by Pedro Marrot for said McQueen, dated February 3, 1792, marked A; which are ordered to be filed.

Francis P. Fatio presented his memorial to this board, praying confirmation of title to ten thousand acres of land, lying on the east side of the river St. John's, about sixty miles from its mouth, and thirty miles from the city of St. Augustine, with a plat and certificate of survey made by Pedro Marrot, and dated November 25, 1791, and marked A. This is a British grant, and the grant is lost; which are ordered to be filed.

Roque Leonardy's heirs presented their memorial to this board, praying confirmation of title to one thousand four hundred acres of land, lying on the west side of the North river, twelve miles north of the city of St. Augustine, with a plat and certificate of survey made by Andrew Burgevin, dated 28th of April, 1819, marked exhibit A; a royal title to memorialists, by Governor Coppinger, dated 25th of May, 1821; which are ordered to be filed.

Francis Ferreira presented his memorial to this board, praying confirmation of title to an island known by the name of Bacas, and four small islands adjoining, situated to the south of Cape Florida, and known as one of the Florida Keys, with a concession to memorialist, made by Governor Kindelan, and dated the 5th of January, 1814; which are ordered to be filed.

The board then adjourned until Thursday, the 20th instant, at 4 o'clock in the evening.

THURSDAY, *November* 20, 1823.

The board met pursuant to adjournment. Present, the Hons. David Floyd and William W. Blair.

Edgar Macon, Esq., United States' attorney for the district of East Florida, attended the board this day, under their order.

Michael Lynch presented his memorial to this board, praying confirmation of title to three hundred and thirty-five acres of land, lying between Halifax river and Tomoke creek, to the west and south-west of lands now or late belonging to Henry Yonge, and west of the canal on which was formerly a sugar plantation, with a certified copy of concession to memorialist, made by Governor White, and dated 22d of June, 1805, marked M. L.; which are ordered to be filed.

Andrew Atkinson presented his memorial to this board, praying confirmation of title to one hundred acres of land, lying on St. John's river, with a certified copy of concession for a piece of land, made to memorialist by Governor Quesada, and dated 4th of February, 1792, marked W. A.; which are ordered to be filed.

Hibberson and Yonge presented their memorial to this board, praying confirmation of title to two thousand acres of land, lying in two tracts of one thousand acres each, on Front creek swamp, with two plats and certificates of survey, made by George J. F. Clarke, and dated 24th of June, 1821, and 21st of March, 1816, marked H. Y.; and a certified copy of concession to memorialist, made by Governor Kindelan, and dated 23d of February, 1815, marked H. Y.; and memorial and order of survey, dated 20th of June, 1821; which are ordered to be filed.

Thomas Yonge presented his memorial to this board, praying confirmation of title to one thousand one hundred acres of land, lying at Mosquito, and known by the name of Bisset's plantation, with a certified copy of royal title to Isaac Wilks, by Governor Coppinger, and dated 31st of March, 1818, and marked W; which are ordered to be filed.

George Atkinson presented his memorial to this board, praying confirmation of title to seventy-five acres of land, lying on the south side of the river St. John's, at a place known by the name of Springfield, with a certified copy of concession made to John Strain by Governor White, dated 17th April, 1806, marked S, and assignment thereof to George Atkinson, dated 7th of May, 1806; which are ordered to be filed.

Hannah Nobles presented her memorial to this board, praying confirmation of a title to one thousand acres of land, lying in Twelve-mile swamp, about four miles from the lake or pond of St. Mark's, on the west, with a certified copy of concession made to Robert Cowan by Governor White, and dated 3d of July, 1799, marked H; which are ordered to be filed.

Hannah Nobles presented her memorial to this board, praying confirmation of title to one hundred acres of land, lying on Wills's swamp, on the south side of the river St. John's, with a certified copy of royal title made to memorialist by Governor Coppinger, dated the 26th of March, 1819, marked G; which are ordered to be filed.

Hannah Nobles presented her memorial to this board, praying confirmation of title to two hundred and eight acres of land, lying on St. John's river, with a certified copy of plat and certificate of survey made by Pedro Marrot, dated 20th of December, 1791, marked P; and a certified copy of royal title made to Robert Cowan by Governor Kindelan, dated 24th of April, 1815, and marked L; which are ordered to be filed.

Zephaniah C. Gibbs presented his memorial to this board, praying confirmation of title to one hundred and twenty-one acres of land, more or less, on the head of Guana river, to the west, on the St. Diego plains, with a plat and certificate of survey made by Roberto McHardy, dated 12th of September, 1818; and a certified copy of royal title in favor of Francisco X. Sanchez, made by Governor White, and dated 12th of February, 1811, marked Z; which are ordered to be filed.

Mary Dewees presented her memorial to this board, praying confirmation of title to five hundred acres of land, lying on the south side of the St. John's river, with a certified copy of a royal title in favor of the heirs of Roberto Clarke Maxey, made by Governor Coppinger, and dated 18th of May, 1821, and transfer to Mary Dewees by Peter Maxey, dated 1st February, 1822; which are ordered to be filed.

John G. Rushing presented his memorial to this board, praying confirmation of title to eighty acres of land, lying on the north side of St. John's river, on Clapboard creek, with a plat and certificate of survey made by George J. F. Clarke, dated 8th of February, 1817, marked C; which are ordered to be filed.

John G. Rushing presented his memorial to this board, praying confirmation of title to one hundred and twenty-five acres of land, lying on the north side of the river St. John's, with a plat and certificate of survey made by George J. F. Clarke, dated 1st of February, 1818, marked B, and a certified copy of concession made by Governor Estrada, for two hundred and five acres, dated 27th of November, 1815, marked A; which are ordered to be filed.

Jesse Newton presented his memorial to this board, praying confirmation of title to three hundred and fifty acres of land, lying on the south side of St. Mary's river, on Live-oak landing, with a plat and certificate of survey, made for said Newton by George J. F. Clarke, dated the 27th of November, 1817; which are ordered to be filed.

Joseph Haddock presented his memorial to this board, praying confirmation of title to two hundred and fifty acres of land, lying in Cabbage swamp, on the river St. Mary's, with a plat and certificate of survey, made for memorialist by George J. F. Clarke, dated 20th November, 1817; which are ordered to be filed.

Ezekiel Haddock presented his memorial to this board, praying confirmation of title to one hundred and fifty acres of land, lying in Cabbage swamp, on the river St. Mary's, with a plat and certificate of survey, made for memorialist by George J. F. Clarke, dated 20th November, 1817, and marked A; which are ordered to be filed.

Zachariah Haddock presented his memorial to this board, praying confirmation of title to two hundred acres of land, lying on the river St. Mary's, at a place formerly occupied by John Raine, near Will's swamp, with a plat and certificate of survey, made by George J. F. Clarke, dated 20th of February, 1816, marked A; and a certified copy of concession, made by Governor White, dated 24th of September, 1803, marked B; which are ordered to be filed.

Francis P. Fatio presented his memorial to this board, praying confirmation of title to one thousand acres of land, lying on the east side of St. John's river, at a place known by the name of Beresford; which is ordered to be filed.

José Alvarez presented his memorial to this board, praying confirmation of title to three hundred and fifty-five acres of land, lying at a place known by the name of Thomas's swamp, near Nassau river, with a plat and certificate of survey, made by George J. F. Clarke, dated 2d of February, 1817, marked A; a royal title, made by Governor Coppinger, dated 9th of September, 1816, marked B; and a certified copy of concession, of same date, marked C; which are ordered to be filed.

Francisco Barbe presented his memorial to this board, praying confirmation of title to five hundred acres of land, lying on the head of the river Nassau, on Cedar creek, at a place called Thomas's swamp, with a plat and certificate of survey, made by George J. F. Clarke, dated the 8th of February, 1817, marked A; a certified copy of royal title, made to memorialist by Governor Coppinger, dated the 27th of March, 1819, marked B; and a certified copy of concession to memorialist, dated 10th of April, 1817, marked C; which are ordered to be filed.

Joseph Sanchez's heirs presented their memorial to this board, praying confirmation of title to twelve acres of land, lying at the end of fifteen hundred varras or Spanish yards north of St. Augustine, with a plat and certified copy of royal title to the widow and heirs of Joseph Sanchez, deceased, made by Governor Coppinger, dated the 10th of June, 1818; which are ordered to be filed.

William Hobkirk presented his memorial to this board, praying confirmation of title to three hundred and fifty acres of land, lying on Bell's creek, with a certified copy of a royal title to memorialist, made by Governor Coppinger, dated 24th September, 1816, marked A; which are ordered to be filed.

William Hobkirk presented his memorial to this board, praying confirmation of title to a town lot in Fernandina, numbered square 18, and lots 3 and 4, with a certified copy of a royal title to memorialist, made by Governor Coppinger, dated 13th January, 1816, marked A; which are ordered to be filed.

William Hobkirk presented his memorial to this board, praying confirmation of title to three hundred and twenty-five acres of land, lying on the St. Mary's river, in East Florida, with a certified copy of a royal title to memorialist, made by Governor Coppinger, dated 24th of September, 1816; which are ordered to be filed.

Michael Crosby's heirs presented their memorial to this board, praying confirmation of title to two thousand acres of land, lying at Mount Tucker, on the west side of the river St. John's, with a plat and certificate of survey, made by George J. F. Clarke, dated 12th of April, 1818, and marked A; a certified copy of a royal title to Michael Crosby, made by Governor Coppinger, and dated 2d of March, 1813, marked B; which are ordered to be filed.

Michael Crosby's heirs presented their memorial to this board, praying confirmation of title to five hundred acres of land, lying at Mount Tucker, on the east side of the river St. John's, with a plat and certificate of survey, made by George J. F. Clarke, dated 10th of April, 1818, marked A; and a certified copy of a royal title made to memorialist, dated 2d of March, 1818, made by Governor Coppinger; which are ordered to be filed.

James Riz presented his memorial to this board, praying confirmation of title to five hundred acres of land, lying in a tract of four thousand acres, with a conveyance from Joseph R. Rattenbury to memorialist, dated 24th of August, 1820; and a certified copy of naturalization of said Riz, marked A; and a passport of Governor Coppinger to said Riz, marked B; and a confirmation of the attorney of the executors of James Alexander, deceased, marked C; which are ordered to be filed.

Zephaniah Kingsley presented his memorial to this board, praying confirmation of title to two thousand five hundred and sixty acres of land, lying between the creeks called Boggy swamp and Clapboard creek, adjoining to lands on the south of Charles Seton and Tilano Edwards, with a concession for sixteen thousand acres, made to memorialist, by Governor Coppinger, dated 2d December, 1816, and marked S; also, a plat and certificate of survey of two thousand five hundred and sixty acres, made by George J. F. Clarke, and dated the 27th of March, 1818, marked V; which are ordered to be filed.

Zephaniah Kingsley presented his memorial to this board, praying confirmation of title to two thousand five hundred and sixty acres of land, lying on the west side of the Twelve-mile swamp, with a plat and certificate of survey, made by George J. F. Clarke, and dated 2d of April, 1818, marked R; which are ordered to be filed.

Zephaniah Kingsley presented his memorial to this board, praying confirmation of title to ten thousand eight hundred and eighty acres of land, lying on the north side of St. John's river, and north and west of Doctor's lake with a plat and certificate of survey, made by George J. F. Clarke, and dated the 8th of February, 1821, marked T; which are ordered to be filed.

Zephaniah Kingsley presented his memorial to this board, praying confirmation of title to fifty acres of land, lying on St. John's bluff, on the south side of the said river, with a plat and certificate of survey, made by George J. F. Clarke, dated 15th of April, 1817, marked M; and a conveyance from Francisco Estacholy to memorialist, dated 27th of March, 1817, marked N; also, a certified copy of a royal title to said Francisco Estacholy, made by Governor Coppinger, and dated 15th of March, 1817, marked O; which are ordered to be filed.

Zephaniah Kingsley presented his memorial to this board, praying confirmation of title to one hundred acres of land, lying on the south side of St. John's river, at a place commonly called St. John's bluff, with a plat and certificate of survey, made by George J. F. Clarke, dated the 15th of April, 1817, marked A; conveyance from Manuel Castilla, agent of Isabel Rodriguez, widow of Manuel Romero, dated 27th of March, 1817, to memorialist, marked B; also, a memorial of said Kingsley to the Spanish Government, and answer thereto, relating to a claim of Antonio Suarez for part of said land, marked No. 2; a certified copy of royal title to the widow and heirs of Manuel Romero, made by Governor Coppinger, and dated 7th of March, 1817; which are ordered to be filed.

Zephaniah Kingsley presented his memorial to this board, praying confirmation of title to three hundred acres of land, lying on Doctor's creek, on the river St. John's, called *Fuento del Alamo*, with a plat and certificate of survey, made by Pedro Marrot, dated 30th November, 1791, marked E; a conveyance from Isabel Kane, widow of William Kane, dated 1st of September, 1809, marked F; a power of attorney from Elizabeth, Margaret, and Anna Kane, daughters of William Kane, to Isabel Kane, their mother, to sell said land, dated 1st of September, 1809; a certified copy of royal title to William Kane for said land, made by Governor White, dated 19th of August, 1809; a bond from Elizabeth Kane to Timothy Hollingsworth, dated 5th of February, 1806, and a relinquishment from said Hollingsworth to Zephaniah Kingsley, dated 18th of January, 1807; which are ordered to be filed.

Zephaniah Kingsley presented his memorial to this board, praying confirmation of title to five hundred acres of land, lying on the south side of St. Mary's river, which it parts, fronts to the north, with a plat and certificate of survey, made by George J. F. Clarke, dated 10th of January, 1816, and marked M; a certified copy of royal title to the widow and heirs of Burrows Higginbottom, made by Governor Coppinger, and dated 16th of April, 1819, marked E; a conveyance from Isabella Higginbottom to Zephaniah Kingsley, dated the 30th of January, 1822; a power of attorney to Isabella Higginbottom from Elijah, Joseph, David, and Thomas Higginbottom, children of Burrows Higginbottom, deceased, to sell said lands, dated the 8th of February, 1820; and a bond of indemnity from Isabella Higginbottom and James Crosier to Zephaniah Kingsley, dated 30th January, 1822; which are ordered to be filed.

Zephaniah Kingsley presented his memorial to this board, praying confirmation of title to one thousand acres of land, lying on the St. Mary's river, on the south side thereof, with a plat and certificate of survey made by George J. F. Clarke, dated the — day of ——; also, a certified copy of royal title, made to memorialist by Governor Estrada, and dated the 22d of December, 1815, marked I; which are ordered to be filed.

Zephaniah Kingsley presented his memorial to this board, praying confirmation of title to three hundred acres of land, lying on Spanish river, a branch of St. Mary's river, and White Oak creek, with a conveyance from James Martinelly to memorialist, dated 13th of May, 1818; and a receipt of Pedro Miranda, for payment of a tract of land of three hundred acres, purchased by Z. Kingsley, and dated 3d of April, 1818; which are ordered to be filed.

Zephaniah Kingsley presented his memorial to this board, praying confirmation of title to a lot in the town of Fernandina, with a certified copy of royal title, made to memorialist by Governor Estrada, and dated the 7th of July, 1815, and marked A; which are ordered to be filed.

Zephaniah Kingsley presented his memorial to this board, praying confirmation of title to two thousand acres of land, lying in Twelve-mile Swamp, with a plat of survey, marked G., and a certified copy of royal title to memorialist, made by Governor Coppinger, and dated the 18th of January, 1816; which are ordered to be filed.

Zephaniah Kingsley presented his memorial to this board, praying confirmation of title to three hundred acres of land, lying at the head of Saw-mill creek, with a plat of survey, marked H; and a certified copy of royal title in favor of memorialist, made by Governor Coppinger, and dated the 18th of January, 1816, and marked H; which are ordered to be filed.

Zephaniah Kingsley presented his memorial to this board, praying confirmation of title to two thousand acres of land, lying on the island called Drayton island, at the entrance of lake George, with a certified copy of royal title in favor of memorialist for one thousand five hundred acres, made by Governor Kindelan, and dated the 7th of January, 1815, marked K; which are ordered to be filed.

Zephaniah Kingsley presented his memorial to this board, praying confirmation of title to five hundred and sixty-five acres of land, lying on the east side of St. John's river, being half of eleven hundred and thirty acres, with a certified copy of conveyance from Francisco Roman Sanchez to memorialist, dated the 16th March, 1819, marked A; which are ordered to be filed.

Zephaniah Kingsley presented his memorial to this board, praying confirmation of title to one hundred and fifty acres of land, lying on the west side of the river St. John's, opposite the mouth of Dunn's creek, known by the name of Orange Grove, in the swamp, with a bond for conveyance from William Hartley, made by Governor Coppinger, dated 13th of December, 1817, marked B; also, a plat and certificate of survey made for said Hartley by Andres Burgevin, and dated the 10th of April, 1818, and marked C; which are ordered to be filed.

Zephaniah Kingsley presented his memorial to this board, praying confirmation of title to seven hundred and thirteen acres of land, lying on the northeast side of the river St. John's, at its mouth, being the whole of an island called Fort George, with a certified copy of conveyance by George J. F. Clarke, agent of John H. McIntosh, to memorialist, with appendant documents; which are ordered to be filed.

The board then adjourned until Monday next, the 24th instant, at 4 o'clock, P. M.

MONDAY, *November* 24, 1823.

The board met according to adjournment. Present, all the members.

Susannah Cashen presented her memorial to this board, praying confirmation of title to one thousand and fifty acres of land, lying on St. Mary's river, at a place known by the name of Cabbage swamp, with a certified copy of royal title made to James Cashen by Governor Coppinger, and dated the 23d of February, 1816; also, a plat and certificate of survey made for James Cashen by George J. F. Clarke; which are ordered to be filed.

Susannah Cashen presented her memorial to this board, praying confirmation of title to five hundred acres of land, situated on the west side of the river St. John's, at a place known by the name of Hawk's or Fleming island, with a certified copy of plat and certificate of survey made for James Cashen by Andres Burgevin, and dated the 15th of June, 1821; also, a certified copy of royal title made to James Cashen by Governor Coppinger, and dated the 12th of February, 1821; which are ordered to be filed.

Susannah Cashen presented her memorial to this board, praying confirmation of title to two hundred and fifty acres of land, lying on Amelia island, near the lands formerly granted to her late husband by the Spanish Government, with a plat and certificate of survey made for James Cashen by Juan Purcell, dated the 30th of November, 1807, and marked No. 2; also, a conditional concession, made to James Cashen by Governor White, dated the 7th of October, 1805, and marked No. 2; which are ordered to be filed.

Susannah Cashen presented her memorial to this board, praying confirmation of title to two hundred and thirty acres of land, lying on the banks of the river St. Mary's, at a place known by the name of Old Township, with a conveyance from Joseph Reed and Nancy Reed to Moses Harral, dated 5th of February, 1811, and marked A; and conveyance from Moses Harral to James Cashen, dated the 12th of November, 1811, and marked B; also, a certified copy of concession made to José Reed by Governor White, dated 13th of July, 1804; which are ordered to be filed.

Susannah Cashen presented her memorial to this board, praying confirmation of title to seven hundred acres of land, situated on the west side of Amelia island, at a place known by the name of Plum Orchard, with a certified copy of a plat and certificate of survey made for James Cashen by Andres Burgevin, dated the 12th of July, 1820, and marked No. 1; also, a certified copy of royal title made to James Cashen by Governor Kindelan, dated the 11th of June, 1824, and marked C; which are ordered to be filed.

Susannah Cashen presented her memorial to this board, praying confirmation of title to one hundred acres of land, lying on Amelia island, on Beach creek, with a certified copy of concession made to Juan D. Kerr, and dated the 29th of July, 1801; which are ordered to be filed.

Susannah Cashen, on behalf of the orphan children of Samuel Meers, deceased, presented her memorial to this board, praying confirmation of title to two hundred acres of land, situated on Tyger island, in East Florida, with a certified copy of royal title made to the widow and heirs of the said Samuel Meers, deceased, by Governor Estrada, dated the 17th of October, 1811, and marked M; which are ordered to be filed.

Susannah Cashen presented her memorial to this board, praying confirmation of title to one hundred acres of land, lying on Amelia island, at a place called Red bay, at the head of Beach creek, between the sand hills and the pine barren, with a certified copy of concession made to Solomon Miller by Governor White, and dated the 26th of June, 1802; also, a conveyance from said Miller to James Cashen, dated the 24th of February, 1804, and marked C; which are ordered to be filed.

Domingo Acosta, by his attorney, B. Segui, presented his memorial to this board, praying confirmation of title to six hundred and ninety-five acres of land, lying in three surveys, as follows: two hundred and fifty acres on the east side of St. John's river, at a place called Mount Tucker; two hundred and fifty acres on the east side of lake George; and one hundred and ninety-five acres on the east side of the river St. John's, at the first point above a place called Mount Royal, with a plat and certificate of survey of each, made for memorialist by George J. F. Clarke, dated the 1st of June and 10th of April, 1821, and 30th of May, 1820, and marked A, B, C; also, a certified copy of royal title, made to the memorialist by Governor Coppinger, dated the 20th of March, 1817, and marked E; which are ordered to be filed.

Eleanor Pritchard presented her memorial to this board, praying confirmation of title to two hundred and seventy acres of land, lying on the east side of the river St. John's, at a place called Beauclerk's Point; which is ordered to be filed.

Valentine Fitzpatrick's heirs, by their agent, James Hall, presented their memorial to this board for twenty-five acres of land, situated on Matanzas river, at a place known by the name of Sam's Hammock, about fifteen miles south of the city of St. Augustine; which is ordered to be filed.

Robert Pritchard's heirs, by their agent, James Hall, presented their memorial to this board, praying confirmation of title to two hundred and fifty acres of land, lying on the east side of the river St. John's, at a place called Goodby's lake, with a certified copy of plat and certificate of survey, made for Thomas Bowden by Pedro Marrot, and dated the 19th of December, 1791; which are ordered to be filed.

Robert Pritchard's heirs, by their agent, James Hall, presented their memorial to this board, praying confirmation of title to sixteen thousand acres of land lying on Julington creek, which empties into the river St. John's, on the east side, with a plat and certificate of survey made for Robert Pritchard by George J. F. Clarke, dated the 20th of July, 1819, and marked Z; and a certified copy of concession made to Robert Pritchard by Governor White, dated the 10th of October, 1803, and conditional confirmation by Governor Coppinger to the heirs of said Robert Pritchard, dated the 5th of June, 1818, and marked A; which are ordered to be filed.

Juana Pareds presented her memorial to this board, praying confirmation of title to sixty-nine acres of land, lying on the North river, at a place known by the name of Alligator Point, with a plat of survey made for memorialist by Andres Burgevin, dated the 3d of April, 1819, and marked A; also a certified copy of royal title made to memorialist by Governor Coppinger, dated the 17th of April, 1809, and marked B.

Francis de Medicis, agent for Mariano Fontan, presented his memorial to this board, praying confirmation of title to twenty-six acres of land, lying at the point of the river Juanes, on the east side of the North river, with a certified copy of concession made to Mariano Fontan by Governor White, dated the 29th of January, 1808, and marked F; also a general power of attorney from Mariano Fontan and Clara Salom to memorialist, dated the 10th of January, 1810, and marked S; which are ordered to be filed.

Antonio Pons's widow and heirs, by their agent, Richard Murray, presented their memorial to this board, praying confirmation of title to one hundred and seventy-five acres of land, situated at the mouth of the river Halifax, to the southward of St. Augustine, with a plat and certificate of survey made for Antonio Pons by Robert McHardy, dated the 20th of May, 1819, and marked P; also a certified copy of royal title made to the widow and heirs of Antonio Pons, deceased, by Governor Coppinger, dated the 27th of May, 1819, and marked B; which are ordered to be filed.

John Herault presented his memorial to this board, praying confirmation of title to one hundred and forty-five acres of land, situated about seven miles north of St. Augustine, on Red-house branch creek, with a plat and certificate of survey made for memorialist by George J. F. Clarke, and dated 20th of April, 1818, marked F; also a certified copy of concession made to memorialist by Governor White, dated the 25th of September, 1806, and marked I, A; which are ordered to be filed.

Patrick Lynch presented his memorial to this board, praying confirmation of title to one thousand one hundred acres of land, lying near Tomoca, between the Haul-over and Smith creeks, with a certified copy of a royal title made to memorialist by Governor Coppinger, and dated the 10th ———, 1818; which are ordered to be filed.

Mary Kunen presented her memorial to this board, praying confirmation of title to two hundred acres of land near Tomoca, one-half on each side of Smith creek, with a certified copy of royal title made to memorialist by Governor Coppinger, and dated the 10th of June, 1818; also a plat and certificate of survey made for memorialist by Robert McHardy, and dated the 20th of April, 1818; which are ordered to be filed.

Nicolas Rodriguez presented his memorial to this board, praying confirmation of title to one hundred acres of land, lying on St. Anastasia island, with a certificate by the notary of the Government, stating that memorialist came into possession of said lands as one of the heirs of his deceased father, Lorenzo Rodriguez, and dated the 26th of February, 1817; also a certified copy of royal title to Lorenzo Rodriguez, by Governor White, dated the 9th of January, 1805; which are ordered to be filed.

Stephen M. Ingersol presented his memorial to this board, praying confirmation of title to one hundred acres of land, lying in the Twelve-mile swamp, at a place formerly occupied and cultivated by Lewis Schofield, with a concession to Lewis Schofield by Governor White, dated the 13th of March, 1799; and a conveyance from said Schofield and Susannah, his wife, to memorialist, dated the 29th of March, 1819; which are ordered to be filed.

Estevan Cheves presented his memorial to this board, praying confirmation of title to two hundred acres of land, lying on the river Matanzas, and known by the name of Tom Johnson, with a certified copy of concession in favor of memorialist, by Governor White, and dated the 14th of November, 1797; which are ordered to be filed.

Stephen M. Ingersol presented his memorial to this board, praying confirmation of title to one hundred acres of land, lying north of St. Augustine, and joining lands of Manuel Marcial and Barbara Hainsman, with a certified copy of concession made in favor of Lewis Schofield, dated the 16th of June, 1796, by Governor White; which are ordered to be filed.

William Pengree's heirs, by their agent, Julius Alford, presented their memorial to this board, praying confirmation of title to one thousand acres of land, lying near the head of the creek called Nepomuceno, and near Doctor's lake, with a certified copy of concession made in favor of William Pengree, by Governor Quesada, and dated the 29th of January, 1793, marked P.

Rebecca Pengree's heirs, by their agent, Julius Alford, presented their memorial to this board, praying for confirmation of title to five hundred acres of land, lying adjoining the said Rebecca Pengree's plantation, on the river St. John's, formerly owned by Mrs. Jones, with a certified copy of concession made to Rebecca Pengree by Governor White, dated the 9th of May, 1798, and marked 4; which are ordered to be filed.

George F. and Oliver Palmes presented their memorial to this board, praying confirmation of title to nine hundred and ninety-nine and three-fourths acres of land, lying at a place called Turnbull, on both sides of Spruce creek, in the territory of Mosquitos, with a certified copy of conveyance from Robert McHardy to Paul Dupon of said lands, and dated the 2d of June, 1818; which are ordered to be filed.

George F. and Oliver Palmes presented their memorial to this board, praying confirmation of title to two hundred and forty-five acres of land, lying on San Diego plains, with a plat and certificate of survey made for Joseph Delespine by Robert McHardy, dated the 12th of September, 1816, and marked A; a certified copy of conveyance from Joseph Walles to Paul Dupon, dated the 27th of May, 1818; and a conveyance from Paul Dupon to memorialists, dated the 1st of April, 1819; which are ordered to be filed.

George Fleming's heirs, by Sophia Fleming, his widow and relict, presented their memorial to this board, praying confirmation of title to one thousand acres of land, lying on the west side of the river St. John's, on an island known by the name of Fleming's island, with a plat and certificate of survey made for George Fleming by Andres Burgevin, dated the 16th of November, 1818, and marked A; also a certified copy of royal title made in favor of George Fleming by Governor Coppinger, dated the 8th of March, 1816, and marked F; which are ordered to be filed.

George Fleming's heirs, by Sophia Fleming, his widow and relict, presented their memorial to this board, praying confirmation of title to twenty thousand acres of land, lying on Indian river, at the mouth of St. Sebastian creek, with a plat and certificate of survey made for George Fleming by Andres Burgevin, dated 3d of February, 1820; which are ordered to be filed.

George Fleming's heirs, by his widow and relict, Sophia Fleming, presented their memorial to this board, praying confirmation of title to nine hundred and eighty acres of land, situated in two tracts, one on the west side of the river St. John's, at a place called Langley Bryan; the other lies in Coco swamp, about one mile west of Buena Vista fort: the first contains seven hundred and eighty acres, the other two hundred acres, with a plat and certificate of survey of the first made for George Fleming, dated the 2d of December, 1818, marked D; also a plat and certificate of the second survey made for said Fleming, dated 16th November, 1818, marked E; which plats and certificates were made by Andres Burgevin; also certified copy of royal title made in favor of George Fleming by Governor Coppinger, dated the 5th of April, 1816, and marked G. F.

George Fleming's heirs, by his widow and relict, Sophia Fleming, presented their memorial to this board, praying confirmation of title to a lot of ground, lying in Fernandina, designed as lot No. 7, in square No. 7, with a concession made in favor of George Fleming by Governor Estrada, dated the 2d of May, 1811, marked B; which are ordered to be filed.

Gabriel W. Perpall presented his memorial to this board, praying confirmation of title to six hundred and sixty acres of land, lying at a place called the Big Hammock, about forty miles west of Buena Vista, and on the west side of the river St. John's, with a plat and certificate made for memorialist by Andres Burgevin, dated the 9th of September, 1819; also a certified copy of royal title made in favor of memorialist by Governor Coppinger, dated the 12th of January, 1818; which are ordered to be filed.

Gabriel W. Perpall presented his memorial to this board, praying confirmation of title to thirteen hundred and forty acres of land, lying on the west side of the river St. John's, opposite a place called Rowlestown, with a plat and certificate made for memorialist by George J. F. Clarke, dated the 15th of April, 1818; also a certified copy of royal title made in favor of memorialist by Governor Coppinger, and dated the 22d of February, 1817; which are ordered to be filed.

Gabriel W. Perpall presented his memorial to this board, praying confirmation of title to two hundred and eighty acres of land, situated at the head of Matanzas river, at a place called Sam's hammock, with a plat of the same; which are ordered to be filed.

Gabriel W. Perpall presented his memorial to this board, praying confirmation of title to five hundred acres of land, lying in Turnbull's swamp, about twelve miles north of St. Augustine, with a plat and certificate made for memorialist by Andres Burgevin, dated the 17th of August, 1818; also, certified copy of royal title made in favor of memorialist by Governor Coppinger, for seven hundred and eighty acres, and dated the 19th of June, 1818; which are ordered to be filed.

Gabriel W. Perpall presented his memorial to this board, praying confirmation of title to fifteen or more acres of land, lying at the Little Matanzas bar, known by the name of Barataria island, with a certified copy of conveyance made to memorialist by Joseph Hughes, and dated the 27th of January, 1818; which are ordered to be filed.

Gabriel W. Perpall presented his memorial to this board, praying confirmation of title to six hundred acres of land, lying at Matanzas bar, to the south of the Orange Grove, called Buen Retiro, with a plat of survey of seven hundred acres; also, a certified copy of conveyance from José Bonely to memorialist, dated 30th of December, 1803; and certified copy of concession in favor of said Bonely, by Governor White, dated the 16th of January, 1799, and (Buen Retiro, No. 2;) also a petition from memorialist to this board, dated August, 1823; which are ordered to be filed.

Gabriel W. Perpall presented his memorial to this board, praying confirmation of title to a small island containing about one acre, lying on the river opposite the Orange Grove of Buen Retiro, with a certified copy of royal title made in favor of memorialist by Governor Coppinger, dated the 15th of January, 1818; which are ordered to be filed.

Gabriel W. Perpall presented his memorial to this board, praying confirmation of title to three hundred and thirty-five acres of land, lying at a place called Trumbull, about twelve miles northwest of St. Augustine, with a plat and certificate of survey made for José Maria Bousquet by Andres Burgevin, dated the 13th of August, 1818; also, a certified copy of conveyance from said Bousquet to memorialist, dated the 20th of October, 1818; which are ordered to be filed.

Gabriel W. Perpall presented his memorial to this board, praying confirmation of title to six hundred and forty acres of land, lying on the river St. Sebastian, about one mile in a southwest direction from this city, with a certified copy of conveyance from Fernando de la Maza Arredondo, Sen., as agent and attorney of George Taylor, to memorialist, dated the 18th of March, 1809; which are ordered to be filed.

Gabriel W. Perpall presented his memorial to this board, praying confirmation of title to sixteen acres of land, about one mile north of St. Augustine, with a plat and certificate of survey made for Diego Carreras by Andres Burgevin, dated the 15th of February, 1819; also, a certified copy of royal title made in favor of Diego Carreras, by Governor Coppinger, dated the 10th of June, 1818, and a certified copy of conveyance from said Carreras, to memorialist, dated the 3d of April, 1819; which are ordered to be filed.

Gabriel W. Perpall presented his memorial to this board, praying confirmation of title to twenty acres of land, lying about one mile and a half to the north of the city of St. Augustine, and in front of the stockades, with a plat and certificate of survey made for the widow and heirs of José Sanchez, deceased, by Andres Burgevin, dated the 1st of March, 1820; also, a certified copy of royal title made in favor of the widow and heirs of said Sanchez by Governor Coppinger, dated the 10th of June, 1818; and a certified copy of conveyance from Christina Hill to memorialist, dated the 12th of June, 1820; which are ordered to be filed.

Gabriel W. Perpall presented his memorial to this board, praying confirmation of title to twenty-five acres of land, with a certified copy of concession made in favor of Pedro Triay by Governor White, dated the 30th of September, 1806; also, a receipt of Lucas Munoz to memorialist for twenty dollars, dated 20th of February, 1820; and also a receipt for the same amount from Pedro Triay, and dated the 13th of January, 1820; which are ordered to be filed.

Gabriel W. Perpall presented his memorial to this board, praying confirmation of title to five hundred and thirty-five acres of land, lying at the head of Matanzas river, and known by the name of Sam's hammock, with a plat of survey and certified copy of royal title made in favor of memorialist by Governor Kindelan, and dated 24th of May, 1815; which are ordered to be filed.

Gabriel W. Perpall presented his memorial to this board, praying confirmation of title to one hundred and fifty acres of land, lying on the river Halifax, opposite to Mount Oswold, with a certified copy of royal title made in favor of memorialist by Governor Kindelan, and dated the 23d of May 1815; which are ordered to be filed.

Gabriel W. Perpall presented his memorial to this board, praying confirmation of title to one hundred acres of land, lying at the Little Matanzas bar, joining Buen Retiro, and opposite the lands of Francis Pellicer, with a certified copy of concession, made in favor of John Daly by Governor White, dated the 15th of March, 1779; also, a conveyance from Maria Daly to memorialist, dated the 10th of June, 1808; which are ordered to be filed.

Pedro R. de Calas, executor of G. W. Perpall, presented his memorial to this board, praying confirmation of title to five hundred acres of land, lying in the Territory of the Mosquitos, adjoining the lands of Antoine Alvarez, on the south side, and on the west side of Hillsborough river, with memorial and order of survey dated the 3d of September, 1818, and plat and certificate of survey dated the 15th of September, 1815; also a certified copy of royal title made in favor of memorialist by Governor Coppinger, for services, dated the 27th of January, 1818; which are ordered to be filed.

Pedro R. de Calas, executor of G. W. Perpall, presented his memorial to this board, praying confirmation of title to two hundred acres of land, lying in San Diego swamp, at a place known by the name of Clarke's rice plantation, and on the south of the lands of the late Francis Sanchez, deceased, with a certified copy of concession made to Thomas Ellerby for head-rights, by Governor Quesada, dated the 20th of October, 1791; also a certified copy of concession for the same on account of the death of said Ellerby, and certain debts due to memorialist by Governor White, dated the 4th of August, 1803, and marked P. R.; which are ordered to be filed.

Elizabeth, widow of Samuel Burch, deceased, by her attorney, G. W. Perpall, presented her memorial to this board, praying confirmation of title to one hundred acres of land, lying on the river Halifax, near Pelican inlet, with a certified copy of concession made in favor of Samuel Burch, by Governor White, dated the 3d of June, 1806, and marked S. B.; which are ordered to be filed.

Lazaro Ortega, by his agent, G. W. Perpall, presented his memorial to this board, praying confirmation of title to eighty-eight acres of land, lying on the North river and Guana creek, which lands were transferred to him by Thomas Travers, with a plat and certificate of survey made for memorialist by Andrew Burgevin, dated the 30th of January, 1819, and marked L. O.; which are ordered to be filed.

Mariano Berta, by his attorney, G. W. Perpall, presented his memorial to this board, praying confirmation of title to one hundred and sixty-six and two-thirds acres of land, lying on Cartel Point neck, and on the north of lands belonging to Andrew Paceti, with a certified copy of plat and certificate of survey made by Andres Burgevin, dated the 27th of April, 1819; and a certified copy of conveyance from Andres Paceti to Manuel Fernandez Bendicho, dated the 29th of May, 1804; also, a certified copy of conveyance from Thomas Andrew to memorialist, dated the 15th of April, 1819; which are ordered to be filed.

Mariano Berta, by his attorney, G. W. Perpall, presented his memorial to this board, praying confirmation of title to two hundred acres of land, lying on Cartel Point neck, and adjoining lands belonging to memorialist, with a certified copy of plat and certificate of survey made by Andres Bergevin, dated the 27th of April, 1819; also, a certified copy of conveyance from Juan Capo to Manuel Fernandez Bendicho, dated the 14th of September, 1804; and certified copy of conveyance from Thomas Andrew to memorialist, dated the 15th of April, 1819; which are ordered to be filed.

John Frazer's executors presented their memorial to this board, praying confirmation of title to five hundred acres of land, lying on the St. Mary's river, about twelve miles from Amelia island; which are ordered to be filed.

Mary Dewees, by her attorney, George Gibbs, presented her memorial to this board, praying confirmation of title to two thousand six hundred and thirty-three acres and a third of land, lying on the south side of St. John's river, and on the east side of San Pablo creek, with a certified copy of royal title in favor of Catalina Chicken, widow of Andrew Dewees, of sixty-nine caballerias, made by Governor White, and dated 4th of May, 1804, marked D.; which are ordered to be filed.

George Atkinson, by his attorney, George Gibbs, presented his memorial to this board, praying confirmation of title to a lot of ground in the town of Fernandina, with a concession to George Clarke, made by Governor White, dated 31st January, 1811; a certificate of George J. F. Clarke, marked G. A.; which are ordered to be filed.

George Atkinson, by his attorney, George Gibbs, presented his memorial to this board, praying confirmation of title to a lot, No. 7, in the town of Fernandina, containing, front, fifty feet, and depth, one hundred feet, with a concession to memorialist made by Governor White, and dated the 12th of September, 1810; and a certificate of George J. F. Clarke, marked G. A.; which are ordered to be filed.

George Atkinson, by his attorney, George Gibbs, presented his memorial to this board, praying confirmation of title to a lot in the town of Fernandina, with a concession to Antonia Estephanopoly, made by Governor White, dated 27th February, 1811; and a certificate of Lopez attached thereto, and also certificate of George J. F. Clarke, marked G. A., 10; which are ordered to be filed.

George Atkinson presented his memorial to this board, praying confirmation of title to a lot in the town of Fernandina, with a concession from Juan Fernandez, made by Governor Estrada, and dated the 29th of April, 1811, and a certificate of Justo Lopez attached thereto, marked G. A.; which are ordered to be filed.

George Atkinson, by his attorney, George Gibbs, presented his memorial to this board, praying confirmation of title to a lot in the town of Fernandina, with a concession to Maria Mitchel, made by Governor White, and dated 14th of November, 1810, with a certificate of Justo Lopez, and a certificate of George J. F. Clarke, G. A., 6; which are ordered to be filed.

Hibberson and Young, by their attorney, George Gibbs, presented their memorial to this board, praying confirmation of title to a lot in the town of Fernandina, seventeen yards in front, and seventeen yards deep, with a certified copy of a royal title by Governor Kindelan, dated 31st January, 1814, marked X; which are ordered to be filed.

Hibberson and Young, by their attorney, George Gibbs, presented their memorial to this board, praying confirmation of title to a lot in the town of Fernandina, with a concession made to them by Governor Estrada, and dated 4th December, 1811, and a certificate of Justo Lopez attached thereto, marked U; which are ordered to be filed.

George Atkinson, by his attorney, George Gibbs, presented his memorial to this board, praying confirmation of title to a lot in the town of Fernandina, seventeen yards in front, and thirty-four yards deep, with a certified copy of royal title made to memorialist by Governor Kindelan, dated the 16th of August, 1814, marked G. A.; which are ordered to be filed.

Lindsey Todd's executors, by George Gibbs, their attorney in fact, presented their memorial to this board, praying confirmation of title to a lot in the town of Fernandina, seventeen yards in front, and thirty-four in depth, with a certified copy of a royal title to Lindsey Todd, made by Governor Kindelan, and dated the 7th of June, 1814, marked W; which are ordered to be filed.

Hibberson and Young, by their attorney, George Gibbs, presented their memorial to this board, praying confirmation of title to one and three-quarters acres of high land and two and a half acres of marsh, in the town of Fernandina, with a certified copy of royal title made to them by Governor Coppinger, dated the 1st of February, 1816, marked Z; which are ordered to be filed.

George Atkinson, by his attorney, George Gibbs, presented his memorial to this board, praying confirmation to a lot in the town of Fernandina, seventeen yards in front, and thirty yards deep, with a certified copy of royal title to memorialist, made by Governor Coppinger, dated the 7th of May, 1817, marked R; which are ordered to be filed.

George Atkinson, by his attorney, George Gibbs, presented his memorial to this board, praying confirmation of title to a lot in the town of Fernandina, seventeen yards in front, and thirty-four in depth, with a certified copy of royal title to memorialist, made by Governor Coppinger, dated the 7th of May, 1817, marked P; which are ordered to be filed.

Hibberson and Yonge, by their attorney, George Gibbs, presented their memorial to this board, praying confirmation of title to a lot in the town of Fernandina, consisting of thirty-four yards of marsh land, with a certified copy of royal title made to memorialists by Governor Coppinger, and dated the 1st of February, 1816, marked H; which are ordered to be filed.

Hibberson and Yonge, by their attorney, George Gibbs, presented their memorial to this board, praying confirmation of title to a lot in the town of Fernandina, consisting of thirty-four yards of marsh land, with a certified copy of royal title to memorialists, made by Governor Coppinger, dated 1st of February, 1816, marked Y; which are ordered to be filed.

Peter Miranda presented, by his attorney, Waters Smith, his memorial to this board, praying confirmation of title to two thousand acres of land, lying on the west of the river St. John's, at a place called Bernard, with a certified copy of royal title to memorialist by Governor Coppinger, and dated the 12th of December, 1817; which are ordered to be filed.

Peter Miranda, by Waters Smith, his attorney, presented his memorial to this board, praying confirmation of title to two thousand acres of land, lying on a creek or river called Big Spring, on the west of the river St. John's, about twenty-five miles south of lake George, with a certified copy of royal title to memorialist, made by Governor Coppinger, dated 11th of April, 1821, for services; which are ordered to be filed.

James Arnau, by his attorney, Waters Smith, presented his memorial to this board, praying confirmation of title to one hundred and twenty-five acres of land, lying on the North river, nineteen miles from St. Augustine, with a certified copy of concession to memorialist, made by Governor White, and dated 13th of April, 1807, marked A; memorial and order of survey dated 15th of June, 1818, marked B; and a plat and certificate of survey made by Andres Burgevin, and dated 30th of June, 1818, marked C; which are ordered to be filed.

Clara Pretos Arnau, by her attorney, Waters Smith, presented her memorial to this board, praying confirmation of title to one hundred and seventy-five acres of land, lying on the North river, about nineteen miles from St. Augustine, on the south side of Roque Leonardy's lands, with a certified copy of concession to Francisco Arnau, made by Governor White, and dated the 24th of April, 1807, marked A; a memorial and order of survey dated

15th of April, 1818, marked B; and plat and certificate of survey made by Andres Burgevin, dated April 1, 1819, marked C; which are ordered to be filed.

Henry Eckford, by his attorney, George Murray, presented his memorial to this board, praying confirmation o title to forty-six thousand and eighty acres of land, lying on the waters of Hillsborough bay, with a deed of conveyance from Joseph Delespine and Philo Andrews, attorneys in fact of Pedro Miranda, dated the 13th of November, 1823, marked A; which are ordered to be filed.

Alexander M. Muir et al., by their attorney, George Murray, presented their memorial to this board, praying confirmation of title to thirty thousand seven hundred and twenty acres of land, lying in the district of Alachua, and is an undivided part of a grant of two hundred eighty-nine thousand six hundred and forty-five English acres and five-sevenths of an acre, made to F. M. Arredondo and José M. Arredondo, with a conveyance from grantees to memorialist, dated 30th of October, 1823; which are ordered to be filed.

Thomas Forbes's heirs, by their agent, William Travers, presented their memorial to this board, praying confirmation of title to five hundred acres of land, lying on the west side of the river St. John's, on lake George, near the springs, with a plat and certificate of survey made by Benjamin Lord, and dated 26th of November, 1799, marked B; also, a British grant made to Thomas Forbes, by Governor Tonyn, and dated 3d of February, 1780, marked A; which are ordered to be filed.

Thomas Forbes's heirs, by their agent, William Travers, presented their memorial to this board, praying confirmation of title to five hundred acres of land, lying on the west side of the river St. John's, on lake George, with a plat and certificate of survey made by Benjamin Lord, and dated 23d of November, 1799, marked B; and a copy of a British grant made to Thomas Forbes by Governor Tonyn, dated 3d of February, 1780, marked A; which are ordered to be filed.

Thomas Forbes's heirs, by their agent, William Travers, presented their memorial to this board, praying confirmation of title to five hundred acres of land, lying on Cedar swamp, on the west side of St. John's river, with a plat and certificate of survey made by Benjamin Lord, dated 5th of October, 1780, marked B; and a copy of a British grant made to Thomas Forbes by Governor Tonyn, dated 15th of February, 1781, marked A; which are ordered to be filed.

William Panton's representatives, by their agent, William Travers, presented their memorial, praying confirmation of title to five hundred acres of land, lying on the head of Spring creek, about six miles east of St. John's river, and seventy miles southwardly from St. Augustine, with a plat and certificate of survey thereof, made by Benjamin Lord, dated the 23d of November, 1779; and a copy of a British grant made to William Panton, by Governor Tonyn, dated 3d of February, 1780, marked A; which are ordered to be filed.

Thomas Forbes's heirs, by their agent, William Travers, presented their memorial to this board, praying confirmation of title to five hundred acres of land, lying on an island in lake Lomand, in the St. John's river, seventy-five miles southwardly from St. Augustine, with a plat and certificate of survey made by Benjamin Lord, dated 9th of February, 1782, marked B; and a copy of a British grant made to Thomas Forbes by Governor Tonyn, dated 11th November, 1782, marked A; which are ordered to be filed.

Thomas Forbes's heirs, by their agent, William Travers, presented their memorial to this board, praying confirmation of title to seven hundred and fifty acres of land, lying on the St. John's river, about half a mile above Hester's Bluff, and is river marsh, with a certified copy of a British grant made to Thomas Forbes by Governor Tonyn, dated the 11th of November, 1782, and certificates attached thereto; which are ordered to be filed.

William Panton's heirs, by their agent, William Travers, presented their memorial to this board, praying confirmation of title to five hundred acres of land lying on Cedar Swamp, west side of St. John's river, with a certified copy of a British grant made to William Panton's heirs by Governor Tonyn, dated the 15th of February, 1781, with appendant certificates; which are ordered to be filed.

William Panton's heirs, by their agent, William Travers, presented their memorial to this board, praying confirmation of title to two thousand acres of land, lying on Cedar Swamp, bounded northwest by the lands of William Panton and Thomas Forbes, with a plat and certificate of survey, dated 3d of May, 1780, made by Samuel Wilkins, marked Q; and a copy of a British grant made to William Panton by Governor Tonyn, and dated 16th of June, 1782, marked I; which are ordered to be filed.

Nehemiah Brush, Jun., by his attorney, George Murray, presented his memorial to this board, praying confirmation of title to thirty thousand acres of land, lying in the Alachua district, and is an undivided part of F. M. Arredondo and son's grant, in that district; for two hundred and eighty-nine thousand six hundred and forty-five acres of land, with a conveyance from grantees to memorialist, dated 4th of September, 1821, and certificates attached thereto; which are ordered to be filed.

John B. Entralgo, by his attorney, George Murray, presented his memorial to this board, praying confirmation of title to one thousand acres of land, lying about thirty miles west of the post of Buena Vista, with a certified copy of royal title made to memorialist by Governor Coppinger, dated 15th November, 1817, marked A; also, a plat and certificate of survey made by Andres Burgevin, dated 9th of September, 1819; which are ordered to be filed.

John B. Entralgo, by his attorney, George Murray, presented his memorial to this board, praying confirmation of title to one thousand acres of land, lying on the east side of St. John's river, at a place called Rollestown, with a certified copy of royal title made to memorialist by Governor Coppinger, dated the 5th of May, 1821, for services marked A; also, a plat and certificate of survey made by Andres Burgevin, dated the 7th of April, 1821, marked B; which are ordered to be filed.

John B. Entralgo, by his attorney, George Murray, presented his memorial to this board, praying confirmation of title to three thousand four hundred acres of land, lying at the Big Spring, twenty-five miles south of lake George, with a certified copy of royal title to Pedro Miranda, for services, made by Governor Coppinger, dated 11th of April, 1821; and conveyance from said Miranda to memorialist, dated 5th of December, 1821, attached thereto, marked A; and a plat and certificate of survey made by Andres Burgevin, dated 5th of April, 1821; which are ordered to be filed.

William Travers, by his attorney, George Murray, presented his memorial to this board, praying confirmation of title to one thousand acres of land, lying at a place called Santo Thomas, on the St. John's river, with a certified copy of royal title made to Doctor Thomas Travers by Governor White, dated 27th September, 1818; which are ordered to be filed.

William Travers, by his attorney, George Murray, presented his memorial to this board, praying confirmation of title to seven hundred and fifty and a third acres of land, lying on the St. John's river, at a place called Glorat, with the documents marked No. 13; which are ordered to be filed.

John Bolton presented his memorial to this board, praying confirmation of title to two thousand acres of land, lying in Turnbull's Back Swamp, in the territory of Mosquitos, with a certified copy of royal title to John Atkinson, made by Governor Coppinger, for services, dated 7th of December, 1817; a deed from said Atkinson, to George Atkinson, dated the 17th of May, 1820; and a deed from George Atkinson to William Cook, dated 6th of June, 1820; and conveyance from said Cook to the memorialist, dated the 4th of April, 1823; plat and certificate of survey made by Robert McHardy, dated 2d of May, 1818; which are ordered to be filed.

John Bellamy, by A. Bellamy, his attorney, presented his memorial to this board, praying confirmation of title to three hundred acres of land, with certified copy of royal title made to Robert Hutchinson by Governor Coppinger, and dated the 31st July, 1816; which are ordered to be filed.

John Bellamy, by A. Bellamy, his attorney, presented his memorial to this board, praying confirmation of title to fifty acres of land, lying at Jacksonville, on the St. John's river, with a certified copy of royal title made by Governor Coppinger to John Mestre, dated 3d December, 1816; ordered to be filed.

William Hollingsworth presented his petition to this board, praying confirmation of title to one hundred and fifty acres of land, lying at the mouth of Goodby's lake, on the north side, and on the river St. John's, being the half of a tract of land of three hundred acres granted to George Whitmore and William Valentine, with a certified copy of concession made to Guillermo Valentine, by Governor Quesada, and dated the 4th April, 1792; also, a document of William Valentine, purporting to bind himself in the penalty of $1,000 to said Hollingsworth, if he does not make good and sufficient title for said land; which are ordered to be filed.

Magwood, administrator of Isaac Sasportas, deceased, presented his memorial to this board, praying confirmation of title to four hundred and twenty-five acres of land, lying on the river St. John's, at a place called Scipio's swamp, with a certified copy of royal title made by Governor Coppinger to Eusebio Maria Gomez, dated 6th May, 1811; a certified copy of conveyance from said Gomez to Pablo Dupon, dated 5th February, 1819; also, copy and plat of certificate of survey of said land by Andres Burgevin, dated 1st of October, 1818; and a conveyance of Paul Dupon to Isaac Sasportas, dated Darien, 5th March, 1819; which are ordered to be filed.

John Houston, by A. Bellamy, his attorney, presented his memorial to this board, praying confirmation of title to ninety-two acres of land, lying on Talbot island, with a certified copy of royal title made by Governor White to Spicer Christopher, dated the 12th of April, 1809; which are ordered to be filed.

John Houston, by A. Bellamy, his attorney, presented his memorial to this board, praying confirmation of title to six hundred acres of land, lying on the north side of the island of Talbot, which he derives from a decree made to Spicer Christopher by Governor Quesada, dated 2d December, 1795, as will be seen by reference to the decree in the keeper of the public archives' office; ordered to be filed.

John Houston, by A. Bellamy, his attorney, presented his memorial to this board, praying confirmation of title to the island and marshes of Little Talbot, which island memorialist derives from a decree made by Governor White in favor of Spicer Christopher, dated 31st January, 1798, as will be seen by a reference to the decree in the keeper of the public archives' office; ordered to be filed.

John Christopher, by A. Bellamy, his attorney, presented his memorial to this board, praying confirmation of title to five hundred acres of land, lying on or near the mouth of the river Nassau, at a place called Santa Maria, with a certified copy of royal title made to Spicer Christopher by Governor White, dated the 8th of April, 1809; ordered to be filed.

Joseph Higginbottom, by A. Bellamy, his attorney, presented his memorial to this board, praying confirmation of title to three hundred acres of land, lying on Spell swamp, a branch of the Nassau river, in Duval county, with a certified copy of plat and certificate of survey made to memorialist by George J. F. Clarke, dated 16th November, 1817; ordered to be filed.

Robert Harrison, by his attorney, John Drysdale, presented his memorial to this board, praying confirmation of title to seven hundred and seventy-five acres of land in East Florida, on an island in the river Nassau, near a place called the Roundabout, with a certified copy of concession made by Governor Coppinger to memorialist, dated 10th of May, 1816, marked exhibit A; and a certified copy of a plat and certificate of survey made to memorialist by George J. F. Clarke, dated 20th of April, 1821, marked exhibit B; which are ordered to be filed.

Estevan Arnau, by his attorney, John Drysdale, presented his memorial to this board, praying confirmation of title to two hundred acres of land, lying at a place called the Black General, a little distance from St. Mark's lake, about seven miles north of the city of St. Augustine, with a certified copy of royal title made to memorialists by Governor Coppinger, dated 19th of June, 1808, marked exhibit A; which are ordered to be filed.

Horatio S. Dexter, by John Drysdale, his attorney, presented his memorial to this board, praying confirmation of title to two hundred acres of land, lying on the east side of St. John's river, in East Florida, between Little lake and lake George, and known by the name of Mount Royal, with a certified copy of concession made to George Petty by Governor Kindelan, dated 5th of April, 1815; a certified copy of plat and certificate of survey made by George J. F. Clarke to said Petty, dated the 1st of May, 1821; a conveyance from the said Petty to Mrs. Abby Dexter, dated the 21st of May, 1821; and a note of hand for two hundred and fifty dollars from Horatio S. Dexter, payable to George Petty, for his right, title, interest, and property in Mount Royal, dated January 26, 1820, erased by a pen; which are ordered to be filed.

Horatio S. Dexter, by his attorney, John Drysdale, presented his memorial to this board, praying confirmation of title to two hundred acres of land, lying at a place called McCullough's point, on the river St. John's, about seven miles south of Picolata, with a certified copy of concession made by Governor Kindelan to William Bardin, dated the 17th of March, 1815, with a plat; also, a conveyance from said Bardin to memorialist, dated the 23d of December, 1819; which are ordered to be filed.

Peter Mitchell, by his attorney, John Drysdale, presented his memorial to this board, praying confirmation of title to a lot of ground, with the buildings and improvement on the same, situated at the south corner of the public square, with a conveyance for the same from Francisco P. Sanchez to memorialist, bearing date ——— day of October, in the present year, one thousand eight hundred and twenty-three; which said conveyance has been duly recorded in the office of the clerk of the county court: ordered to be filed.

John McQueen's heirs, by John Drysdale, their attorney, presented their memorial to this board, praying confirmation of title to ten thousand acres of land, lying and being near the bay of Tampa, in East Florida, with an affidavit of Peter Mitchell attached thereto: ordered to be filed.

Samuel Harrison, by his attorney, John Drysdale, presented his memorial to this board, praying confirmation of title to two hundred acres of land, lying at the west point of Amelia island, and has never been surveyed, with a certified copy of concession made to memorialist by Governor White, dated the 16th of May, 1799: ordered to be filed.

Samuel Harrison, by his attorney, John Drysdale, presented his memorial to this board, praying confirmation of title to five hundred acres of land, lying on Amelia island, in Duval county, and is known by Harrison's Old Field's, with a certified copy of concession made to memorialist by Governor White, dated 12th of November, 1807, marked A; a certified copy of plat and certificate of survey, made by Juan Purcell for memorialist, dated the 15th of April, 1807, marked B: ordered to be filed.

Peter Miranda, by his attorneys, John Drysdale and John Rodman, presented his memorial to this board, praying confirmation of title to three hundred and sixty-eight thousand six hundred and forty acres of land, lying on Tampa and Hillsborough bays, in East Florida, which has never been surveyed, with a certified copy of concession made to memorialist by Governor White, dated the 26th of December, 1810: ordered to be filed.

Robert Isaac, by his attorney, John Drysdale, presented his memorial to this board, praying confirmation of title to three lots in the city of St. Augustine, as by deed bearing date the 10th of October, 1823, conveyed by Octavius Mitchell, by his attorney, Peter Mitchell, to memorialist in fee simple, absolute, and recorded in the office of the clerk of the county court for the county of St. John's: ordered to be filed.

Sophia Fleming, on behalf of herself as widow, and the heirs of George Fleming, deceased, and William Gibson, presented her memorial to this board, praying confirmation of title to ten thousand seven hundred and sixty-two acres of land, lying on the south side of the branch of Nassau river, about ten miles above the forks, with a British grant made to Robert Paris Taylor by Governor Grant, dated 18th of April, 1771; also, articles of agreement between said Taylor and Daniel Wagenfield, dated 15th of February, 1767, and an assignment of said agreement by said Wagenfield to John Thomas, dated 10th of July, 1770; also, a mutilated release of property in said ten thousand acres, made by Robert P. Taylor to John Thomas, dated on or about the 24th of July, 1770, which said Thomas, by release bearing date the 10th of August, 1770, did convey all his interest and title in said lands to Francis P. Fatio and Joachim Noel Farnen, herewith exhibited; also, a patent from the British Government, executed by Governor Tonyn, for seven hundred and sixty-two acres, in favor of Francis P. Fatio, adjoining said ten thousand acres, dated 27th day of March, 1775; also, a certified copy of plat and certificate of survey made by Pedro Marrot, by order of the Spanish Government, dated 29th of March, 1793; all of which are ordered to be filed.

Stephen Pierce and wife, by their attorney, John Drysdale, presented their memorial to this board, praying confirmation of title to three hundred acres of land, lying in south branch of, and about four miles distant from the river St. Mary's, about ninety miles distant from the city of St. Augustine, with a British grant made to Thomas Mills, dated — of May, 1767; a certified copy of plat and certificate of survey (mutilated) made by Brahm unto Thomas ———, dated 14th of November, 1765: ordered to be filed.

Hannah Drayton and others, by their attorney, John Drysdale, presented their memorial to this board, praying confirmation of title to a tract of land in the Territory of East Florida, with an order of survey from Governor Tonyn to F. G. Mulcaster, Surveyor General, "to lay unto William Drayton, Esq., a plantation or tract of one thousand acres," dated the 11th of February, 1775; also, another order of survey from Governor Tonyn to F. G. Mulcaster, Surveyor General, to "measure and lay out unto William Drayton, Esq., a tract of one thousand acres of land, 11th day of February, 1775;" also, a certified copy of plat and certificate of survey of one thousand acres of land, made for William Drayton by John Funk, deputy surveyor, certified the 20th of February, 1775; all of which being labelled and marked exhibits A, 34.

Also, a British grant for one hundred acres of land, lying at the Matanzas, west side of Crooked creek, to William Drayton, dated October 1, 1772, and signed by Arthur Gordon, Attorney General, with two orders of survey bearing date the 16th of February, 1771, directed to Frederick George Mulcaster, Surveyor General, by Governor James Grant; and a certified copy of plat and certificate of survey of one hundred acres of land, certified the 18th of May, 1771, by John Funk, deputy surveyor; all of which being labelled, and marked exhibits B, 33.

Also, a British grant for one hundred acres of land, lying on Matanzas river, about twenty miles southeastward from St. Augustine, to William Drayton, dated 1st October, 1772, and signed by Arthur Gordon, Attorney General, with two other orders of survey bearing date the 29th of June, 1771, directed to F. G. Mulcaster, Esq., Surveyor General, by Governor John Moultrie, and a certified copy of plat and certificate of survey of one hundred acres of land, certified the 8th September, 1772, by John Funk, deputy surveyor; all of which being labelled and marked exhibits C, 32.

Also, a British grant for two hundred acres of land, lying on Northwest creek, about twenty miles southeast from St. Augustine, to William Drayton, dated May 14, 1772, signed by Arthur Gordon, Attorney General, with a warrant of survey by James Grant, directed to F. G. Mulcaster, Surveyor General, dated 26th December, 1770, and an order of survey by said Governor Grant, dated 26th December, 1770; and a certified copy of plat and certificate of survey, certified the 18th May, 1771, by John Funk, deputy surveyor; all of which being labelled and marked exhibits D, 31.

Also, a British grant for three hundred acres of land, lying on the north side of the Northwest creek running into the Little Matanzas, to William Drayton, dated 14th May, 1772, signed by Arthur Gordon, Attorney General, with a warrant of survey by Governor James Grant, directed to F. G. Mulcaster, Surveyor General, dated 8d of December, 1770; all of which being labelled and marked exhibits E, 30.

Also, a warrant of survey by Governor James Grant, directed to William G. De Brahm, Surveyor General, "to survey one hundred acres of land on Rain's Cowpens creek, opposite to his former tracts," dated 19th September, 1769; and an order of survey from said Governor Grant, dated 19th of September, 1769, and a certified copy of plat and certificate of survey certified the 19th December, 1770, by Andrew May, deputy surveyor; all of which being labelled and marked exhibits F, 29.

Also, a warrant of survey by Governor Grant, directed to William Gerard De Brahm, Esq., Surveyor General, "to measure, or cause to be admeasured and laid out unto William Drayton, Esq., a plantation or tract of land, containing five hundred acres of land, situated on the west line of a tract petitioned for by Mr. Coursorvie, on Rain's Cowpens creek," dated 24th of July, 1769; and an order of survey from said Governor Grant, dated 24th of July, 1769, and a certified copy of plat and certificate of survey, certified the 1st of September, 1769, by Andrew May, deputy surveyor; all of which being labelled and marked exhibits G, 28.

Also, a warrant of survey by Governor Grant, directed to William Gerard De Brahm, Esq., Surveyor General, "to measure, or cause to be admeasured and laid out, unto William Drayton, Esq., a plantation or tract of land, containing five hundred acres of land, situated on Rain's Cowpens, adjoining his former five hundred acre tract," dated 3d of August, 1769; and a certified copy of plat and certificate of survey, certified the 2d of September, 1769, by Andrew May, deputy surveyor; all of which being labelled and marked exhibits H, 27.

Also, a warrant of survey by Governor Grant, directed to William Gerard De Brahm, Esq., Surveyor General, "to measure, or cause to be admeasured and laid out, unto William Drayton, Esq., two hundred and fifty acres, situated on a cypress swamp, about eight miles west from St. Augustine, near his tract of fifty acres," dated 13th of January, 1768; and an order of survey from the said Governor Grant, dated 13th of January, 1768; and a certified copy of plat and certificate of survey, certified the 15th of February, 176–, by John Funk, deputy surveyor; all of which being labelled and marked exhibits I, 26.

Also, a warrant of survey by Governor Grant, directed to William Gerard De Brahm, Esq., Surveyor General, "to measure, or cause to be admeasured and laid out, unto William Drayton, Esq., fifty acres, situated in a swamp about eight miles west from St. Augustine, near a tract of Mr. Jollies'," dated 4th January, 1768; an order of survey from the said Governor Grant, dated 4th January, 1768, and a certified copy of plat and certificate of survey, certified the 14th of February, 1769, by John Funk, deputy surveyor; all of which being labelled and marked exhibits J, 25.

Also, a British grant for one hundred acres of land, lying northwestwardly five miles from St. Augustine, to William Drayton, dated 14th October, 1768, and signed by James Box, Attorney General, with a warrant of survey directed to William Gerard De Brahm, Surveyor General, dated 22d June, 1767; all of which being labelled and marked exhibits K, 24.

Also, a British grant for one thousand three hundred and two acres of land, lying and being an island situated in lake George, to William Drayton, dated the 3d October, 1768, and signed by James Box, Attorney General, with a warrant of survey directed to William Gerard De Brahm, Esq., Surveyor General, dated 22d of June, 1767, and a certified copy of plat and certificate of survey, certified 2d of August, 1767, by John Funk, deputy surveyor; all of which being labelled and marked exhibits L, 23.

Likewise, a certified will of William Drayton, marked M; a certificate of James D. Mitchell, ordinary, specifying that William Drayton did administer on the estate and effects of Jacob Drayton, marked N. Memorialist further presented, for the consideration of the board, certified copies of eleven British grants obtained from the British Colonial Department in London; which, with the exhibits already referred to, are ordered to be filed.

Nicol Turnbull, and other heirs of Andrew Turnbull, deceased, by their attorney, John Drysdale, presented their memorial to this board, praying confirmation of title to *fourteen grants* of land, to wit:

The first grant of three hundred acres, lying on Hillsborough river opposite the north side of his (Andrew Turnbull's) tract of twenty thousand acres, with a warrant of survey for the said land, directed to William Gerard De Brahm, Surveyor General, by Governor James Grant, dated the 17th January, 1767; an order of survey, same date; a certified copy of plat and certificate of survey, dated 18th January, 1767, signed by John Funk, deputy surveyor, referred to, and marked exhibit A, No. 1.

The second grant for one thousand three hundred acres of land, lying on Spruce creek, with a warrant of survey for the said land directed to William G. De Brahm, Surveyor General, by Governor James Grant, dated 3d December, 1770; a certified copy of plat and certificate of survey, dated 4th day of January, 1771, signed by John Funk, deputy surveyor, referred to, and marked exhibit B, No. 2.

The third grant of one thousand acres of land, lying on Don Pablo's creek, opposite to Mr. Wooldridge's land, with a warrant of survey for the said land, directed to William G. De Brahm, Surveyor General, by Governor James Grant, the 16th April, 1770; an order of survey, same date; a certified copy of plat and certificate of survey, dated 20th April, 1771, signed by James Delaire, deputy surveyor, referred to, and marked exhibit C, No. 3.

The fourth grant of two hundred acres of land, lying on an island swamp, about two miles west from the Stockades fort, with a warrant of survey for the said land directed to William G. De Brahm, Surveyor General, by Governor James Grant, dated 17th January, 1767; a grant signed by James Box, Attorney General, dated 21st January, 1767, for said land; and a certified copy of plat and certificate of survey, dated 20th January, 1767, signed by John Funk, deputy surveyor, referred to, and marked exhibits D, No. 4.

The fifth grant of ten thousand acres of land, lying on the south side of the forks of Nassau river, with a warrant of survey for the said land, directed to Frederick George Mulcaster, Surveyor General, by Governor John Moultrie, dated 5th April, 1773; with a plat of survey having no date, referred to, and marked exhibits E, No. 5.

The sixth grant of one hundred acres of land, lying about seventy miles southwardly from St. Augustine, with a warrant of survey for the said land directed to Frederick George Mulcaster, Surveyor General, by Governor Pat. Tonyn, dated 18th October, 1774; an order of survey, same date; and a certified copy of plat and certificate survey, dated 24th ———, 1774, referred to, and marked exhibits F, No. 6.

The seventh grant of fifty acres of land, lying between Halifax river and the sea beach, about three-quarters of a mile to the northward of the Mosquito inlet, with a warrant of survey directed to F. G. Mulcaster, Surveyor General, by Governor Tonyn, bearing date 18th October, 1774; an order of survey, of same date; and a certified copy of plat and certificate of survey by John Funk, deputy surveyor, dated 2d January, 1775, referred to, and marked exhibits G, No. 15.

The eighth grant of one hundred acres of land, lying on the east side of Hillsborough river, and a little to the northward of the Mosquito inlet, with an order of survey, dated 7th June, 1773, "signed John Moultrie," and a certified copy of plat and certificate of survey by John Funk, deputy surveyor, dated 8th June, 1773, referred to, and marked exhibits H, No. 7.

The ninth grant of twenty thousand acres of land, lying two miles and three-quarters from the Mosquito inlet, with a *mandamus* for twenty thousand acres of land, dated the 18th day of June, 1766; a warrant of survey directed to William Gerard De Brahm, Surveyor General, by Governor James Grant, dated 15th January, 1767; a grant signed by James Box, Attorney General, dated 17th January, 1767; and certified copy of plat and certificate of survey by John Funk, deputy surveyor, dated January 15, 1767, referred to, and marked exhibits I, No. 9.

The tenth grant of one thousand acres of land, lying about sixty miles south from St. Augustine, on the head of Fishing creek, a branch of the river Halifax, with a mutilated warrant of survey directed to William Gerard De Brahm, Surveyor General, by Governor James Grant, dated the 25th of June, 1767; and a certified copy of plat and certificate of survey by John Davis, deputy surveyor, dated 29th December, 1768, referred to, and marked exhibits J.

The eleventh grant of three thousand six hundred acres of land, lying on Sugar island, about twenty miles to the southward of Mr. Elliot's plantation, with a warrant of survey directed to Frederick George Mulcaster, Surveyor General, by Governor Tonyn, dated 21st January, 1775; an order of survey of same date, and a certified copy of plat and certificate of survey by John Funk, deputy surveyor, dated the 17th of March, 1775, referred to, and marked exhibits K.

The twelfth grant of two hundred and fifty acres of land, lying on the west side of Tomoka creek, adjoining on the south line of lands surveyed for the children of the late James Moultrie, Esq., with a warrant of survey directed to Frederick George Mulcaster, Surveyor General, by Governor Grant, dated the 16th of February, 1771; an order of survey, same date; also, a certified copy of plat and certificate of survey by John Funk, deputy surveyor, dated 20th February, 1771, referred to, and marked M.

The thirteenth grant of two hundred acres, lying on the west side of Tomoka creek, adjoining Mr. Alert's line, with a warrant of survey directed to William Gerard De Brahm, Surveyor General, by Governor Grant, dated 9th of August, 1770; an order of survey, same date; and a certified copy of plat and certificate of survey, dated 4th of January, 1771, by John Funk, deputy surveyor, referred to, and marked exhibits N.

The fourteenth grant of two hundred acres, lying on the west side of Tomoka creek, opposite an island in the said creek, with a warrant of survey directed to F. G. Mulcaster, Surveyor General, by Governor Grant, dated 11th October, 1770; an order of survey same date, and a certified copy of plat and certificate of survey, dated 4th January, 1771, by John Funk, deputy surveyor, referred to, and marked exhibits O.

And Robert Harvey, one of the heirs of the aforesaid Andrew Turnbull, claims title to a tract of land granted to his mother, Mary Turnbull, daughter of the said Andrew Turnbull, before her marriage with the father of memorialist, consisting of five thousand acres of land, lying on the east side of lake George, adjoining the south line of Nicholas Turnbull, with an order of survey, signed James Grant, dated 19th day ——, 1768; a grant for the land, dated 29th March, 1769, signed by James Box, Attorney General; a certified copy of plat and certificate of survey by John Funk, deputy surveyor, dated 2d February, 1769, referred to, and marked P.

And John Holland and Jane Holland, heirs of the aforesaid Andrew Turnbull, claim title to a tract of land granted to the said Jane, daughter of said Andrew Turnbull, before her marriage with the said Holland, consisting of five thousand acres, lying on the great fork of Nassau river, with an order of survey signed James Grant, dated 5th day of May, 1769; and a certified copy of plat and certificate of survey by James Delaire, dated 14th April, 1770, referred to, and marked exhibits Q.

And Nichol Turnbull, one of the heirs of the aforesaid Andrew Turnbull, claims title to a tract of land granted to him, consisting of five thousand acres, on the east side of lake George, with the following exhibits: A warrant of survey directed to William Gerard De Brahm, Surveyor General, by Governor Grant, dated 19th September, 1768; an order of survey same date; a grant signed by James Box, Attorney General, dated 29th March, 1769; two certified copies of survey; one by John Funk, deputy surveyor, dated 1st of February, 1769, the other by R. Romans, deputy surveyor, dated 27th February, 1769, referred to, and marked exhibits R.

And Elihu Hall Bay and Margaret Bay, formerly Margaret Turnbull, daughter of the aforesaid Andrew Turnbull, likewise heirs to said Turnbull, claim title to a tract of land granted to the said Margaret, before her marriage, consisting of five thousand acres, lying across the heads of the middle branches of Nassau river, with the following exhibits: A warrant of survey directed to William G. De Brahm, Surveyor General, by Governor Grant, dated 5th day of May, 1769; a grant signed W. Owens, Attorney General, dated 13th February, 1779; a *mandamus* for five thousand acres, dated the 13th day of May, 1767; an order of survey, dated 5th May, 1769; and certified copy of plat and certificate of survey by James Delaire, dated 16th July, 1770, referred to, and marked S.

And the memorialist further presented two affidavits, marked U and V., purporting that the original grants could not be procured; that no compensation was ever received from the British Government; that Andrew Turnbull was a citizen of the United States, by the certificate of Judge Burke. The memorialist further presented, for the consideration of this board, certified copies of fifteen grants from the Department of the Secretary of State for the Colonial Department in London; all of which documents are ordered to be filed.

Nichol Turnbull, by his attorney, John Drysdale, presented his memorial to this board, praying confirmation of title to a lot of ground lying in this city, situated on the south side of Convent lane, with a copy of a British grant made by Governor Tonyn for memorialist, and dated 2d August, 1783, marked exhibit A; also, a warrant of survey by Governor Grant for one acre, dated 15th January, 1767; certified copies of plat and certificates of survey by John Funk, deputy surveyor; no date; a certified copy of survey by Benjamin Lord, assistant surveyor general, dated the 21st of June, 1783, referred to as exhibits A and B, in exhibit B: ordered to be filed.

James Marshall, by his attorney, John Drysdale, presented his memorial to this board, praying confirmation of title to five hundred acres of land, lying on the east side of Rain's cowpen, with a warrant of survey made by Governor Moultrie, dated 3d May, 1773; a plat and certificate of survey, and a representation of Edwin C. Holland attached thereto, dated Charleston, April 1, 1819, referred to, and marked exhibit A; an attested copy of a British grant made by Governor Pat. Tonyn, bearing date 18th October, 1774, obtained from England, in favor of Abraham Marshall, referred to, in exhibit T: ordered to be filed.

Elihu Hall Bay and wife presented, by their attorney, John Drysdale, their supplementary memorial to this board, praying confirmation of title to five thousand acres of land, lying across the heads of the branches of Nassau river, already petitioned for, with an attested copy of a British grant dated the 16th of February, 1771, made by Governor James Grant to Margaret Turnbull, obtained from England, referred to, in exhibit T: ordered to be filed.

The board then adjourned until Thursday afternoon, November 27, at 4 o'clock.

Thursday, November 27, 1823.

The board met pursuant to adjournment. Present, Hons. Davis Floyd and William W. Blair.

Edgar Macon, Esq., United States' attorney for the district of East Florida, attended the sitting of the board, under their order.

William Drummond presented his memorial to this board, praying confirmation of title to five hundred acres of land, lying on the north of the river St. John's, on Cedar creek, at a place named *Mount Agreeable*, with a certificate of concession to John Youngblood by Governor White, dated 19th February, 1799: ordered to be filed.

William Drummond presented his memorial to this board, praying confirmation of title to four hundred acres of land, lying at a place called White House, in the St. Mary's river, with a conveyance from David Lang to memorialist, dated 24th February, 1817; a memorial from said Lang to Governor Coppinger, dated the 6th of February, 1816; and a certified copy of plat and certificate of survey made by George J. F. Clarke, dated 7th October, 1818; ordered to be filed.

William Drummond presented his memorial to this board, praying confirmation of title to two hundred acres of land, lying at a place called Bird Pond, on the bank of the river St. Mary's, near Cabbage swamp, with a certified copy of plat and certificate of survey made by George J. F. Clarke for memorialist, dated 20th of November, 1817: ordered to be filed.

William Drummond presented his memorial to this board, praying confirmation of title to four hundred acres of land, lying in Wilder's swamp, on the banks of the river St. Mary's, with a certified copy of plat and certificate of survey made by George J. F. Clarke for memorialist, dated 1st November, 1817; which are ordered to be filed.

William Drummond presented his memorial to this board, praying confirmation of title to five thousand seven hundred and sixty acres of land, lying on a creek called Buck branch, on the banks of the river St. Mary's, with a certified copy of concession to memorialist by Coppinger, dated 12th September, 1816: ordered to be filed.

Matthias Pons's heirs, by Francis Marin, administrator, presented their memorial to this board, praying confirmation of title to four hundred acres of land, lying on the river Matanzas, known by the name of *Casapula*, to the south of St. Augustine, with a certified copy of royal title made to Matthias Pons by Governor Kindelan, dated 7th September, 1814; ordered to be filed.

Daniel Hurlbert presented his memorial to this board, praying confirmation of title to two hundred acres of land, lying four miles north of the city of St. Augustine, with a certified copy of sale of said land by Government, by Governor Coppinger, dated the 23d July, 1818: ordered to be filed.

Daniel Hurlbert presented his memorial to this board, praying confirmation of title to one hundred and twenty-five acres of land, lying on Secret Swamp branch, to the southward of the city of St. Augustine, with a certified copy of concession made to memorialist by Governor White, dated 3d September, 1805: ordered to be filed.

Fernando de la Maza Arredondo, Jun., presented his memorial to this board, praying confirmation of title to two hundred acres of land, lying on the east side of St. John's river, about thirty miles to the west of the city of St. Augustine, with a certified copy of concession of said land made to Francis P. Fatio by Governor Quesada, dated the 21st November, 1771: ordered to be filed.

Fernando de la Maza Arredondo, Jun., presented his memorial to this board, praying confirmation of title to twenty-one caballerias and twenty acres, (about seven hundred and twenty acres of land,) and two small islands of marsh in front of the river St. John's, on the east side thereof, about forty-five miles northwestward from St. Augustine, with a certified copy of plat and certificate of survey by Pedro Marrot, dated March 9, 1793.

Fernando de la Maza Arredondo, Jun., presented his memorial to this board, praying confirmation of title to five hundred acres of land on the east side of Maxwell's creek, emptying into St. John's river near Jacksonville, with a British grant made to Francis P. Fatio by Governor Tonyn, of said land, dated the 28th day of March, 1775; and a British certified copy of plat and certificate of survey by Frederick George Mulcaster, Surveyor General, dated the 16th of February, 1775: ordered to be filed.

Fernando de la Maza Arredondo, Jun., presented his memorial to this board, praying confirmation of title to a lot of land, lying in the suburbs of the city of St. Augustine, on the west side of the Powder-house street, with a certified copy of concession by Governor Estrada, dated 7th of March, 1812: ordered to be filed.

Peter Miranda presented his memorial to this board, praying confirmation of title to a lot of land, situated in the south suburbs of the city of St. Augustine, on the east side of Burnt-barrack street, with a certified copy of concession made by Governor Estrada to said Miranda, dated 12th of May, 1812, with an order of survey dated 4th of April, 1821, by Governor Coppinger, and a certificate of survey dated 30th April, 1821: ordered to be filed.

George Webber, by George Gibbs, his agent, presented his memorial to this board, praying confirmation of title to one hundred and fifty acres of land, lying on the edge of the marsh of Graham's creek, about two miles southwest of the plantation of Dupont, with a certified copy of concession made by Governor White, dated 21st January, 1804: ordered to be filed.

George Atkinson, by his attorney, George Gibbs, presented his memorial to this board, praying confirmation of title to a lot of ground in the town of Fernandina, Island of Amelia, with a license to Antonio Triay, made by Governor White, dated 31st January, 1811: ordered to be filed.

Mary Dewees, by George Gibbs, her attorney, presented her memorial to this board, praying confirmation of title to a lot of ground consisting of five hundred and thirty-two square feet, in the town of Fernandina, Amelia island, with a certified copy of concession made to Joseph Fenwick by Governor Kindelan, dated the 2d of March, 1814, referred to, and marked S: ordered to be filed.

Andrew Atkinson, by George Gibbs, his attorney, presented his memorial to this board, praying confirmation of title to two hundred acres of land, lying between Dunn's creek and Front creek, on the west side of St. John's river, with a certified copy of concession made to memorialist by Governor Coppinger, dated 17th November, 1817: ordered to be filed.

Zephaniah Kingsley, by George Gibbs, his agent, presented his memorial to this board, praying confirmation of title to two thousand six hundred and eleven acres of land, lying on the west side of the St. John's river, and on the south by Doctor's lake, or creek called *Laurel Grove*, with a certified copy of conveyance from Rebecca Pengree to memorialist, dated the 26th of November, 1803, marked Z. K.: ordered to be filed.

Hannah Kingsley, by George J. F. Clarke, presented her memorial to this board, praying confirmation of title to three hundred and fifty acres of land; two hundred and twenty-five being on Dunn's lake on the east side, and one hundred and twenty-five on St. John's river, with a certified copy of concession by Governor Coppinger, dated 12th January, 1816: ordered to be filed.

Moses Elias Levy, by his attorney, Isaac N. Cox, Esq. presented his memorial to this board, praying confirmation of title to an undivided fourth part of a tract consisting of *ten miles square on each wind*, lying on the Manate and Tolosatachy rivers, on the bay of Espirito Santo, containing, in the whole, two hundred and fifty-six thousand acres, with a deed of conveyance from Fernando de la Maza Arredondo to memorialist, dated St. Augustine, 24th of January, 1822, certified by Edmund Law, Esq., on the same day; which are ordered to be filed.

John Foulk's heirs, by their attorney, Isaac N. Cox, Esq., presented their petition to this board, praying confirmation of title to three hundred and fifty acres of land, lying on the river St. John's, at a place called Mulberry Grove, south of the ancient post of *Buena Vista*, with a certified copy of a concession made by Governor White to John Foulk, dated 17th of March, 1803: ordered to be filed.

Moses Elias Levy, by his attorney, Isaac N. Cox, Esq., presented his memorial to this board, praying confirmation of title to *thirty-eight thousand* acres of land, lying on Alligator creek, in the county of St. John, with the following exhibits: a certified copy of concession for said lands made by Governor Coppinger to Fernando de la Maza Arredondo, dated the 24th March, 1817, in the Spanish language, marked A; a translation of the same, marked B; a certified copy of conveyance from said Arredondo to Hernandez and Chauviteau, with other accompanying documents in the Spanish language, marked C; a translation of the same, marked D; a declaration of Hernandez and Chauviteau, marked E; lease and release of Moses E. Levy and A. Cohen, marked F; a power of attorney from Hernandez and Chauviteau to Moses E. Levy, marked G; which are ordered to be filed.

Peter Miranda, by his attorney, Waters Smith, presented his memorial to this board, praying confirmation of title to one hundred acres of land, situated on the river St. Mary's, at the place called *Montford* or *Lowford*, with a certified copy of royal title to memorialist by Governor Coppinger, dated the 28th of November, 1816: ordered to be filed.

Fernando de la Maza Arredondo, by his attorney, Isaac N. Cox, presented his memorial to this board, praying confirmation of title to a tract of land consisting of *ten miles on each wind*, situated between the rivers Tolosatachy and the Manaté, in the bay of *Espirito Santo*, with a certified copy of the proceedings relating to said tract at the Havana, referred to, and marked A; and an affidavit of William Reynolds, keeper of the public archives, dated 11th December, 1823; which are ordered to be filed.

Fernando M. Arredondo and son, by their attorney, Isaac N. Cox, Esq., presented their memorial to this board, praying confirmation of title to one-half part of a tract of land, consisting of thirty-eight thousand acres of land, lying on Alligator creek, in the county of St. John's, with a certified copy of a power of attorney from Joseph M. Arredondo to memorialists, referred to, and marked A: ordered to be filed.

Moses E. Levy, by Isaac N. Cox, Esq., his attorney, presented his memorial to this board, praying confirmation of title to fourteen thousand five hundred acres of land, lying at a place called Hope Hill, with a certified copy of concession made to Fernando de la Maza Arredondo by Governor Coppinger, dated the 9th of August, 1819, marked A; a certified copy of plat and certificate of survey made by Andres Burgevin, dated the 5th August, 1819, marked B: ordered to be filed.

Francis de Medicis presented his memorial to this board, praying confirmation of title to four hundred acres of land, lying on the west side of the North river, about nine miles from St. Augustine, with a certified copy of concession, dated the 27th September, 1798, made to John Salon; also, a quit claim to memorialist by Miguel Salon, one of the heirs of Juan Salon, dated the 23d March, 1820, marked C; and a conveyance from Lewis Ricardo to memorialist, dated 18th May, 1822, marked B; which are ordered to be filed.

Charles Edmonston, by his agent, Peter Poirier, presented his memorial to this board, praying confirmation of title to five hundred acres of land, lying on the east side of St. John's river, with a certified copy of conveyance from Francisco Gué to Augusto Poujaud, dated 6th February, 1821; also, a certified copy of conveyance from Augusto Poujaud to memorialist, dated 11th May, 1821, and a certified copy of plat and certificate of survey made by Andres Burgevin for Francisco Gué, dated 14th August, 1818: ordered to be filed.

Charles Edmonston, by his agent, Peter Poirier, presented his memorial to this board, praying confirmation of title to five hundred acres of land, lying on the west side of St. John's river, opposite his tract on the east side of said river, with a certified copy of royal title made to Francis Gué by Governor Coppinger, dated 12th of June, 1818; a conveyance from said Gué to Augusto Poujaud, dated 6th of February, 1821; a conveyance from Poujaud to memorialist, dated 11th May, 1821; a certified copy of plat and certificate of survey made by Andres Burgevin for Francisco Gué, dated the 14th August, 1818: ordered to be filed.

José Youngblood presented his memorial to this board, praying confirmation of title to six hundred acres of land, lying on the river St. Mary's, at the place formerly occupied by the rebel John Bayley, with a certified copy of concession made to him by Governor White, dated 7th February, 1798, and a plat of survey of D. Garvin, of June 17, 1816: ordered to be filed.

Philip R. Yonge, trustee of Josiah Starkey, presented his memorial to this board, praying confirmation of title to four hundred and fifty-five acres of land, situated on the St. Mary's river, in East Florida, with a certified copy of plat and certificate of survey made by George J. F. Clarke, for Charles Sibbald, dated 8th July, 1816, and a conveyance from said Sibbald and wife to memorialist, in trust for J. Starkey, bearing date the 1st of January, 1818: ordered to be filed.

John Batchelot presented his memorial to this board, praying confirmation of title to a small island of marsh near that of the *Doctor*, with a certified copy of concession made to him by Governor White, dated 29th November, 1800: ordered to be filed.

John Batchelot presented his memorial to this board, praying confirmation of title to three hundred acres of land, lying on the north point of Amelia island, with a certified copy of royal title made to him by Governor Coppinger, dated 10th June, 1816, with plats and certificates: ordered to be filed.

John Batchelot presented his memorial to this board, praying confirmation of title to three hundred acres of land, lying on Amelia island, at a place called White Point, with a certified copy of royal title made to him, dated 10th June, 1816: ordered to be filed.

Ezekiel Hudnell's heirs, by John B. Strong, their attorney, presented their memorial to this board, praying confirmation of title to two hundred acres of land, lying at the south head of San Pablo creek, with a certified copy of concession to Selby Taylor by Governor Coppinger, dated 14th of April, 1817; also, a conveyance from said Taylor to Hudnell, bearing date 28th November, 1821; and a certified copy of plat and certificate of survey made by George J. F. Clarke to Selby Taylor, dated 7th June, 1821: ordered to be filed.

Ezekiel Hudnell's heirs, by John B. Strong, their attorney, presented their memorial to this board, praying confirmation of title to one hundred acres of land, lying on St. John's river, and east side thereof, at a place called Falck, with a certified copy of royal title to José Garcia, dated the 5th of December, 1817; and a conveyance from José Garcia to Ezekiel Hudnell, dated the 29th November, 1821; also, a certified copy of plat and certificate of survey, made by George J. F. Clarke, dated 8th June, 1821: ordered to be filed.

Ezekiel Hudnell's heirs, by John B. Strong, their attorney, presented their memorial to this board, praying confirmation of title to two hundred and fifty acres of land, lying on the north bank of the river St. John's, nearly opposite the fort of St. Nicholas, with a certified copy of concession made to Daniel Hogan, 18th March, 1817, by Governor Coppinger, with a conveyance from Hogan to Hudnell, dated 11th November, 1818; a certified copy of plat and certificate of survey made by George J. F. Clarke, dated 9th May, 1817: ordered to be filed.

Ezekiel Hudnell's heirs, by John B. Strong, their attorney, presented their memorial to this board, praying confirmation of title to nine hundred acres of land, lying at the mouth of lake George, on the south part of the river St. John's, with a certified copy of concession made to E. Hudnell by Governor Coppinger, dated 3d June, 1817; and a certified copy of plat and certificate of survey made by George J. F. Clarke, dated 1st April, 1821: ordered to be filed.

James Darley, by his attorney, George Murray, presented his memorial to this board, praying confirmation of title to five hundred acres of land in Turnbull's swamp, in the territory of Mosquito, with a certified copy of concession to memorialist of one thousand acres, made by Governor Coppinger, dated 15th June, 1817, referred to, and marked B; and a certified copy of plat and certificate of survey made by Robert McHardy, dated 20th June, 1818: ordered to be filed.

James Darley, by his attorney, George Murray, presented his memorial to this board, praying confirmation of title to five hundred acres of land, lying in the territory of Mosquito, with a certified copy of plat and certificate of survey made by Robert McHardy, dated the 25th June, 1818: ordered to be filed.

Henry Yonge, by his agent, Peter Mitchell, presented his memorial to this board, praying confirmation of title to one hundred and ninety acres of land, lying in Lofton's swamp, with a certified copy of plat and certificate of survey made by George J. F. Clarke, dated 8th June, 1817: ordered to be filed.

William P. Yonge, by his agent, Peter Mitchell, presented his memorial to the board, praying confirmation of title to five hundred acres of land, lying on St. Mary's and Little St. Mary's river, with a certified copy of plat and certificate of survey by George J. F. Clarke, dated 3d April, 1816, for Henry Yonge: ordered to be filed.

Ezekiel Hudnell's heirs, by John B. Strong, their attorney, presented their memorial to this board, praying confirmation of title to five hundred acres of land, lying in the place known as the *Baranca de las Calabazas* to the south, and near the mouth of the river Nassau, with a certified copy of concession made by Governor White to Hudnell, dated the 29th January, 1802; which are ordered to be filed.

John P. Williamson, by his agent, Peter Mitchell, presented his memorial to this board, praying confirmation of title to eight hundred and fifty acres of land, lying about two miles from the junction of the rivers Tomoka and Halifax, and with no exhibit for the same: ordered to be filed.

William P. Yonge, by his agent, Peter Mitchell, presented his memorial to this board, praying confirmation of title to four hundred and eighty acres of land, lying on St. Mary's river, with a certified copy of plat and certificate of survey, made by George J. F. Clarke, dated 1st April, 1816: ordered to be filed.

Francis Kinloch, of South Carolina, by his attorney, Richard B. Furman, presented his memorial to this board, praying confirmation of title to five hundred acres of land, lying on the east side of the river St. John's, about twenty-eight miles from the town of St. Augustine, with a certified copy of plat and certificate of survey made by John Funk, deputy surveyor, dated 30th of May, 1766: ordered to be filed.

Thomas Napier, by his attorney, Richard B. Furman, presented his memorial to this board, praying confirmation of title to eight hundred acres of land, lying and being in the territory of Mosquitos, in the passage called Paulano, of the west of Turnbull, about three miles to the west of New Smyrna, with a conveyance from Isaac Wickes to memorialist, dated 22d of April, 1820; also, a certified copy of conveyance from Juan de Entralgo to Isaac Wickes, dated 20th August, 1818; also, a certified copy of royal title by Governor Coppinger to said Entralgo, dated 15th November, 1817; also, a certified copy of concession by Governor Coppinger to the aforesaid Entralgo for three thousand eight hundred acres, dated 20th May, 1817; also, a memorial of Entralgo to Governor Coppinger to have the eight hundred acres recorded in the archives, dated 26th February, 1818; and a certified copy of plat and certificate of survey, made by George J. F. Clarke to said Entralgo, dated 20th February, 1818: ordered to be filed.

Thomas Napier, by Richard B. Furman, his attorney, presented his memorial to this board, praying confirmation of title to three thousand acres of land, in three tracts, to wit: one tract of one thousand acres, granted to George J. F. Clarke, lying and being on the west side of the Mosquito, South Lagoon or Hillsborough river; one tract of one thousand, being the southernmost moiety of two thousand acres granted to William Garvin the 26th of November, 1817, lying on the west side of the river Ys or Indian river; one tract of one thousand acres of land, or moiety of two thousand acres, granted to Charles Clarke the 10th of June, 1816, lying at Chacala, in the territory of Alachua, with a deed of conveyance from George J. F. Clarke to Thomas Napier, dated the —— day of ——, 1823, recorded in the office of the clerk of the county court July 17, 1823; and three plats of survey, translated from the Spanish language: all of which are ordered to be filed.

Domingo Reys, by his attorney, Isaac N. Cox, Esq., presented his memorial to this board, praying confirmation of title to two thousand acres of land, at a place known by the name of Spring Garden, on the river Halifax, with a certified copy of royal title made by Governor Coppinger to memorialist, dated 5th of May, 1820, referred to, and marked A A: ordered to be filed.

Andrew R. Govan, by his attorney, Edward R. Gibson, presented his memorial to this board, praying confirmation of title to sixteen hundred acres of land, lying on the east side of St. John's river, and named Orange Grove, and near Buena Vista, with no exhibits: ordered to be filed.

Artemas E. Ferguson's heirs, by Susan Sleigh, his widow, presented their memorial to this board, praying confirmation of title to thirty-four caballerias and seventeen acres of land, adjoining Doctor's creek and Negro creek, being the plantation called Armonia, with a certified copy of royal title made to them by Governor Estrada, dated the 5th of October, 1811, referred to, and marked A: ordered to be filed.

Artemas E. Ferguson's heirs, by Susan Sleigh, his widow, presented their memorial to this board, praying confirmation of title to forty-three and one-third acres of land lying on Doctor's creek, adjoining the plantation of Armonia, belonging to memorialists, with a certified copy of royal title made to memorialist by Governor Estrada, dated the 7th of October, 1811, referred to, and marked B: ordered to be filed.

Artemas E. Ferguson's heirs, by Susan Sleigh, his widow, presented their memorial to this board, praying confirmation of title to five hundred and seven acres of land, lying on St. John's river, being a plantation known by the name of San Onces, with a certified copy of royal title made them by Governor Estrada, dated 5th October, 1811, referred to: ordered to be filed.

William Walker presented his memorial to this board, praying confirmation of title to one hundred and seventy-five acres of land, lying on a little island in the northern branch of Nassau river, at a place known by the name of Cypress Grove, with a certified copy of royal title made to him by Governor Coppinger, dated 16th of February, 1816: ordered to be filed.

John Baptiste Gaudry presented his memorial to this board, praying confirmation of title to three thousand acres of land, lying on the river St. John's, at a place known by the name of Spring Garden, with a certified copy of concession made to memorialist, dated 8th of October, 1817, and the proceedings to obtain royal title; also, a certified copy of royal title by Governor Coppinger, dated 14th of May, 1818; and a certified copy of plat and certificate of survey by Robert McHardy, dated 12th of December, 1817: ordered to be filed.

Charles W. Clarke presented his memorial to this board, praying confirmation of title to sixteen thousand acres of land, in four tracts: First contains four thousand acres, situate on the west side of Alachua pond; second contains four thousand acres, situate at Fatio's negro town, to the south of Payne's town; third contains four thousand acres, on the west side of Indian river; fourth contains four thousand acres, on Black creek, St. John's river; with a certified copy of concession made to memorialist, by Governor Coppinger, for a mill-seat on Black creek, dated the 29th of October, 1817: ordered to be filed.

Charles W. Clarke presented his memorial to this board, praying confirmation of title to three hundred and seventy-five acres of land, lying on the south side of Dunn's lake, at a place known by the name of Cowing's old field, with a certified copy of concession made to him by Governor Coppinger, dated 15th December, 1815: ordered to be filed.

Charles W. Clarke presented his memorial to this board, praying confirmation of title to five hundred acres of land, lying in Graham's swamp, between the heads of the Matanzas and Halifax rivers, with no exhibits: ordered to be filed.

Charles W. Clarke presented his memorial to this board, praying confirmation of title to two thousand three hundred acres of land in five tracts; the first consisting of eight hundred and eighty acres, situate on the east side of St. George's lake; the second consisting of four hundred and four acres, on the east side of St. George's lake; the third consisting of two hundred and ninety-two acres, on the east side of St. George's lake; the fourth consisting of two hundred acres, on the east side of St. George's lake, which memorialist has sold to Doctor Weightman; and the fifth, consisting of five hundred and twenty-four acres, likewise, memorialist has sold to Andrew Stores, lying on the east side of lake George; with a certified copy of concession made by Governor Coppinger to memorialist, dated 12th of February, 1817: ordered to be filed.

George J. F. Clarke presented his memorial to this board, praying confirmation of title to four thousand acres of land in six tracts, to wit: The first contains one thousand acres at a place called Spring Grove, west side of St. George's lake, and south of Spring creek; the second contains one thousand acres, on the west of the river Hillsborough, at a place called McDougall's old field, in Turnbull's swamp, which memorialist has sold to Thomas Napier; the third contains five hundred acres, at the Big bend of Durbin's swamp; the fourth contains five hundred acres at the Big bend of Durbin's swamp, adjoining the foregoing tract; the fifth contains five hundred acres, at the Big bend of Durbin's swamp; the sixth contains five hundred acres, at the Big bend of Durbin's swamp; this tract the memorialist has sold and conveyed to James G. Forbes, now absent from this Territory. The memorialist, therefore, claims title to two thousand five hundred acres of the said four thousand acre tract, with a concession made to him by Governor Coppinger, dated 3d May, 1816; all which are ordered to be filed.

George J. F. Clarke presented his memorial to this board, praying confirmation of title to one thousand acres of land, lying at the head of Matanzas river, and place called Big Savannah, east of Graham's swamp, with a certified copy of concession made to him by Governor White, dated 28th December, 1815: ordered to be filed.

George J. F. Clarke presented his memorial to this board, praying confirmation of title to one thousand acres of land, lying on Picolata swamp, on the west side of St. John's river, and south of the road going to Alachua, with a certified copy of royal title made to him by Governor Coppinger, dated 27th August, 1818: ordered to be filed.

George J. F. Clarke presented his memorial to this board, praying confirmation of title to one thousand acres, five hundred acres thereof lying on the head of Durbin's swamp, to the west part of said swamp; and the other five hundred acres lie on Picolata swamp, on the west side of the river St. John's, with a certified copy of concession by Governor Kindelan, dated 9th May, 1815: ordered to be filed.

George J. F. Clarke presented his memorial to this board, praying confirmation of title to one hundred acres of land, lying on Amelia island, to the north-east of the town of Fernandina, by the name of Willow pond, with a certified copy of concession made by Governor Estrada, dated the 15th December, 1815: ordered to be filed.

George J. F. Clarke presented his memorial to this board, praying confirmation of title to two thousand acres of land, lying on Cedar, alias Bugg's hammock, on the south of Mizell's lake, with a certified copy of concession made by Governor White to memorialist, dated the 7th of February, 1811: ordered to be filed.

George J. F. Clarke presented his memorial to this board, praying confirmation of title to two thousand acres of land, one thousand of which lie in Chachala hammock, at the westernmost part of Payne's savannah; five hundred acres lying in Twelve-mile swamp, adjoining on the south to lands belonging at the time of survey to Charles and George Clarke; and another five hundred acres adjoining to the next above described, in Twelve-mile swamp, with a certified copy of concession made by Governor Kindelan to memorialist, dated the 10th July, 1814: ordered to be filed.

George J. F. Clarke presented his memorial to this board, praying confirmation of title to sixteen thousand acres of land in different tracts, eight thousand of which lie on the west shore of St. John's river, along the said river from the former ferry, called Picolata ferry, where the road leading to Alachua commences on that side of said river, and down to Buckley creek, including the place named White spring; a tract containing three thousand acres, situate in about Cone's hammock, to the south of Mizell's, alias Orange lake; a tract containing five thousand acres lying in Lang's hammock, on the south side of Mizell's, alias Orange lake; which said five thousand acres, and one thousand of the next preceding tract here described, the memorialist has sold and conveyed to Colonel Duncan L. Clinch, leaving memorialist in possession of ten thousand acres of land, with a certified copy of royal title made by Governor Coppinger, dated 6th April, 1816; also two memorials of survey, one dated the 29th December, 1818, with the order of survey, dated 11th January, 1819; the other memorial of survey dated 25th of January, 1819, with the order of survey dated same date: ordered to be filed.

James Clarke presented his memorial to this board, praying confirmation of title to five hundred acres of land, lying on the east head of Springer's branch, about ten miles to the west northwest from St. Augustine, with a certified copy of concession made by Governor White, dated 12th April, 1810: ordered to be filed.

Flora Leslie presented her memorial to this board, praying confirmation of title to five hundred acres of land, lying in Lang's hammock, on the south of Mizell's lake, with a certified copy of concession made by Governor Coppinger, dated 17th December, 1817: ordered to be filed.

Thomas Clarke presented his memorial to this board, praying confirmation of title to five hundred acres of land, lying on Lang's hammock, on the south of Mizell's lake, with a certified copy of concession made by Governor Coppinger, dated 17th December, 1817: ordered to be filed.

Daniel Clarke presented his memorial to this board, praying confirmation of title to five hundred acres of land, lying on the north part of the Big bend, in Durbin's swamp, and on the west of the road going from hence to St. John's bluff, with a certified copy of concession made by Governor Coppinger, dated the 17th December, 1817.

Francis Richard presented his memorial to this board, praying confirmation of title to four hundred and sixty-six acres of land, lying at a place called Branchester, on St. John's river, with a royal title made by Governor Kindelan, dated 20th March, 1815: ordered to be filed.

Francis Richard presented his memorial to this board, praying confirmation of title to two hundred and thirty acres of land, lying at a place called Vargue, on St. John's river, with a certified copy of royal title made to memorialist by Governor Kindelan, dated 20th March, 1815: ordered to be filed.

Francis Richard presented his memorial to this board, praying confirmation of title to one hundred and ten acres of land, lying on the St. John's river, at a point called Santa Esabela, with a certified copy of royal title made by Governor Coppinger, dated the 27th January, 1818: ordered to be filed.

George Atkinson presented his memorial to this board, praying confirmation of title to fifteen thousand acres of land, in different tracts, to wit: a tract of six thousand acres lying near the Santa Fé river, at Darcey's creek, on Ray's trail; a tract of four thousand acres lying on the north of Dunn's creek, that communicates with St. John's river; a tract of three thousand acres of land on the middle branch of Han creek, running into Dunn's lake; a tract of two thousand acres lying on Dixon's hammock, on the south-east of Bowleg's savannah, with a certified copy of concession made to memorialist by Governor Coppinger, dated 20th October, 1816: ordered to be filed.

John Low presented his memorial to this board, praying confirmation of title to sixteen thousand acres of land, in two tracts, to wit: a tract of six thousand acres of land, lying on Bell's river, at a place called Doctor's branch; and a tract of ten thousand acres, lying on the northwest of the head of Indian river, on the west of the savannahs of North creek, with a certified copy of concession made to memorialist, by Governor Coppinger, and dated the 6th of April, 1816: ordered to be filed.

John Brevard presented his memorial to this board, praying confirmation of title to sixteen thousand acres of land, in different tracts, seven thousand of which lie between Cedar creek and Dunn's creek, on the north side of St. John's river; three thousand lie on the north side of St. John's river, and on the east of the road to St. Mary's river; four thousand acres lie on the south side of Dunn's creek, that connects Dunn's lake with St. John's river, at a place called Cabbage hammock; two thousand acres lie at Sugartown, Cedar swamp, on the west of St. John's river, with a certified copy of concession, made by Governor Coppinger, dated 24th April, 1816: ordered to be filed.

Domingo Fernandez presented his memorial to this board, praying confirmation of title to sixteen thousand acres of land, in different tracts, six thousand of which are situated about Cooley's hammock, on the northeast of Ray's trail; four thousand acres are situated on the west side of St. John's river, above Bernard's ford, and below the Semfeloky ford, and bounded on the south by another tract belonging to memorialist; three thousand acres are situated on the west side of St. John's river, next above the preceding four thousand, and at the place where Semfeloky road fords said river; three thousand acres lie in Moody's hammock, to the southeast of Payne's town, with a certified copy of concession, made by Governor Coppinger, dated 16th December, 1817: ordered to be filed.

George J. F. Clarke, on behalf of the estate of William Garvin, presented his memorial to this board, praying confirmation of title to three thousand acres of land, in two tracts; two thousand thereof lie on the west side of Indian river, at a place called Flounder creek; the other thousand acres lie in Youngblood's hammock, on the southeast of Ray's trail, which said Garvin sold to George J. F. Clarke; the remaining two thousand acres are now claimed, with a certified copy of concession, made by Governor Coppinger, dated 26th November, 1817: ordered to be filed.

Christopher Minchin presented his memorial to this board, praying confirmation of title to four hundred acres of land, situated in Durbin's swamp, to the eastward of Twenty-mile house, with a certified copy of concession, made to memorialist by Governor Coppinger, dated the 10th November, 1817: ordered to be filed.

Charles Clarke presented his memorial to this board, praying confirmation of title to three hundred acres of land, lying on the east of St. George's lake, with a certified copy of concession, made by Governor Coppinger, dated 2d October, 1817: ordered to be filed.

Elizabeth Wiggins presented her memorial to this board, praying confirmation of title to three hundred acres of land, lying on the east side of lake St. George, with a certified copy of grant, made by Governor Estrada, dated 6th August, 1815: ordered to be filed.

Pedro Ponce presented his memorial to this board, praying confirmation of title to eight hundred and seventy-five acres of land, situated in mill swamp, on the river Nassau, with a certified copy of royal title, made to him by Governor Coppinger, dated 4th June, 1817: ordered to be filed.

George J. F. Clarke, for the estate of Job Wiggins, presented his memorial to this board, praying confirmation of title to one thousand two hundred acres of land, lying near Rowle's town, on St. John's river, with a certified copy of plat and certificate of survey, made by Pedro Marrot, bearing date the 10th of November, 1791: ordered to be filed.

Domingo Acosta presented his memorial to this board, praying confirmation of title to eight thousand acres of land, in different tracts; a tract of one thousand five hundred acres in Ibbin's hammock, on the southwest of Ray's trail; a tract of four thousand acres, situated on the west side of Indian river, at Flounder's creek; a tract of one thousand five hundred acres on the north of Dunn's lake, that communicates with St. John's river; a tract of one thousand acres at Bowleg's old field, west of Payne's town, with a certified copy of concession, made by Governor Coppinger, the 20th May, 1816: ordered to be filed.

Jane Meers, by Belton A. Copp, her attorney, presented her memorial to this board, praying confirmation of title to two hundred acres of land, in Duval county, on Tiger island, with no exhibits: ordered to be filed.

Joseph Hull, by Belton A. Copp, his agent, presented his memorial to this board, praying confirmation of title to five hundred acres of land, in two tracts; the first situated at the mouth of Nassau river, in Duval county, and known by the name of Hammock, containing one hundred acres, the other situated in the same county, west of the St. John's, on the bank of said river, fronting a place called E. A. Ferguson's plantation, with no exhibit: ordered to be filed.

William Berrie, by his agent, Belton A. Copp, presented his memorial to this board, praying confirmation of title to one hundred acres of land, lying in the county of Duval, north and west of the river St. John's, called Miller's old field, with a certified copy of concession, made by Governor White, dated 16th June, 1801, to memorialist; also, a certified copy of plat and certificate of survey, dated 15th March, 1807: ordered to be filed.

William Berrie, by his agent, Belton A. Copp, presented his memorial to this board, praying confirmation of title to one hundred acres of land, lying north of a place called Lofton's, said place called Turkey island, with a certified copy of concession, made by Governor White to Thomas Mann, dated the 3d July, 1799; also, a relinquishment of said Mann to memorialist, dated November 2, 1805: ordered to be filed.

William Hart's heirs, by their agent, Belton A. Copp, presented their memorial to this board, praying confirmation of title to fourteen hundred acres of land, lying in Duval county, on the west side of St. John's river, between Smith's and Six-mile creek, with no exhibits: ordered to be filed.

Belton A. Copp presented his memorial to this board, praying confirmation of title to fifteen hundred acres of land, lying in that tract called Alachua, west of Alachua pond, being part of a two thousand acre tract, with a conveyance from George J. F. Clarke to memorialist, dated 19th November, 1823, with a plat of survey attached thereto: ordered to be filed.

William Frink presented his memorial to this board, praying confirmation of title to three hundred and twenty-one acres of land, lying on the St. Mary's, at Camp Pinckney ferry, at a place called McGirt's neck, with no exhibits: ordered to be filed.

Francisco Ramon Sanchez, by his attorney, B. A. Copp, presented his memorial to this board, praying confirmation of title to five hundred acres of land in Alachua, on the branches of Hogtown creek, with a certified copy of plat and certificate of survey, made by George J. F. Clarke, dated 16th November, 1819: ordered to be filed.

Nathaniel Wilds, by Abraham Bellamy, his attorney, presented his memorial to this board, praying confirmation of title to one hundred and eighty-four acres of land, adjoining the lands of memorialist, near the mouth of Little St. Mary's, on the St. Mary's river, with a certified copy of plat and certificate of survey, made by George J. F. Clarke, dated 8th of May, 1818: ordered to be filed.

John Bellamy, by Abraham Bellamy, his attorney, presented his memorial to this board, praying confirmation of title to five hundred acres of land, lying on McGirt's creek and its head waters, at a place called Gravelly hill, with a certified copy of plat and certificate of survey, made by George J. F. Clarke, dated 28th October, 1820: ordered to be filed.

Francis Ramon Sanchez presented his memorial to this board, praying confirmation of title to four hundred acres of land, lying on Hogtown creek, in Alachua, with a certified copy of plat and certificate of survey, made by George J. F. Clarke, for Simeon Sanchez, dated the 8th of December, 1819: ordered to be filed.

John Sanchez presented his memorial to this board, praying confirmation of title to four hundred acres of land in Alachua, lying on a creek called Hogtown creek, with a certified copy of plat and certificate of survey, made by George J. F. Clarke, dated 6th December, 1819: ordered to be filed.

Louisa Ann Christopher, by Abraham Bellamy, her attorney, presented her memorial to this board, praying confirmation of title to one hundred and eighty acres of land, lying on the river St. John's, on the east side of said river, at a place called Dame's creek, with a certified copy of plat and certificate of survey, made by George J. F. Clarke for John Houston, dated the 9th April, 1817; also, a conveyance from said Houston to memorialist, dated 3d June, 1822: ordered to be filed.

John Houston, by his attorney, Abraham Bellamy, presented his memorial to this board, praying confirmation of title to one hundred and seventy acres of land, situated on the river Nassau, with a certified copy of plat and certificate of survey, made by George J. F. Clarke for John Houston, dated the 16th May, 1816; also, a conveyance from John C. Houston to memorialist, dated 3d June, 1822: ordered to be filed.

Thomas Suarez, administrator of Antonio Suarez, presented his memorial to this board, praying confirmation of title to five hundred acres of land, lying on Mill's swamp, a branch of Nassau river, near the crossing-place of the public road in Duval county, with a certified copy of plat and certificate of survey, made by George J. F. Clarke, dated 1st March, 1817, for Antonio Suarez: ordered to be filed.

Theophilus Williams presented his memorial to this board, by Abraham Bellamy, his attorney, praying confirmation of title to two hundred acres of land, lying on St. Mary's river, two miles below Camp Pinckney, at a place called *Cattle Hickory Hill*, with a Spanish paper signed by Fernando de la Puente, purporting to be a permission to memorialist to occupy said lands for the purpose of grazing cattle: ordered to be filed.

Duncan L. Clinch presented his memorial to this board, praying confirmation of title to one thousand acres of land in Alachua, on the south side of Mizell's, alias Orange lake, in Cone's hammock, with a certified copy of plat and certificate of survey, made by Andres Burgevin, dated 12th March, 1819: ordered to be filed.

Duncan L. Clinch presented his memorial to this board, praying confirmation of title to five thousand acres of land in Alachua, on the south side of Mizell's, alias Orange lake, called Long's hammock, with a certified copy of plat and certificate of survey, by Andres Burgevin, dated 10th March, 1819, for George J. F. Clarke; also, a conveyance from Clarke to memorialist, dated 24th November, 1823: ordered to be filed.

George Morrison, by Duncan L. Clinch, his agent; presented his memorial to this board, praying confirmation of title to one hundred and fifty acres of land, lying in Duval county, at the St. Mary's river, on the point formed by the Big and Little St. Mary's, with a certified copy of concession made by Governor White, dated 2d May, 1805: ordered to be filed.

Duncan L. Clinch presented his memorial to this board, praying confirmation of title to one thousand acres of land, lying in Chacala hammock, on the western side of Payne's savannah, Alachua, with a certified copy of plat and certificate of survey made by George J. F. Clarke, dated 1st November, 1817; also, a conveyance made by George J. F. Clarke, dated 24th November, 1823, to memorialist: ordered to be filed.

John H. McIntosh presented his memorial to this board, praying confirmation of title to eight hundred acres of land, lying on the St. John's river, opposite the Cow ford, with a certified copy of concession made to Philip Dell, dated the 11th February, 1801: ordered to be filed.

Thomas Suarez, administrator of Antonio Suarez, deceased, presented his memorial to this board, praying confirmation of title to five hundred acres of land lying on the island of Amelia, at a place called Black point, with a certified copy of royal title made by Governor White, dated the 27th July, 1809, to Antonio Suarez: ordered to be filed.

Elijah Higginbottom presented his memorial to this board, praying confirmation of title to three hundred and fifty acres of land, lying on Little St. Mary's, seven miles from its junction with Little St. Mary's, with a certified copy of plat and certificate of survey made by George J. F. Clarke, dated 19th December, 1818: ordered to be filed.

William Hogan presented his memorial to the board, praying confirmation of title to three hundred acres of land, lying on the public or King's road from St. Augustine to the river St. Mary's, with a certified copy of plat and certificate of survey made by J. F. Clarke, dated 13th May, 1818: ordered to be filed.

Samuel Spicer Christopher presented his memorial to this board, praying confirmation of title to five hundred acres of land, lying on the river St. Mary's, at a place called Old Township, with no exhibits; which is ordered to be filed.

Samuel Russell, Sen., presented his memorial to this board, praying confirmation of title to two tracts of land, consisting of three hundred and fifty acres—one tract of one hundred and fifty acres, on Brass swamp, two miles from the Old Township, on St. Mary's river; the other, of one hundred and fifty acres, on the north side of the river Nassau, two miles below John Christopher's plantation, called Santa Maria, near the mouth of said river, with no exhibits: ordered to be filed.

Joseph Rain and William Bailey, by their attorney, Abraham Bellamy, presented their memorial to this board, praying confirmation of title to one thousand acres of land, lying on Front creek, where the road leading from St. Augustine to the State of Georgia crosses in Duval county, with a certified copy of British survey made the 15th day of February, 1773, by John Funk, surveyor, for Frederick Rolfe; also, a deed of conveyance from John Haley, provost-martial, to Peter Bagley, dated 1779; also, a lease for one year from Benjamin Dodd to Arthur Gordon; also, a release from said Dodd to said Gordon; also, a deed of conveyance from John Hollingsworth to Joseph Rain and William Bailey; also, a deed of conveyance from Elizabeth Bagley to Joseph Rain and William Bailey; all of which are ordered to be filed.

The heirs of Joseph Peavett, deceased, by their agent, William Travers, and George Murray, his attorney, presented their memorial to this board, praying confirmation of title to five hundred acres of land, lying on the branches of Pablo creek, twenty-five miles west from St. Augustine, with a British grant, dated the 29th April, 1771, made by Governor Grant to Robert Payne, marked A; a deed of conveyance from said Payne to Henry Sowerby, dated the 5th December, 1780, marked C; a paper from Henry Sowerby to Joseph Peavett, dated 24th January, 1781, marked D: ordered to be filed.

The heirs of Joshua Yellowly, deceased, by their agent, William Travers, and George Murray, his attorney, presented their memorial to this board, praying confirmation of title to five hundred acres of land, lying on Durbin's swamp, about three-fourths of a mile to the eastward of St. John's river, with a British grant made by Governor Tonyn to Joshua Yellowly, dated 23d April, 1777, marked A: ordered to be filed.

The heirs of Joseph Peavett, deceased, by their agent, William Travers, and George Murray, his attorney, presented their memorial to this board, praying confirmation of title to five hundred acres of land, lying near the Three Runs of Pablo creek, with a British grant made by Governor Tonyn to Joseph Peavett, dated 11th March, 1782, marked A: ordered to be filed.

The heirs of Joseph Peavett, deceased, by William Travers, their agent, and George Murray, his attorney, presented their memorial to this board, praying confirmation of title to two hundred and fifty acres of land, lying near the Three Runs, with a British grant made to Joseph Peavett by Governor Tonyn, dated 14th April, 1783, marked A: ordered to be filed.

The heirs of Joseph Peavett, deceased, by William Travers, their agent, and George Murray, his attorney, presented their memorial to this board, praying confirmation of title to five hundred acres of land, lying on a fork made of Durbin's swamp, and a branch made of Julinton creek, with a British grant made to Joseph Peavett by Governor Tonyn, dated 12th February, 1783, marked A: ordered to be filed.

The board then adjourned to Friday afternoon next, at 3 o'clock, November 28, 1823.

FRIDAY, *November* 28, 1823.

The board met pursuant to adjournment. Present, all the members.

Maria Mabrity, widow of John Andrew, deceased, presented her memorial to this board, praying confirmation of title to four caballerias and twenty-eight, or one hundred and sixty-one and one-third acres, lying on the North river and Guena creek, at a place called Oyster bank, with a certified copy of royal title made by Governor White to Juan Andrew, dated 10th July, 1814; also, a certificate of the division, by the notary of Government, of the estate of said Andrew; also, a certified copy of plat and certificate of survey made by Pedro Marrot for Juan Andrew, dated 24th May, 1793: ordered to be filed.

The heirs of Cornelius Griffiths presented their memorial to this board, praying confirmation of title to one hundred acres of land, lying on a small branch of the waters of Front creek, east side of said creek, being a branch of the St. John's, with a certified copy of concession made by Governor White to Edward Crosson, to Samuel Betts, dated 7th day of September, 1803; a conveyance from Samuel Betts to Cornelius Griffiths, dated 4th February, 1807: ordered to be filed.

Samuel and George Brennan presented their memorial to this board, praying confirmation of title to three hundred acres of land, lying at a place called the Forks of Black creek, on the west side of the river St. John's, with a certified copy of plat and certificate of survey made by George J. F. Clarke, dated 29th September, 1819: ordered to be filed.

Andrew Brennan presented his memorial to this board, praying confirmation of title to four hundred acres of land, lying on Black creek, at a place called Brown's fort, with a certified copy of plat and certificate of survey, made by George J. F. Clarke for Andres Brennan, dated 4th October, 1819: ordered to be filed.

William Drummond presented his memorial to this board, praying confirmation of title to one hundred acres of land, situated on Front creek, a water of St. John's river, with a certified copy of plat and certificate of survey, made by George J. F. Clarke for Henry Groves, dated 12th November, 1818; also, a conveyance from said Groves to memorialist, dated 5th November, 1821: ordered to be filed.

William Drummond presented his memorial to this board, praying confirmation of title to five hundred acres of land, lying on the north side of St. John's river, known by the name of Green hill, with a certified copy of concession made by Governor Quesada to Solomon King, dated 3d January, 1792; also a certified copy of the will of Sarah King, widow of said Solomon King, dated 30th April, 1808; also a deed of conveyance from Solomon King Rain to memorialist, dated 19th of February, 1823: ordered to be filed.

Absalom Beardon and wife presented their memorial to this board, praying confirmation of title to one hundred and fifty acres of land, lying on the east side of St. John's river, in St. John's county, being the place granted to Aaron Travers for head-rights, with a paper: ordered to be filed.

John Salome, by his attorney, John B. Strong, presented his memorial to this board, praying confirmation of title to three hundred and forty-seven acres of land, situate on the St. John's river, in the plantation called Montpelier, with a certified copy of plat and certificate of survey made by Pedro Marrot, dated 6th January, 1792; also a petition from memorialist to Governor White, dated 22d January, 1800: ordered to be filed.

William T. Hall, by his attorney, John B. Strong, presented his memorial to this board, praying confirmation of title to two thousand acres of land in two tracts; one of twelve hundred acres, lying between Indian and Mosquito rivers, called the Haul-over; the other tract of seven hundred and thirty acres, lying in McDougall back swamp, with a memorial to have the lands surveyed, dated May 23, 1818; an order of survey by Governor Coppinger, dated June, 1818; a certified copy of plat and certificate of survey made by Robert McHardy for memorialist, dated 24th July, 1818; a translation of a memorial and decree of 18th October, 1819, and 20th October, 1819: ordered to be filed.

Sarah Tate, by John B. Strong, her attorney, presented her memorial to this board, praying confirmation of title to four hundred and fifty acres of land, on the Tomoka river, with a certified copy of concession made by Governor White to John Edward Tate, father of the memorialist, dated July 8, 1803; also a deposition of James Arnon, attested by James S. Tingle, clerk of the superior court; an order of survey from Juan de Pierra, dated 24th January, 1804, to Juan Purcell, surveyor; and a certified copy of plat and certificate of survey, dated 10th September, 1804, made by Juan Purcell for Juan E. Tate: ordered to be filed.

Robert Gilbert, by John B. Strong, his attorney, presented his memorial to this board, praying confirmation of title to one hundred acres of land, lying on Matanzas river, and has not been surveyed, with a certificate of Juan de Pierra, dated 1st March, 1798: ordered to be filed.

Joseph S. Sanchez, by John B. Strong, his attorney, presented his memorial to this board, praying confirmation of title to twenty acres of land, lying on Anastasia island, and has not been surveyed, with a certified copy of concession by Governor White to Francis Xavier Sanchez, father of memorialist, dated 8th July, 1802: ordered to be filed.

Moses E. Levy presented his memorial to this board, praying confirmation of title to one thousand acres of land, lying on the west bank of the river Matanzas, to the southward of St. Augustine, with a certified copy of plat and certificate of survey made by George J. F. Clarke, dated 15th March, 1818; also a certified copy of royal title to Fernando de la Maza Arredondo, Jun., by Governor Coppinger, dated 7th March, 1816; and a deed of conveyance from said Arredondo to Moses E. Levy and James R. Hanham, dated 5th May, 1822: ordered to be filed.

Moses E. Levy presented his memorial to this board, praying confirmation of title to two hundred acres of land, lying on Moses or Pelica creek, on Matanzas river, south of St. Augustine, with a certified copy of plat and certificate of survey made by George J. F. Clarke, dated 20th of July, 1819: ordered to be filed.

Francis de Medicis presented his memorial to this board, praying confirmation of title to eighty-three and a third acres of land, lying on the east side of the river St. John's, a mile and a half from Picolata fort, being the third part, with a certified copy of concession made by Governor White to Isabel Cain, dated 23d December, 1802; a conveyance from Margaret Cain, daughter of Isabel Cain, to memorialist, dated 8th of September, 1808: ordered to be filed.

John Addison presented his memorial to this board, praying confirmation of title to one thousand eight hundred acres of land, lying on the river Tomoka, at a place called Carrickfergus, to the southward of St. Augustine, with a certified copy of royal title made by Governor Coppinger, dated the 8th June, 1816, to memorialist: ordered to be filed.

Isaac Hendricks, by Abraham Bellamy, presented his memorial to this board, praying confirmation of title to four hundred and fifty acres of land, lying on St. John's river and Coy's creek, a branch of said river, one mile above Jacksonville, with no exhibits: ordered to be filed.

George Anderson, by George Murray, his attorney, presented his memorial to this board, praying confirmation of title to four hundred and fifty acres of land, lying on the west side of the Tomoka river, with no exhibits: ordered to be filed.

John Silcock presented his memorial to this board, praying confirmation of title to three hundred acres of land, lying three miles from the road of Nassau river, in Duval county, with a certified copy of plat and certificate of survey made by Pedro Marrot, dated 18th March, 1792: ordered to be filed.

Francis Marein presented his memorial to this board, praying confirmation of title to two thousand acres of land, lying on the west side of the river St. John's, at a place known by the name of Cabbage hammock, with a certified copy of concession made to him the 15th November, 1815, by Governor Estrada; and a certified copy of plat and certificate of survey made by George J. F. Clarke, dated 24th April, 1821: ordered to be filed.

Gabriel Priest presented his memorial to this board, praying confirmation of title to five hundred acres. of land, lying on Black creek, with a certified copy of concession made to John M. Fontané by Governor Estrada, dated the 5th January, 1816: ordered to be filed.

Mary Fontané, administratrix of the estate of Joseph Fontané, deceased, presented her memorial to this board, praying confirmation of title to four hundred and ninety-five acres of land, lying at the head of Moultrie creek, with a certified copy of royal title made to Joseph Fontané by Governor Coppinger, dated 4th April, 1816: ordered to be filed.

Francis Pellicer presented his memorial to this board, praying confirmation of title to one thousand one hundred acres of land, in the territory of Matanzas, at a place called Pellicer's plantation, with a certified copy of royal title made to memorialist by Governor Kindelan, dated 30th March, 1815: ordered to be filed.

Farquhar Bethune presented his memorial to this board, praying confirmation of title to four hundred and twenty-five acres of land, situate on the river St. Mary's, at a place called Cabbage swamp, with a certified copy of royal title made by Governor Coppinger, dated 22d April, 1817, to memorialist; and a certified copy of plat and certificate of survey, made by George J. F. Clarke for memorialist, dated 10th June, 1818: ordered to be filed.

Farquhar Bethune presented his memorial to this board, praying confirmation of title to four caballerias and eleven acres, equal to about one hundred and forty-five acres, lying on the river St. John's, with a certified copy of royal title made by Governor White to Francis Xavier Hill, dated 30th January, 1811: ordered to be filed.

Farquhar Bethune presented his memorial to this board, praying confirmation of title to one hundred and seventy-two acres of land, lying in Spell's swamp, Nassau river, with a certified copy of concession made to memorialist by Governor Estrada, dated 25th August, 1815; also a certified copy of plat and certificate of survey made by George J. F. Clarke, dated 13th December, 1818: ordered to be filed.

Domingo Fernandez presented, by his attorney, Farquhar Bethune, his memorial to this board, praying confirmation of title to eleven hundred and fifty acres of land, lying on Big Dunn's creek, St. John's river, with a certified copy of royal title made to him by Governor Coppinger, dated 10th April, 1817, marked A: ordered to be filed.

Domingo Fernandez, by Farquhar Bethune, his attorney, presented his memorial to this board, praying confirmation of title to one hundred acres of land, on Amelia island, with a certified copy of conveyance from Isabella Jourdine to memorialist, dated 28th July, 1810: ordered to be filed.

Domingo Fernandez, by his attorney, Farquhar Bethune, presented his memorial to this board, praying confirmation of title to two hundred and twenty-eight acres of land, lying on the west side of Amelia island, with a certified copy of royal title made to him by Governor Coppinger, dated 10th April, 1817: ordered to be filed.

Domingo Fernandez, by his attorney, Farquhar Bethune, presented his memorial to this board, praying confirmation of title to two hundred and forty-five acres of land, lying near the mouth of the river Nassau, on Amelia river, with a certified copy of royal title made to Lewis Matteir by Governor Coppinger, dated 4th February, 1820; marked B; also a certified copy of conveyance from Lewis Matteir to memorialist, dated April 11, 1820, marked A: ordered to be filed.

Domingo Fernandez, by his attorney, Farquhar Bethune, presented his memorial to this board, praying confirmation of title to one hundred and fifty acres of land, lying on Amelia island, with a certified copy of royal title made by Governor White, dated the 19th August, 1807, to memorialist, marked A: ordered to be filed.

Domingo Fernandez, by his attorney, Farquhar Bethune, presented his memorial to this board, praying confirmation of title to a lot in the town of Fernandina, by the number of two, square number eighteen, with a certified copy of a royal grant made by Governor Coppinger, dated 27th March, 1818: ordered to be filed.

Domingo Fernandez, by his attorney, Farquhar Bethune, presented his memorial to this board, praying confirmation of title to a lot in the town of Fernandina, by the number four, square number twenty-three, with a certified copy of a royal grant made by Governor Coppinger, dated 10th April, 1817: ordered to be filed.

Domingo Fernandez, by his attorney, Farquhar Bethune, presented his memorial to this board, praying confirmation of title to three hundred acres of land, lying on Amelia island, with a certified copy of royal title made by Governor Coppinger, dated 11th April, 1817: ordered to be filed.

Pedro Estopa presented his memorial to this board, praying confirmation of title to fifteen and three-tenths acres of land, lying at a place known by the name of Stockade, one mile and three quarters north of St. Augustine, with a certified copy of concession made by Governor Quesada to memorialist, dated the 23d September, 1793; also a plat and certificate of survey made by Gamaliel Darling.

Domingo Fernandez, by his attorney, Farquhar Bethune, presented his memorial to this board, praying confirmation of title to three hundred acres of land, called Myrtle Grove, situated on Amelia island, with a certified copy of conveyance from Isabella Jourdine to memorialist, dated 4th May, 1809: ordered to be filed.

Domingo Fernandez, by his attorney, Farquhar Bethune, presented his memorial to this board, praying confirmation of title to one hundred acres of land, lying on Amelia island, with a certified copy of royal title made by Governor Kindelan to memorialist, dated 1st September, 1813, referred to, and marked A: ordered to be filed.

Domingo Fernandez, by his attorney, Farquhar Bethune, presented his memorial to this board, praying confirmation of title to four half lots in the town of Fernandina, numbers 5, 6, 7, and 8, of square number 23, with a certified copy of royal title made by Governor Coppinger to memorialist, dated 10th April, 1817, marked A: ordered to be filed.

Domingo Fernandez, by his attorney, Farquhar Bethune, presented his memorial to this board, praying confirmation of title to two hundred acres of land, lying on the main land opposite Amelia island, and known by the name of Orange Grove, with a certified copy of royal title made by Governor White to the heirs of Maria Matteir, dated the 25th April, 1807, marked A; a certified copy of conveyance from Lewis Matteir to memorialist, dated 11th April, 1820, marked B: ordered to be filed.

Bartholome de Castro y Ferrer, by John B. Strong, his attorney, presented his memorial to this board, praying confirmation of title to two thousand acres of land, lying at San Pablo, in the county of St. John's, with the following exhibits, to wit: a certified copy of a decree, dated 24th January, 1818, by Governor Coppinger; also a certified copy of royal title by Governor Coppinger, dated 28th February, 1818; and a certified copy of a plat and certificate of survey, dated 16th June, 1818, by Andres Burgevin: ordered to be filed.

Belton A. Copp presented his memorial to this board, praying confirmation of title to one thousand acres of land, lying in the county of St. John's, on the east side of the river of that name, from six to ten miles above lake George, with schedule B, containing a certified copy of the royal title made by Governor Coppinger to Captain Francisco Rivera, dated 31st October, 1818; also a conveyance from said Rivera to Gabriel Guillermo Perpall, dated the 2d November, 1818; also a conveyance from Gabriel G. Perpall to memorialist, dated 23d August, 1821; also a certified copy of plat and certificate of survey by Andres Burgevin, dated 6th February, 1819; likewise schedule A, containing a certified copy of concession of said one thousand acres of land, by Governor Coppinger, to the said Captain Francisco Rivera, dated 27th February, 1818: ordered to be filed.

Francisco P. Sanchez, by his attorney, John Drysdale, presented his memorial to this board, praying confirmation of title to one thousand acres of land, lying on Indian river, to the east of said river, with the following exhibits, to wit: a certified copy of concession by Governor Coppinger, dated 31st October, 1818, marked exhibit A; also a certified copy of royal title to memorialist, by Governor Coppinger, dated 3d April, 1818, marked exhibit B; also an order of survey by Governor Coppinger, dated 2d September, 1818, marked exhibit C; and a certified copy of plat and certificate of survey, dated 15th September, 1818, by Robert McHardy, marked exhibit D; which are ordered to be filed.

Andrew McDowell and Alexander Black, by John Drysdale, their attorney, presented their memorial to this board, praying confirmation of title to one thousand acres of land, lying on the St. John's river, on the east side of Dunn's lake, in the middle branch, called Han creek, with the following exhibits, to wit: a certified copy of concession, by Governor Coppinger to William Travers, dated 14th May, 1818, marked exhibit A; also a certified copy of plat and certificate of survey, by Andres Burgevin for William Travers, dated 5th November, 1818, marked exhibit B; also a certified copy of royal title made by Governor Coppinger to William Travers, dated 6th November, 1818, marked exhibit C; also a certified copy of conveyance by William Travers to Francisco P. Sanchez, dated 20th October, 1820, marked exhibit D; and also an attested copy of conveyance from Francisco P. Sanchez to memorialist, of said land, dated 11th June, 1823, marked exhibit E; which are ordered to be filed.

Petrona Martinez, and other heirs of Matthias Martinez, deceased, by their attorney, John Drysdale, presented their memorial to this board, praying confirmation of title to one thousand acres of land, lying at a place called the Big Hammock, about forty miles westward of Buena Vista, with a certified copy of royal title made by Governor Coppinger to Matthias Martinez, dated the 26th January, 1818, marked exhibit A; also a certified copy of concession by Governor Coppinger, dated 24th January, 1818, marked exhibit B; also an explanatory document, marked exhibit C, dated the 26th of January, 1818: ordered to be filed.

Moses Elias Levy presented his memorial to this board, praying confirmation of title to two thousand acres of land, lying on the west bank of Indian river, opposite the Haul-over, with a certified copy of royal title made by Governor Coppinger to Thomas Lorente, dated 26th June, 1818; also a memorial and order of survey, made the 28th April, 1819, and a certified copy of plat and certificate of survey, made by Andres Burgevin, dated the 24th May, 1819, for said Lorente; also a deed of conveyance from the said Thomas Lorente to memorialist, dated in the Havana, the 14th of November, 1821: ordered to be filed.

Moses Elias Levy presented his memorial to this board, praying confirmation of title to five hundred acres of land, lying on Jupiter island, with a certified copy of royal title made by Governor Coppinger in favor of Joaquim Sanchez, dated 15th June, 1818; also a conveyance from Joaquim Sanchez to Antonio Mier, dated 22d January, 1822: and a conveyance from Antonio Fernandez Mier, dated 22d January, 1822: ordered to be filed.

In a resolution adopted by the board upon the 15th of September, 1823, two blanks were filled, the first by inserting the words "to any person;" the second by inserting the word "person;" and the following words were erased by the board, to wit: "*and living in the vicinity of the witness.*" The said resolution then read as follows:

"*Resolved*, That claimants desiring to obtain the testimony of any witness residing without the Territory of Florida, shall file, with the secretary, their interrogatories; and that the district attorney, under the direction of the board, shall, if required, annex cross-interrogatories on behalf of the United States; and that, in all cases where the witnesses are resident within the Territory, the claimants may file depositions, taken *ex parte*, as the said witnesses are subject to the jurisdiction of the commissioners, leaving it optional with the claimants to proceed by filing interrogatories; and that a commission, with the interrogatories so annexed, shall be directed to any person authorized to administer oaths, sealed by the secretary, and delivered to the party so making application; and it shall be the duty of said person to take the answers of said witness to all such interrogatories, and none other, and to certify the same, and whether the said commission was sealed when delivered."

Which resolution was adopted by the board.

The board then adjourned until to-morrow morning, at 9 o'clock, November 29th, 1823.

SATURDAY, *November* 29, 1823.

The board met pursuant to adjournment. Present, all the members, and adjourned until Monday, December 8th, 1823.

The following claims were received this day:

John Salome, claim for two hundred acres of land, lying on the head of Five-mile Branch of Trout creek, St. John's river, with a certified copy of plat, and certificate of survey, made by George J. F. Clarke, dated the 18th March. Filed.

Jeremiah Wingate, claim for four hundred and twenty acres of land, in different tracts; two hundred thereof on the north side of Nassau river; one hundred and twenty in Plummer's Swamp; one hundred in Plummer's Swamp, Nassau river, with three plats and certificates of survey, by George J. F. Clarke, referred to, and dated 2d and 23d December, and 6th October, 1818. Filed.

John Wingate, claim for two hundred acres of land, lying on Lofton's Swamp, Nassau river, with a certified copy of plat, and certificate of survey, by George J. F. Clarke, dated 4th October, 1818. Filed.

Lewis Bailey, claim for three hundred and ninety-two acres of land, lying on Turkey Branch, St. Mary's river, with a certified copy of plat, and certificate of survey, made by George J. F. Clarke, dated 5th November, 1818. Filed.

Ellis Stafford, claim for five hundred acres of land, in two tracts, three hundred thereof lying at the mouth of Dunn's creek, St. Mary's river; two hundred acres on Dunn's creek, St. Mary's river, with two certified copies of plats, and certificates of surveys, by George J. F. Clarke, dated 12th October, 1818, and 4th November, 1818. Ordered to be filed.

Frederick Hartley, claim for four hundred acres of land, lying at the head of Nassau river, with no exhibit. Filed.

Frederick Hartley, claim for six hundred acres of land, lying on Old Field Branch, Julington creek, St. John's river, with a certified copy of plat, and certificate of survey, by George J. F. Clarke, dated 8th July, 1819. Filed.

Charles Homer, claim for two hundred acres of land, lying on Boggy Swamp, Nassau river, with a certified copy of plat, and certificate of survey, by George J. F. Clarke, dated 14th April, 1821. Ordered to be filed.

Horatio Low, claim for four hundred acres of land, lying on St. Mary's river, in front of Colerain, with a certified copy of plat, and certificate of survey, made by George J. F. Clarke, dated 12th June, 1821. Filed.

William McCully, claim for three hundred acres of land, on St. Mary's river, high up, with a certified copy of plat, and certificate of survey made by George J. F. Clarke, dated 8th September, 1818. Filed.

Westley Low, claim for four hundred acres of land, lying on Plummer's swamp, Nassau river, with a certified copy of plat, and certificate of survey, made by George J. F. Clarke, dated 19th June, 1821. Filed.

James Woods, claim for seventy-five acres of land, lying on the north of Mill's swamp, and east of the King's road, with a certified copy of plat, and certificate of survey, made by George J. F. Clarke, dated 13th December, 1818. Filed.

Thomas Moy, claim for three hundred and fifty acres of land, lying at Row's Bluff, Bell's river, with a certified copy of plat, and certificate of survey, by George J. F. Clarke, dated 21st September, 1819. Filed.

Thomas King, claim for three hundred and fifty acres of land, in two tracts, viz: two hundred and fifty-seven acres of which lie at Live Oak Landing, St. Mary's river, and one hundred acres on Walker's Swamp, St. Mary's river, with two plats, and certificates of surveys, by George J. F. Clarke, dated 26th November, 1818, and 27th January, 1821. Filed.

Martha Dell, claim for four hundred and fifty acres of land, lying on St. Mary's river, with a certified copy of plat, and certificate of survey, by George J. F. Clarke, dated 26th May, 1818. Filed.

Simeon Dell, claim for six hundred and ninety-six acres of land, in three tracts, four hundred lie on the north side of Payne's savannah; two hundred lie on Boggy Swamp, Nassau river; and ninety-six lie on Meely's creek, St. Mary's, with three plats, and certificates of surveys, by George J. F. Clarke, dated 14th May, 1818, 25th of August, 1820, and 10th of November, 1820. Filed.

William and John Lofton, claim for three hundred acres of land, lying on the north of Julington creek, St. John's river, with a certified copy of plat, and certificate of survey, by George J. F. Clarke, dated 6th July, ——. Filed.

Joseph Prevatt, claim for four hundred acres of land, lying in Turner's swamp, with a certified copy of plat, and certificate of survey, by George J. F. Clarke, dated 10th October, 1818. Filed.

Joseph Summerall, claim for two hundred acres of land, lying on St. Mary's river, with a certified copy of plat, and certificate of survey, by George J. F. Clarke, dated 18th January, 1820. Filed.

James Bradley, claim for four hundred and fifty acres of land, in two tracts, two hundred and fifty thereof lie on Cedar swamp, and two hundred on Black creek, both on the waters of St. John's river, with a certificate of permission by George J. F. Clarke, dated 16th August, 1820. Filed.

Thomas Prevatt, claim for five hundred and fifty acres of land, lying on the St. Mary's river, with a certified copy of plat, and certificate of survey, by George J. F. Clarke, dated 14th May, 1818.

William Eubanks, claim for one hundred acres of land, lying below the mouth of Trout creek, St. John's river, with a certified copy of plat, and certificate of survey, by George J. F. Clarke, dated 12th of December, 1818. Filed.

William Hartley, claim for two hundred and fifty acres of land, lying on Willis's Swamp, Julington creek, St. John's river, with a certified copy of plat, and certificate of survey, by George J. F. Clarke, dated 10th July, 1819. Filed.

George Hartley, claim for four hundred acres of land, lying on Old Field Branch, Julington creek, St. John's river, with a certified copy of plat, and certificate of survey, by George J. F. Clarke. Filed.

Daniel Plummer, claim for six hundred acres of land, lying on St. Mary's river, at the place called Old Township; no exhibits, but reference to the public archives for the grant and survey. Filed.

Edward Dixon, claim for one hundred acres of land, lying on Pigeon creek, St. Mary's river, with a certified copy of plat, and certificate of survey, made by George J. F. Clarke. Filed.

William Garvin's heirs, claim for sixteen thousand acres of land, lying in the neighborhood of the head of Oklawaha creek, with a certified copy of concession of a square of land, five miles in length, by Governor Coppinger, dated 21st October, 1817. Filed.

Theophilus Woods, Sen., claim for three hundred and seventy acres of land, in two tracts; two hundred and twenty lie on Deep creek, St. Mary's river, and one hundred and fifty on Reedy Branch, St. Mary's river, with two certified copies of plats, and certificates of survey, by George J. F. Clarke, dated 9th November, 1818, and 10th December, 1820. Filed.

Theophilus Woods, Jun., claim for two hundred and fifty acres of land, in two tracts; one hundred and sixty lie on St. Mary's river, and ninety-six lie, likewise, on St. Mary's river, with two certified copies of plats, and certificates of survey, dated 11th December, 1820, and 12th December, 1820, by George J. F. Clarke. Filed.

Delia Broadway presented her memorial for two thousand five hundred acres of land, lying on Dunn's creek, with a certified copy of concession, by Governor Estrada, dated the 15th September, 1815, to memorialist. Filed.

John Birks, claim for three hundred acres of land, lying on Front creek, east side of St. John's river, with a certified copy of plat, and certificate of survey, dated 11th June, 1817, by George J. F. Clarke. Filed.

Joseph Gaunt, claim for three hundred and twenty-five acres of land, lying in Turnbull's swamp, west of Hillsborough river, with a concession made to memorialist, by Governor Coppinger, dated 12th October, 1816. Filed.

Maxey Dill, claim for seven hundred acres of land, in two tracts; four hundred thereof lie on the north of Payne's savannah, and three hundred lie on Dunn's creek, St. Mary's river, with two certified copies of plats, and certificates of survey, dated 13th May, 1818, and 9th July, 1819, by George J. F. Clarke. Filed.

Isaac Tucker, claim for two hundred acres of land, in two tracts; one hundred lie on Coy's creek, St. John's river; and one hundred lie on St. John's river, in two surveys of fifty each, with a certified copy of concession for one hundred acres of land, by Governor White, dated 24th May, 1804, and two certified copies of plats, and certificates of survey, by George J. F. Clarke, dated 6th April, 1821, and 10th April, 1821. Filed.

Thomas Higginbottom, claim for two hundred acres of land, lying on St. Mary's river, with a certified copy of plat, and certificate of survey, made by George J. F. Clarke, dated 17th October, 1818. Filed.

Joseph Hagens, claim for four hundred acres of land, lying in two tracts; two hundred lie on the forks of Cormorant creek and Julington creek, St. John's river; the other two hundred on the north of Julington creek, St. John's river, with certified copies of two plats, and certificates of survey, by George J. F. Clarke, both dated 15th September, 1819. Filed.

William Thomas, claim for two hundred acres of land, lying on a branch of Little St. Mary's, with a conveyance from John Hall to William Thomas, dated the 12th April, 1823, and an affidavit of said Hall of the same date. Filed.

Stephen Eubanks, Jun., claim for four hundred and fifty acres of land, lying on the north side of Thomas's Swamp, near Snake Bluff, Nassau river, with a certified copy of plat, and certificate of survey, dated 17th December, 1818. Filed.

James Plummer, Jun., claim for three hundred acres of land, on the north of Julington creek, St. John's river, with a certified copy of plat and certificate of survey by George J. F. Clarke. Filed.

Hartwell Leath, claim for three hundred acres of land in two tracts; two hundred lie on Big creek, St. Mary's river, and one hundred on Sweet spring branch, St. Mary's river, with two copies of plat and certificates of survey by George J. F. Clarke, both dated 11th of November, 1818. Filed.

John Mizell, claim for eight hundred acres of land, lying in different tracts; four hundred lies on Long's hammock, on the south side of Mizell's lake; two hundred lie on Hickory Bluff, St. Mary's river; and two hundred on Brandy creek, St. Mary's river, with three copies of plats and certificates of survey, certified by George J. F. Clarke, and dated as follows: one, 6th of May, 1818, and the other, 10th of November, 1818. Filed.

Charles Hovey, claim for four hundred acres of land, lying on Plummer's swamp, Nassau river, with a certified copy of plat and certificate of survey dated 18th June, 1818, by George J. F. Clarke. Filed.

William Nelson, claim for three hundred and fifty acres of land in two tracts; two hundred and fifty lie on St. Mary's river, Mills's ferry, and one hundred acres between said river St. Mary's and river Nassau, with a permission of George J. F. Clarke, dated 8th of October, 1818. Filed.

John Dixon, claim for three hundred and fifty acres of land in two tracts; two hundred lie on St. Mary's river, and one hundred and fifty acres lie on Pigeon creek, with two plats and certificates of survey, certified by George J. F. Clarke, dated 12th and 13th of May, 1818. Filed.

Peter Swelly, claim for one hundred and fifty acres of land, lying on Long bay, about seven miles to the northwest of St. Augustine, with certified copy of plat and certificate of survey, by George J. F. Clarke. Filed.

David Scurry, claim for three hundred acres of land, lying on the east of Godsby's lake, St. John's river, with a certified copy of plat and certificate of survey, by George J. F. Clarke, dated 26th of July, 1820. Filed.

George Long's heirs, claim to three hundred and fifty acres of land, lying at the head of Matanzas river, west side of Graham's creek: not been surveyed, and with no exhibits. Filed.

William Sparksman, claim for three hundred acres of land, on the north side of the crossing place of Boggy swamp: no survey. Filed.

George J. F. Clarke, claim for three hundred and fifty acres of land, lying in Graham's swamp, at the head of Matanzas river, with a concession of Governor Quesada, dated the 23d of February, 1792, and a memorial from Honoria Clarke to the Government, dated the 19th of September, 1787, praying confirmation of certain documents; and a certified copy of plat and certificate of survey, by George J. F. Clarke, dated the 12th of May, 1818. Filed.

James Clarke, claim for three hundred acres of land, lying on Graham's swamp, at the head of Matanzas river, with a certified copy of plat and certificate of survey by George J. F. Clarke, dated 10th of May, 1818. Filed.

James and George J. F. Clarke, claim to five hundred acres of land, lying on the west of Matanzas river, with a British grant by Governor Tonyn to Honoria Clarke, dated 29th of September, 1780. Filed.

Charles W. and George J. F. Clarke, claim three hundred acres of land, on the Matanzas river, at a place called Worcester, with a British grant by Governor Grant, dated 2d of April, 1770. Filed.

Charles and George J. F. Clarke, claim for one thousand acres of land in different tracts; three hundred acres of which lie on the Matanzas river, at a place called Johnson's; three hundred acres lie at Emery's, on the Matanzas river; three hundred acres lie at Durbin's swamp, near the Twenty-mile house, with a certified copy of concession by Governor Quesada, dated 6th of February, 1792. Filed.

George J. F. Clarke, claim for two thousand acres of land, lying on the northwest of Payne's savanna in Alachua, with a certified copy of concession made by Governor Coppinger to C. W. Clarke, dated the 10th of June, 1816; also, a conveyance from Charles W. Clarke to Duncan L. Clinch, dated 24th of November, 1823; and a conveyance from Duncan L. Clinch to the memorialist, dated the 24th of November, 1823. Filed.

John Low, claim for seven hundred and fifty acres of land, lying at Bell's old field, or Bell's river, with a certified copy of royal title, dated the 30th of January, 1812, by Governor Estrada, made to memorialist. Filed.

Daniel O'Hara, claim for fifteen thousand acres of land, lying on the heads of Nassau river, on Alligator swamp, and Mill's swamp, with a certified copy of concession, dated 5th of September, by Governor White. Filed.

George Henning, claim for two hundred acres of land, lying on Bell's river, near Row's Bluff, with a certified copy of concession by Governor White, dated 2d of October, 1805. Filed.

James Lewis, Jun., claim for three hundred acres of land in two tracts; fifty of which lie at Buena Vista, on St. John's river, and two hundred and fifty lie in Caucah swamp, east side of St. John's river, with a certified copy of concession for fifty acres by Governor White, dated 22d of December, 1806; and a reference for the two hundred and fifty acres to the public archives. Filed.

James Dell, claim for sixteen thousand acres of land, lying in different tracts, to wit: eight thousand acres lie on Santa Fé river, or creek, three thousand lie on Brushy creek, at St. Mary's river, and five thousand lie on Turnbull's swamp, near the head of Indian river, with a certified copy of concession made by Governor Coppinger, dated 24th of March, 1816. Filed.

Sarah Brevard, claim for three hundred acres of land in different tracts, to wit: one hundred and sixty acres, lying on the waters of Nassau river, at a place called Doctor's island; thirty-eight acres lie near the head of Pumpkinhill creek, and one hundred acres at Pumpkinhill swamp, with a certified copy of concession made to John Brevard by Governor Coppinger, dated 7th of August, 1817; also a certified copy of royal title made by Governor Coppinger, dated 13th of February, 1816, to the heirs of Francisco Brevard. Filed.

James Dell presented his memorial for five hundred acres of land, lying on the north part of Payne's savanna, at a place called Hagan's point, with a certified copy of concession by Governor Coppinger, dated 16th of December, 1816. Filed.

James Dell, claim for five hundred acres, lying on the south of Mizell's, alias Orange lake, with a plat and certificate of survey, certified by George J. F. Clarke, dated 8th of January, 1818. Filed.

John Hampton, claim for five hundred and thirty-five acres, lying in front of Trader's hill, on St. Mary's river, with a plat and certificate of survey, certified by George J. F. Clarke, dated 8th of May, 1818. Filed.

John Lowe, claim for two hundred and fifty acres of land, lying on Bell's river, with a certified copy of royal title made by Governor Coppinger to William Carney, dated 4th of April, 1816. Filed.

Moses Harrold, claim for three hundred and ninety-five acres of land, lying on the river Nassau, with a certified copy of royal title made by Governor Coppinger to memorialist, dated the 8th of May, 1821, and a reference to the public archives for plat and certificate of survey. Filed.

Stephen Eubanks, Jun., claim for three hundred and twenty-five acres in two tracts; two hundred and ten acres lie on Trout creek, St. John's river; the other, one hundred and fifteen acres, has not been surveyed; with a certified copy of concession made by Governor Coppinger, dated 18th of March, 1817. Filed.

Stephen Eubanks, Sen., claim to two hundred and fifty-five acres of land on Nassau river, with no exhibit, but a reference to the public archives for the grant. Filed.

William Eubanks presented his claim for two hundred acres of land in two tracts; one hundred and seventy lie on Big Cedar creek, the other thirty acres lie on Burton island, Nassau river, with a certified copy of concession by Governor Coppinger, dated 18th of March, 1817. Filed.

John Creighton, claim to three hundred and five acres of land, lying on Plym's island, on the west of St. John's river, with a certified copy of concession by Governor White, dated 29th of October, 1803. Filed.

Alexander Creighton, claim for two hundred and fifty-four acres of land, lying on St. John's river, at a place called Lovett's, with a certified copy of plat and certificate of survey by Pedro Marrot and John Samuel Eastlake, dated 14th of November, 1792. Filed.

Charles Brevard, claim for two hundred and fifty acres of land, lying on Cedar creek, of St. John's river, with a certified copy of concession by Governor Coppinger, dated the 18th of November, 1817. Filed.

Charles Brevard, claim for one hundred acres of land, lying on Lofton's branch, south side of Nassau river, with a plat and certificate of survey, certified by George J. F. Clarke, dated 14th of December, 1818. Filed.

Francis Richard, claim for sixteen thousand acres of land, lying on Pottsburg creek and Cedar swamp, about a mile distant from McQueen's mills, with a certified copy of concession by Governor Coppinger, dated 4th of June, 1817. Filed.

Abraham Hannean, claim for fifty acres of land, lying at Little Grove, on the east side of St. John's river, and north of the military station of Buena Vista, has never been surveyed, with a certified copy of concession by Governor Coppinger, dated 18th of September, 1816. Filed.

Ezekiel Tucker, claim for one hundred and fifty acres of land, lying on Tucker's creek, Nassau river, with a certified copy of concession by Governor Coppinger, dated 18th March, 1817. Filed.

Eugenia Brant, claim for two hundred and fifty acres of land, lying at Row's bluff, on Bell's river with a certified copy of concession made by Governor White to Stephen Brant, her deceased husband, dated 18th April, 1803. Filed.

Heirs of David Garvin, claim for five hundred acres of land, lying on Pope's hammock, west of St. John's river, with a certified copy of plat and certificate of survey by George J. F. Clarke, dated 4th of December, 1817. Filed.

John Jennings, claim for five hundred and fifty acres of land, lying at a place called Belly, south of St. Mary's river: no exhibit. Filed.

James Bose, claim to twenty-five acres of land, lying in Pivet's swamp, four miles west from St. Augustine, with a certified copy of concession by Governor White, dated 15th September. Filed.

James Woodland, claim to two hundred acres of land, lying on Sample's creek, Nassau river, with a deed of conveyance from Susannah Blunt to Robert Rollings, dated the 2d July, 1821; also another deed of conveyance from Robert Rollins to memorialist, dated 30th July, 1822; and also a reference to the archives for the original grant. Filed.

Mrs. Collier, widow of Thomas Collier, claim for one thousand two hundred acres of land, lying on Tomoka river, with a certified copy of concession by Governor White, dated the 8th May, 1804. Filed.

Pedro Cocifacio, by George Murray, his attorney, presented his claim for two thousand acres of land, lying north of the post of Buena Vista, with a certified copy of royal title made to him by Governor Estrada, dated 12th of October, 1815. Filed.

James Darley, by his attorney, George Murray, presented his claim to twenty-three thousand acres of land, lying on the west side of Dunn's lake, with a certified copy of concession made by Governor Coppinger, dated the 10th November, 1817; and a certified copy of plat and certificate of survey by George J. F. Clarke, dated the 21st December, 1817. Filed.

John Bunch, claim to one thousand one hundred and sixty acres of land, lying in the territory of Mosquito, at a place called Moultrie and Moncrief, with a certified copy of royal title made to memorialist by Governor Coppinger, dated the 24th April, 1819. Filed.

William Travers, claim to eight thousand acres of land, lying on the west side of Long lake, west part of St. John's river, about forty miles south of lake George, with the following exhibits, to wit: a certified copy of royal title made, by Governor Coppinger, dated the 22d February, 1817, to Felipe Robert Yonge; a certified copy of concession by the same Governor to said Yonge, dated 11th February, 1817; order of survey dated 25th May, 1818; and a conveyance from said Yonge to memorialist, dated the 22d December, 1820. Filed.

William Travers, claim to twelve thousand acres of land, lying at the lagoon called *Second*, south of lake George, on St. John's river, with a conveyance from Filipe Robert Yonge, dated the 22d December, 1820. Filed.

William Travers, administrator of Thomas Travers, deceased, claim to one hundred and seventy-two acres of land, lying on the river St. John's, at a place called *St. Patricio*, with a certified copy of royal title by Governor White, dated 27th September, 1808. Filed.

William Travers, agent for John Forbes and Co., claim to one thousand nine hundred acres of land and twenty-five perches, lying on San Pablo creek, with a certified copy of royal title, made by Governor White for Catalina Chicken, and other heirs of Andrew Dewees, dated the 4th May, 1804; likewise a certified copy of conveyance from Catalina Chicken to John Forbes, dated 5th June, 1811. Filed.

William Travers, administrator of Thomas Travers, deceased, claim for one hundred and twenty-five acres of land, lying on St. John's river, at a place called St. *Patricio*, with a certified copy of royal title, made to Thomas Travers by Governor White, dated 28th September, 1808, and a reference to the public archives for certificate of survey. Filed.

William Travers, one of the heirs of Thomas Travers, deceased, claim for one thousand acres of land, at a place called the *Old Savannah*, where Mr. Mann had a rice plantation, with a certified copy of royal title, made by Governor Coppinger to the heirs of Thomas Travers, dated the 9th July, 1819. Filed.

Fernando de la Maza Arredondo, Jun., claim for fifteen hundred acres of land, lying five miles east of Spring garden, with a certified copy of royal title by Governor Coppinger to memorialist, dated the 9th August, 1820. Filed.

Fernando de la Maza Arredondo, Jun., by George Murray, presented his claim for fifteen thousand acres of land, lying on the west side of Lake George, in East Florida, with a certified copy of royal title, made by Governor Coppinger to memorialist for services, dated the 9th August, 1819. Filed.

Fernando de la Maza Arredondo, by his attorney, George Murray, presented his claim for *fifty thousand acres of land*, lying about forty miles west of the St. John's river, with a certified copy of *royal title* (merced) to him, dated the 24th April, 1810, by Governor White. Filed.

Fernando de la Maza Arredondo, by his attorney, presented his claim for five hundred acres of land, lying on the south side of Nassau river, about ten miles from its mouth, with a certified copy of concession, made by Governor White to Samuel King, dated 9th March, 1803; a certified copy of transfer from said King to memorialist, dated 9th June, 1808. Filed.

Joseph M. Arredondo, by his attorney, George Murray, presented his claim for twenty thousand acres of land, lying in Alachua, about eighty miles from St. Augustine, at a place called Big Hammock, with a certified copy of royal title, by Governor Coppinger to him, dated 30th March, 1817. Filed.

José M. Arredondo, by his attorney, George Murray, presented his claim for forty thousand acres of land, lying on the river Oklawaha, on both sides of the river, with a certified copy of royal title to him by Governor White, dated 2d January, 1811. Filed.

Pedro Cocifacio, claim for five hundred and twenty-two acres of land, with a certified copy of royal title by Governor Estrada to memorialist, dated the 2d October, 1815. Filed.

Juan B. Entralgo, by his attorney, George Murray, presented his claim for four thousand acres of land, lying at a place called Big Spring, on the river St. John's, and about twenty-five miles south of Lake George, on the west bank, with a certified copy of royal title, made by Governor Coppinger to Pedro Miranda, dated the 11th April, 1821; also a renunciation of said title to the aforesaid land by Pedro Miranda to memorialist, dated 5th December, 1821. Filed.

Juan B. Entralgo, by his attorney, George Murray, presented his claim to ten thousand four hundred acres of land, lying on the St. John's river to the west, and about twelve miles south of lake George, with a certified copy of royal title, made by Governor Coppinger, dated the 10th April, 1821, to Antonio Huertas; a renunciation of Huertas to memorialist, dated the 4th December, 1821; a certified copy of plat and certificate of survey by Andres Burgevin, dated the 5th April, 1821. Filed.

Juan B. Entralgo, by George Murray, his attorney, presented his claim to four thousand acres of land, lying on Black creek, with the following exhibits: a certified copy of royal title by Governor Coppinger to Fernando de la Maza Arredondo for ten thousand acres of land, (four thousand of which lie on Black creek,) dated 9th August, 1820; also another certified copy of royal title, made by same Governor to F. M. Arredondo, dated 9th August, 1820, for four thousand acres; a certified copy of conveyance from F. M. Arredondo to memorialist, dated 5th January, 1821. Filed.

José Cone, claim for one hundred and fifteen acres of land, lying on St. Mary's river, at a place called Upper Dunn's creek, with a certified copy of concession, made to him, dated the 29th May, 1805. Filed.

Francis Miles, a minor, by John M. Hanson, presented his claim for three hundred acres of land, lying on the river St. John's, at place called *Terios*, with a certified copy of royal title, made to the heirs of Francisco Xavier Sanchez by Governor White, dated 4th February, 1811. Filed.

Francis Miles, a minor, by John M. Hanson, presented his claim for two hundred acres of land, lying on the North river, with a certified copy of plat and certificate of survey by Pedro Marrot, for Barbara Strasburghy Hainsman, dated the 2d June, 1793, and a conveyance (certified copy of) from Barbara Hainsman to Francisco Xavier Sanchez, dated 11th September, 1797. Filed.

Samuel Miles, claim for sixteen thousand acres of land, lying at the mouth of St. Lucia river, with a certified copy of concession made by Governor Kindelan to him, dated the 19th July, 1813; and a certified copy of plat and certificate of survey by Robert McHardy, dated the 7th May, 1815. Filed.

James R. Hanham, claim to one hundred and seventy-five acres of land, lying between the North river and Guana river, called *El Burgos*, with a certified copy of plat and certificate of survey by Pedro Marrot and Josiah Dupont, dated the 26th May, 1793, and a translation thereof by A. Gay, and a deed of conveyance from Andres Pacety to the memorialist, dated the 20th May, 1822. Filed.

Nicholas Gomez's heirs, by George Murray, their attorney, presented their claim for twelve hundred acres of land, lying in the territory of Mosquito, on Hillsborough river, at a place called "Ross's Place," with a certified copy of royal title by Governor Coppinger, for the heirs of Donna Nicolasa Gomez, dated the 5th November, 1818. Filed.

James and Emanuel Ormond, by George Murray, presented their claim for two thousand acres of land, at Tomoka, at a place called Damietta, with a certified copy of royal title made by Governor Coppinger, dated 18th April, 1816; also a memorial and order of survey, dated 10th February, 1816; and a copy of a certified copy of plat and certificate of survey of Robert McHardy, dated 19th February, 1816. Filed.

George Murray, claim to an island called Key West, *Cayo Hueso*, consisting of eight thousand acres of land, at the extremity of the Florida reef, in the county of Monroe, and has ever been known by the name of *Cayo Hueso*, or Key West, until recently it has received the name of Thompson's island, with a certified copy of conveyance from John P. Sallas to John B. Strong, dated the 24th September, 1821, referred to, and marked B; and a certified copy of conveyance from John B. Strong to memorialist, dated 11th February, 1822, referred to, and marked C. Filed.

James G. Smith, claim for five hundred acres of land, lying in McQueen's swamp, on St. Mary's river, with a certified copy of plat and certificate of survey by George J. F. Clarke, dated the 3d October, 1818. Filed.

Philip R. Yonge, by his attorney, Farquhar Bethune, presented his claim for five hundred acres of land, lying on the river St. John's, with a certified copy of plat and certificate of survey by Pedro Marrot, dated the 17th December, 1791. Filed.

Ferdinand McDonald, claim for eight hundred and fifty acres of land, lying at Sr. Stout, Matanzas, near the bars, with a certified copy of concession made to Guillermo McHenry by Governor Quesada, dated 8th October, 1790; also a certificate of Tomas de Aguilar, dated 19th December, 1817. Filed.

Thomas Andrew, on behalf of himself and sister, heirs of Robert Andrew, deceased, by his attorney, Farquhar Bethune, presented his claim for five hundred acres of land, lying at San Diego, with a certified copy of royal title made by Governor White to father of memorialists, dated the 6th April, 1809, referred to, and marked B; a certified copy of plat and certificate of survey by Pedro Marrot, dated 12th May, 1793, referred to, and marked A. Filed.

Farquhar Bethune presented his claim for sixteen thousand acres of land, in three different parts, viz: nine thousand five hundred and seventy-two acres on Black creek, St. John's river; five thousand acres in Turnbull's swamp, Mosquito; fourteen hundred and twenty acres in Cabbage swamp, near the river St. Mary's, with a certified copy of concession made by Governor Coppinger, dated the 22d April, 1817; and three certified copies of plat and certificate of survey of said lands, dated 3d July, 1817, 19th February, 1820, and 19th May, 1820. Filed.

James Pelot, by his attorney, Farquhar Bethune, presented his claim for six hundred and twenty acres of land on Amelia island, with a certified copy of concession by Governor White to John Francis Pelot, son of memorialist, dated 20th December, 1823, marked A; and a certified copy of plat and certificate of survey, dated 16th July, 1816, by George J. F. Clarke, marked B. Filed.

Ferdinand D. McDonald, by his attorney, Farquhar Bethune, presented his claim for eight hundred and fifty-five acres of land, with a decree of Governor Coppinger, dated 24th May, 1819, and a certificate from the Government notary, dated 25th May, 1819. Filed.

Maria Mills, for herself and children, by her attorney, Farquhar Bethune, presented her claim for one hundred and fifty acres of land, contiguous to Johnson's creek, with a certified copy of royal title by Governor Coppinger, for the widow and heirs of William Mills, dated 9th July, 1819, and a reference to the archives for the survey. Filed.

Thomas Andrew, guardian of the grandchildren of Margaret O'Neale, by Farquhar Bethune, presented his claim for three hundred acres of land, lying on Langford creek, with a certified copy of royal title by Governor White to the children and heirs of Margaret O'Neale, deceased, dated 15th June, 1810. Filed.

Thomas Andrew, guardian of the grandchildren of Margaret O'Neale, deceased, by Farquhar Bethune, their attorney, presented his claim for three hundred and seven acres of land, lying on Langford creek, near Amelia island, with a certified copy of royal title by Governor White to Margaret O'Neale, dated 12th March, 1807. Filed.

Thomas Andrew, on behalf of himself and sisters, heirs of Robert Andrew, deceased, by Farquhar Bethune, his attorney, presented his claim for two hundred acres of land, lying on the northwest side of the river St. John's, with a certified copy of plat and certificate of survey, dated 20th April, 1807, by Juan Purcell, marked B, and a certified copy of concession by Governor White, dated 23d September, 1803, marked A. Filed.

James Pelot, by his attorney, Farquhar Bethune, presented his claim for ten caballerias and twenty acres of land, lying on Pumpkin hill, river Nassau, with a certified copy of plat and certificate of survey by Pedro Marrot and Josiah Dupont, dated March 31, 1793. Filed.

James Pelot, by his attorney, Farquhar Bethune, presented his claim for fourteen caballerias and twenty-nine acres of land, or about four hundred and ninety-six acres, lying on Pelot's island, St. John's river, with a certified copy of plat and certificate of survey made by Pedro Marrot and Josiah Dupont, dated 14th April, 1793. Filed.

Domingo Fernandez, claim for three hundred and twenty-two acres of land; has not been located with a reference to the public archives for decrees. Filed.

John W. Simonton, by his attorney, John Rodman, presented his claim to a tract of land, being the island of Key West, known also by the name of Thompson's island, with a reference to the public archives for the grant, and a certified copy of the grant, dated the 26th August, 1815. Filed.

Teresa Rodriguez, on behalf of herself and children, by her attorney, John W. Simonton, presented her claim for five thousand five hundred acres of land, lying on two margins of a creek running from the west, and empties into the river St. John's, about two miles north of a lake known by the name of *Long lake*, and has never been surveyed—with reference to the public archives in this city for the grant, and a certified copy of concession by Governor Estrada, dated 18th October, 1815. Filed.

Geronima Martinelly, claim for three hundred and sixty-six and two-thirds acres of land, lying at Guana creek, being the plantation known as San Genaro, with a certified copy of royal title made by Governor Coppinger to Jose Peso de Burgo, father of memorialist, dated the 28th February, 1818; and a certificate of Bernardo Segui, Charles Robion, and F. Arredondo, stating that the above tract fell to memorialist on a division of the estate of Jose Peso de Burgo, her father. Filed.

Eusebio M. Gomez, claim for twelve thousand acres of land, lying on the rivers Jupiter and Santa Lucia; never been surveyed; with a certified copy of concession by Governor Estrada, dated the 17th July, 1815. Filed.

John M. Sanchez, claim for eleven hundred and thirty-six acres of land, on the St. John's river, being the plantation called San Jose, with a reference to the public archives for proofs. Filed.

James Richards, claim for two hundred acres of land, lying on Amelia island, adjoining the lands of Harrison and Lamb, with reference to the public archives for proof. Filed.

Peter Mitchell *et al.*, claim for five hundred and fifty acres of land, on the Oklawaha, in lieu of fifteen hundred varras in the town of Fernandina, or a confirmation of either of them, with plat of survey by said Mitchell, marked exhibit B; and a document, purporting to be the proceedings in relation to the land in Fernandina, marked exhibit A. Filed.

Peter Mitchell, agent for Robert Mitchell, presented his claim for a lot of land within the limits of the city of St. Augustine, known as Mitchell's Grove, with reference to the archives and the clerk of the superior court for proofs; likewise a plat of survey of said grove. Filed.

Robert Mitchell and John P. Williamson, assignees of Carnochan L. Mitchell, by Peter Mitchell, presented their claim for two lots in the town of Fernandina, Nos. 2 and 3, with reference to the public archives. Filed.

Robert Mitchell, trustee for the children of Julia Scarborough, by Peter Mitchell, his agent, presented his claim for six thousand seven hundred and eighty-eight acres of land, or a section and a half, in Alachua, with reference to the public archives for proofs; likewise, reference to the office of this board for vouchers filed by Peter Mitchell and Moses E. Levy; and, likewise, reference to the clerk of the superior court for the conveyance by F. M. Arredondo and son. Filed.

Peter Mitchell, agent for Henry Yonge, presented his claim to sixteen thousand acres of land, lying on Black creek, river St. John's, with a reference to the public archives for the concession, and a certified copy of plat and certificate of survey by George J. F. Clarke, dated 15th June, 1816, referred to, and marked exhibit A. Filed.

Anthony L. Molyneaux, by Peter Mitchell, his agent, presented his claim to a lot in this city, with reference to the public archives. Filed.

Scipio, a free black, claims to twenty-five acres of land on the east side of the river St. John's, at a place known by the name of Podan Aram, twenty-eight miles west of St. Augustine, with a certified copy of concession by Governor White, dated 9th October, 1809. Filed.

Peter Mitchell, for himself and Ogden, Day, and Co., and Anthony L. Molyneaux, presented his claim for three thousand five hundred acres of land lying at a place called Volusia, on the St. John's river, with a copy of two surveys referred to, and marked exhibit A; and sundry documents relating to said land, referred to, and marked exhibit B. Filed.

Joseph Delespine, by John Drysdale, his attorney, presented his claim for two hundred acres of land, lying south of Turtle mount, district of Mosquito, east bank of the Hillsborough river, with a reference to the public archives for evidence. Filed.

Francis P. Sanchez presented his claim, by his attorney, John Drysdale, for twenty-five acres of land in St. John's county, at Moultrie, with reference to the public archives. Filed.

Francis P. Sanchez, by John Drysdale, his attorney, presented his claim for one hundred acres of land in St. John's county, on the North river and Guana creek, with a reference to the public archives and the clerk of the superior court of St. John's county. Filed.

Manuel Marshall, by his attorney, John Drysdale, presented his claim for two hundred and fifty acres of land; never been surveyed, lying on St. Mark's pond, nine miles from the city of St. Augustine, with reference to the public archives. Filed.

J. Allen Smith, by John Drysdale, presented his claim to a lot in this city, with reference to the public archives and the clerk of the county court. Filed.

J. Allen Smith, by John Drysdale, his attorney, presented his claim to a lot in this city, with reference to the public archives. Filed.

Magdalena Joanada, for herself and heirs of Nicholas Sanchez, deceased, by her attorney, John Drysdale, presented her claim for three hundred acres of land, lying in Diego plains, at a place called Qui Qui, with a certified copy of concession made by Governor White to Nicholas Sanchez, dated 3d February, 1800, referred to, and marked exhibit A, also, a certified copy of plat and certificate of survey by Juan Purcell, dated 23d June, 1809, referred to, and marked B; and a certified copy of royal title by Governor Coppinger to the heirs of Nicholas Sanchez, dated 2d April, 1819, marked exhibit C.   Filed.

Francis P. Sanchez, by his attorney, John Drysdale, presented his claim for two thousand acres of land, lying at a place called Oklawaha, on a creek of the river St. John's, with a certified copy of concession to Francisco de Medicis by Governor Estrada, dated 14th December, 1815, referred to, and marked exhibit A; also, a certified copy of an order of survey by Governor Estrada, dated 25th December, 1815, referred to, and marked exhibit B. Filed.

Francis P. Sanchez, by his attorney, John Drysdale, presented his claim to two thousand acres of land, lying at a place called Oklawaha, on the margin of a creek of the river St. John's, with a certified copy of concession by Governor Estrada to Juan Percheman, dated 12th December, 1815.   Filed.

Andrew McDowell and Alexander Black, by their attorney, John Drysdale, presented their claim to four hundred and fifty acres of land, lying on Graham's swamp, between the heads of Halifax and Matanzas rivers, with a reference to the public archives; also, a plat and certificate of survey by George J. F. Clarke, dated 12th March, 1818, referred to, and marked exhibit A; also, a certified copy of conveyance from José M. Ugarté, agent of Margarita Clarke, to F. M. Arredondo, dated the 23d August, 1820, referred to, and marked exhibit B; also, a certified copy of conveyance from F. M. Arredondo to Francis P. Sanchez, dated 25th August, 1820, referred to, and marked exhibit C; and a reference to the records of the clerk of the county court.   Filed.

Joseph Simeon Sanchez, for himself and other heirs of Francisco Xavier Sanchez, by his attorney, John Drysdale, presented his claim for one thousand acres of land, lying in Diego plains, at a place called Montes de San Juan, with a certified copy of plat and certificate of survey by Robert McHardy, in four parts, dated the 26th May, 1819, referred to, and marked exhibit A; also, a certified copy of royal title by Governor Coppinger, dated 5th June, 1821, for the heirs of the deceased Francisco Xavier Sanchez, referred to, and marked exhibit B.   Filed.

Joseph Simeon Sanchez, for himself and other heirs of Francisco Xavier Sanchez, by his attorney, John Drysdale, presented his claim for one hundred acres of land lying in Diego plains, at a place called Montes de Puercos, with a certified copy of concession by Governor White to Francisco Xavier Sanchez, dated 4th August, 1801, marked exhibit A; also, a certified copy of plat and certificate of survey by Andres Burgevin, dated 30th March, 1819, marked exhibit B; and a certified copy of royal title by Governor Coppinger to the heirs of Francisco Xavier Sanchez dated the 5th June, 1821, marked exhibit C.   Filed.

William G. Saunders, by his attorney, John Drysdale, presented his claim for thirty-six caballerias, or twelve hundred acres of land, lying at a place called Russelltown, on the St. John's river, with a certified copy of royal title made by Governor Quesada to memorialist's father, dated 10th December, 1791, referred to, and marked exhibit A.   Filed.

Heirs of William Mills, by their attorney, John Drysdale, presented their claim for five hundred acres of land, situated on the south side of St. Mary's river, at a place called Mill's ferry, and has never been surveyed, with reference to the public archives for proof.   Filed.

Samuel Harrison, on behalf of himself and other heirs of Samuel Harrison, deceased, by John Drysdale, his attorney, presented his claim to eighteen caballerias, or six hundred acres of land, lying on Seymour point, Nassau river, with a certified copy of concession by Governor Quesada, dated 1st October, 1791, referred to, and marked exhibit A; also, a certified copy of plat and certificate of survey by Pedro Marrot and Samuel Eastlake, dated 14th February, 1792, referred to, and marked exhibit B.   Filed.

Thomas Murphy, claim to three thousand acres of land, lying on St. John's river, on the eastern branch thereof, and known as Murphy's island, with a reference to the public archives, and a certified copy of plat and certificate of survey by Andres Burgevin, dated the 4th July, 1818.   Filed.

Octavius Mitchell, by his attorney, John Drysdale, presented his claim to two thousand acres of land, lying in the Territory of Mosquito, with a memorial and order of survey by Governor Coppinger, dated 2d June, 1818, referred to, and marked exhibit A; also, a certified copy of plat and certificate of survey by Robert McHardy, dated 25th of July, 1818, referred to, and marked exhibit B; and a reference to the public archives for concession. Filed.

George J. F. Clarke, claim to two thousand acres of land, lying in Yallahasasa, west of the river St. John's, on the road to Alachua, with a certified copy of concession by Governor Quesada, dated 12th January, 1812.   Filed.

George J. F. Clarke, claim to four thousand acres of land, lying in different tracts, (being the remainder of a twenty-six thousand acre tract,) with a certified copy of concession by Governor Coppinger, dated 17th December, 1817.   Filed.

Peter Mitchell, by John Rodman and John Drysdale, his attorneys, presented his memorial, claiming title to a tract of land, lying on Alachua, with reference to the public archives and a plat.   Filed.

John Drysdale and John Rodman, by their attorney, Thomas F. Cornell, presented their claim to two thousand two hundred and sixty-two acres of land, lying in Alachua, with reference to the public archives, the memorial of Peter Mitchell, and the clerk of the county court of St. John's county.   Filed.

Jasper Ward, by John Drysdale, his attorney, presented his claim to the moiety, or half part, of the Alachua grant, with a reference to the public archives.   Filed.

Antonio Huertas, by John Rodman, his attorney, presented his claim to ten thousand acres of land, lying on Six-mile creek, with reference to the public archives for documents relating to the said land.   Filed.

Horatio S. Dexter's claim to the Alachua country, with the exception of Peter Mitchell's part, with no reference or exhibits.   Filed.

Horatio S. Dexter, by John Rodman, his attorney, presented his claim to two thousand acres of land, being an undivided part of the tract commonly known by the name of Volusia tract, with reference to the public archives. Filed.

Horatio S. Dexter, by John Rodman, his attorney, presented his claim to a tract of land three miles square, lying on Indian river, with no reference or exhibits.   Filed.

Horatio S. Dexter, by John Rodman, his attorney, presented his claim to a tract of land containing a mill-seat, and two thousand five hundred and sixty acres of land, lying on Moultrie creek, and known by the name of Bushnell's mill-seat, with a certified copy of conveyance by Robert Cain to memorialist, dated 10th September, 1818; also, a plat of the same, and a reference to the public archives.   Filed.

Horatio S. Dexter, by John Rodman, his attorney, presented his claim to sixteen thousand acres of land, lying on Indian river, with a certified copy of a plat and certificate of survey, by George J. F. Clarke, dated 15th August, 1819.   Filed.

James Curtis, by John B. Lancaster, his attorney, presented his claim for four hundred acres of land, lying on the North river, eight miles from St. Augustine, with a certified copy of plat and certificate of survey by Benjamin Lord, dated 20th day of May, 1784, and sundry other British papers relating to said land.   Filed.

Paul Dupon, by John Rodman, his attorney, presented his claim for three thousand acres of land, lying on an island on the eastern side of the river St. John's, with a certified copy of royal title to memorialist by Governor Coppinger, dated the 26th April, 1819; a certified copy of plat and certificate of survey by Andres Burgevin, dated 3d June, 1818. Filed.

Andrew Drouillard, by his attorney, John Rodman, presented his claim for three thousand acres of land on Dunn's lake, at a place called Old Field, with a certified copy of concession by Governor Coppinger, dated 10th January, 1818; also, a certified copy of plat and certificate of survey by George J. F. Clarke, dated 15th April, 1818. Filed.

Josiah Smith, by John Rodman, his attorney, presented his claim for 40,824 square yards within the precincts of this city, with a reference to the public archives; also, a certified copy of plat and certificate of survey by Andres Burgevin, dated 9th December, 1819. Filed.

Josiah Smith, by John Rodman, his attorney, presented his claim for four hundred acres of land, lying on Nassau river, at a place called Spell's old fields, with a certified copy of concession by Governor White to Archibald Atkinson, dated 12th July, 1804. Filed.

Josiah Smith, by John Rodman, his attorney, presented his claim for one thousand acres of land, lying at a place called Row's bluff, on St. Mary's river, with a certified copy of royal title by Governor Coppinger to him, dated 24th April, 1820; also, a plat. Filed.

Hannah Smith, by her attorney, John Rodman, presented her claim to three hundred and eighty-nine and two-thirds acres of land, lying at a place called St. Lucia, with a reference to the public archives.

Antelm Gay, by John Rodman, his attorney, presented his claim for five hundred acres of land, lying on Indian river, front of the Barrederos, with a certified copy of conveyance from Lewis Matteir, dated the 19th of February, 1821; also a certified copy of royal title to Lewis Matteir, by Governor Coppinger, dated 3d January, 1821; and a certified copy of plat and certificate of survey by Andres Burgevin, dated the 30th December, 1820. Filed.

Antelm Gay, by John Rodman, his attorney, presented his claim for five hundred acres of land, situated eighteen miles north of this city, at a place called Governor Grant, with a certified copy of royal title by Governor Coppinger to Joaquim Sanchez, dated the 16th May, 1820; also a certified copy of conveyance from said Sanchez to memorialist, dated the 19th May, 1820, and a plat of the tract. Filed.

Marie Rose François Felix, marquis de Fourgeres, by his attorney, John Rodman, presented his claim for sixteen thousand acres, in two tracts, six thousand acres of which lie on Black creek, and six thousand on Indian river, with a certified copy of concession by Governor Coppinger to Don José Argote Villalobos, dated 29th October, 1817; also a certified copy of conveyance by Villalobos, with the proceedings thereon under the Spanish Government; also a certified copy of plat and certificate of survey for lands on Indian river, by George J. F. Clarke, dated the 15th December, 1817; and another certified copy of plat and certificate of survey by George J. F. Clarke, dated 1st December, 1817, for lands on Black creek. Filed.

John Geddes, Duke Goodman, and William Lance, executors of the will and testament of Charles A. Bulow, deceased, on behalf of the heirs of said Bulow, by John Rodman, their attorney, claim title to two thousand acres of land, lying at Tomoka, with a certified copy of royal title to Francisco Pellicer, by Governor Coppinger, dated the 22d July, 1818; also a certified copy of plat and certificate of survey, by Robert McHardy for Pellicer, dated 14th March, 1818, and a reference to the public archives; likewise to the public records kept by Mr. Tingle. Filed.

John Geddes, Duke Goodman, and William Lance, executors of the will and testament of Charles W. Bulow, deceased, on behalf of the heirs of said Bulow, presented their claim, by John Rodman, their attorney, to four thousand six hundred and seventy-five acres of land, in three different tracts: the first tract lies on Graham's swamp, between the Matanzas and Tomoka rivers, and contains three thousand four hundred and eighty-six acres; the second tract, of five hundred and fourteen acres, lies the west side of the river Halifax; the third tract, of six hundred and seventy-five acres, lies on the west side of Halifax river; with a reference to the public archives for evidence, and the public records of this city kept by Mr. Tingle. Filed.

John Geddes, Duke Goodman, and William Lance, executors of the last will and testament of Charles W. Bulow, deceased, on behalf of the heirs of said Bulow, by John Rodman, their attorney, presented their claim to a dwelling-house in St. Augustine, with a certified copy of conveyance from Donna Maria de la Conception Miranda, and proceedings thereon, dated the 4th of April, 1821. Filed.

John Geddes, Duke Goodman, and William Lance, executors of the last will and testament of Charles W. Bulow, deceased, on behalf of the heirs of said Bulow, presented their claim to six acres of land, and an orange grove within the precincts of the city of St. Augustine, with a certified copy of royal title by Governor Kindelan to Matthias Pons, dated 9th April, 1813; also a reference to the public archives, and a certified copy of plat and certificate of survey by Andres Burgevin, dated 23d May, 1821. Filed.

William Gibson, of St. Mary's Georgia, executor of the last will and testament of Ambrose Hull, deceased, for and on behalf of the heirs of said Hull, by John Rodman, his attorney, presented his claim to three hundred acres of land, lying at a place called Colonel Plummer, west side of the river St. John's, with a certified copy of royal title, by Governor Coppinger to Daniel Plummer, dated 23d December, 1819. Filed.

William Gibson, of St. Mary's, Georgia, executor of the last will and testament of Ambrose Hull, deceased, for and on behalf of the heirs of the said Hull, by John Rodman, his attorney, presented his claim to two hundred acres of land, situated on the west side of the river St. John's, with a certified copy of royal title by Governor Coppinger, dated the 18th January, 1816, to James Hull, and reference to the public archives. Filed.

William Gibson, of St. Mary's, Georgia, executor of the last will and testament of Ambrose Hull, deceased, for and in behalf of the heirs of said Hull, by John Rodman, his attorney, presented his claim for two thousand six hundred acres of land, in two tracts, as follows: fifteen hundred is situated in the district of Mosquito, at a place named Turnbull's eastern hammock, or New Smyrna, with a certified copy of royal title, made by Governor Estrada to Ambrose Hull, dated the 2d February, 1812, and certified copies of memorials, orders of surveys, certificates of surveys, and plats, and a reference to the public archives. Filed.

The heirs of Andrew Dewees, by John Rodman, their attorney, presented their claim to eighteen hundred and nine acres and twenty-five perches of land, lying at Pablo, county of St. John's, with reference to the public archives. Filed.

Joseph M. Hernandez presented his claim to this board for eight hundred acres of land, lying on Graham's swamp, with reference to the public archives for proofs of grant and survey. Filed.

Joseph M. Hernandez, claim for six hundred and thirty-five acres of land, lying at Matanzas, at a place called Buyck's hammock, with reference to the public archives for evidence of concession. Filed.

Joseph M. Hernandez, claim to one hundred acres of land, lying on the west side of the river Halifax, at a place called Old Chimneys; with no reference. Filed.

Joseph M. Hernandez, claim to four hundred and fifty-five acres of land, situated on the Northwest creek, a branch of the river Matanzas, otherwise called Pellicer's creek, with reference to the public archives for evidence of possession. Filed.

Joseph M. Hernandez, claim to three hundred and seventy-five acres of land, situated at Matanzas, with reference to the public archives. Filed.

Joseph M. Hernandez, claim to ten thousand acres of land, lying at the place known as the Salt spring, west side of lake George, with reference to the public archives. Filed.

Joseph M. Hernandez, claim for five thousand acres of land, situated between Buffalo bluff and Mount Tucker, being the half of a grant of ten thousand acres granted to him, with reference to the public archives for proofs of grant, royal title, and survey. Filed.

Joseph M. Hernandez, claim for five thousand acres of land, lying on the west side of the river St. John's, being the half of a grant of ten thousand acres made to him, with reference to the public archives for grant, royal title, and survey. Filed.

Joseph M. Hernandez, claim for about seventy acres of land, being a small island fronting the Little Matanzas bar, and has not been surveyed, with reference to the public archives. Filed.

Joseph M. Hernandez, claim, as attorney for Samuel Williams, deceased, for three thousand two hundred acres of land, situated on Halifax river, with reference to the public archives for grant, royal title, and survey. Filed.

Joseph M. Hernandez, claim to a house and lot in this city, situated in St. George street, with reference to the public archives. Filed.

Joseph M. Hernandez, claim to a house and lot in this city, with reference to the public archives for conveyance. Filed.

Joseph M. Hernandez, agent for Thomas Backhouse, presented his claim to five hundred acres of land on Indian river, near the St. Lucia river, with a certified copy of royal title by Governor Coppinger to T. B. Backhouse, dated the 20th June, 1818. Filed.

Joseph M. Hernandez, attorney for Martin Hernandez, presented his claim for three houses and lots in this city, with no exhibits. Filed.

Joseph M. Hernandez, for George Anderson, presented his memorial for a house and lot in this city, with no exhibits. Filed.

Joseph M. Hernandez, attorney in fact for Martin Hernandez, presented his claim for five hundred acres of land, lying on the river Halifax, south of lands belonging to G. W. Perpall, with reference to the public archives. Filed.

Joseph M. Hernandez, attorney in fact for Martin Hernandez, presented his claim for five hundred acres of land, lying in Cypress swamp, north side of Picolata road, with reference to the public archives. Filed.

Joseph M. Hernandez, attorney in fact for Martin Hernandez, presented his claim to twenty acres of land, lying on the river St. Sebastian, called the Ferry, with reference to the public archives. Filed.

Joseph M. Hernandez, attorney in fact for Martin Hernandez, presented his claim for ten and one-quarter acres and one perch of land, lying within the present limits of this city, with reference to the public archives. Filed.

Joseph M. Hernandez, attorney in fact for Martin Hernandez, presented his claim for one thousand acres of land, lying at the head of the Northwest creek, commonly called Pellicer's creek, Matanzas, with no exhibits. Filed.

Fernando de la Maza Arredondo, Jun., presented his claim for one hundred and seventy-five acres, lying on the west side of the river St. Sebastian, about three miles west from St. Augustine, with a certified copy of royal title by Governor Coppinger to Prince, a free black, dated 9th March, 1816, and a certified copy of conveyance from Flora, widow of Prince, to memorialist, dated 30th June, 1821. Filed.

Mrs. Ann Campbell, by Isaac N. Cox, Esq., her attorney, presented her claim to a town lot in this city. Filed.

The heirs of Richard Malpas, claim for two hundred acres of land, lying on the east side of the river St. John's, at a place called Terrios, about thirty-eight miles from this city, with a reference to the public archives.

Charles Robion, claim for seven hundred and ninety acres of land, lying on the west side of the river Matanzas, south of St. Augustine, with a certified copy of plat and certificate of survey, by George J. F. Clarke, dated the 18th March, 1818. Filed.

Margaret Scofield, by Isaac N. Cox, Esq., her attorney, presented her claim to three hundred acres, lying at a place called Springfield, in the Twelve-mile swamp, with a certified copy of concession by Governor White, dated the 7th June, 1798; also, a certified copy of plat and certificate of survey, by Andres Burgevin, dated the 24th of February, 1823. Filed.

Joseph F. White, by his attorney, Isaac N. Cox, Esq., presented his claim to two hundred and fifty acres of land, lying in Graham's swamp, with a certified copy of concession by Governor White to Alexander Watson, dated the 28th July, 1803; also, a certified copy of a decree by said Governor, dated the 28th June, 1804; and a conveyance from the aforesaid Watson to memorialist, dated 22d March, 1820. Filed.

Fernando de la Maza Arredondo and son, by their attorney, Isaac N. Cox, Esq., presented their claim to *two hundred and eighty-nine thousand six hundred and forty-five acres of land*, situated and known by the name of the *Alachua country*, with a certified copy of concession by Alexander Ramirez, Intendant General of the Island of Cuba, dated 22d December, 1817. Filed.

Felipe Solano, by Antonio Alvarez, presented his claim for one hundred acres of land, lying at Moultrie, about four miles, from St. Augustine, and has not been surveyed, with reference to the minutes of the common council of this city during the Spanish domination. Filed.

John A. Cavedo, claim for three hundred and fifty acres of land, lying on Black creek, with a certified copy of concession by Governor Estrada to him, dated 4th January, 1816. Filed.

Antonio Huertas, by Antonio Alvarez, his attorney, presented his claim for one thousand five hundred acres of land on the St. John's river, to the west, and about twelve miles south of lake George, with a certified copy of royal title, by Governor Coppinger, dated the 10th April, 1821, to memorialist, referred to, and marked A. Filed.

Antonio Huertas, by Antonio Alvarez, his attorney, presented his claim for two thousand five hundred acres of land, lying on the river St. John's, to the west, about twelve miles south of lake George, with a certified copy of royal title, by Governor Coppinger, to memorialist, dated the 10th April, 1821, referred to, and marked A, and a reference to the public archives for survey. Filed.

Geronimo Alvarez, by Antonio Alvarez, presented his claim to two half lots in the town of Fernandina, seventeen yards in front, and thirty-four in depth, with a certified copy of royal title, by Governor Coppinger to memorialist, dated 26th March, 1818. Filed.

Geronimo Alvarez, by Antonio Alvarez, presented his claim for a lot in the town of Fernandina, seventeen yards in front, and thirty-four in depth, with a certified copy of royal title to memorialist, by Governor Coppinger, dated the 26th March, 1818. Filed.

Joseph Simeon Sanchez, claim to six hundred acres of land in Diego plains, with a certified copy of royal title, to the heirs of Francisco X. Sanchez, deceased, dated the 12th February, 1811. Filed.

Joseph Simeon Sanchez, claim for five hundred acres of land, lying on the North river, with a certified copy of and from the treasurer of this city, Don Bartoleme Benitez y Galvez to Francisco X. Sanchez, dated 12th April, 1792. Filed.

Joseph Simeon Sanchez, claim for a town lot in Fernandina, with a certificate of George J. F. Clarke, dated 2d February, 1817. Filed.

Antonio Huertas, by Isaac N. Cox, Esq., his attorney, presented his claim for eight hundred acres of land, lying on the west bank of St. Sebastian river, with a certified copy of royal title, by Governor Kindelan to him, dated 26th October, 1813. Filed.

The heirs of Francis Goodwin, deceased, by L. H. Coe, their attorney, presented their claim to thirteen hundred acres of land, lying at a place called Bailey in the time of the British, four miles north of St. Vincent Ferrer, two miles north of John McIntosh's lands, with reference to the public archives. Filed.

The heirs of Francis Goodwin, deceased, by L. H. Coe, their attorney, presented their claim to thirteen hundred acres of land, lying on the east side of St. John's river, on Pablo creek, at a place called Dutch settlement, on McGirt's encampment, with reference to the public archives. Filed.

Ynez Gomez, by her attorney, Waters Smith, presented her claim to one thousand and seventy-five acres of land, lying on the river St. John's, with a certified copy of concession, by Governor Coppinger to memorialist's husband, dated the 4th of June, 1817. Filed.

William Bardin, by his attorney, Waters Smith, presented his claim for six lots of land, lying on the St. John's river, at a place called St. Anthony, with a certified copy of royal title, by Governor Kindelan to Uriah Bowden, dated the 17th April, 1815, and a reference to the public archives for the survey. Filed.

William Hobkirk, by Waters Smith, his attorney, presented his claim for a tract of land of five miles square, lying on St. Mary's river, near John Forbes's lines, with a certified copy of concession, by Governor Coppinger, dated the 18th September, 1816, marked A; an order from George J. F. Clarke, to survey, dated 20th December, 1816, marked B; also, a certificate of George Atkinson, dated 1st January, 1816, marked C. Filed.

Farquhar Bethune, claim for a lot in the town of Fernandina, No. 7, with a bill of sale of George Atkinson to memorialist, dated the 1st of September, 1815, marked A; and a certified copy of royal title, by Governor Kindelan to George Atkinson, dated the 16th August, 1814. Filed.

Farquhar Bethune, claim to a lot in the town of Fernandina, No. 10, with reference to public archives. Filed.

Farquhar Bethune, claim to a lot in the town of Fernandina, No. 5, with a concession, by Governor Estrada to Andrew Atkinson, dated 2d May, 1811. Filed.

Farquhar Bethune, claim for a lot of land in Fernandina, No. 9, with a concession from Governor White to Francisco Entralgo, dated 31st January, 1811. Filed.

John Middleton, by Farquhar Bethune, his attorney, presented his claim for a lot in the town of Fernandina, No. 6, with a certified copy of royal title by Governor Kindelan to James Cashen, dated the 13th March, 1814, referred to, and marked A; a conveyance from James Cashen, and Susannah his wife, to Middleton and Selby, dated the 20th November, 1817. Filed.

Maria Mills, by Farquhar Bethune, her attorney, presented her claim to a lot in the town of Fernandina, No. 12, with a certified copy of royal title by Governor Coppinger to the heirs of William Mills, dated 19th December, 1818. Filed.

Maria Mills, by Farquhar Bethune, her attorney, presented her claim to two half lots in the town of Fernandina, Nos. 1 and 2, with a certified copy of royal title by Governor Kindelan to Samuel Betts, dated 2d March, 1814. Filed.

William T. Hall, claim for twelve hundred and sixty-five acres of land, lying in the territory of Mosquito, at a place called Haul-over, between Indian and Hillsborough rivers, with reference to the public archives for evidence of possession. Filed.

William T. Hall, claim for seven hundred and sixty-five acres of land, lying in McDougall's back swamp, in the territory of Musquito, with reference to the public archives. Filed.

Charles Gobert, claim to two thousand acres of land lying on St. John's river, about ten miles south of Rollstown, at the entrance of Dunn's lake, with a certified copy of concession by Governor White to memorialist, dated the 12th November, 1804. Filed.

Joseph M. Sanchez, claim to two hundred acres of land, lying at Mosquito, on the river Mosquito, at a place called Sorragney, on the river Hillsborough, with a certified copy of concession by Governor White to Gertrude Carrello, dated 4th February, 1804, and a decree of said Governor, dated 27th March, 1804; also, a conveyance from John M. Fontané to memorialist, dated the 23d of May, 1822. Filed.

Lewis Guibert, by Thomas F. Cornell, his attorney, presented his claim for four hundred acres of land lying to the east of the river St. John's, with reference to the public archives. Filed.

Edward M. Wanton, by Thomas F. Cornell, his attorney, presented his claim for three hundred and fifty acres of land, lying on the east of the river St. John's, and known by the name of Picolata Ferry, with reference to the public archives, and a certified copy of plat and certificate of survey by George J. F. Clarke, dated the 17th November, 1819, marked D. Filed.

Edward M. Wanton, by Thomas F. Cornell, his attorney, presented his claim to three hundred acres of land, lying on the creek called Coleson's branch, on the east of the river St. John's, with reference to the public archives, and a certified copy of plat and certificate of survey by George J. F. Clarke, dated the 17th November, 1819, marked C. Filed.

Edward M. Wanton, by Thomas F. Cornell, his attorney, presented his claim to two hundred acres of land, lying on the east of the river St. John's, with reference to the public archives, and a certified copy of plat and certificate of survey by George J. F. Clarke, dated 17th November, 1819, marked A. Filed.

Edward M. Wanton, by Thomas F. Cornell, his attorney, presented his claim for one hundred and fifty acres of land situated on the east of the river St. John's, and known by the name of Wanton's plantation, with reference to the public archives, and a certified copy of plat and certificate of survey by George J. F. Clarke, dated the 17th November, 1819, marked B. Filed.

John Creyon, executor of Lucas Creyon, deceased, by John M. Fontané, presented his claim for one thousand acres of land in the territory of Mosquito, with reference to the public archives. Filed.

Joseph Wales, by John B. Strong, his attorney, presented his claim to two thousand three hundred and seventy-five acres of land, lying in McDougall's back swamp, with a memorial of memorialist to the Government, dated

6th October, 1817, and a concession of Governor Coppinger, dated 8th October, 1817, for lands in Spring Garden; likewise, a memorial from memorialist to change location, dated 5th February, 1818; likewise a decree from Governor Coppinger, dated 1st April, 1818, granting his request; and a certified copy of plat and certificate of survey by Robert McHardy, dated the 25th July, 1818. Filed.

Daniel Hurlbert, claim for three hundred acres of land, lying about six miles north of this city, and is called Levet, with a certified copy of the proceedings of a public sale by order of Government, and a conveyance from Francis P. Sanchez to memorialist, dated 12th April, 1823. Filed.

Daniel Hurlbert, claim for two hundred acres of land, lying about three miles from this city, on the savannas and marshes of Casacola, with a certified copy of the proceedings of a public sale by order of Government. Filed.

William Harvey, claim for two hundred acres of land, lying on Front creek, emptying into the river St. John's, at a place called Mult, with a certified copy of royal title, by Governor Coppinger to memorialist, dated 9th ——, 1818. Filed.

William Harvey, claim for eight hundred and fifty-one acres of land, lying on Petas creek, with a certified copy of royal title by Governor Coppinger, to Hannah Moore, mother of memorialist, dated 8th June, 1818; likewise a plat. Filed.

John Uptagrove, by George Gibbs, his attorney, presented his claim for one hundred acres of land on Amelia island, with reference to the public archives. Filed.

Philip R. Yonge and Zephania Kingsley, executors of John Frazus, deceased, by George Gibbs, their attorney, presented their claim for a tract, consisting of less than three thousand acres, with a reference to the public archives. Filed.

Hiberson and Yonge, by Governor Gibbs, their attorney, presented their claim for forty-five acres of land, lying north of Fernandina, and north of a creek called Viega, on Amelia island, with certified copies of concession by Governor White, dated 27th January, 1810, marked Y. Filed.

Zephaniah Kingsley, by George Gibbs, his attorney, presented his claim to a marsh lot in the town of Fernandina, with a certified copy of a memorial and decree, dated the 8th July, 1815, marked A; and a certified copy of royal title by Governor Coppinger, dated the 26th March, 1817. Filed.

Cyrus Briggs, by Abraham Bellamy, presented his claim for two hundred and fifty acres of land, lying on the river Nassau, adjoining Lofton's creek, with no exhibits. Filed.

Robert Shepherd, by John B. Strong, his attorney, presented his claim for one hundred acres of land, lying on the Mosquito river, and has never been surveyed, with a certified copy of concession, by Governor White to memorialist, dated 30th December, 1803. Filed.

Cyrus Briggs, by Abraham Bellamy, his attorney, presented his claim for one hundred acres of land, lying on Nassau river, at a place called Pearcent island, with no exhibits. Filed.

Robert Walker, by John B. Strong, his attorney, presented his claim for one hundred acres of land, lying on the river Mosquito, and has not been surveyed, with a certified copy of concession by Governor White to memorialist, dated 14th May, 1803. Filed.

The heirs of Henry Martin, deceased, by John B. Strong, their attorney, presented their claim for four hundred acres of land, praying confirmation of title to the same, lying at the Mosquito, and has not been surveyed, with a certified copy of concession, by Governor White to memorialist, dated the 3d September. Filed.

Sarah Petty, by John B. Strong, her attorney, presented her claim for two hundred acres of land, lying on the river St. Mary's, with a certified copy of plat and certificate of survey by Pedro Marrot and Samuel Eastlake, dated the 13th April, 1792. Filed.

Seymour Pickett, by John B. Strong, his attorney, presented his claim to three hundred and fifty acres of land, lying on the Mosquito river, at a place called New Smyrna, with a certified copy of concession by Governor White, to memorialist, dated 3d September, 1803; also, a certified copy of plat and certificate of survey by Juan Purcell, dated 24th May, 1804. Filed.

Seymour Pickett, by John B. Strong, his attorney, presented his claim to two hundred and fifty acres of land, lying at a place called Hodquin plantation, with a certified copy of royal title, by Governor Kindelan, to Reuben Hogans, dated 26th May, 1815, and an instrument purporting to be a conveyance from Reuben Hogans to memorialist. Filed.

Thomas Briggs and John Robertson, by their attorney, Edward R. Gibson, presented their claim for one thousand eight hundred acres of land, lying on Halifax river, with reference to the public archives and the public records of St. John's county. Filed.

Stephen Pearce and wife, on behalf of themselves and other heirs of William Mills deceased, presented their claim for two hundred and fifty acres of land, by John Drysdale, their attorney, with a mutilated copy of a British grant made to William Mills by Governor Grant; likewise, a mutilated copy of a plat and certificate of survey, dated 28th July, 1768. Filed.

Geronimo Alvarez, by George J. F. Clarke, presented his claim to five hundred acres of land, lying on the west side of Hillsborough river, with a certified copy of royal title, by Governor Coppinger to memorialist, dated 12th January, 1818. Filed.

Antonio Triay, by George J. F. Clarke, presented his claim to one thousand five hundred acres of land, situate at Mount Tucker, on river St. John's, with a certified copy of royal title, by Governor Coppinger to memorialist, dated 9th April, 1821. Filed.

Antonio Alvarez, by George J. F. Clarke, presented his claim for one thousand five hundred acres of land, situated on the west side of Ocklawaha creek, with a certified copy of royal title by Governor Coppinger to him of said land, dated the 7th December, 1817. Filed.

Pablo Sebate, by Antonio Alvarez, presented his claim for two hundred acres of land, lying at San Diego, at a place known by the name of *Plantage de Arroze de Clarke*, and has not been surveyed, with a certified copy of concession by Governor White, dated 21st May, 1803, marked A. Filed.

Pablo Sebate, by Antonio Alvarez, presented his claim for a tract of land six miles in length, situated at a place called Cascola, between Indian creek and Araguez creek, emptying into the North river, and has not been surveyed, with a reference to the public archives, and a certified copy of conveyance from the widow of Bryan Conner, deceased, to memorialist, dated the 7th of September, 1809, marked A. Filed.

Estevan Arnau, by Antonio Alvarez, presented his claim for one hundred acres of land, lying on Hillsborough river, with a certified copy of royal title by Governor Coppinger to him, dated the 19th June, 1818, marked B; and a certified copy of plat and certificate of survey by Robert McHardy, dated the 20th October, 1818, marked A. Filed.

Pablo Sebate, by Antonio Alvarez, presented his claim for two thousand five hundred acres of land, lying about seven miles from St. Augustine, with an order of survey by Governor Coppinger, of 18th June, 1818; a certified copy of plat and certificate of survey by Andres Burgevin, dated the 30th June, 1818; and a certified copy of royal title by Governor Coppinger, dated 2d April, 1818. Filed.

Felipe Solana, by Antonio Alvarez, presented his claim for thirty acres of land, situated at a place called Moultrie, with a certified copy of concession by Governor White to Pedro de Cala, dated 10th March, 1807, and a conveyance from said Cala to memorialist, dated the 30th June, 1821, marked A and B. Filed.

Francis Richard, by Antonio Alvarez, presented his claim for one thousand and twenty-five acres of land, lying on the west side of lake George, seven miles from Drayton's island, near the place known by the name of the Big Spring, with a certified copy of concession by Governor Coppinger to memorialist, dated the 10th January, 1818, marked A. Filed.

Felipe Solana, by Antonio Alvarez, presented his claim for two hundred and forty-five acres of land, at a place called Two Sisters, on Diego plains, with a certified copy of royal title to memorialist, dated May 6, 1816. Filed.

Francis Richard, by Antonio Alvarez, presented his claim for six hundred and fifty acres of land, lying at a place known by the name of Dudley, on the east side of the St. John's river, and north of Pottsburg creek, with a certified copy of concession by Governor Quesada to Samuel Russell, dated the 2d December, 1795, marked A; and an order of survey of Governor Coppinger, dated 5th June, 1821, marked B; likewise, a certified copy of plat and certificate of survey, dated 4th November, 1820, by George J. F. Clarke, marked C. Filed.

Francis Richard, by Antonio Alvarez, presented his claim for two hundred and fifty acres of land, situated on St. John's river, near the Cow Ford, at a place known by the name of Red Bay Hammock, with a certified copy of concession by Governor Coppinger, dated the 7th November, 1817, marked B; and a certified copy of plat and certificate of survey by D. S. H. Miller, dated the 22d March, 1819. Filed.

Francis Richard, by Antonio Alvarez, presented his memorial for three hundred and fifty acres of land, lying at a place called Strawberry hill, and has not been surveyed, with a certified copy of royal title to Reuben Hogans by Governor Coppinger, dated the 17th of April, 1817, marked A. Filed.

Francis Richard, by Antonio Alvarez, presented his claim for two hundred acres of land, lying on the east side of St. John's river and head of Pottsburg creek, known by the name of *Tiger Hole*, with a certified copy of concession by Governor Coppinger to Louis Zachariah Hogans, dated the 12th June, 1817, marked B; and a certified copy of plat and certificate of survey by George J. F. Clarke, dated the 26th June, 1818. Filed.

Gabriel Triay presented his claim for one of the Keys, known by the name of *Key Vacas*, with a certified copy of concession by Governor Coppinger to memorialist, dated 3d January, 1818, marked A. Filed.

Francis Philip Fatio, assignee of Samuel Betts, deceased, presented his claim for two thousand acres of land, lying in the territory of Mosquito, south of Ambrose Hull, and north of New Smyrna, with reference to the public archives. Filed.

Francis Philip Fatio, assignee of Samuel Betts, deceased, presented his claim for eighteen hundred acres of land, lying in the territory of Matanzas, with reference to the records, and an instrument conveying the said lands, together with the above tract, to Messieurs Arredondo, Fatio, and Fleming, in trust. Filed.

James Toole, claim to nine hundred and forty-five acres of land, lying in Graham swamp, on the Matanzas, with a certified copy of concession by Governor White, dated January 7, 1804. Filed.

Joseph M. Hernandez, claim to eight hundred acres of land, lying on the river Matanzas, with the following exhibits: 1st, a certified copy of proceedings to the grant to Dupont, and the title of Miguel Crosby, dated 31st May, 1805; 2d, a certified copy of regulations of Governor White, dated 12th October, 1803; 3d, a certified copy of grant to Miguel Crosby, dated 3d February, 1804; and a certified copy of plat and certificate of survey by Robert McHardy, dated 4th September, 1818. Filed.

Francis Ferreira, claim to fourteen acres of land, lying without the old lines, three-fourths of a mile north of this city, with a certified copy of concession by Governor White to Juan Bautista Ferreira, dated 27th July, 1803. Filed.

Benjamin Chair, claim to five hundred acres of land, lying at the head of the North river, at a place known by the name of Cabbage swamp, with a deed of conveyance by the heirs of Robert Andrew, deceased, dated the 16th August, 1822. Filed.

Andres Papy's claim to one hundred and twenty-six acres of land, lying at a place by the name of San Diego, north of this city, with a certified copy of conveyance from Philip Solana to Ana Pons, dated 9th February, 1819; a certified copy of plat and certificate of survey by Pedro Marrot, dated 13th May, 1793, and a reference to the public archives for royal title. Filed.

Joseph Baya, claim to one hundred and thirty acres of land, more or less, situated about two miles north of St. Augustine, known by the name of Moses, with a deed of conveyance from Bartoleme de Castro y Ferrer, attorney for Gumana Soria, to memorialist, dated the 21st June, 1823. Filed.

Richard Murray, administrator of Francis Brady, deceased, presented his claim for one hundred and forty-five acres of land, lying on the east side of St. John's river, on the west side of an arm of Trout creek, with a certified copy of concession by Governor White, dated 22d December, 1803, to John Wright; a deed of conveyance from Adam and Molly Wright to said Brady, dated 11th July, 1821; a certified copy of plat and certificate of survey by George J. F. Clarke, dated the 5th July, 1821. Filed.

Susannah Cashen, claim to three hundred acres of land, lying on Plym's island, on the river St. John's, with no exhibit. Filed.

Charlotte Gobert, by her trustee, Gabriel W. Perpall, presented her claim to one hundred acres of land, lying on the west side of San Marcos, nine or ten miles northwest from St. Augustine, with a certified copy of concession by Governor White to Charles Hill, (a free black,) dated the 4th December, 1806. Filed.

Robert Hutchinson presented his claim for one hundred and fifty acres of land, lying on the banks of Little St. Mary's river, with a certified copy of concession by Governor Estrada to the memorialist, dated the 11th September, 1811. Filed.

Antonio Williams, (a free black,) claim for three hundred acres of land, lying on St. Mark's lake, with a certified copy of concession by Governor White to memorialist, dated the 1st December, 1801. Filed.

Edward Ashton, claim for two hundred and forty-five acres of land, situated at the head of the creek called Turnbull, northwest from this city, with a certified copy of royal title by Governor Coppinger, dated the 18th of January, 1816. Filed.

John B. Strong, attorney for the estate of Ezekiel Hudnall, deceased, presented his claim for six hundred acres of land, lying on Amelia island, at a place known by the name of Beech Hammock, with a certified copy of concession by Governor White, dated 4th August, 1802. Filed.

John B. Strong, attorney for the estate of Ezekiel Hudnall, deceased, presented his claim for one hundred acres of land, lying on St. John's river, at a place known by the name of St. Nicholas, with a certified copy of conveyance by David S. Miller to Hudnall, dated the 11th February, 1819; also, a certified copy of plat and certificate of survey, by D. S. H. Miller, dated the 16th October, 1818. Filed.

Ezekiel Hudnall's estate, by John B. Strong, the attorney, presented their claim to two hundred and fifty-five acres of land, lying on the north bank of the river St. John's, nearly opposite the Fort of St. Nicholas, and on the east of a creek called Hogan's creek, with a certified copy of concession by Governor Coppinger to Daniel Hogan, dated the 18th March, 1817. Filed.

John B. Strong, attorney for the estate of Ezekiel Hudnall, deceased, presented his claim for two wooden houses at St. Nicholas, on the St. John's river, with a conveyance from Juan Jose Robles to Hudnall, dated May 6, 1818. Filed.

John B. Strong, attorney for the estate of Ezekiel Hudnall, deceased, presented his claim for a house and lot at St. Nicholas, on St John's river, with a conveyance from Ann Munroe, dated 17th October, 1818. Filed.

William Travers, by George Murray, his attorney, presented his claim for five hundred acres of land, four miles west of St. Augustine, with sundry British documents, and a memorial and order of survey by the Spanish Government, dated the 16th day of September, 1819; and a certified copy of plat and certificate of survey by Andres Burgevin, dated 20th December, 1819. Filed.

José Bernardo Reyes, claim for one thousand acres of land, lying on the east side of the Ocklawaha river, at a place known by the name of Bella Vista, near Chicochati ferry, west side of St. John's river, in St. John's county, with a certified copy of concession by Governor Coppinger to him, dated the 1st of June, 1818; also, a certified copy of plat and certificate of survey by Robert McHardy, dated 3d October, 1818, marked A. Filed.

At a meeting of the Board of Land Commissioners on Monday, the 8th December, 1823, pursuant to adjournment. Present, all the members.

Joseph B. Lancaster came before the board, and tendered his resignation as assistant secretary of this board; which was accepted.

James Bosley vs. the United States. Walters Smith, agent of said Bosley, being called on to answer if this claim was prepared for trial, declared it was not: whereupon, it is ordered that the same stand continued for further order of this board.

Edgar Macon, Esq. attended, by order of this board.

John H. McIntosh vs. the United States, claim for six thousand, three thousand, six hundred, three hundred, and one thousand acres, on Indian river: this day this case came on to be heard, and George Morrison, James Hall, and George J. F. Clarke, were examined as witnesses in the same; but, the board not being sufficiently advised, it is ordered that the same be continued until to-morrow.

The board then adjourned until to-morrow morning at nine o'clock.

TUESDAY, *December* 9, 1823.

The board met pursuant to adjournment. Present, all the members.

Edgar Macon, Esq., district attorney for East Florida, attended this day, under order of this board.

Lewis Hugeron was this day admitted and sworn in as assistant secretary of this board, well and truly and faithfully to perform the duties required of him by the Board of Land Commissioners.

Mr. Hamilton objected to either of the commissioners administering oaths when the board is not in session; that, depositions taken before either of the commissioners receive a consequence and importance from their official situation, that may mislead the judgment of Congress, as it will be presumed that the commissioners will have asked all pertinent and necessary questions.

Ordered, That the Secretary be directed, forthwith, to record the minutes of this board in a well-bound book.

Ordered, That the marshal of the United States for the district of East Florida be directed to prepare the Government house for the reception of this board.

It is ordered, That the rules of evidence governing courts of law govern this board for the future, viz: That the party calling the witness, first examine him, and then turn him over to the district attorney; and, when he has finished, the board can ask him any pertinent question which they conceive to have been omitted; but the party examining the witness cannot be interrupted without he is putting an improper question.

Mr. Hamilton dissented as to any restraint on the board in its examination.

The board then resumed the consideration of the case of John H. McIntosh, which was postponed until this day, and examined sundry witnesses, to wit: Gabriel W. Perpall, Antonio Alvarez, and Joseph M. Hernandez, and re-examined George J. F. Clarke.

At half past two o'clock, P. M., the board adjourned until to-morrow morning, at nine o'clock, A. M.

WEDNESDAY, *December* 10, 1823.

The board met this day pursuant to adjournment. Present, all the members.

Edgar Macon, Esq., district attorney for East Florida, attended this day, under order of this board.

Elias B. Gould presented his account to this board for printing and stationary, amounting to seventy-one dollars and twenty-five cents; which was approved, and ordered to be certified.

The board resumed the consideration of the case of John H. McIntosh, which was postponed until this day, and re-examined the former witnesses, viz: George Morrison and George J. F. Clarke.

At two o'clock, P. M., the board adjourned until to-morrow morning at nine o'clock, A. M.

THURSDAY, *December* 11, 1823.

The board met this day pursuant to adjournment. Present, all the members.

Edgar Macon, Esq., district attorney for East Florida, attended this day, under order of this board.

George J. F. Clarke presented to this board seven bundles of plats and certificates of surveys, and a register of the town of Fernandina; said surveys commencing in 1811, and ending in 1821; which are ordered to be put in the care of the secretary of this board.

The board resumed the consideration of the claim of John H. McIntosh, and re-examined therein George J. F. Clarke, and examined ———— Turnbull. At two o'clock, P. M., not being sufficiently advised of and concerning the said claim, adjourned the further consideration thereof until to-morrow.

The board adjourned until to-morrow, ten o'clock, A. M.

FRIDAY, *December* 12, 1823.

The board met this day pursuant to adjournment. Present, all the members.

Edgar Macon, Esq., district attorney for East Florida, attended this day, under order of this board.

On motion of Isaac N. Cox, a commission was issued to John Mountain, Collin Mitchell, and Daniel Osgood, or any one of them, in the city of Havana, for the purpose of obtaining the deposition of Thomas de Aguilar, in the case of F. M. Arredondo, Jun. vs. the United States; and cross-interrogatories were filed by the district attorney, under direction of the board.

The board resumed the consideration of the claim of John H. McIntosh, and re-examined therein George J. F. Clarke. At half past two o'clock, P. M., not being sufficiently advised of and concerning the said claim, adjourned the further consideration until to-morrow.

The board adjourned until to-morrow at 10 o'clock, A. M.

SATURDAY, *December* 13, 1823.

The board met this day pursuant to adjournment. Present, all the members.

Edgar Macon, Esq., district attorney for East Florida, attended this day, under order of this board.

The board then resumed the consideration of the claim of John H. McIntosh, and examined therein Bernard Segui. At one o'clock, P. M., not being sufficiently advised of and concerning the said claim, adjourned the further consideration thereof until Monday next.

The board adjourned until Monday next at 10 o'clock, A. M.

MONDAY, *December* 15, 1823.

This day the board met pursuant to adjournment. Present, all the members.

Edgar Macon, Esq., district attorney for East Florida, attended this day, under order of the board.

Resolutions were offered by Mr. Hamilton for the adoption of the board, in the words and figures, to wit:

"*Resolved*, That in all cases the board will direct their secretary to obtain from the keeper of the public archives the original documents upon which claims are founded, previous to their adjudications.

"*Resolved*, That the secretary be directed to procure from the keeper of the public archives the original documents in the case of James Bosley and John H. McIntosh, the first claims on the docket;" which, after due deliberation, was overruled; Messrs. Floyd and Blair both voting against its adoption.

The board resumed the consideration of the claim of John H. McIntosh, and re-examined therein Gabriel W. Perpall; at two o'clock, P. M., not being sufficiently advised of and concerning the said claim, adjourned the further consideration thereof until to-morrow.

The board adjourned until to-morrow at 10 o'clock, A. M.

TUESDAY, *December* 16, 1823.

The board met this day pursuant to adjournment. Present, all the members.

Edgar Macon, Esq., district attorney for East Florida, attended this day, under order of this board.

The board resumed the consideration of the claim of John H. McIntosh, and examined therein Andrew Burgevin; and, at 12 o'clock, P. M., not being sufficiently advised of and concerning the said claim, the further consideration thereof is postponed until to-morrow.

The board then adjourned until to-morrow, at 10 o'clock, A. M.

WEDNESDAY, *December* 17, 1823.

The board met this day pursuant to adjournment. Present, all the members.

Edgar Macon, Esq., district attorney for East Florida, attended this day, under order of this board.

Mr. Hamilton presented a resolution to the board in the following words and figures, to wit:

"*Resolved*, That the board will direct their secretary to select the claims presented to this board under the royal order of 1790, when the claims are supported by royal titles;" the consideration of which was postponed until to-morrow.

The board resumed the consideration of the claim of John H. McIntosh, and examined therein Daniel Hurlbut; but, not being sufficiently advised of and concerning the same, and good cause herefor appearing, they postponed the further consideration thereof until Monday, the 22d instant.

James Marshall *vs.* the United States, for five hundred acres. Upon motion of the claimant, by his attorney, John Drysdale, leave is given him to file interrogatories, to be propounded to Nicol Turnbull, a resident of Chatham county, in the State of Georgia; and that a commission be awarded to James M. Wayne, judge of the superior court of the eastern district of Georgia, and John P. Williamson, one of the justices of the inferior court of the said county of Chatham, or either of them, to take the answers of said Turnbull to said interrogatories.

The affidavits of Adam Tunno, and J. M. Davis, and Adam Tunno, and John Maynard Davis, proving the legitimate heirs of Doctor Andrew Turnbull, formerly of East Florida, deceased, were allowed to be withdrawn from the claims filed by John Drysdale, attorney for Nicol Turnbull.

John Love *vs.* the United States, for three hundred acres. Upon the calling of this claim, it appearing to the satisfaction of this board that the same is not prepared for adjudication, it is ordered that it be continued until a further day, and leave is given to introduce documents.

Samuel Fairbanks *vs.* the United States, for a lot in the city of St. Augustine. Upon the calling of this claim, it appearing to the satisfaction of this board that the same is not prepared for adjudication, it is ordered that it be continued until a further day, and leave is given to introduce documents.

Duncan L. Clinch *vs.* the United States, for five hundred acres. This claim not being prepared for adjudication, on motion of his attorney, it is ordered that it be continued until a further day.

Samuel Fairbanks *vs.* the United States, for eighty acres. This claim being called, and it appearing to this board that the same is not prepared for adjudication, it is ordered that it be continued until a further day, and leave is given to introduce documents.

Pedro Miranda *vs.* the United States, claim for one thousand acres. This day this claim came on to be heard; and, on motion, the papers were submitted to the board for their decision.

Bernard Segui *vs.* the United States, claim for seven thousand acres. This claim being called, and not being prepared for adjudication, it is ordered that it be continued until a further day.

Mary Ann Davis *vs.* the United States, claim for five hundred acres. This claim being called, and not being prepared for adjudication, it is ordered that it be continued until a further day.

Moses Elias Levy *vs.* the United States, claim for thirty-six thousand acres. This claim being called, and not being prepared for adjudication, on motion of his attorney, it is continued until to-morrow morning.

The board adjourned until to-morrow morning, at 10 o'clock, A. M.

THURSDAY, *December* 18, 1823.

The board met this day pursuant to adjournment. Present, all the members.

Edgar Macon, Esq., district attorney for East Florida, attended this day, under order of this board.

The form of a docket, exhibiting the character and circumstances of each claim, submitted by Mr. Hamilton, was adopted by the board; and that Mr. Macon, the United States' attorney, be authorized to employ as many persons as he may think proper to make out the same, aided by the secretary of the board.

To the decision of the commissioners in favor of the admission of the claims of Antelm Gay and others to record and adjudicate, Mr. Hamilton dissents; and states, as the grounds of his disagreement, that, by the treaty all grants, concessions, and orders of survey, dated subsequently to the 24th of January, 1818, are declared null and void; and that, unless expressly and specially revived by the acts of Congress, the commissioners can have no authority to take the said claims into consideration, inasmuch as the documents on which these claims are predicated bear date subsequent to 24th January, 1818.

On motion of Mr. Drysdale, the following rule was adopted by a majority of the board, viz:

"*It is ordered*, That, hereafter, commissions for the taking of testimony may issue in blank as to the names of the witness or witnesses to be examined: provided, that the claimant shall, in all such cases, whenever he can do so, name to the board, as commissioner, a judge of one of the courts of the United States, or a judge or justice of the superior, circuit, or county courts of the State in which the commission is to be executed."

Mr. Hamilton dissents to the issuing of any commission to ——— witness, unless the same be directed to a judge of the United States, or a judge or justice of the superior, circuit, or county courts of the State in which the commission is to be executed. Mr. Hamilton not being willing to issue blank commissions to any person or persons authorized to administer oaths, such as justices of the peace, notaries public, &c.

The board then adjourned until to-morrow morning, at 10 o'clock, A. M.

FRIDAY, *December* 19, 1823.

This day the board met pursuant to adjournment. Present, all the members.

Edgar Macon, Esq., district attorney for East Florida, attended this day, under order of this board.

On motion of Mr. Cox, leave is given him to amend his memorial in the case of Arredondo and son *vs.* the United States, for two hundred and eighty-nine thousand six hundred and forty-five acres and five-sevenths of an acre.

This day the United States' attorney made a motion, "whether the board considered themselves authorized to adjudicate and make a final decision upon a claim over which they had this power, which claim was a part of a grant for a greater number of acres of land than this board can finally act upon?" which was postponed for further consideration.

The board took into consideration the claim of Moses E. Levy for thirty-six thousand acres of land; and the documents marked with red ink, A, B, C, D, E, G, H, F, and J, being read, as well also as the deposition of E. M. Wanton, the board then proceeded to examine therein Thomas Murphy. At 2 o'clock, P. M., not being sufficiently advised of and concerning the said claim, adjourned the further consideration thereof until to-morrow.

The board adjourned until to-morrow morning, at 10 o'clock, A. M.

SATURDAY, *December* 19, 1823.

The board met this day pursuant to adjournment. Present, all the members.

Edgar Macon, Esq., district attorney for East Florida, attended this day, under the order of this board.

The consideration of the motion made by the United States' attorney on the ——— instant, was, on motion of Mr. Hamilton, brought up, and was postponed by the board until Saturday next, the 27th instant, Mr. Hamilton dissenting.

Ordered, That the testimony of Hypolite Chateauneuf, as taken in the claim of Moses E. Levy *vs.* the United States, for thirty-six thousand acres of land, be read in evidence in all cases under the Alachua grant.

The board resumed the consideration of the claim of Moses E. Levy, and re-examined therein Thomas Murphy, and examined Hypolite Chateauneuf. At 4 o'clock, P. M., not being sufficiently advised of and concerning the said claim, adjourned the further consideration thereof until Monday next.

The board adjourned until Monday next, at 10 o'clock.

MONDAY, *December* 22, 1823.

The board met this day pursuant to adjournment. Present, all the members.

Edgar Macon, Esq., district attorney for East Florida, attended this day, under order of this board.

The board resumed the consideration of the claim of Moses E. Levy.

A certified copy of the royal order of the 3d of September, 1817, from the secretary's office of the Intendant of the Havana, was offered as evidence by Moses E. Levy; and satisfactory proof being made by the testimony of Antonio Alvarez, John Cavedo, and E. M. Gomez, sworn and examined, that Juan Nepomuceno de Arrocha, who certifies the same, is secretary of said office; that he has no seal of office, as well, also, as proof identifying his signature, it is resolved, upon due deliberation by the board, unanimously, that the said copy of the royal [order] of the 3d of September, 1817, and the certificate of said Arrocha, secretary as aforesaid, be received and allowed as evidence in the claim of said Levy; and that the same, together with the certificate of John Mountain, vice-commercial agent of the United States at Havana, thereto appendant, be filed.

The board adjourned until to-morrow morning at 10 o'clock.

TUESDAY, *December* 23, 1823.

The board met this day pursuant to adjournment. Present, all the members.

Edgar Macon, Esq., district attorney for East Florida, attended this day, under order of the board.

The board then proceeded to the appointment of an assistant or minuting secretary; and John H. Lawrence was appointed.

The board resumed the consideration of the claim of Moses E. Levy for thirty-six thousand acres of land, and examined therein James Riz. At 1 o'clock, P. M., not being sufficiently advised of and concerning said claim, adjourned the further consideration thereof until to-morrow morning.

Before adjournment the board resolved that the depositions of all witnesses in the case of Moses E. Levy be admitted in all cases under the Alachua grant represented before this board; upon condition, however, that the whole of each deposition should be taken, or the whole rejected.

The board then adjourned until to morrow morning, 10 o'clock, A. M.

WEDNESDAY, *December* 24, 1823.

The board met this day pursuant to adjournment. Present, the Hons. Davis Floyd and Alexander Hamilton.

Edgar Macon, Esq., district attorney for East Florida, attended this day, under order of the board.

The board resumed the consideration of Moses E. Levy's claim for thirty-six thousand acres, and examined therein George J. F. Clarke, Gabriel W. Perpall, and Francis P. Sanchez. At 2 o'clock, P. M., not being sufficiently advised of and concerning said claim, adjourned the further consideration thereof until Friday the 26th instant.

The board then adjourned until Friday the 26th instant, at 10 o'clock, A. M.

FRIDAY, *December* 26, 1823.

The board met this day pursuant to adjournment. Present, all the members.

Edgar Macon, Esq., district attorney for East Florida, attended this day, under order of the board.

The board resumed the consideration of the claim of Moses E. Levy, and examined therein Anthony Rutant and William Simmons. It was then submitted for final decision, with leave to introduce the evidence of Frederick Warburg, if thought fit.

The board then took into consideration James Bosley's claim for five hundred acres of land; the papers and documents of which having been read, the secretary was ordered to translate the concession of said claim, and the case was laid over for further consideration.

Mr. Strong made a motion to make an amendment in the memorial of Samuel Fairbanks for eighty acres of land; which amendment was admitted. The amendment was as follows: " Samuel Fairbanks, for himself, claims two-thirds of two hundred and forty acres of land, and on behalf of Polly Beardon, wife of William Beardon, for the remaining one-third; and files the following documents, viz: A deed from Robert Gilbert and his wife for one-third part of the above two hundred and forty acres, the affidavit of Joseph Summerall, and the affidavit of William Lofton."

The board adjourned until Monday, the 29th instant, at 10 o'clock.

MONDAY, *December* 29, 1823.

The board met this day pursuant to adjournment. Present, all the members.

Edgar Macon, Esq., district attorney for East Florida, attended this day, under order of the board.

The board then took into consideration the claim of Mary Ann Davis for five hundred acres of land, and examined therein William Beardon, Edward R. Gibson. The case was then submitted.

The board then took into consideration the claim of Samuel Fairbanks, for eighty acres; which was also submitted.

The board took into consideration Duncan L. Clinch's claim for five hundred acres of land; which was laid over.

The board then took into consideration Bernardo Segui's claim for seven thousand acres. Submitted.

The board then took into consideration the claims of Antelm Gay, for one hundred and sixty, four hundred, seven hundred, six hundred, four hundred, five thousand, three hundred, and two thousand acres; all of which were submitted.

Mr. Hamilton made a motion that a letter should be addressed to the Secretary of the Treasury, reporting the proceedings of this board up to this meeting; which motion was overruled.

The board then adjourned until to-morrow morning, at 10 o'clock A. M.

TUESDAY, *December* 30, 1823.

The board met this day pursuant to adjournment. Present, all the members.

Edgar Macon, Esq., district attorney for East Florida, attended this day, under order of the board.

The board again took into consideration Antelm Gay's claim for two thousand acres, which was submitted; also, another claim of Antelm Gay, for five thousand acres, which was likewise submitted.

The question then arose, " What should constitute an actual settlement under construction of the second section of an act amending and supplementary to the act for ascertaining claims and titles to land in the Territory of Florida, and to provide for the survey and disposal of public lands in Florida?" and it was decided that a residence in the Territory, and not the occupation of land, constituted the actual settlement; the majority of the board agreeing therein, and Mr. Hamilton dissenting.

On motion of Mr. Hamilton, it was resolved that all royal orders and correspondence of Governors, and all the rules of the Governors, in relation to lands, omitting all facts which have no relation to lands, be recorded on the minutes of the board.

The board then adjourned until to-morrow morning, at 10 o'clock.

WEDNESDAY, *December* 31, 1823.

The board met this day pursuant to adjournment. Present, all the members.

Edgar Macon, Esq., district attorney for East Florida, attended this day, under order of the board.

The board then took into consideration the claim of Sarah Tate for four hundred and fifty acres of land, which was submitted.

The board then took into consideration the two claims of the heirs of Lorenzo Capo, one for fifty acres, and the other for one hundred and fifty-seven acres. These claims interfere with the claim of Pablo Sabate.

The memorial of Charles Seton, Domingo Acosta, and Francisco Ponce, in behalf of the inhabitants of Fernandina, was read, and, upon motion of Mr. Hamilton, it was resolved that the district attorney be directed to address a letter to the memorialists upon the subject of their memorial, stating to them that the board will receive testimony with regard to their case.

The board then adjourned until 10 o'clock to-morrow.

THURSDAY, *January* 1, 1824.

The board met this day pursuant to adjournment. Present, all the members.

Edgar Mocon, Esq., district attorney of East Florida, attended this day, by order of the board.

The board then adjourned until to-morrow morning, at 10 o'clock.

FRIDAY, *January* 2, 1824.

The board met this day pursuant to adjournment. Present, all the members.

Edgar Macon, Esq., district attorney for East Florida, attended this day, under order of the board.

The board certified to the account of Elias B. Gould, of seventy-one dollars and twenty cents for printing and stationery.

The board then took into consideration the claim of Robert Miller and wife to Martin's island; which was laid over.

Memorial No. 14, entered for a reference by the request of Mr. Hamilton.

It appears by the concession of Governor Coppinger to Jehu Underwood, dated the 17th October, 1821, that the license for a mill-seat was considered as a permission only to use the timber.

The board took into consideration the claim of Samuel Fairbanks to eighty-two acres of land; which was submitted.

The board then took into consideration the claim of William Williams, and co-heirs of William Williams, deceased, for one hundred and eighty acres of a grant of two thousand two hundred acres of land at New Smyrna, and another for two thousand and twenty acres of land at Spring garden, which is claimed by virtue of an exchange of a like number of acres of the grant of two thousand two hundred acres at New Smyrna; and examined therein George W. Perpall and Andrew Burgevin. The claim was then submitted.

Mr. Hamilton moved that the deponent, Joseph Summerall, in the case of William Williams and co-heirs, be summoned to appear before this board, inasmuch as that the deposition of said Joseph Summerall was taken before J. B. Strong, Esq., attorney for claimants; which was agreed to, Judge Blair dissenting.

Mr. Strong, attorney for claimants, moved that he be allowed to withdraw the deposition of Joseph Summerall, which was agreed to, Mr. Hamilton dissenting.

The board then took into consideration the claim of Joseph Simeon Sanchez, and examined therein Daniel Hurlbert and Charles W. Clarke. The claim was then submitted.

Francis Roman Sanchez's claim for four thousand acres of land was then taken into consideration, and Daniel Hurlbert and Charles W. Clarke examined therein. The claim submitted.

The following motion was made by Mr. Hamilton, and rejected by the majority of the board: " That the board would take into consideration the regulations of Governor White of the 12th of October, 1803, in relation to the granting possession and forfeiture of lands, and decide whether the said regulations be respected by the board as the regulations of the Spanish Government.

The board adjourned till ten o'clock to-morrow morning.

SATURDAY, *January* 3, 1824.

The board met this day pursuant to adjournment. Present, all the members.

Edgar Macon, Esq., district attorney for East Florida, attended this day, under order of the board.

The board then took into consideration the claim of Belton A. Copp for twelve hundred acres; which was then submitted.

The claim of Moses E. Levy, for fourteen thousand five hundred acres of land at Hope hill, was then taken into connsideration, and submitted.

Ordered, That the secretary produce the original concession, or a transcript thereof, in the case of Belton A. Copp for twelve hundred acres.

The board then took into consideration the claim of Sarah Tate, heiress of John E. Tate, deceased, for four hundred and fifty acres of land on the river Tomoka; the papers of which having been read, the claim was submitted.

Mr. Macon submitted cross interrogatories to be propounded to William Gibson in the case of Fernando de la Maza Arredondo *vs.* the United States.

Mr. Cox, attorney for claimant, moved that the said cross-interrogatories be put by two or more persons of the highest judicial authority in the place where Mr. Gibson should be found; which was agreed to.

Ordered, That the memorial, concession, and order of survey referred to in the royal title exhibited by the claimant, and also the power of attorney from Hernandez and Chauviteau to Moses E. Levy, be translated by the secretary, and furnished to this board; and, in the mean time, the further consideration of this case be postponed.

George J. F. Clarke appeared, at the request of Mr. Hamilton, by virtue of a *subpœna duces tecum*, and presented his instructions from the Government as Surveyor General, with a translation of the same; which are ordered to be filed.

Judge Blair offered the following resolution:

" *Resolved*, That, hereafter, when a claim is presented to the consideration of the board, it shall be the duty of the party, or his attorney, if present, if not, then the secretary officiating, to read all the papers and documents; and if the board shall determine that the deraignment in English is not sufficient, then the case shall be returned to the secretary, and an order made requiring the production of such other papers; and so, also, in cases where the party or district attorney shall require further parol evidence; and in all cases where the party is absent, and has not an attorney, such order requiring further evidence shall be published in the East Florida Herald for two weeks successively.

" In all cases hereafter submitted, the commissioners will deliver a final decree, or opinion only."

This resolution was laid over, upon motion of Mr. Hamilton.

The board then adjourned till Monday morning, the 5th instant, at 10 o'clock.

MONDAY, *January*, 5, 1824.

The board met this day pursuant to adjournment. Present, all the members.

The board then adjourned until to-morrow morning, 10 o'clock.

TUESDAY, *January* 6, 1824.

The board met this day pursuant to adjournment. Present, all the members.

Edgar Macon, Esq., district attorney for East Florida, attended this day, under order of the board.

Mr. George J. F. Clarke appeared before the board, and presented a paper containing notes explanatory of the instructions of general survey presented on Saturday by him; which explanation was ordered to be filed.

The board then adjourned until to-morrow morning, at 10 o'clock.

WEDNESDAY, *January* 7, 1824.

The board met pursuant to adjournment. Present, the Hons. Davis Floyd and Alexander Hamilton.

Edgar Macon, Esq., attended this day, under order of the board.

Frederick Warburg, witness in case of Moses E. Levy for thirty-six thousand acres at Alachua, was then introduced; a part of whose evidence was taken—the further examination postponed.

The board adjourned till 10 o'clock to-morrow morning.

THURSDAY, *January* 8, 1824.

The board met this day pursuant to adjournment. Present, the Hons. Davis Floyd and Alexander Hamilton.

Edward Macon, Esq., district attorney for East Florida, attended under order of the board.

William Berrie's claim was then taken into consideration by the board, and submitted.

John Huertas's claim was taken into consideration, and also submitted.

The board then took into consideration the claim of Joseph Delespine for five hundred and sixty acres of land, which was submitted—Francisco Ferreira having been examined therein; also, another claim of Joseph Delespine for six hundred acres—Francis Ferreira examined therein; which was submitted.

The following letter was inserted by order of the board:

January 8, 1824.

Inasmuch as the commissioners will be able to make final decision of but few claims, and as much time will be necessary to investigate and report sundry rules and regulations and customs prevalent in the province relative to granting land, and as the time when we must make report to Congress will shortly elapse, I would propose for consideration whether it would not be proper to take all the claims, now in a state of readiness, into consideration; have them recorded, and finally decided; and whether we would be able to devote more of our time, and our secretary, to the investigation of new cases; or whether, probably, the whole time may not be necessary for the preparation of those before us.

Yours,

DAVIS FLOYD.

To ALEXANDER HAMILTON, Esq.

The board then took into consideration the claim of Francis J. Avice, for five hundred acres; which was submitted.

The claim of Avice and Viel for one thousand acres of land was taken up and submitted.

The board then adjourned until to-morrow morning, at 10 o'clock.

FRIDAY, January 9, 1824.

The board met pursuant to adjournment. Present, the Hons. Davis Floyd and Alexander Hamilton; the Hon. Wm. W. Blair being indisposed.

Edgar Macon, Esq., district attorney for East Florida, attended under order of the board.

The board then took into consideration the claim of Charles Hogan for two hundred acres; which was submitted.

Reuben Hogan's claim for three hundred and eighty-five acres, was taken into consideration, and submitted.

The board then adjourned till to-morrow morning, 10 o'clock.

SATURDAY, January 10, 1824.

The board met pursuant to adjournment. Present, the Hons. Davis Floyd and Alexander Hamilton.

There being no business before the board, they adjourned until Monday morning, the 12th instant, at 10 o'clock.

MONDAY, January 12, 1824.

The board met this day pursuant to adjournment. Present, the Hons. Davis Floyd and Alexander Hamilton.

Edgar Macon, Esq., district attorney for East Florida, attended under order of the board.

The board then took into consideration the claim of Fernando de la Maza Arredondo for fifty thousand acres; which was submitted.

Peter Bagley's claim for two hundred acres was taken into consideration, and submitted.

José M. Arredondo's claim for twenty thousand acres was taken into consideration, and laid over.

Mr. Hamilton presented a letter addressed to Davis Floyd, Esq., being an answer to one addressed by him to Mr. Hamilton on the 8th instant.

The board then adjourned until to-morrow morning, at 10 o'clock.

TUESDAY, January 13, 1824.

The board met this day pursuant to adjournment. Present, the Hons. Davis Floyd and Alexander Hamilton.

Edgar Macon, Esq., district attorney for East Florida, attended under order of the board.

Francis J. Avice's claim for one hundred and fifteen acres of land was taken into consideration, and submitted.

The claim of James and Emanuel Ormond for two thousand acres of land on Halifax river was taken into consideration, and submitted.

The board then adjourned until to-morrow morning, at 10 o'clock.

WEDNESDAY, January 14, 1824.

The board met this day pursuant to adjournment. Present, the Hons. Davis Floyd and Alexander Hamilton.

Edgar Macon, Esq., district attorney for East Florida, attended this day, under order of the board.

The board then took into consideration the claim of Eliza Robinson for one hundred and five acres of land; which was submitted.

The claim of Joseph Summerall for one hundred and fifty acres was taken into consideration, and submittted.

The board then adjourned until to-morrow morning, at 10 o'clock.

THURSDAY, January 15, 1824.

The board met this day pursuant to adjournment. Present, all the members.

Edgar Macon, Esq., district attorney for East Florida, attended, under order of the board.

There being no business before the board, they adjourned until 10 o'clock to-morrow morning.

FRIDAY, January 16, 1824.

The board met pursuant to adjournment. Present, all the members.

Edgar Macon, Esq., district attorney for East Florida, attended, under order of the board.

The board then took into consideration the claim of Don Ramon de Fuentes; and having examined therein, Nicholas Rodriguez, Charles W. Clarke, Pedro Miranda, and Francisco Medicis, declared as follows:

Ramon de Fuentes vs. *the United States.* This is a claim for a house and lot in the city of St. Augustine, known and designated in the schedule of the buildings and lots in the said city as lot No. 203, in square 28, measuring upon its front, from east to west, fifteen Spanish yards, and in depth, from north to south, sixty Spanish yards, with its improvements and appurtenances.

Upon this day this cause came on to be heard; and, upon the exhibits therein filed, and the testimony of Peter Miranda, Charles W. Clarke, Nicholas Rodriguez, Francisco Medicis, and Antonio Alvarez, being therein taken, the board being sufficiently advised of and concerning the premises, do order and decree that all claim of the United States of and to said lot be released to said claimant; which decree was ordered to be recorded.

The board then adjourned until to-morrow morning, at 10 o'clock.

SATURDAY, January 17, 1824.

The board met pursuant to adjournment. Present, all the members.

Edgar Macon., Esq., district attorney for East Florida, attended, under order of this board.

The board then took into consideration the claim of Joseph Wales for two thousand three hundred and seventy-five acres, which was laid over, having first examined therein Samuel Miles.

The claim of Samuel Fairbanks for a lot in St. Augustine, was submitted.

The board then adjourned until Monday morning, 19th instant, at 10 o'clock.

The board met pursuant to adjournment. Present, the Hons. Davis Floyd and Alexander Hamilton.

Edgar Macon, Esq., district attorney for East Florida, attended, under order of this board.

The board then took into consideration the claim of James Bosley for final adjudication; which was laid over.

Farquhar Bethune was introduced, sworn, and examined, in the case of John H. McIntosh.

The board then adjourned till to-morrow morning, at 10 o'clock.

The board met pursuant to adjournment. Present, all the members.

Edgar Macon, Esq., district attorney for East Florida, attended, under order of the board.

James Bosley's claim was again taken into consideration. This claim was for five hundred acres of land, and it was confirmed.

John H. McIntosh's claim for six thousand acres was submitted, and advised for the confirmation of Congress.

The majority of the board refusing to establish, preliminarily, what was to be considered as the law of the land under the Spanish Government, as governing the decisions of the board, Mr. Hamilton declines interfering in the adjudication of claims.

John H. McIntosh's claim for three hundred acres was submitted, and advised for the confirmation of Congress.

John H. McIntosh's claim for one thousand acres of land was submitted for the confirmation of Congress.

John H. McIntosh's claim for three thousand two hundred and seventy-four acres and two-thirds of an acre was submitted, and advised for confirmation.

Pedro Miranda's claim for one thousand acres was submitted and confirmed.

Bernardo Segui's claim for seven thousand acres was submitted, and advised to Congress for confirmation.

Mary Ann Davis's claim for five hundred acres was submitted and confirmed.

Samuel Fairbanks's claim for a lot in St. Augustine submitted and confirmed.

Samuel Fairbanks's claim for one hundred and sixty acres submitted and confirmed: eighty acres were also confirmed to William Beardon and wife.

Moses E. Levy's claim for thirty-six thousand acres was submitted, and advised for confirmation.

The board then adjourned till to-morrow morning, at 10 o'clock.

The board met pursuant to adjournment. Present, all the members.

Edgar Macon, Esq., district attorney for East Florida, attended, under order of the board.

The board then proceeded to the consideration of the claims of Antelm Gay, the first of which, being for one hundred and sixty acres, was confirmed.

The second claim of Antelm Gay was taken into consideration and rejected, with the condition that the claimant, whenever he is able to procure additional testimony, may move the board to a reconsideration of the case.

Antelm Gay's third claim for seven hundred acres was likewise rejected, with the above conditions.

Antelm Gay's fifth claim for six hundred acres, was also rejected conditionally, as above.

No. 6 of Antelm Gay's claim was taken into consideration, and confirmed.

The board took into consideration, and advised for confirmation, No. 7 of Antelm Gay's claim.

No. 8 of same claim was taken into consideration, and confirmed.

No. 9 came under consideration of the board, and was rejected under conditions as of 2, 3, and 5.

The 10th number of Gay's claim was taken up, but the board not being sufficiently advised of and concerning said claim, it was ordered to be held under further advisement.

Antelm Gay's claim, No. 12, for two lots in St. Augustine, was taken into consideration, and laid over for further consideration.

The board then proceeded to the consideration of Belton A. Copp's claim for one thousand and two hundred acres, which was ordered to be recommended for confirmation.

The board then adjourned till to-morrow morning at 10 o'clock.

The board met this day pursuant to adjournment. Present, all the members.

Edgar Macon, Esq., district attorney for East Florida, attended under order of the board.

The board then took into consideration the claim of William Berrie for three hundred and fifty acres; which was confirmed.

The board then took into consideration the claim of John Huertas for fifteen thousand acres; which was recommended for confirmation.

The claim of Francis J. Avice, for five hundred acres was taken under consideration; and, on motion of claimant's attorney, the board gave leave to introduce an amended memorial, which was ordered to be filed. The case was then laid over for further consideration.

Avice and Viel's claim for one thousand acres was then taken into consideration, and rejected for want of evidence, with leave to move the board for a reconsideration of the case when sufficient evidence can be procured.

The claim of Eliza Robinson for one hundred and five acres was taken into consideration and confirmed.

The claim of Samuel Fairbanks and others for two thousand acres was taken into consideration and confirmed.

The board then took into consideration the claim of Samuel Fairbanks for five hundred acres, which was confirmed.

The claim of Peter Bagley for two hundred acres was taken up and confirmed.

The board then took into consideration, and confirmed, the claim of Charles Hogan for two hundred acres.

Reuben Hogan's claim for three hundred and eighty-five acres was also taken into consideration, and confirmed by the board.

Francis R. Sanchez's claim for four thousand acres was taken up, which was recommended for confirmation.

Joseph Delespine's claim for five hundred and sixty acres was taken under consideration, and confirmed.

Another claim of Joseph Delespine for six hundred acres was taken up and confirmed.

Sarah Tate's claim for four hundred and fifty acres, upon the St. John's, having been laid before the board, was confirmed.

The board then adjourned till to-morrow, at 10 o'clock, A. M.

The board met this day pursuant to adjournment. Present, all the members.

Edgar Macon, Esq. district attorney for East Florida, attended this day, under order of the board.

The board then entered upon the consideration of the case of Peter Fouchard for fifteen hundred acres, which was confirmed.

The claim of Williams's heirs for one hundred and eighty acres was taken under consideration, of which the board, not being sufficiently advised, order it to be held under further advisement.

The claim of Williams's heirs for two thousand and twenty acres was taken into consideration, and was recommended for confirmation.

The board then entered upon the adjudication of the claim of Eusebio Bushnell for six hundred acres, which was confirmed.

The board then took into consideration the claim of the heirs of Lorenzo Capo for one hundred and fifty-seven acres, which was rejected.

The claim of James and Emanuel Ormond for two thousand acres of land was taken under consideration, which was confirmed.

The claim of Moses E. Levy for fourteen thousand five hundred acres was taken under consideration, and recommended for confirmation.

The claim of F. M. Arredondo, Jun., for fifty thousand acres was taken under consideration of the board, and was laid over for further advisement.

The claim of Sarah Tate for four hundred and fifty acres on Tomoka river was taken into consideration, upon which Mr. Floyd and Mr. Blair forming different conclusions, and Mr. Hamilton refusing his opinion thereon, it was ordered to be reported to Congress.

The board then adjourned until to-morrow morning, at 10 o'clock.

SATURDAY, *January* 24, 1824.

The board met this day, pursuant to adjournment. Present, all the members.

Edgar Macon, Esq., district attorney for East Florida, attended this day, under order of the board.

Resolved, That, in the future decisions of the board, there being only two members of the board who act in the adjudication, that, in case of a disagreement, the case will be reported to Congress, with the facts attending it, for their decision.

John B. Strong, attorney for the heirs of Lorenzo Capo, petitions the board of commissioners for a re-hearing in said case, and exhibits the deposition of Anthony Hindsman, which is herewith filed, and prays that the former decree, rejecting said claim, may be set aside, and a decree of confirmation entered thereon.

JOHN B. STRONG, *Attorney for claimant.*

The board then, agreeably to the said petition, reversed the decree of rejection upon said case, and granted thereon a confirmation.

Ordered by the board, that, in the case of Antelm Gay for four hundred acres, the decree of rejection be set aside, and a reconsideration of the case be allowed.

Ordered by the board, that, in the case of Antelm Gay for six hundred acres, the decree of rejection be set aside, and a reconsideration of the case be allowed.

Ordered by the board, that, in the case of Antelm Gay for two thousand acres, the decree of rejection be set aside, and a reconsideration of the case be allowed.

Ordered by the board, that, in the case of Avice and Viel for one thousand acres, the decree of rejection be se aside, and a reconsideration of the case be allowed.

John B. Strong, attorney for Sarah Tate, only heiress of John E. Tate, deceased, respectfully represents, that he expects to be able to give testimony in this case which will satisfy the honorable the board of commissioners of the justice of the claim of the petitioner or claimant to the land in question, by proving that Governor Coppinger offered to give other lands in lieu thereof. Your petitioner, therefore, prays that the board will vacate the decision or order heretofore made in this case, and permit the petitioner to introduce the testimony which he expects will show that the Spanish Government have considered the claimant's father legally entitled to the land in question, since the grant made to him in 1811, on the St. John's river.

JOHN B. STRONG, *Attorney for claimant.*

ST. AUGUSTINE, *January* 24, 1824.

Agreeable to the request of the petitioner, ordered by the board, that, in the case of Sarah Tate for four hundred and fifty acres, the decree of rejection be set aside, and a reconsideration of the case be allowed.

The board then adjourned until Thursday morning, the 29th instant, at 10 o'clock.

THURSDAY, *January* 29, 1824.

The board met pursuant to adjournment. Present, all the members.

Edgar Macon, Esq., district attorney for East Florida, attended, under order of the board.

The board then entered upon the reconsideration of the case of Antelm Gay for four hundred acres of land, which was confirmed.

The claim of Antelm Gay for seven hundred acres was then taken up and reconsidered, and was confirmed.

Antelm Gay's claim for six hundred acres was then taken up for reconsideration, and ordered to be reported to Congress, for their consideration.

The claim of Antelm Gay and Francis J. Avice for two thousand acres was then taken up and reconsidered; upon which, the board being fully advised, it was confirmed.

The claim of Avice and Viel for one thousand acres was taken up and reconsidered; upon which the board ordered that the case be reported to Congress, with the facts attending it, and opinion that the same should be confirmed.

The claim of Michael Crosby's heirs for two thousand acres was taken into consideration, and confirmed.

The claim of Michael Crosby's heirs for five hundred acres was taken under advisement, and confirmed.

The board was then adjourned until Saturday morning, the 31st instant, at 10 o'clock.

SATURDAY, *January* 24, 1821.

The board met pursuant to adjournment. Present, the Hons. Davis Floyd and Alexander Hamilton.

The board then examined, in the case of Joseph Wales for two thousand three hundred and seventy acres of land, James Pellicer, José B. Reyes, and Peter Mitchell.

Edgar Macon, Esq., United States' attorney for the district of East Florida, attended, under order of the board.

The board adjourned until Monday morning, the 2d instant, at 10 o'clock.

MONDAY, *February* 2, 1824.

The board met pursuant to adjournment. Present, the Hons. Davis Floyd and Alexander Hamilton.

Edgar Macon, Esq., district attorney for East Florida, attended, under order of the board.

There being no business before the board, they adjourned until Thursday morning, the 5th instant, at 10 o'clock.

THURSDAY, *February* 5, 1824.

The board met pursuant to adjournment. Present, the Hons. Davis Floyd and William W. Blair.

Edgar Macon, Esq., United States' attorney for the district of East Florida, presented his account against the United States for his attendance upon the board of land commissioners up to this day; which said account was ordered to be certified.

The board then entered upon the reconsideration of the case of Joseph Wales, and examined therein Francis J. Fatio and Joseph M. Sanchez; the case was then submitted.

The board then adjourned until Monday, the 9th instant, at ten o'clock.

MONDAY, *February* 9, 1824.

The board met pursuant to adjournment. Present, the Hons. Davis Floyd and William W. Blair.

Edgar Macon, Esq., United States' attorney, attended this day, under order of the board.

Waters Smith, Esq., United States' marshal, presented to the board two accounts, marked Nos. 1 and 2.

No. 1, being for the summoning and attendance of witnesses, amounting to forty-six dollars; which was certified.

No. 2, being an account for stationary and other supplies and contingencies of the board, amounting to three hundred and thirty dollars ninety-five cents; which was also certified.

Joseph M. Sanchez presented his account to the board for house rent for three months, at thirty dollars per month, amounting to ninety dollars; which was likewise certified.

Waters Smith presented No. 3 of his accounts, being a compensation allowed him for subpœnaing witnesses, amounting to twenty-three dollars and forty-five cents; was also certified.

The board then adjourned *sine die.*

ST. AUGUSTINE, *February* 2, 1824.

In conformity to the provision of the act of Congress passed the 3d of March, 1823, requiring of this board to make a return of their proceedings to the Secretary of the Treasury, to be laid before Congress, we certify that the foregoing is a correct and full copy from the minutes of the board.

DAVIS FLOYD.
W. W. BLAIR.

FLORIDA LAND CLAIMS RECOMMENDED FOR CONFIRMATION.

No. 1.

AUGUST 29, 1823.

To the honorable the Commissioners appointed to try claims and titles to land in East Florida.

The memorial of Belton A. Copp, a citizen of the United States, residing in the county of Camden, in Georgia, showeth:

That your memorialist claims title to a tract of land, situated on the west side of the river St. John's, opposite New Buena Vista, and known by the name of Guy's place or Pelitka, first line commencing on the river St. John's, and running north 45 degrees, west 120 chains; second line running north 45 degrees, east 120 chains; third line running south 54 degrees, east 80 chains; and the fourth line bounded on the east by the river St. John's, as per survey thereof, in schedule B, will more fully appear, which said tract of land contains twelve thousand acres; and was granted to one Bernardo Segui on the 22d day of January, 1818, as will appear by exhibit A, by virtue of the royal order of the 29th March, 1815, which concession was carried into royal grant on the 3d of August, 1818, which will appear by exhibit B; and which said tract of land, on the 18th of January, 1819, was conveyed, in fee, by the said Bernardo Segui, for the consideration of $1,200, to one George Fleming, a Spanish subject, and a resident of Florida, till the 23d of August, 1821; and after, as per exhibit B, will also appear that, on that day last mentioned, the said George conveyed the said tract of land to your memorialist, which conveyance also forms a part of exhibit B. Your memorialist further says that he is *in actual possession* of said tract of land, and that a part of it is in cultivation; all which is humbly submitted.

BELTON A. COPP.

ST. AUGUSTINE, FLORIDA, *December* 16, 1817.

Don Bernardo Segui, a native and inhabitant of this city, to your excellency, respectfully showeth:

Being advised of the royal clemency of his Majesty, by his royal order of the 29th of March, 1815, his having acceded to the gifts proposed by the Government of this province, that, to the faithful subjects of the same, who occupied themselves in the defence thereof during the last invasion, lands should be granted them in absolute property.

The services rendered by the memorialist in all that period are well known and notorious; and although he did not take up arms and undergo the fatigues of a militiaman, yet he exercised the duties of police officer, and discharged other trusts peculiar to the royal service, which your excellency's predecessors thought proper to charge me with, and which I performed to their satisfaction. These limited services, and the sight of a large family which surround him, obliges him to resort to the said royal clemency, and by it prays that your excellency will be pleased to grant him, in absolute property and dominion, a tract of vacant land containing twelve hundred acres, opposite a place known by the name of *Joe Gres,* and situated on the opposite sides of the bank of the river St. John's, in this said province, bounded on the north and west by vacant lands, and on the south by those belonging to Don Gabriel Perpall, which he hopes to receive from the known justice of your excellency.

BERNARDO SEGUI.

To the GOVERNOR.

ST. AUGUSTINE, *January* 22, 1818.

Grant the memorialist the twelve hundred acres of land in the place pointed out, of which there will be given him a title, in form, by the Government notary and royal finance.

COPPINGER.

I certify the foregoing to be a true and correct translation from a document in the Spanish language.

F. J. FATIO, *S. B. L. C.*

Title in favor of Don Bernardo Segui to twelve hundred acres of land on the opposite side of the banks of the river St. John's.

ST. AUGUSTINE, FLORIDA, *August* 3, 1818.

Don José Coppinger, colonel of the royal armies, civil and military Governor, and chief of the royal finance in the city of St. Augustine, Florida, and its provinces, by his Majesty:

Whereas, by royal order of the 29th March, 1815, his Majesty has been pleased to approve the gifts and premiums proposed by my predecessor, the Brigadier General Don Sebastian Kindelan, for the officers and soldiers, both of the line as well as of the local militia, and other individuals of this province who contributed to its defence at the time of the rebellion, being one of said gifts, the distribution of lands, according to the number of family each individual may have, Don Bernardo Segui having presented himself, and making known his services rendered in said defence, he petitioned, in virtue of them and the aforesaid gifts, for the concession of twelve hundred acres of land which were granted him by my decree of the 22d January of the present year, opposite the place known by name of *Joe Gres*, and situated on the opposite side of the banks of the river St. John's, bounded on the north and west by vacant lands, and on the south by those of Don Gabriel Perpall, the dimensions of the said lands being as follows: the first line begins at an oak, and runs north 45 degrees west, 120 chains, and ends at a pine; the second line commences at the said pine, and runs north 45 degrees east, 120 chains, and ends at another pine; the third line begins at the last mentioned pine, and runs south 45 degrees east, 80 chains, and ends at a cypress, as is fully seen in the proceedings brought forward by the said Don Bernardo Segui, filed in the office of the notary of Government. Wherefore, I have thought proper to grant, and by these presents do grant, in the name of his Majesty and his royal justice, which I administer to the said Don Bernardo Segui, the aforesaid one thousand two hundred acres of land, without injury to a third person, in the place already pointed out, for himself, his heirs, and successors, in absolute property; and I hereby, and by these presents, deliver him the corresponding title, by which I separate it from the royal domains, from the right and dominion it held in said land; and I cede and transfer it to the said Bernardo Don Segui, his heirs and successors, that in consequence thereof they may possess it as their own, make use of and enjoy it free from any claim whatever, with all its entrances, outlets, uses, customs, rights, privileges, and all and in general, which hath, doth, or in any manner by right may belong or pertain thereto; and, it being their wish, they may sell, cede, transfer, barter, or alienate it at their will and pleasure. To all of which I interpose my authority, as far as possible, and according to law, in compliance with the sovereign will.

Given under my hand, and countersigned by the undersigned notary of Government and royal finance in this said city of St. Augustine, Florida the 3d of August, 1818.

JOSE COPPINGER.

By order of his Excellency:

JUAN DE ENTRALGO,
Notary of Government and Royal Finance.

ST. AUGUSTINE, FLORIDA, *August* 3, 1818.

Conformable to the original filed in the archives under my charge, to which I refer, and at the request of the party, do seal and sign the present copy on two leaves of ordinary paper, stamps not being used.

JUAN DE ENTRALGO,
Notary of Government and Royal Finance.

In virtue of the order, dated the 11th of July last past, which was communicated to me by Don Joseph Coppinger, colonel of the royal armies, civil and military Governor of this city and its province, I certify that I have measured and laid off for Don Bernardo Segui a tract of land, situated on the west of the river St. John's, opposite the place on which there is a military post; which land contains one thousand two hundred acres, its figures and demarcations being the same as represented in the preceding plat, [See plate 3, fig. 1,] and give this certificate, which I sign in St. Augustine, Florida, the 1st day of August, 1818.

ANDRES BURGEVIN.

The foregoing plat is copied from the original, but on a double scale, to which I refer.

A. BURGEVIN.

I certify that the foregoing is a true and correct translation from a document in the Spanish language.

F. J. FATIO, *S. B. L. C.*

CONVEYANCE.

Know ye, that I, Don Bernardo Segui, resident of this city, do sell to George Fleming, inhabitant of this province, one thousand two hundred acres of land, which I possess as my property, opposite the place known by the name of Joe Gres, and situated upon the opposite side of the banks of the river St. John's, bounded on the north and west by vacant lands, and on the south by those of Don Gabriel Perpall, the first line beginning at an oak, and running N. 45°, W. 120 chains, and ending at a pine. The second line begins at said pine, and runs N. 45°, E. 120 chains, and ends at another pine. The third line commences at the last mentioned pine, and runs S. 45°, east 80 chains, and ends at a cypress; which lands appertain to me in absolute property, by a concession made to me by this Government on the 22d January, 1818, and of which there was given me corresponding title on the 3d of August of the same year, as a recompense for my services rendered at the time of the insurrection of this province, agreeable to the royal order on the subject; and I sell him the said one thousand two hundred acres of land, under the boundaries and dimensions already explained, with all its entrances, outlets, usages, customs, rights, and privileges, which it has or may belong to it, free from any incumbrance, (as I, the said notary, do certify as results from the register of mortgages under my charge, which, to that effect, I examined,) in the sum of one thousand two hundred dollars, which the purchaser has paid me in cash, of which sum I acknowledge the receipt, of my own free will, renouncing the proof, laws of delivery, exception for pecuniary misreckoning, fraud, and other circumstances of the case, whereof I acknowledge a formal receipt. In virtue of which I separate myself from the right of possession, title, and whatever other rights, real and personal, I had, or may have, to said lands, which I cede, renounce, and transfer in favor of the purchaser, and whomsoever may represent him, that he may, as his own, possess, sell, and alienate the same at his will, in virtue of this deed, which I make in his favor, as a sign of real delivery, with which will be proved his having acquired possession without the necessity of further proof, from which I relieve him; and I bind myself, to the eviction and goodness of this sale, in sufficient form, and in the most formable manner to the purchaser, with my present and future property, with power and submission to the tribunals of His Majesty, that they may compel me to the fulfilment thereof, as by sentence agreed to and passed by virtue of an adjudged cause, upon which I renounce all laws, customs, rights, and privileges in my favor, and the general in form which it prohibits. And I, the said Don George Fleming, being present, do accept in my favor this deed, and by it receive as purchased the aforesaid one thousand two hundred acres of land, in the price and manner it has been sold me, which I acknowledge to have received of my free will, renouncing the proof, laws of delivery, those of the things not seen, nor received, fraud, and all other things in the matter, of which I give a receipt in form. In testimony whereof, it is dated in this city of St. Augustine, Florida, the 18th of January, 1819.

I, the notary, do attest and know the parties who signed, being witnessess. Don Fernando de la Maza Arredondo, Jun., Don Pedro Miranda, and Don Guillermo Travers, residents, present.

BERNARDO SEGUI.
GEORGE FLEMING.

Before me, Juan de Entralgo, *Notary of Government.*

Conformable to its original, filed in the archives under my charge, to which I refer, and at the request of the party, do seal and sign this present copy on two leaves of ordinary paper, stamps not being used. St. Augustine, Florida, this day of the acknowledging thereof.

JUAN DE ENTRALGO, *Notary of Government.*

I certify the foregoing to be a true and correct translation from a document in the Spanish language.

F. J. FATIO, *S. B. L. C.*

Territory of East Florida, *city of St. Augustine:*

Know all men by these presents, that I, George Fleming, for and in consideration of one cent to me in hand well and truly paid by Belton A. Copp, the receipt whereof is acknowledged, hath bargained and sold, and hereby do bargain, and sell, and transfer to said Belton A. Copp all my right, title, and interest in the lands to which the plat on the other side, and A. Burgevin's certificate opposite to it, refers, which were conveyed to me by Bernardo Segui, as by the documents herewith appears, to have and to hold, to said Belton, his heirs and assigns, without warranty on my part.

In witness whereof I have hereunto set my hand and seal, on this twenty-third day of August, eighteen hundred and twenty-one.

GEORGE FLEMING.

In the presence of Daniel D. Copp.

No. 2.

St. Augustine, Florida, *December* 18, 1815.

Don Francisco Roman Sanchez, native and inhabitant of this province, with due respect to your excellency, showeth that, on the south part of the river known by the name of Santa Fé, about ten miles to the westward of the Alachua road to St. Mary's, there is great quantity of vacant lands adapted for cultivation and raising of stock, to which he intends dedicating himself for the purpose of increasing the same; and, as the petitioner has not obtained any concession of lands on which he can establish himself as he wishes, with all his family and slaves, he therefore prays your excellency will be pleased to grant him four thousand acres of land at said place, bounded on the north by said river Santa Fé, and on the other sides by vacant lands; which quantity of acres are necessary, not only on account of the number of negroes he owns, but also for the said raising of stock, and many other purposes relating to a planter; being a favor which he hopes to merit from the goodness of your excellency.

FRANCIS R. SANCHEZ.

To the Governor.

DECREE.

St. Augustine, *December* 18, 1815.

In consideration of the urgent necessity there is of settling this province by all possible measures, and for the purpose of raising horned cattle, on account of the scarcity thereof, which is daily observed, grant the petitioner the four thousand acres of land in the place where he prays for, without injury to a third person; and for his security, grant him a certified copy from the secretary's office of this memorial and decree.

ESTRADA.

I certify the foregoing to be a true and correct translation from a document in the Spanish language.

F. J. FATIO, *S. B. L. C.*

Roman Sanchez vs. United States.

Witter Clarke sworn and examined. Deposed that he had always heard that there were Indians at Santa Fé; he thinks it would have been unsafe to establish a plantation or carry stock there: that the Indians stopped him while about attempting a survey, and would not let him proceed, but threatened him if he did attempt it.

Daniel Hurlbut sworn and examined. Deposeth that it was considered unsafe, even on the St. John's, to settle there on account of the Indians.

No. 3.

To the honorable the Commissioners appointed to ascertain claims and title to lands in East Florida:

The memorial of Francis Julian Avice and Prosper Viel respectfully showeth, that your memorialists claim title to a tract of land consisting of one thousand acres, situated on the river St. Sebastian, opposite the city of St.

Augustine, which were granted to José Peso de Burgo by the Spanish Government, the eleventh of September, one thousand seven hundred and ninety-eight, in virtue of the royal order of the 29th of October, 1790, and for which lands the said Peso de Burgo received a title from Governor Coppinger upon the twenty-fourth of February, one thousand eight hundred and eighteen; which title and plat of the survey of said tract of land are herewith filed, and marked M. and N. And your memorialists further showeth, that they became the proprietors of said tract of land by virtue of a bill of sale from the widow Peso de Burgo to your memorialists, dated upon the twenty-second of October, in the year one thousand eight hundred and twenty-two; which is also herewith exhibited, and marked O. Your memorialists further showeth, that they are actually seized and possessed of said land, that they are citizens of the United States, and residents of the city of St. Augustine. All of which are respectfully submitted, &c.

FRANCIS J. AVICE.
PROSPER VIEL.

To the honorable the Commissioners appointed by law to ascertain claims and titles to lands in East Florida.

Francis J. Avice and Prosper Viel, with leave, amend their memorial before this board for one thousand acres of land lying on the west side, and on the bank of the St. Sebastian river, to the following effect: They state that, in the year 1794, a concession for an undefined quantity of land at St. Sebastian river, was made to Francis and John Triay by Governor Quesada, which they herewith exhibit. That, on the 11th of September, 1798, the said Francis and John Triay exchanged their said lands to José Peso de Burgo for lands which he had at a place called Governor Grant. That no steps were taken, at any time, to ascertain the quantity of said lands till after the 24th of January, 1818, but that the same was in the possession of the original grantee from 1785 until the exchange aforesaid, which was permitted by Governor White; which said exchange, and Governor White's permission for the same, are herewith exhibited. That, after the exchange, the said lands were always in the possession and cultivation of the aforesaid José Peso de Burgo until 1819, when he died, and afterwards in the possession of his widow until the time of the purchase by memorialists from her, since which time they have been actual occupants. They aver that the said lands were as head-rights to said José Peso de Burgo, and that, for many years before his death, his head-rights would have entitled him to more than one thousand acres.

J. B. LANCASTER, *Attorney for claimant.*

[TRANSLATION.]

Memorial to the Governor and Commander-in-chief.

FLORIDA, *August 19, 1794.*

Francis and John Triay, brothers, and residents of this city, to your excellency most humbly and respectfully show, that, in the year 1785, at their request, they were granted, by your excellency's predecessor, some arable lands, which belonged to the Englishman Don John Forbes, situated on the west of the river St. Sebastian, as will be seen by the annexed memorial and its decree: and believing that, with the anterior permission, they could enjoy the right of a good and legitimate property, they have since understood that, unless they could obtain the authorization and new license of your excellency, they had no right to said lands: in virtue of which they humbly pray that you will be pleased, not only to excuse this unforeseen circumstance, but also to grant them the necessary license, in order to show the same whenever it is required; in which your excellency will be pleased to interpose your authority for its greater validity—a favor which they hope to obtain from the humane heart of your excellency. For the petitioners,

RAFAEL SAAVEDRA DE ESPINOSA.

DECREE.

ST. AUGUSTINE, *August 26, 1794.*

The parties may continue in the enjoyment of the lands on which they are situated, until, in the general survey, they be allowed whatever portion may appertain to them.

QUESADA.

A certificate was delivered.

RENGIL.

I certify the foregoing to be a true and correct translation from a document in the Spanish language.

F. J. FATIO, *S. B. L. C.*

SENOR GOVERNOR: ST. AUGUSTINE, *September 14, 1798.*

Don Peso de Burgo and Francisco and John Triay, with the respect due to your excellency, say, that the former, having possession of the land lying nine miles to the north of this town, at a place known by the name of Governor Grant, and the latter other lands on the west of the river called St. Sebastian, which were granted to them by this Government to be cultivated, as is shown by the annexed certificates; and the aforesaid Don José Peso de Burgo and Francis and John Triay having agreed to exchange the said lands one for the other, for the conveniences and advantages that can result to both parties; therefore, beg your excellency to allow them the said exchange, by which means they will settle themselves on said lands without further difficulties. By so doing you will confer a favor which they expect from your kindness.

For Francis and John Triay, who do not know how to write,

JUAN DE ENTRALGO.
JOSE PESO DE BURGO.

ST. AUGUSTINE, *September 11, 1798.*

It is granted to the above interested petitioners to do the exchange of lands they ask for; which exchange is to take place, with the knowledge of the commanding engineer, and the same to be recorded in the office of the Government; at which office the necessary certificates will be delivered.

WHITE.
LICE. ORTEGA.

I certify the foregoing to be a true and correct translation from a document in the Spanish language.

F. J. FATIO, *S. B. L. C.*

[TRANSLATION.]

Title of property for one thousand acres of land in favor of Don José Peso de Burgo.

Don José Coppinger, colonel of the royal armies, civil and military, Governor *pro tem.*, and chief of the royal finance of this city of St. Augustine, Florida, and its province, by His Majesty:

Whereas, by the royal order, communicated to this Government the 29th of October, 1790, by the Captain General of the island of Cuba and two Floridas, it is provided, among other things, that, to those strangers who, of their own free will, shall present themselves to swear allegiance to our sovereign, lands should be measured for them free of expense, in proportion to the number of laborers each family may have; Don José Peso de Burgo having presented himself, he solicited of, and was granted by the Government, the 11th of September, 1798, in consequence of a transfer made by him with Francisco and Juan Triay of a quantity of land, without specifying the quantity, on the west side of the river St. Sebastian, which belonged to Don John Forbes at the time this province was under the British dominion; which, according to the number of the family of the said Peso de Burgo, shall consist of a thousand acres of land, in the following form: fifteen acres front towards the said river, and the rest in depth, until the quantity of the said one thousand acres be complete; on the west and low pine barren, under the following boundaries: on the east and south of the said river St. Sebastian, and on the west and north by the pine barren, as will be seen by the documents and memorial presented by the said Don José Peso de Burgo, attached to the proceedings instituted for the purpose of obtaining the title of property of said one thousand acres of land, all of which remain filed in the archives of the present notary; and, as no title whatever had been given to the said Don José Peso de Burgo for the security and evidence of his possession of the said land in the form adopted towards others, that more than ten years' uninterrupted possession have elapsed, to obtain possession of said lands in fee simple and absolute property, on which he has built houses, cultivated the same, and complied with all the conditions established by the Government for the gifts and concessions of this nature, as is seen in the titles given to other settlers, and is set forth in the same proceeding: Wherefore, and in consideration thereof, I have granted, and by these presents do grant, in the name of His Majesty, and of his royal justice, which I administer to the said Don José Peso de Burgo, the above-mentioned one thousand acres of land, for him, his heirs, and successors, in absolute property; and I hereby, and by these presents, deliver him the corresponding title, by which I separate it from the royal domain, from the right and dominion it held to said land; and I cede and transfer it to the said Don José Peso de Burgo, his heirs, and successors, that in consequence thereof they may possess it as their own, make use of and enjoy it free from any claim whatever, with all its entrances, outlets, uses, customs, rights, and hereditaments, and all and in general which hath, doth, or in any manner may belong or pertain thereto; and, being their wish, they may sell, cede, transfer, and alienate, at their will and pleasure: To all of which I interpose my judicial authority as far as possible, and according to law, in compliance with the sovereign will.

Given under my hand, and countersigned by the undersigned notary of Government and royal finance, in this said city of St. Augustine, Florida, February 28, 1818.

JOSE COPPINGER.

By order of His Excellency:

JUAN DE ENTRALGO,
Notary of Government and Royal Finance.

Conformable to the original filed in the archives under my charge, to which I refer, and, at the request of the party, do seal and sign the present copy on two leaves of ordinary paper, stamps not being used. St. Augustine, Florida, 28th February, 1818.

JUAN DE ENTRALGO,
Notary of Government and Royal Finance.

Don Andres Burgevin, of this city, private surveyor: I certify that, by virtue of the decree of this Government of the 10th May of the present year, I have measured and laid off for Donna Maria Maberty, widow of the deceased Don José Peso de Burgo, a tract of land containing one thousand acres, situated on the opposite side of the river St. Sebastian, and in front of this city, and being conformable, in all other circumstances, to the following plat. [See plate 3, fig. 2.] I give the present, which I sign in St. Augustine, Florida, December 29, 1820.

ANDRES BURGEVIN.

A copy of the original to which I refer.

A. BURGEVIN.

I certify the foregoing to be a true and correct translation from two documents in the Spanish language.

F. J. FATIO, *S. B. L. C.*

TERRITORY OF FLORIDA, *county of St. John's:*

This indenture, made the 22d day of October, in the year of our Lord one thousand eight hundred and twenty-two, between Maria Maberty de Burgos, widow of José Carlos Peso de Burgos, deceased, and Maria de Burgos, wife of Don Miguel Papy, and Geronima de Burgos, wife of Don James Martinely, Magdalina de Burgos, wife of Don José Ximenes, and Pedro de Burgos, children and heirs of the said José Carlos Peso de Burgos, of the first part; and Prosper Viel, and Francis Julian Avice, of the second part, witness: That the said parties of the first part, for and in consideration of the sum of one thousand eight hundred dollars to them in hand paid by the said parties of the second part, and of the further sum of one thousand dollars secured to be paid to the said Maria Maberty de Burgos, by the said parties of the second part, at or before the sealing and delivery of these presents, have granted, bargained, sold, alienated, released, and confirmed, and by these presents do grant, bargain, sell, alien, release, and confirm, unto the said parties of the second part, as tenants in common, and to their heirs and assigns, all that tract or parcel of land, situate, lying, and being, in the aforesaid county of St. John's, in the territory aforesaid, on the west side of the river St. Sebastian, opposite the city of St. Augustine, in the said county, known commonly by the name of the "Ferry tract," containing one thousand acres, more or less, and having such boundaries as in and by the annexed plat are described; and also all the houses, out-houses, edifices, buildings, improvements, groves, advantages, hereditaments, rights, members, and appurtenances, whatsoever, to the said tract or parcel of land above mentioned belonging, or in anywise appertaining; and the reversion and reversions, remainder and remainders, rents, issues, and profits of the said premises, and of every part and parcel thereof, and all the estate, right, title, interest, claim, and demand, whatsoever, of the said parties of the first part, in and to the said tract or parcel of land and premises, and every part thereof; to have and to hold the said tract or parcel of land, and all and singular other the premises above mentioned, and every part and parcel thereof, with the appurtenances, unto the said Prosper Viel and Francis Julian Avice, the said parties of the second part, as tenants in common, and to their and each of their heirs and assigns, forever; and to the only proper use, benefit, and behoof of the said Prosper Viel and Francis Julian Avice, their and each of their heirs and assigns forever. And the said parties of the first part, for themselves, respectively, and for their respective heirs, executors, and administrators, the aforesaid tract or parcel of land, and all and singular other the aforesaid premises, and every part and parcel thereof, against them, and each of them, respectively, and their and each of their respective heirs, and against all and every other person or persons whomsoever, to the said parties of the second part, their and each of their heirs and assigns, shall and will warrant and defend forever by these presents. And the said parties of the first part, for themselves, respectively, and for their respective heirs, executors, and administrators, do further covenant, promise, and agree, to and with the said parties of the second part, and their heirs and assigns, that they, the said parties of the second part, and their and each of their heirs and assigns, shall and may, from time to time, and at all times forever hereafter, peaceably and quietly have, hold, occupy, possess, and enjoy, the aforesaid tract or parcel of land, and all and singular other the premises mentioned to be hereby granted and sold, and to receive and take the rents, issues, and profits thereof, to and for their own use and uses, without the let, suit, hinderance, interruption, or denial of them, the said parties of the first part, or any of them, or of their or any of their heirs or assigns, or of any other person or persons claiming, or to claim, by, through, or under them, or any of them, or of any other person or persons whomsoever lawfully claiming, or to claim the said tract of land and premises, in any manner or way whatsoever.

In witness whereof, the parties to these presents have hereto set their hands and seals, the day and year first above written.

MARIA M. DE BURGOS, her ✕ mark.
MARIA B PAPY, her ✕ mark.
GERONIMA B. Y MARTINELY.
MAGDALENA B. XIMENES.
PEDRO DE BURGOS, *by attorney in fact.*
MARIA M. DE BURGOS, her ✕ mark.

Sealed and delivered in the presence of
> MEYNARDIE DE NADALIE,
> CHARLES ROBION,
> JOHN DRYSDALE.

TERRITORY OF FLORIDA, *St. John's county:*

Received of and from the within named Prosper Viel and Francis Julian Avice, the sum of $2,800, the consideration in the within deed mentioned to have been paid, or secured by them to us by the payment in money of $1,800, and by a mortgage on the within mentioned land and premises.

OCTOBER 22, 1822.

MARIA M. DE BURGOS, her ✕ mark.
MARIA B. PAPY, her ✕ mark.
GERONIMA B. MARTINELY.
MAGDALENA B. XIMENES.
PEDRO DE BURGOS, *by attorney in fact.*
MARIA M. DE BURGOS, her ✕ mark.

Witnesses: MEYNARDIE DE NADALIE,
> CHARLES ROBION.

TERRITORY OF FLORIDA, *county of St. John's:*

Know all men by these presents that we, Miguel Papy, James Martinely, and John Ximenes, do respectively assent to, and approve of the foregoing deed, as and for the act of our respective wives, for the purposes therein mentioned; and we do, and each of us doth, by these presents, relinquish, release, quit-claim, and conform unto the said Prosper Viel and Francis Julian Avice, and unto their heirs and assigns, forever, all our, and each of our estate, right, title, interest, and demand, of every kind whatsoever, of, in, to, and upon, the land and premises in the said aforegoing deed mentioned.

In witness whereof, we have hereunto set our hands and seals, this ——— day of October, 1822.

MIGUEL PAPY.
JAMES MARTINELY.
JOSE XIMENES.

Sealed and delivered in the presence of
> P. PORRIER,
> MEYNARDIE DE NADALIE,
> CHARLES ROBION.

Proved by Charles Robion and Meynardie.
OCTOBER 24, 1822.

TERRITORY OF FLORIDA, *county of St. John's, ss:*

Be it remembered, that, on this 24th day of October, Anno Domini 1822, the annexed deed of bargain and sale, from Maria Maberty de Burgos, and others, children and heirs of José Carlos Péso de Burgos, parties of the first part, to Prosper Viel and Francis J. Avice, parties of the second part, was presented to me in my office and proved to be the act and deed of the parties of the first part, for the purposes therein mentioned, by the oath of John Drysdale and Charles Robion, witnesses thereto, (they being duly sworn by me for that purpose,) and the said deed admitted to record according to law; and on the same day the within deed of release from Miguel Papy, James Martinely, and José Ximenes, to the said Prosper Viel and Francis J. Avice, was proved by the oath of Charles Robion and Menardie de Nadalie, to be the act and deed of the said Papy, Martinely, and Ximenes, for the purposes therein, the said Robion and Menardie de Nadalie being subscribing witnesses thereto, and being by me duly sworn; which said deed of release is admitted to record.

Witness my hand, as clerk of the circuit court for the county aforesaid, the day and year aforesaid.

JAMES S. TINGLE, *Clerk.*

Francisco J. Avice and Prosper Viel vs. United States. For one thousand acres.

The claimants, by their counsel, pray a new trial, on the ground that they have, as they believe, a good title, emanating to their grantees, through whom they claim, anterior to the 24th January, 1818, which they had supposed it was not necessary to exhibit, as the royal title, dated after that date, specially referred to it; and they exhibit, as evidence upon which they claim a new trial, an amended memorial, and the documents therein referred to.

J. B. LANCASTER, *Attorney for claimants.*

Avice and Viel vs. *the United States.*

Bernardo Segui sworn and examined on the part of claimant, January 24, 1824.

I know Mr. Burgos. He occupied the land in question for about twenty years. His family consisted of about fifteen or twenty negroes, himself, his wife, and four children.

G. W. Perpall sworn and examined.

I have known Mr. Burgos. He occupied the land for about twenty years. The Messrs. Triay occupied it before him. I know not how long. I know they did occupy it. Mr. Burgos's family consisted of about fifteen negroes, himself, his wife, and four children. This was, I believe, the number of his family at the time of his death, and long before. His youngest child is, I presume, more than twenty.

Avice and Viel vs. *the United States.*

Gabriel W. Perpall sworn and examined on the part of claimant, January 24, 1824.

Witness says, I have known Mr. Burgos. He occupied the land for about twenty years. The Messrs. Triay occupied it before. I know not how long, but I know they did occupy it. Mr. Burgos's family consisted of about fifteen negroes, himself, his wife, and four children. This was, I believe, the number of his family at the time of his death, and long before. His youngest child is, I presume, more than twenty years of age.

Bernardo Segui, being sworn and examined, says I know Mr. Burgos. He occupied the land in question for about twenty years. His family consisted of about fifteen or twenty negroes, himself, his wife, and four children.

No. 4.

Title of property in favor of Don Juan Huertas of fifteen thousand acres of land.

Don José Coppinger, colonel of the royal armies, civil and military Governor *pro tem.*, and chief of the royal finance of this city and province, by His Majesty:

Whereas, by royal order, communicated to this Government the 29th of October, 1790, by the captain general of the island of Cuba and two Floridas, among other things it is provided that, to strangers, who, of their own free will, shall present themselves to swear allegiance to our Sovereign, lands should be laid out for them free of expense, in proportion to the number of laborers each family may have. That Don Juan Huertas having presented himself, he solicited of this Government the concession of fifteen thousand acres of land as a compensation for his well-known services, and for the purpose of establishing a cowpen, and the raising of black cattle, which was granted him the 26th August, 1814, in consideration of the truth of his petition, according to the following boundaries: five thousand acres at a place called Tocoy, five miles above Picolata, bounded on the north by the lands of Don Manuel Solano, on the southwest by vacant lands, and on the west by the river St. John's; and the remaining ten thousand acres on the banks of the river, about twelve miles above a place called the Ferry, below B. Rayant's, bounded on the south by the lands of John Mure, and from thence east to the head of Deep creek, taking in the east and west banks of the said creek, and bounded on the north by the southwest line of Tocoy, and on the west by the river St. John's, as results from a certificate given by the secretary of this said Government, with the said date of the 26th of August, 1814, which is found attached to the proceedings instituted by the above mentioned Don Juan Huertas, praying that the corresponding title of the said land be given him. Therefore, and in consideration that the above mentioned Don Juan Huertas has fully proved his having established said cowpen, and that he employs himself in the raising of cattle, complying with the object of said concession, as is seen by the said proceedings filed in the archives of the present notary; and, according to my decree of the present month, I have, therefore, granted, and by these presents do grant, in the name of His Majesty, to the said Don Juan Huertas, his heirs and successors, the said fifteen thousand acres of land in absolute property; and I hereby, and by these presents, deliver him the corresponding title, by which I separate it from the royal domain, from the right and domain it held in said land, and I cede and transfer it to the aforesaid Don Juan Huertas, his heirs and successors, that in consequence thereof they may possess it as their own; make, use, and enjoy it, free from any claim whatever, with all its entrances, outlets, uses, customs, rights, appurtenances, and all, and in general, which hath, doth, or may belong or pertain thereto; and, it being their wish, they may sell, cede, transfer, barter, and alienate it at their will and pleasure. To all of which I interpose my authority, as far as possible, and according to law, in virtue of the sovereign will.

Given under my hand, and countersigned by the undersigned notary of Government and royal finance, in the city of St. Augustine, Florida, the 24th of December, 1817.

JOSE COPPINGER.

By order of His Excellency:

JUAN DE ENTRALGO,
Notary of Government and Royal Finance.

St. Augustine, *April* 19, 1820.

Conformable to the original filed in the archives under my charge, to which I refer, and at the request of the party, I do seal and sign the present copy on two leaves of ordinary paper, stamps not being used.

JUAN DE ENTRALGO, *Notary of Government and Royal Finance.*

I certify the foregoing to be a true and correct translation from a document in the Spanish language.

F. J. FATIO, *S. B. L. C.*

No. 5.

PETITION.

St. Augustine, Florida, *December* 19, 1815.

Don Bernardo Segui, notary public *pro tem.* of the town of Fernandina, resident in this city, respectfully showeth:

That, with the permission of your lordship, he has come to this capital, with solely the object of making known to you, as he has already done verbally, the deplorable situation and condition of that population, originating from a want of commerce, in consequence of the declaration of peace between Great Britain and the United States of America. In May, of the present year, your memorialist was appointed by your lordship's predecessor, Don Sebastian Kindelan, to the office he now holds in said town; and, as he thought to have obtained by it the greatest advantages, he abandoned in this city, as is well known, the business which he had for the support of himself and family, resulting thereby his leaving a certainty for an uncertainty, and, consequently, at present, without any means whatever. The town of Fernandina, as he has already stated, is in such a deplorable situation, on account of there not being any trade whatever, that your memorialist passes entire weeks without obtaining a half rial in fees. If, therefore, a fact so positive, adding thereto the limited services he has performed, merit the consideration of your lordship, he hopes to obtain from your well-known justice, and in virtue of the superior orders of His Majesty, (whom God preserve,) in which he recommends that lands be granted gratis to Spanish subjects, that you be pleased, therefore, to grant him, in absolute property, the quantity of seven thousand acres of land on the east side of the river St. John's, between the place called Dunn's lake and that known as Horse Landing, including in said tract of land the place called Buffalo Bluff, which was latterly given up to the Government by the house of Don Juan Forbes & Co. in exchange for other lands. Therefore, your memorialist prays that your lordship may be pleased to grant him the said quantity of seven thousand acres of land in the place mentioned, not doubting that he will obtain them from the well-known justice of your lordship.

BERNARDO SEGUI.

To the Governor.

DECREE.

St. Augustine, Florida, *December* 20, 1815.

The renunciation made by Don Juan Forbes & Co. of the lands mentioned by the interested in this memorial, being certain, and in virtue of the reasons which he indicates to this Government, let there be granted to him, in absolute dominion, the seven thousand acres of land which he petitions for, under the boundaries which he points out, without injury to a third person, despatching for his security a certified copy of this concession, which will serve him in every event for a title in form.

ESTRADA.

Don Andres Burgevin,
      Private Surveyor in this city of St. Augustine, East Florida.

St. Augustine, Florida, *September* 10, 1818.

I certify that, in virtue of the permission of this Government, I have measured and marked the boundaries of a tract of land containing seven thousand acres, more or less, situate on the east of the river St. John's, at the place known as Buffalo bluff, and running south, bounding the waters of said river, as is more fully seen by the annexed plat, (see plate 4, fig. 1,) which piece of land belongs to Don Bernardo Segui, by a concession made to him by this Government, the 19th December, 1815.

ANDRES BURGEVIN.

No. 6.

To the honorable the Commissioners appointed to ascertain claims and titles to land in East Florida:

The memorial of Antelm Gay, a citizen of the United States, and actual resident of the city of St. Augustine, East Florida, and who was such citizen and resident at the time of the cession of Florida to the United States, respectfully showeth:

That your memorialist claims title to a tract of land, consisting of five thousand acres, situate on the east side of the river St. John's, near Tocoy, bounded on the north by lands now or late of Don Manuel Solana, on the southeast by vacant lands, and on the west by the river St. John's; the same being a part of a grant of fifteen thousand acres made by the Spanish Government, on the 26th August, 1814, to Don Juan Huertas, in virtue of the royal order of the 29th of October, 1790, as appears by the certificate of full title given by Governor Coppinger on the 24th of December, 1817, herewith presented; and the title of your memorialist is derived from a purchase of the said five thousand acres of land made from the grantee, the said Don Juan Huertas, on the 7th day of July, 1821; from which time your memorialist has been in possession of said land.

In confirmation of the said title of your memorialist, the following documents are respectfully presented herewith:

1. Certificate of full title and grant by Governor Coppinger.
2. Conveyance from grantee to your memorialist.
3. Certificate of survey and plat.
      All which is respectfully submitted.

ANTELM GAY.
JOHN RODMAN.
By his attorney,

St. Augustine, *August* 20, 1823.

[TRANSLATION OF CONVEYANCE.]

Know ye that I, Don Juan Huertas, resident of this city, do really sell to Don Antelmo Gay, also a resident, five thousand acres of land, which I possess as my property in this province, situate at a place called Tocoy, five miles above Picolata, bounded on the north by the lands of Don Manuel Solano, on the south-west by vacant lands, and on the west by the river St. John's; which lands were granted me by a decree of this Government of the 26th of August, 1814, and of which there was a title of absolute property on the 24th of December, 1817; the said land being known by the following dimensions and limits:

The first line commences on the banks of said river St. John's, near the mouth of Tocoy creek, at a cypress marked H, thence south 70 degrees, east 160 chains; the second, likewise, begins at a pine marked H, at which the former line ends, and runs thence south 110 chains, to a swamp; third line crosses said swamp, and runs east 100 chains; and the fourth begins at a pine marked as the former, runs south 130 chains, and ends on the margin of Deep creek, as is seen by a certified plat by Don Andres Burgevin, private surveyor, dated the 19th of September, 1818; which I herewith deliver to the said Don Antelm Gay; and I sell him the said five thousand acres of land under the boundaries and dimensions already explained, with all its entrances, outlets, uses, customs, rights, and privileges which it has, or may belong to it, free from any incumbrance, (as I, the said notary, do certify, as results from the register of mortgages under my charge, which, to that effect, I examined,) for the sum of $5,000, which the purchaser has paid me in cash, of which sum I acknowledge the receipt, of my own will, renouncing the proof, laws of delivery, exception for pecuniary misreckoning, fraud, and other circumstances of the case, whereof I acknowledge a formal receipt; in virtue of which I separate myself from the right of possession, title, and whatever other right, real and personal, I had, or may have, to said five thousand acres of land, which I cede, renounce, and transfer, in favor of the purchaser, and whomsoever may represent his cause and right, that he may, as his own, possess, sell, and alienate the same, at his will, in virtue of this deed, which I make in his favor, and consent to, as a sign of real delivery, with which will be proved his having acquired possession, without the necessity of further proof, from which I relieve him. And I bind myself to the eviction and goodness of this sale, in sufficient form, and in the most favorable manner to the purchaser, with my present and future property, with power and submission to the tribunals of His Majesty, that they may compel me to the fulfilment thereof, as by sentence agreed to and passed by virtue of an adjudged cause, upon which I renounce all laws, customs, rights, and privileges in my favor, and the general in form which prohibits.

And I, the said Antelm Gay, being present, do accept in my favor this deed, and by it receive as purchased the said five thousand acres of land, in the price and manner it has been sold me, which I acknowledge to have received of my free will, renouncing the proof, laws of delivery, those of the thing not seen nor received, fraud, and all other things in the matter, of which I give a receipt in form.

In testimony whereof it is dated in this city of St. Augustine, Florida, the 7th of July, 1821.

I, the notary, do attest and know the parties who signed, being witnesses, Don Francisco Pascual Sanchez, Don Fernando de la Maza Arredondo, Jun., and Don Francisco José Fatio, residents present.

JUAN HUERTAS.
ANTELMO GAY.

Before me,

JUAN DE ENTRALGO, *Notary of Government.*

St. Augustine, Florida, *the same day of its date.*

Conformable to its original remaining in the archives under my charge, to which I refer, and at the request of the party do seal and sign the present copy on two leaves of ordinary paper, stamps not being used.

JUAN DE ENTRALGO, *Notary of Government.*

I certify the above to be a true and correct translation from a document in the Spanish language.

F. J. FATIO, *S. B. L. C.*

[TRANSLATION.]

Title in favor of Don Juan Huertas of fifteen thousand acres of land.

Don José Coppinger, colonel of the royal armies, civil and military governor *pro tem.*, and chief of the royal finance of this city and province, by His Majesty:

Whereas, by royal order communicated to this Government the 29th of October, 1790, by the captain general of the island of Cuba and two Floridas, among other things it is provided that to strangers, who, of their own free will, shall present themselves to swear allegiance to our sovereign, lands should be laid out for them free of expense, in proportion to the number of laborers each family may have; that Don Juan Huertas having presented himself, he solicited of this Government the concession of fifteen thousand acres of land as a compensation for his well known services, and for the purpose of establishing a cowpen, and raising black cattle, which was granted him the 26th day of August, 1814, in consideration of the truth of his petition, according to the following boundaries: five thousand acres at a place called Tocoy, five miles above Picolata, bounded on the north by lands of Manuel Solano, on the southwest by vacant lands, and on the west by the river St. John's; and the remaining ten thousand acres on the banks of the river, about twelve miles above a place called the Ferry, below B. Rayant's, bounded on the south by the lands of John Mure, and from thence, east to the head of Deep creek, taking in the east and west banks of said creek, and bounded on the north by the southwest line of Tocoy, and on the west by the river St. John's; as results from a certificate given by the secretary of this said Government, with the date of the 26th of August, 1814, which is found attached to the proceedings instituted by the above mentioned Juan Huertas, praying that the corresponding title of the said land be given him. Therefore, and in consideration that the abovementioned Juan Huertas has fully proved his having established said cowpen, and that he employs himself in raising cattle, complying with the object of said concession, as is seen by the said proceedings filed in the archives of the present notary, and according to my decree of the 22d of the present month, I have, therefore, granted, and by these presents do grant, in the name of His Majesty, to the said Juan Huertas, his heirs and successors, the said fifteen thousand acres of land in absolute property; and I hereby, and by these presents, deliver him the corresponding title by which I separate it from the royal domain, from the right and dominion it held in said land, and I cede and transfer it to the aforesaid Don Juan Huertas, his heirs and successors, that in consequence thereof they may possess it as their own, make use of and enjoy it free from any claim whatever, with all its entrances, outlets, uses, customs, rights, privileges, and all and in general which hath, doth, or may belong or pertain thereto; and it being their wish they may sell, cede, transfer, barter, or alienate it at their will and pleasure; to all of which I interpose my authority as far as possible, and according to law, in virtue of the sovereign will.

Given under my hand, and countersigned by the undersigned notary of Government and royal finance, in this city of St. Augustine, Florida, the 24th of December, 1817.

JOSE COPPINGER.

By order of His Excellency:

JUAN DE ENTRALGO,
Notary of Government and Royal Finance.

St. Augustine, Florida, *June* 15, 1821.

Conformable to the original filed in the archives under my charge, to which I refer, and at the request of the party do seal and sign the present copy on two leaves of ordinary paper, stamps not being used.

JUAN DE ENTRALGO,
Notary of Government.

Don Andres Burgevin, surveyor, appointed by a decree of this Government, dated the 3d instant in favor of the interested:

I certify that I have measured and laid off to Don Juan Huertas a tract of land, situated on the east bank of the river St. John's, about six miles to the south of Picolata, containing five thousand acres; the first line of which commences on the bank of the river, near the mouth of Tocoy creek, and at a cypress marked H, and runs south, seventy degrees east, one hundred and sixty chains; the second begins at a pine marked H; then south, one hundred and ten chains, and ends at a swamp; the third crosses the swamp, and runs east one hundred chains; the fourth begins with a pine marked H, and runs south one hundred and thirty chains, and ends on the bank of Deep creek; and, in all its other circumstances, is conformable to the following plat. [See plate 4, fig. 2.]

In witness whereof, I sign the present certificate in St. Augustine, Florida, the 19th of September, 1818.

ANDRES BURGEVIN.

I certify the above to be a true and correct translation from a document in the Spanish language.

F. J. FATIO, S. B. L. C.

No. 6.

To the honorable the commissioners appointed to ascertain claims and titles to land in East Florida.

St. Augustine, *August* 20, 1823.

The memorial of Antelm Gay, a citizen of the United States, and actually a resident of St. Augustine, in the Territory of Florida, and who was such citizen of the United States, and resident in Florida, at the period of the cession of said country to the United States, respectfully showeth:

That your memorialist claims title to a tract of land, consisting of five hundred acres, situated on the west side of Indian river, and at the mouth of St. Sebastian river, bounded on the south by the last named river, the same being part of a grant of twenty thousand acres from the Spanish Government, made by Governor Coppinger, the 29th of September, 1816, to George Fleming, in virtue of the royal order of the 29th of March, 1815; and which said tract of five hundred acres your memorialist purchased from Andrew Burgevin on the 22d of February, 1820, who purchased the same from the original grantee aforesaid on the 21st of February, 1820.

And your memorialist further showeth, that no conditions whatever were annexed to said grant, and that your memorialist is in possession of the five hundred acres aforesaid.

The following documents, in confirmation of the title of your memorialists, is herewith presented:

1st. Original grant to George Fleming of twenty thousand acres.
2d. Survey and plat of the same.
3d. Conveyance of the five hundred acres from George Fleming to A. Burgevin.
4th. Conveyance from Burgevin to your memorialist.
5th. Survey and plat of the same.
All which is respectfully submitted.

ANTELM GAY,
By his attorney, JOHN RODMAN.

Title of property in favor of Don George Fleming of twenty thousand acres of land, on the banks of the river St. Sebastian.

Don José Coppinger, lieutenant colonel of the royal armies, civil and military governor, and chief of the royal finance in this city of St. Augustine, Florida, and its province:

Whereas, in the royal order of 1815, 29th of March, His Majesty has been pleased to approve the gifts and premiums proposed by my predecessor, the Brigadier General Don Sebastian Kindelan, for the officers and soldiers, both of the line as well as the local militia of this province, who contributed to its defence at the time of the rebellion, being one of the said gifts, the distribution of vacant lands; and Don George Fleming, captain of militia, and resident of this city, having set forth his distinguished and extraordinary services, to which he has contributed both with his property and person in the defence of this said province at different periods; sacrificing and abandoning his property, as a faithful subject, worthy of every recompense for his love, fidelity, and patriotism, and according to the powerful reasons which he has made known to me in his memorial, dated the 9th of the present month, I have thought proper, by my decrees of the same day, to accede to his prayer relative to the granting him twenty thousand acres of land, with a title of absolute property, in a place situated on the banks of the river St. Sebastian, to the south of Indian river, or the river Ys, and between the east coast of Florida and the river St. John's, setting forth hereafter with more clearness and precision the dimensions, whenever the surveyor shall measure the same, as will be fully seen in the said memorial and decree filed in the archives of the present notary. Wherefore, and in attention to said recommendable services, agreeably to the will of the sovereign, and as ordered by the laws, to remunerate with distinction those who are worthy, according to the nature of the said services, and of the persons who have performed them, I have thought proper to grant, and, by these presents, do grant, in the name of His Majesty, and according to his royal justice, which I administer, to the said Don George Fleming, the abovementioned twenty thousand acres of land in the place pointed out, without injury to a third, for himself, his heirs, and successors in absolute property; and I hereby, and by these presents, deliver him the corresponding title, by which I separate it from the royal domains, from the right and dominion it held in said land, and I cede and transfer it to the aforesaid Don George Fleming, his heirs and successors, that, in consequence thereof, they may possess it as their own, make use of and enjoy it free from any claim whatever, with all its entrances, outlets, uses, customs, rights, and privileges; and all and in general which hath, doth, or in any manner may, belong or pertain thereto; and it being their wish, they may sell, cede, transfer, barter, or alienate it, at their will and pleasure. To all which I interpose my judicial authority as far as possible, and according to law, in virtue of what has been already explained, and in compliance with the sovereign will.

Given under my hand, and countersigned by the undersigned notary of Government and royal finance, in this said city of Augustine, Florida, the 24th of September, 1816.

JOSE COPPINGER.

By order of His Excellency:

JUAN DE ENTRALGO.
Not. of Gov. and Royal Finance.

St. Augustine, Florida, *June* 15, 1821.

Conformable to the original filed in the archives under my charge, to which I refer, and, at the request of the arty, do seal and sign the present copy on two leaves of ordinary paper, stamps not being used.

JUAN DE ENTRALGO, *Notary Public.*

Don Andres Burgevin of this vicinity, and private surveyor:

I certify that the following plat [see plate 4, fig. 3] represents a tract of land, containing five hundred acres, situated on the west side of the river Ys, Indian river, and near the mouth of the river St. Sebastian, bounded south by the last mentioned river. Said land is a part of a tract of twenty thousand acres which I measured, by order of this Government, for Don George Fleming, and was granted him on the 9th of September, 1816, and being in all other circumstances conformable to the boundaries herein mentioned.

In witness whereof, I sign the present in St. Augustine, Florida, the 3d of February, 1820.

ANDRES BURGEVIN.

I certify that the foregoing is a true and correct translation from two documents in the Spanish language.

F. J. FATIO, *S. B. L. C.*

CONVEYANCE.

Know ye that I, Don George Fleming, resident of this city, and captain of the provincial militia in the same, do really sell to Don Andres Burgevin, likewise a resident, five hundred acres of land, being a part of a concession made to me by this Government as a recompense for services, on the banks of the river Ys, (Indian river,) and St. Sebastian, and of which there was granted me the corresponding title of property on the 24th September, 1816; which five hundred acres are situated at the mouth of the river St. Sebastian, on the north side, and measures one hundred chains front on the river Ys. The first line begins at a palm tree on the banks of said river Ys, and runs, south, forty-five degrees west, fifty chains, and ends at a pine marked ☰. The second line runs, south, forty-five degrees east, and ends at a stake in the river St. Sebastian, measuring one hundred chains: and I sell him the said five hundred acres of land, under the boundaries and dimensions explained, with all its entrances, outlets, uses, customs, rights, and privileges, which it has or may belong to it, free from any incumbrance, (as I, the said notary, do certify, as results from the register of mortgages under my charge, which to this effect I examined,) in the sum of five hundred dollars, which the purchaser has paid me, of which sum I acknowledge the receipt, of my own will, renouncing the proof, laws of delivery, exception for pecuniary misreckoning, fraud, and other circumstances of the case, whereof I acknowledge a formal receipt: In virtue of which I separate myself from the right of possession, title, and whatever other right I had, real and personal, I had or may have to said five hundred acres of land, which I cede, renounce, and transfer in favor of the purchaser, and whomsoever may represent his right, that he may, as his own, possess, sell, and alienate the same, at his will, in virtue of this deed which I make in his favor, and consent to as a sign of real delivery, with which will be proved his having acquired possession, without the necessity of further proof, and being present; and I, the said Don Andres Burgevin, being present, do accept in my favor this deed, and by it receive, as purchased, the aforesaid five hundred acres of land, in the price and manner it has been sold me, which I acknowledge to have received of my free will, renouncing the proof, laws of delivery, those of the thing not seen nor received, fraud, and other things in the matter, of which I give a formal receipt. In testimony whereof, it is dated in this city of St. Augustine, Florida, the 21st day of October, 1820.

I, the notary, do attest and know the parties who signed, being witnesses, Don William Travers, Don Francisco Pasqual Sanchez, and Don Bernardo Segui, residents, present.

GEORGE FLEMING.
ANDRES BURGEVIN.

Before me: JUAN DE ENTRALGO, *Notary of Government.*

ST. AUGUSTINE, FLORIDA, *June* 14, 1821.

Conformable to its original, remaining on file in the archives under my charge, to which I refer, and, at the request of the party, do seal and sign the present copy on two leaves of ordinary paper, stamps not being used.

JUAN DE ENTRALGO, *Notary of Government.*

A true translation.

F. J. FATIO, *S. B. L. C.*

CONVEYANCE.

Know ye that I, Don Andrew Burgevin, resident of this city, do really sell to Don Antelmo Gay, likewise a resident, five hundred acres of land, which I possess as my property, at the mouth of St. Sebastian river, on the north side, and measures one hundred chains front upon the river Ys, or Indian river. The first line begins at a palm tree on the banks of said river Ys, and runs, south, forty-five degrees west, fifty chains, and ends at a pine marked ☰. The second line runs, south, forty-five degrees east, and ends at a stake in the river St. Sebastian, measuring one hundred chains; which said five hundred acres of land I obtained and purchased from Don George Fleming of this vicinity, by deed acknowledged by him before the present notary (yesterday) in this archive; and I sell him the same under the boundaries and dimensions explained, with all its entrances, outlets, uses, customs, rights, and privileges, which it has or may belong to it, free from any incumbrance, (as I, the said notary, do certify, as results from the register of mortgages under my charge, which to this effect I examined,) in the sum of seven hundred and fifty dollars, which the purchaser has paid me in cash, of which sum I acknowledge the receipt of my own free will, renouncing the proof, laws of delivery, exceptions for pecuniary misreckoning, fraud, and other circumstances of the case, whereof I acknowledge a formal receipt: In virtue of which I separate myself from the right of possession, title, and whatever other right, real and personal, I may have or had to said five hundred acres of land, which I cede, renounce, and transfer, in favor of the purchaser, and whomsoever may represent his right, that he may, as his own, possess, sell, and alienate the same at his will, in virtue of this deed, which I make in his favor as a sign of real delivery, with which will be proved his having acquired possession, without the necessity of further proof, from which I relieve him; and I bind myself to the eviction and goodness of this sale in sufficient form, and in the most favorable manner to the purchaser, with my present and future property, with power and submission to the tribunals of His Majesty, that they may compel me to the fulfilment thereof, as by sentence agreed to and passed by virtue of an adjudged cause, upon which I renounce all laws, customs, rights, and privileges in my favor, and the general in form which prohibits it: and I, the said Don Antelm Gay, being present, do accept in my favor this deed, and by it receive, as purchased, the said five hundred acres of land, in the price and manner it has been sold me, which I acknowledge to have received of my free will, renouncing the proof, laws of delivery, those of the thing not seen nor received, fraud, and other things in the matter, of which I give a receipt in form. In testimony whereof, it is dated in this city of St. Augustine, Florida, 22d of February, 1820.

I, the notary, do attest, and know the parties who signed, being witnesses, Don Fernando de la Maza Arredondo, Jun., Don Pedro Miranda, and Don Gabriel W. Perpall, residents, present.

ANDRES BURGEVIN.
A. GAY.

Before me: JUAN DE ENTRALGO, *Notary of Government.*

ST. AUGUSTINE, FLORIDA, *June* 15, 1821.

Conformable to its original, remaining on file in the archives under my charge, to which I refer, and at the request of the party, do seal and sign the present copy on two leaves of ordinary paper, stamps not being used.

JUAN DE ENTRALGO, *Notary of Government.*

I certify the foregoing to be a true and correct translation from a document in the Spanish language.

F. J. FATIO, *S. B. L. C.*

Plan of twenty thousand acres of land [see plate 5, fig. 1] in absolute property to George Fleming, Esquire, on 24th September, 1816, for the services he rendered His Catholic Majesty as captain of the militia of Florida, and other services.   These lands are situated on the river St. Sebastian, precisely at the place where it joins with Indian river, having the advantage of two fronts.   The land is admirably adapted for the cultivation of sugar, cotton, rice, and other productions of the climate; and surveyed by Mr. Andrew Burgevin.

I certify that the above plat is a copy of the original.

ANDREW BURGEVIN.

No. 8.

To the honorable the Commissioners appointed to ascertain claims and titles to lands in East Florida, the memorial of Antelm Gay and Francis J. Avice, citizens of the United States, and actually residents of St. Augustine, in the Territory of Florida, and who were such citizens of the United States and residents of Florida at the period of the cession of said country to the United States, respectfully showeth:

That your memorialists claim title to a tract of two thousand acres of land, situated at Mosquito, bounded on the north by lands of Octavius Mitchell, on the east and west by vacant lands, on the south by lands of Francis P. Sanchez; which tract of land was obtained from the Spanish Government by a grant made by Governor Coppinger on the 14th of October, 1817, to Don Pablo Roseté, in virtue of the royal order of the 29th March, 1815, and which land was purchased by your memorialists from the grantee the 24th November, 1819; and your memorialists are now in possession of said land.   In confirmation of your memorialists' title, the following documents are respectfully presented herewith:

1st. A certified copy of the original grant.
2d. Conveyance from the grantee to your memorialist.
3d. Certificate of survey and plat.
     All of which is respectfully submitted.

ANTELM GAY,
By his attorney,   JOHN RODMAN.
F. J. AVICE.

ST. AUGUSTINE, *August* 20, 1823.

[TRANSLATION.]

Petition of Don Pablo Roseté.

ST. AUGUSTINE, *October* 14, 1817.

Don Pablo Roseté, lieutenant of the army, adjutant of the staff of the whites attached by His Majesty to the battalion of the disciplined militia of the regular infantry of the Havana, and commandant of the two companies of the same which serve as auxiliaries in this place, with due respect to your excellency, represents:

That, being one of those who, in his opinion, are concerned and comprehended in the royal order of the 29th March, 1815, relative to the distribution of lands in consequence of having been in this province from the 13th of March, 1813, at which epoch it was invaded and besieged by rebels of the same, and by parties of the State of Georgia, when the petitioner was appointed to the defence of the redoubt, situated at Solano's ford, with a sergeant, a drummer, two corporals, and fourteen grenadiers of the aforesaid companies, by His Excellency Don Sebastian Kindelan, the predecessor of your excellency; that he rigorously complied with the first duties of his commission, and moreover daily attended His Excellency aforesaid, and his secretary's office, in the capacity of an amanuensis, as will certify the secretary of said office, the lieutenant of the armies Don Thomas de Aguilar, that he rendered those extra services without any salary or emolument being awarded to him for the same: and whereas His Majesty, by his said royal order, has been pleased to approve the rewards which your predecessor aforesaid proposed to be given to such individuals who contributed to the defence of said province until the entire tranquillity thereof was effected, whether they were veterans or voluntarily engaged, and whereas one of the favors or indemnities alluded to consists in a distribution of lands in absolute property: The petitioner, therefore, supplicates your excellency that, as a reward for his laborious services, and in consideration of the services which, by their notoriety, entitles him to that royal favor, you be pleased to grant him two thousand acres on the river Ys, (Indian river,) bounded south by lands granted to Isaac Weeks; which favor your petitioner entertains no doubt of receiving from your excellency.

PABLO ROSETE.

To His Excellency the GOVERNOR.

DECREE.

ST. AUGUSTINE, *October* 14, 1817.

In consideration of the well-known services rendered by the petitioner, the two thousand acres, situated in the place by him mentioned are hereby granted to him, for which the title of absolute property will be issued in his behalf, in the usual form, from the secretary's office of the Government and of the royal domains.

COPPINGER.

I certify the foregoing to be a true and correct translation from a document in the Spanish language.

F. J. FATIO, *S. B. L. C.*

[TRANSLATION.]

Title of property, in favor of Lieutenant Don Pablo Roseté, of two thousand acres of land, at the head of the river Ys, (Indian river.)

Don José Coppinger, colonel of the royal armies, civil and military governor and chief of the royal finance in this city of St. Augustine, Florida, and its province, by His Majesty:

Whereas, in the royal order of the 29th of March, 1815, His Majesty has been pleased to approve the gifts and premiums proposed by my predecessor, the Brigadier General Don Sebastian Kindelan, for the officers and soldiers, both of the line as well as of the local militia, and the other individuals of this province who contributed to its defence at the time of the rebellion, being one of said gifts, the distribution of lands in proportion to the number of family each individual may have; that Don Pablo Roseté, lieutenant in the army, adjutant of the general staff attached by His Majesty to the battalion of infantry of disciplined militia of free blacks of the Havana, and commandant of the two companies of said battalion which remain as auxiliaries in this city, having set forth the merits of his services rendered in the said defence, and soliciting in virtue of the same, and of said gifts, the concession of two thousand acres of land, they were granted him at the head of the river Ys, (Indian river,) bounded on the south by those granted to Don Isaac Weeks, as is proved by my decree of the 14th of October of the year last past, on the memorial of the interested, with the same date, which remains on file in the Government notary's office: wherefore I have granted, and, by these presents, do grant, in the name of His Majesty, and according to his royal justice which I administer, to the said Lieutenant Don Pablo Roseté the above-mentioned two thousand acres of land in the place pointed out, without injury to a third person, for him, his heirs, and successors in absolute property; and I hereby, and by these presents, deliver him the corresponding titles by which I separate it from the royal domains from the right and dominion it held in said land; and I cede and transfer it to the said Lieutenant Don Pablo Roseté, his heirs and successors, that, in consequence thereof, they may possess it as their own, make use of, and enjoy it, free from any claim whatever, with all its entrances, outlets, usages, customs, rights and privileges, and all and in general, which hath, doth, or in any manner, by right, may, belong or pertain thereto; and, it being their wish, they may sell, cede, transfer, barter, or alienate the same at their will and pleasure. To all of which I interpose my judicial authority as far as possible, according to law, and in compliance with the sovereign will.

Given under my hand, and countersigned by the undersigned notary of Government and royal finance in this said city of St. Augustine, Florida, the 17th April, 1818.

JOSE COPPINGER.

By order of His Excellency:

JUAN DE ENTRALGO,
Notary of Government and Royal Finance.

ST. AUGUSTINE, FLORIDA, *June* 15, 1821.

Conformable to the original, filed in the archives, under my charge, to which I refer, and at the request of the party, do seal and sign this present copy on two leaves of ordinary paper, stamps not being used.

JUAN DE ENTRALGO, *Notary Public.*

Don Robert McHardy, planter in the territory of Mosquito, surveyor, appointed by a decree of the Government, of the 14th of May of the present year, at the petition of the interested:

I certify that I have measured and laid off for Don Pablo Roseté a tract of land, containing two thousand acres, situated in the territory of Mosquito, bounded on the north by lands of Don Octavius Mitchell, on the east and west by vacant lands, and on the south by the lands of Don Francisco P. Sanchez, the figures and lines of which are according to the foregoing plat. [See plate 5, figure 2.]

In witness whereof, I sign the present, in St. Augustine, this 25th day of July, 1818.

ROBERT McHARDY.

A copy from the original, to which I refer.

ROBERT McHARDY.

I certify the foregoing to be a true and correct translation from two documents in the Spanish language.

F. J. FATIO, *S. B. L. C.*

CONVEYANCE.

Know ye, that I, Don Pablo Roseté, first adjutant of this city, do really sell to Don Francisco Julian Avice and Don Antelmo Gay, new settlers of this province, two thousand acres of land which I possess as my property in the territory of Mosquito, of this said province, bounded on the north by the lands of Don Octavius Mitchell, on the east and west by vacant lands, and on the south by the lands of Don Francisco P. Sanchez. The first line commences at a pine, marked M and R, and runs south 35°, east, 41 chains 43 links, to another pine marked R. The second line commences at the last mentioned pine, and runs south 65°, west, 141 chains 43 links, to a stake. The third line commences at said stake, and runs north 35°, west, 141 chains 43 links, to a pine marked | | | |. The fourth line runs north 65° east, beginning at the last mentioned pine and ending at the first, where the measurement began, and containing the same number of chains as the others, as is seen by the plat, which, under date of the 25th of July, 1818, was made by Don Robert McHardy, an intelligent person, by permission of the Government; which lands were granted me by a decree of this Government of the 14th of October, 1817, as a recompense for my services, and of which a title of absolute property was given me on the 17th of April of the said year of 1818: and I sell unto them the said two thousand acres of land, under the boundaries and dimensions already explained, with all its entrances, outlets, usages, customs, rights, and privileges, which it has or may belong to it, free from any incumbrance, (as I, the notary, do certify, as results from the register of mortgages under my charge, which, to that effect, I examined,) in the price of $3,000, which the purchasers have paid me in cash, of which sum I acknowledge the receipt of my own will, renouncing the proof, laws of delivery, exception for pecuniary misreckoning, fraud, and other circumstances of the case, whereof I acknowledge a formal receipt, in virtue of which I separate myself from the right of possession, title, and whatever other right, real and personal, I had, or may have to said lands, which I cede, renounce, and transfer in favor of the purchasers, and whomsoever may represent them, that they may, as their own, possess, sell, and alienate the same at their will, in virtue of these writings, which I make in their favor as a sign of real delivery, with which will be proved their having acquired possession without the necessity of further proof, from which I relieve them: and I bind myself to the eviction and goodness of this sale, in sufficient form, and in the most favorable manner to the purchasers, with my present and future property, with power and submission to the tribunals of his Majesty, that they may compel me to the fulfilment thereof, as by sentence agreed to, and passed by virtue of an adjudged cause, upon which I renounce all laws, customs, rights, and privileges in my favor, and the general in form which prohibits it: and we, the said purchasers, being present, do accept, in our favor, this indenture, and by it receive as purchased the aforesaid two thousand acres of land in the price and manner it has been sold us, which we acknowledge to have received of our free will, renouncing the proof, laws of delivery, fraud, and all other things in the matter, of which we give a receipt in form. In testimony whereof, it is dated in this city of St. Augustine, Florida, the 24th of November, 1819. I, the notary, do attest and give faith to the parties who signed, in the presence of the witnesses, Don Fernando de la Maza Arredondo, Jun., Don Antonio Mier, and Don Juan Huertas, residents, present.

PABLO ROSETE.
F. J. AVICE.
A. GAY.

Before me:　　　　JUAN DE ENTRALGO,
　　　　　　　　　　　　Notary of Government.

ST. AUGUSTINE, FLORIDA, *June* 14, 1821.

Conformable to the original remaining in the archives under my charge, to which I refer, and, at the request of the party, do seal and sign the present copy, on two leaves of ordinary paper, stamps not being used.

JUAN DE ENTRALGO, *Not. Pub.*

I certify the foregoing to be a true and correct translation from a document in the Spanish language.

F. J. FATIO, *S. B. L. C.*

Petition for re-hearing.

Antelm Gay *vs.* the United States.—Claim for seven hundred acres of land.
Antelm Gay *vs.* the United States.—Claim for four hundred acres of land.
Antelm Gay *vs.* the United States.—Claim for two thousand acres of land.
Antelm Gay *vs.* the United States.—Claim for a lot in St. Augustine.
Antelm Gay *vs.* the United States.—Twelve acres of arable land, with pine land adjoining.

To the honorable the Board of Commissioners appointed to ascertain claims and titles to land in East Florida:

The petition of Antelm Gay respectfully showeth, that the original concession upon which the royal titles, or absolute grants mentioned in the above claims, respectively, are founded, are severally dated, and were severally made, anterior to the 24th of January, 1818. That the reason they were not produced by the counsel of your petitioner, was, as your petitioner believes, that it was considered that the royal titles in the memorials of your petitioner mentioned, and by him exhibited to this honorable board, would be received as, if not conclusive, at least *prima facie* evidence of the facts they set forth, and especially of the existence of the concessions on which they are founded. Your petitioner represents to this honorable board, that he is able to lay before them the said several concessions on which the said royal titles are founded. Your petitioner, also, further represents, that he was under the impression that, at the time his said claims, which have been rejected, were under the examination of the board, that it was taken as proved and admitted, that your petitioner was an inhabitant and resident of this Territory before, and at the time of, its cession to the United States, and that he has been so ever since. These facts your petitioner has power to prove, to the satisfaction of this honorable board.

Your petitioner, understanding that the failure on his part to produce the aforementioned concessions, or to prove the fact of his having been a resident of this Territory at its cession, has been the cause of the rejection of his claim in the above cases; he, therefore, prays that this honorable board will grant him a re-hearing of his said claims, and thereby afford him an opportunity of introducing his said evidence; and he will ever pray, &c.

A. GAY.

TERRITORY OF FLORIDA, *county of St. John's:*

On this 4th day of February, 1824, personally appeared before me, Elias B. Gould, a justice of the peace for said county, Don Ramon Sanchez, Don Bartolome de Castro y Ferrer, Don Pedro Miranda, who, being duly sworn, upon their oaths, say, that they are severally acquainted with Don Juan Gianople, and that they have been so acquainted with him for twenty-five years now last past. That he was then a man with a numerous family of children, and owned five slaves. And the said deponents further state, that the said Don Juan Gianople has, since their acquaintance with him, been an inhabitant of East Florida, and is an inhabitant thereof at this time.

B. CASTRO Y FERRER.
RAMON SANCHEZ.
PEDRO MIRANDA.

Sworn to before me, the day and year above written.

E. B. GOULD, *Justice of the Peace.*

No. 9.

ST. AUGUSTINE, *August* 5, 1823.

To the honorable the Commissioners appointed to ascertain claims and titles to lands in East Florida, from the memorialist, the subscriber, who declares:

That he resides in the United States, and that he was not in the province of East Florida at the time of the cession of the said province to the United States.

That he resided at a former period in the said province, and that the Government of the same made to him, on the 18th May, 1803, the following concession of lands, as his head-rights, on certain conditions, which, when required, he can prove were complied with, being allowed one hundred acres for himself, and fifty for each of his family and negroes: 1st. A tract of land at the head of Indian river, containing six thousand acres, and bounded by Indian river, and vacant lands were adjoining the same. The same is described by a survey, which is herewith presented. [See plate 6, fig. 1.] 2d. A tract called Stoney point, or Marrot's island, lying on Indian river. The number of acres contained in the same is undefined, both in the memorial which your memorialist made to the

Spanish Government, and in the concession of the same to him, it being considered as containing but a small proportion of good land. A survey of the same is herewith presented. 3d. A tract of land of three hundred acres, situated between north and east, on the north side of Marrot's island, and lies between the lagoon of Indian river, bordering on the said island and the Mosquito lagoon, in front of the other, &c. A survey of the same is herewith presented. 4th. A tract of one thousand acres, called Cabbage swamp, situated to the east of Indian river, opposite the Narrows, so called from its being narrower than any other tract. A survey of the same is herewith presented, together with an official copy of the concession to your memorialist, which enumerates all and each of the said tracts of land.

Your memorialist begs leave to state that he would have required, and probably have obtained, royal titles for the said concessions of lands, previous to the change of Government of said province, but from an insurrection which took place in 1812 in the country, and in which your memorialist, being a principal actor, though pardoned by the King, had raised such an excitement in the minds of those who were devoted to the Spanish Government, that his life might have been taken by some bigoted and malignant assassin, who would the more readily have committed such an act, as he might have calculated to have done it with impunity. Your memorialist can prove that, a short time before the cession of the province, he arrived in a vessel off St. Augustine, wishing to enter the same; but, on inquiring of the Governor whether he would be responsible for the safety of his person, he replied, only " while your memorialist was in his sight." Your memorialist has respectfully further to show that, on the 20th March, 1804, he made a purchase, in conformity to all the forms of the Spanish laws, from the late John McQueen, of two tracts of land, situated on the St. John's river. The one called Fort St. George he has since sold; and the other, called *St. Juan Nepunensana*, containing ninety-eight caballerias and eight acres, having one front on St. John's river, and another on McGirt's creek, and which is very particularly defined in an official copy of the royal title to said John McQueen, who had possession of the same from the year 1790 to that of 1804, and from John McQueen to your memorialist; an official copy of which is also herewith presented.

Your memorialist also purchased from Timothy Hollingsworth, deceased, a tract of land on St. John's river, called Mulberry grove, and containing eight hundred acres, in the year 1805, under a royal title, with all the Spanish forms, in such cases; but, not having a translation of the same, cannot particularly describe it. An official copy of his conveyance to your memorialist is herewith presented; the royal title to him is on record in the office with the archives.

Your memorialist also purchased from the said John McQueen two thousand acres of land on Miami river, but for which he did not receive Spanish titles, from the circumstance of this concession not having been obtained ten years. Your memorialist took Mr. McQueen's obligation to make *titles* for the same, together with a receipt acknowledging to have received a full consideration for this tract, together with the other two tracts which your memorialist had purchased from him, and, subsequently, titles in full for the same; all of which papers are herewith submitted to your board; but none of them being on record, your memorialist requests that they may be taken care of. An official copy of the concession to Mr. McQueen is also presented. Your memorialist having offered to your honorable body a particular statement of his claim and titles for lands in the Territory of Florida, respectfully requests a confirmation of the same; and that, where they exceed three thousand five hundred acres, your honorable board will recommend to Congress to confirm such claims and titles.

And your memorialist will ever pray, &c. &c.

JOHN H. McINTOSH.

To the honorable the Board of Commissioners appointed to ascertain titles and claims to lands in East Florida, from their memorialist, who showeth:

That, in a memorial which he presented to your board on the 5th day of August last, he described one of the tracts of land called Marrot's island, (a part of the concession of land which the Spanish Government had granted to him for his head-rights,) as undefined in its quantity of acres; since which he has ascertained, from seeing an old British grant for the said island, that it contains three thousand six hundred acres: he therefore requests that it may be considered by your honorable board that it does contain the said quantity of three thousand six hundred acres, and act accordingly.

JOHN H. McINTOSH.

[TRANSLATION.]

Don George Clarke, lieutenant of the militia of St. Augustine, Florida, commissioned judge of the northern district, and Surveyor General of the province, by his Government:

St. Augustine, *December 2, 1817.*

I certify that I have measured and laid off for Don Juan McIntosh six thousand acres of land, situated at the head of the river Ys, or Indian river, and on the west side, being part of a larger quantity granted him by the Government the 18th May, 1803, and is conformable in all its parts to the following plat, a copy of which remains in the book of surveys under my charge. [See plate 6, fig. 1.]

GEORGE J. F. CLARKE.

[TRANSLATION.]

Don George Clarke, lieutenant of the militia of St. Augustine, Florida, commissioned judge of the northern district, and Surveyor General of the province, appointed by his Government:

St. Augustine, *December 2, 1817.*

I certify that I have measured and laid off for Don Juan H. McIntosh three hundred acres of land at a place known by the name of Stewart's swamp, situated northeast from the northern point of Marrot's island, between the river Ys, or Indian river, and Hillsborough, being part of a larger quantity granted him by the Government the 18th of May, 1803; and is conformable in all its parts to the following plat, a copy of which remains in the book of surveys under my charge. [See plate 6, fig. 2.]

GEORGE J. F. CLARKE.

[TRANSLATION.]

To the Governor, Don Juan H. McIntosh, recent settler, admitted under the protection of His Catholic Majesty, respectfully showeth:

That he intends removing to this province in the course of twelve months, with his family and slaves, amounting to two hundred and fifty, besides five white men, two of whom have families; and, for the purpose of carrying into effect said intention, he solicits that your excellency will be pleased to grant him the lands which appertain to him, according to the number of his family and slaves as above mentioned, in the following places: an island in the river Ys, (Indian river) known by the name of Stoney point, or Marrot's Island, which name he gave it, having a person residing thereon. Likewise, three hundred acres of land which contain about one hundred and fifty acres of hammock or plantable land, known formerly by the name of Stewart's swamp, situated about northeast from the north part of Stoney point island, and lies between the lake of river Ys, (Indian river,) near said island and Mosquito lake, opposite the other, intersected on the part of the hammock by a creek from said river, on the east of said island. Also, one thousand acres of land which contain from seven to eight hundred acres, called Cabbage swamp, situated on the east side of the river Ys, (Indian river,) opposite the Narrows, so called on account of said river being more narrow there than at any other part, and about twenty miles distant from its mouth. Likewise, six thousand acres of land one mile below the head of river Ys, (Indian river,) on the west side, running north from that to another point two miles; thence, in a direct line south three miles, until it stops in front of the first point, and one mile distant, containing three miles square, comprising the lands described on said lines; a creek empties into the river Ys that runs through said lands; a favor which he doubts not of obtaining from your excellency, and which he will gratefully acknowledge.

[DECREE.]

ST. AUGUSTINE, FLORIDA, *May* 18, 1803.

Grant the memorialist the land he petitions for, without injury to a third; and, until the number of his family he may have for its cultivation is known, let the quantity appertaining to him be surveyed, with the absolute conditions, that he must present a person of property as his security that he will take possession of said lands in the course of the twelve months, and of his having executed the same, will be put in continuation of this, my decree, and that it will be out of his power to claim damages in case of an invasion, or for other motives, in which the royal service demands his retiring into the interior of the province.

WHITE.

NOTE.—The memorialist has presented himself, declaring that the said six thousand acres of land is understood to be situated one mile below the head of river Ys, (Indian river) on the west side, although the boundaries described in the memorial are not very correctly explained, which he sets forth on account of not having seen said land, but has petitioned for them through the information he has obtained. Dated as above.

PIERRA.

ST. AUGUSTINE, FLORIDA, *May* 21, 1803.

The foregoing is a copy of the original filed in this office, under my charge, which I certify.

JUAN DE PIERRA.

[TRANSLATION.]

Don George Clarke, lieutenant of the militia of St. Augustine, Florida, commissioned judge of the northern district, and Surveyor General of the province, appointed by his Government:

ST. AUGUSTINE, *December* 2, 1817.

I certify that I have measured and laid off for Don Juan H. McIntosh one thousand acres of land at a place called Cabbage swamp, on the east side of the Narrows of river Ys, or Indian river, being a part of a larger quantity granted him by the Government the 18th of May, 1803, and is conformable, in all its parts, to the following plat, a copy of which remains in the book of surveys under my charge. [See plate 6, fig. 3.]

GEORGE J. F. CLARKE.

No. 10.

To the honorable the Commissioners appointed to ascertain claims and titles to land in East Florida.

The memorial of Moses Elias Levy respectfully showeth, that your memorialist, in his own behalf, and that of others concerned, claim a title to a portion of land, consisting of one-eighth of the grant hereinafter mentioned, and not less than thirty-six thousand acres of land, situated in Alachua county; which title was acquired by a purchase made by your memorialist from Fernando de la Maza Arredondo and son, as will appear by the attested copy of the covenant and indenture annexed, and marked A, who obtained it by a grant made by the sub-delegate, general superintendent of the island of Cuba and the two Floridas, Alexandro Ramirez, which concession was made by virtue of the powers which the laws of Spain invests his high office with, and other royal orders, particularly that of the 3d of September, 1817, which the grant makes mention of, and by and with the advice and consent of the fiscal or attorney general for the royal or national domain, and the Surveyor General.

Your memorialist further showeth, that the original grantees, and others concerned, were in actual possession at the time of the cession; that, from the date of the purchase, your memorialist was, and is now, in actual occupancy of said lands, as may be attested by Edward M. Wanton, Horatio S. Dexter, Francis P. Sanchez, and others, and that your memorialist is a citizen of the United States, and a resident of Mincope, in Alachua.

Your memorialist further showeth, that the grant alluded to in this memorial, consists of four leagues of ground towards each point of the compass, to be reckoned from the point which is established as the centre; and that this grant was made on the 22d day of December, 1817, as evidenced by the attested copy herewith annexed, and marked B. That the settlement of two hundred families was attached as a condition of the grant, and to be commenced within the period of three years from the date of the grant; that the grantees had a prorogation of one year over and above the aforementioned three years, for the fulfilment of the aforegoing terms, as will appear by the decree of the superintendent, and the correspondence between said superintendent and Coppinger, the then Governor of this province, attested copies are herewith annexed, and marked C, D, and E; that, notwithstanding the extension of this time, the concerned did, in September, 1820, enter into an agreement with William Tudor Hall, to settle, with certain number of other persons, on the said tract of Alachua; and that the said William Tudor Hall, with others, did proceed to the said territory of Alachua, and on or about the 7th day of November, of the same year, actually began the establishment, as will appear by the deposition annexed, and marked F.

Your memorialist begs further to state that, in November, or early in December, of same year, Edward M. Wanton and Horatio S. Dexter were employed and engaged to proceed to the aforesaid territory of Alachua, and established themselves as settlers, as will be attested by the same persons, Francis P. Sanchez and others.

Your memorialist begs leave further to state that, long before the settlement was first established, the territory of Alachua was abandoned by the native Indians of this territory; and that the chiefs, in a talk which they formally held with Governor Coppinger, were apprized of the grant in question, as being made by his superior in authority, to the said Arredondo and son, and that two hundred families were to be established in it. The documents or record of said *talk*, like many other documents, as your honorable body must be well aware, are missing from the archives, and the only means left your petitioner to prove the existence of this talk, and its result, is the deposition of Antonio Alvarez, then first officer of the secretary's office, and now one of the officers of the keeper of the Spanish archives' office, and Pedro Miranda, both present at said talk, as will appear by their affidavits annexed, and marked G and H.

Your memorialist also represents that, although the treaty of cession of 22d February, 1819, ratified by His Catholic Majesty on the 24th October, 1820, in the spirit of which, and according to the literal translation of that on the Spanish side, the 8th article provides, " that the *proprietors* of such lands, who, by reason of the recent circumstances of the Spanish nation, and the revolution in Europe, have been prevented from fulfilling all the conditions of their grants, shall complete them within the terms limited in the same, respectively, from the date of the treaty," &c. &c.; which might have justified the grantees in waiting until the title was confirmed by the Government of the United States, or, at any rate, to defer a settlement calculated to incur immense expense and trouble, as it was to be made in a wild and inhospitable country, seventy miles from the capital, and in the neighborhood of savages, to even as late a period as the 24th of October ensuing.   Yet the grantees, notwithstanding all the disadvantages and hardships they had to contend with, did continue, even after the ratification and promulgation of the treaty, with vigor and zeal, the objects which, from the date of the grant, had been in preparation, and which they actually began to carry into effect on the 7th November, 1820, and have advanced and augmented the establishment to its present respectable footing.

The present settlers, with their families, amount to about forty-seven persons, the most of whom have been transported and maintained at the expense of the concerned; who have, also, at considerable cost, cut a road for wheel carriages of about forty-five miles, leading from the river St. John's to the settlement; have built upon the same eight bridges, erected twenty-five houses, and established three plantations on the tract, of which about three hundred acres are cleared, and now under cultivation.   The present owners of said grant or tract of land, consist of more than seventy individuals, most of them agriculturists from New York, New Jersey, and other parts; many rich and opulent citizens, the major part of whom became purchasers with the intention of settling on the said lands, circumstances publicly well known, and which will be substantiated when the parties present their respective claims before your honorable body.

The proprietors have now prepared materials, and are about erecting a saw-mill; have got out the frames, &c., to build ten or fifteen houses, and are now clearing land for the establishment of eleven farms, as will be made to appear by the annexed affidavit, marked J.   Further testimonies may be obtained from Mr. Edward M. Wanton, and others, settled on the lands.   All of which is respectfully submitted.

M. E. LEVY.

St. Augustine, *August* 14, 1823.

A.

Whereas Messrs. Hernandez and Chauviteau did, some time in the month of August, one thousand eight hundred and twenty, purchase from Don Fernando de la Maza Arredondo, the elder, a concession or tract of land, situated on both sides of Alligator creek, in East Florida, containing about thirty-eight thousand and four hundred acres, a more particular description of which will be seen by reference to the deed and other accompanying documents, bearing date in the month aforesaid; which concession or grant was afterwards transferred to Moses E. Levy for, and in consideration of, the sum of twenty-five thousand dollars, actually paid by Moses E. Levy, who has since that time remained, and still is, the owner of said concession or tract, the one-half or moiety of which he desires to give and grant unto Arredondo and son, of Havana, in exchange for certain lands hereinafter mentioned; and the said Arredondo and son, proprietors of a large portion of a certain grant, or concession of land, made to them, the said Arredondo and son, in and by a decree bearing date at Havana, on or about the twenty-second day of December, one thousand eight hundred and seventeen, commonly called the Alachua grant, situated in East Florida, a more particular description of which will be seen by reference to said grant, have consented, and agreed to give and grant the one-sixteenth part of the said concession to the said Moses E. Levy, in exchange for the lands above mentioned.   *This indenture,* therefore, between Fernando de la Maza Arredondo, the younger, agent and attorney in fact for said Arredondo and son, of the one part, and Moses Elias Levy of the other part, witnesseth: That the said Fernando de la Maza Arredondo, agent and attorney as aforesaid, hath given, granted, aliened, exchanged, and released, and by these presents, doth give, grant, alien, exchange, and release, unto the said Moses Elias Levy, one-sixteenth part of said concession, grant, or tract of land, lying and being in Alachua as aforesaid, to have and to hold the said one-sixteenth part unto him, the said Moses Elias Levy, his heirs and assigns forever, in exchange for the lands hereinafter mentioned, granted by said Levy to said Arredondo and son.   And the said Moses Elias Levy hath given, granted, aliened, exchanged, and released, and doth by these presents give, grant, exchange, and release, unto Fernando de la Maza Arredondo, otherwise called Arredondo and son, one undivided half or moiety of the concession, grant, or tract, lying on Alligator creek as aforesaid: to have and to hold the one-half or moiety of the said concession, grant, or tract, to them, the said Arredondo and son, and their heirs and assigns forever, in exchange for the lands before mentioned and granted, to said Moses Elias Levy.

And the parties to these presents do covenant and agree, that if both of the above mentioned concessions shall be established, and recognised as legal and valid, on or before the first day of April, 1824, they shall reciprocally give and exchange, at the cost of the party requiring them, all further and other assurances which they may deem necessary more effectually to secure the interests hereby meant to be conveyed; and it is further covenanted and agreed that, if the title to Alligator creek tract shall not be established and ratified, and deemed valid by a board of land commissioners, or some other tribunal or commissioners, on or before the day and year last mentioned, then, and in that event, Arredondo and son shall transfer and convey unto Moses E. Levy one other sixteenth part of said Alachua concession, so as to make the whole amount conveyed to said Levy one-eighth part of the whole concession; and, in order the more effectually to secure the same, the said one-sixteenth part set aside for this purpose is, by these presents, placed under the absolute control of said Levy until the said 1st day of April, 1824, or until the title to the Alligator creek tract, which was granted to Arredondo, the elder, shall be recognised; and they further covenant and agree that, if the Alachua concession shall not be deemed valid by a competent tribunal on or before the said 1st day of April, 1824, so as to secure to the said Moses Elias Levy the one-sixteenth or eighth part thereof, according to the contingencies herein mentioned, then, and in that event, the said Moses E. Levy shall be entitled immediately to an equivalent in other lands owned or provided by Arredondo and son, or an equitable indemnity in the manner pointed out by the contracts on the subject of Florida lands heretofore made between F. M. Arredondo, the elder, and Moses E. Levy. And it is further agreed and covenanted, that the said Moses Elias Levy shall continue to exercise the sole and absolute control in all respects, as if he were the sole owner over the whole of the Alligator creek tract, as well as one-eighth of the Alachua, until the question of titles be determined, or until the day and year above mentioned, whichever event may first happen; and the said Arredondo, the younger, agent and attorney as aforesaid, covenants to and with the said Moses Elias Levy that the one-sixteenth part of said concession shall not contain less than eighteen thousand sixty-two and a half acres, and the one-eighth not less than thirty-six thousand one hundred and twenty-five acres, but may, respectively, contain a greater quantity, if the quantity contained in the whole grant will justly allow of a greater to these proportions. And said Arredondo, agent as aforesaid, covenants to reimburse and refund to said Levy any sum or sums of money which he may lay out and expend in and about the premises; and, upon consultation and deliberation, the parties to these presents covenant and agree that the above written covenants and agreements shall be modified and changed in the following manner: that is, if one of the above-mentioned tracts shall, on or before the 1st day of January, which shall be in the year 1826, shall be recognised and deemed valid before any court or tribunal in the United States, and the title of the other tract not determined, then, and in that event, the rights and claims of the parties in the tracts of land, respectively, as settled by this exchange, shall not be altered or changed; and Moses E. Levy shall, in that event, retain his claims on Alachua, and Arredondo and son shall retain their claims on one-half of Alligator creek tract; nor shall Arredondo and son be required to convey to said Moses E. Levy the additional one-sixteenth part of Alachua until the title, grant, or concession of Alligator creek tract shall be annulled; nor shall the said Arredondo and son be required, in the case of either grant, to give an equivalent therefor, as provided by this and their several contracts on the subject of Florida lands, until the said grant shall be actually annulled and determined to be not the property of Arredondo, Levy, or their assigns; and the said Moses E. Levy shall do and perform whatever lies within his power to effect, as early as possible, a legal recognition of said grants. In testimony whereof, they, the said F. M. Arredondo, agent and attorney as aforesaid, and Moses E. Levy, have hereunto affixed their hands and seals, this 22d day of January, 1822, the word "Fernando" in the second page, and word "hundred" on fourth page, being first obliterated.

F. M. ARREDONDO.
M. E. LEVY.

Signed, sealed, and delivered, in presence of
BERNARDO SEGUI.
WM. M. GIBSON.

TERRITORY OF FLORIDA, *county of St. John's:*

I, James S. Tingle, clerk of the county court for the county aforesaid, do certify that the foregoing is a true copy from the records in my office.

JAMES S. TINGLE.

B.

[TRANSLATION.]

[The original appears to have been written on stamped paper, of the second class, valid for the years 1816 and 1817.]

Don Alexandro Ramirez, intendant of the army, superintendent general, sub-delegate of the royal treasury of this island of Cuba and the two Floridas, president of the tribunal of accounts, and of the committee of tithes, superintendent of the crusada, sole judge of arrivadas, protector of the royal lottery, chief director and inspector of the royal monopoly of tobacco, &c.

Whereas Don Fernando de la Maza Arredondo and son, of this city, merchants, have presented a petition, in this Intendancy, and general sub-delegate superintendency, dated the 12th November last, praying for a gratuitous grant of a piece of ground in East Florida, where they have been established, and where the greatest part of their family reside, with much of their property, offering to form an establishment in the territory known by the name of *Alachua*, the same being suitable for the raising of cattle and grain, if cultivated, by two hundred families, which they will, at their expense, transport there; showing, also, other advantages that will result in favor not only of the other inhabitants already established and living in the city of St. Augustine, but likewise of the Creek and Seminole Indians on the boundaries of that country, provided that the said tract of land be granted unto them, with an absolute dominion thereon, it consisting of four leagues of ground to each point of the compass reckoned from the aforesaid establishment of Alachua, which is to be fixed as the central point: which petition having, by my decree of the 12th instant, been referred to the captain of infantry, Don Vincente Sebastian Pintado, Surveyor General of the Floridas, he returned it, on the 15th, with the requisite explanation, advancing the most solid reason to show and demonstrate how convenient and useful it would be to encourage the settling of that province without any expense of the royal treasury, and to accept the proposals of the concerned on account of the importance of the undertaking, and of the great expenses they must make in order to put it into execution. In consequence thereof, and by a decree of the same day, the aforesaid petition and report were passed to the inspection of the King's attorney in the treasury department, who, in his memorial of the 17th, supported the petition of De la Maza Arredondo and son, founding his opinion on the royal orders for the encouragement of settling in these possessions of His Majesty, and consented that the said grant of the tract of land should be made unto them on the terms they propose: in consequence whereof I issued, yesterday, the decree, as follows:

"These proceedings being examined, in consequence, and by virtue of, the royal order of the 3d of September of this year, by which His Majesty, appointing me to the superintendency of the two Floridas, has most expressly ordered that I should endeavor to encourage the settling of those provinces by every means that my prudence and zeal could suggest, in conformity with the opinion of the King's attorney, and the report of the Surveyor General of said provinces, the tract of land called *Lachua*, in the East Florida, is declared unappropriated, and belonging to the King. In consequence thereof, and taking into consideration the notorious honesty and fidelity, as well as the well-known wealth and other good qualities of Don Fernando de la Maza Arredondo and son, I grant unto them that piece of ground which they ask out of the said unappropriated tract of land, in full property, in conformity with the royal orders on the subject, and under the precise condition to which they are bound, there to settle two hundred families, and that they shall be Spanish, together with all other requisites already set forth, and that will be set forth, by this superintendency by virtue of the said royal order; and, also, that they must begin the establishment in the term of three years at furthest, without which this grant shall be void, and that the same must be understood, provided that it will not be prejudicial to the right of any third person, and more especially to the native Indians of that country that may have returned, or may intend to return to it, to cultivate the fields."

Let these proceedings pass to the said Surveyor General, to make the plan of this grant in conformity to his report, and to the extent of four leagues to each point of the compass, as herein granted, in rectilineal figure, with all possible clearness, in order to prevent doubts and lawsuits in future. All which being done, let a title in due form be granted, with the said plan annexed to it, of which a copy must be kept with the proceedings, it being understood that the three years as aforesaid for the commencing the establishment of the families must be reckoned from this day; and that, on the first families being ready to be sent, the concerned will lodge information thereof, with a list of the individuals, their birthright and employment, that the necessary orders and instructions be given to the Government and sub-delegation of the royal treasury in the East Florida, in order that His Majesty may be opportunely informed thereof.

The figurative plan, as aforesaid, being presented by the surveyor, together with the explanation of the survey and admensuration, it appears that the above-mentioned tract of land is situated in the East Florida, fifty-two miles more or less west of the city of St. Augustine, and about thirty-six miles west of the eastern shore of the river San Juan, bounded on all sides by unappropriated land, having in or about its centre the place known by the name of Alachua, which was formerly inhabited by a tribe of Seminole Indians that abandoned it, and according to the dimension and form set forth in the said plan, and the explanations thereto annexed; and taking it into consideration that the leagues used in that province consist of three English miles, and each of them of one thousand seven hundred and sixty yards, or eighty Gunter's chains, the tract of land granted as aforesaid, contains two hundred and eighty-nine thousand six hundred and forty-five English acres and five-sevenths of another, which are equal to three hundred and forty-two thousand two hundred and fifty arpents and one-seventh of another, of those in use in West Florida; the English acre being reckoned at one hundred and sixty poles or perches, and each linear English perch at sixteen and a half London feet, according to the use in the time of the British possession of that country, which has been since tolerated by our Government. Wherefore, and using the faculties which our lord the King (whom God preserve) has conferred upon me in his royal name, I gratuitously grant unto the above-mentioned Don Fernando de la Maza Arredondo é Hijo the number of acres of land above stated, in the direction, boundaries and distances, set forth in the figurative plan, of which a copy must be annexed to this title, that they may possess and enjoy them as sole masters thereof, and in the terms mentioned in my decree herein inserted. In testimony whereof, I have ordered this title to be given, signed by me, sealed with the royal seal of my secretary's department, and countersigned by the Commissary at War, Don Pedro Carrambot, appointed by His Majesty Secretary of this Intendancy, and sub-delegate superintendency.

Given at Havana, on the twenty-second day of December, one thousand eight hundred and seventeen.

                                                              ALEXANDRO RAMIREZ.

PEDRO CARRAMBOT.

The foregoing title was registered in the book for that purpose, in the office under my charge. Havana, dated as above.

                                                              CARRAMBOT.

        A copy: JUAN NEPOM. DE ARROCHA.

C.

[TRANSLATION.]

DON JUAN NEPOMUCENO DE ARROCHA, Secretary of the *Intendencia de Exercito*, (Intendancy of the Army,) general superintendency, sub-delegate of the national domain of this island and the two Floridas:

I certify that his honor, the intendant of the army, superintendent general, sub-delegate of the same national domain, has this day decreed as follows: "Having before me the information received at this office from the Senor *Gobernador* and sub-delegate of San Augustin of Florida, and in consequence of the instructions given him by this general superintendency on the 2d of October, ultimo, and attending to the reasons which the concerned adduced, Don Fernando de la Maza Arredondo and son, they are allowed *prolongation* of one year, which they have solicited for the object proposed; without any prejudice to their interest, let it be given to them, certificates of the secretary's office for the end and purposes which may suit their interest, and let this be communicated to the same senor sub-delegate for his intelligence; and, in conformity of this decree, I give the present in Havana the 2d day of December, 1820.

                                                              JUAN NEPOMUCENO DE ARROCHA.

D.

                                                              HAVANA, *April* 2, 1820.

The annexed memorial which Don Fernando de la Maza Arredondo and son, of this commerce, presented me, with the title of the concession of a lot of land which was granted them by this sub-delegate general superintendency in December, 1817, asks for prolongation of one year to accomplish or carry into effect the establishment of the families which he proposed, and it is convenient that your lordship inform on this particular point. I have, in consequence, so decreed it on this day, accompanying it with a certified copy of the title not to expose the original to the danger of the seas.

        God preserve you for many years,

                                                              ALEXANDRO RAMIREZ.

Don JOSE COPPINGER.

E.

                                                              ST. AUGUSTINE, *October* 23, 1800.

In your lordship's official letter of this current month, you ask me to inform on the subject of one year's prolongation solicited by Don Fernando de la Maza Arredondo and son, of that commerce, for the establishment of the families which he proposed in the territory of Alachua, which gratuitous concession, with a formal title, he obtained of that sub-delegate general superintendency in December, 1817. I must inform your lordship that, as yet, only the copy of the said grant has come to hand, but not the memorial of Arredondo which your lordship speaks of in your said official letter. I have to inform your lordship that I find no obstacle, or have no objection, that the said prolongation shall be granted, because, if this meditated establishment takes place, the benefits that will result from it will be considerable, and will further the prosperity of this province, which our Government so anxiously desires to promote.

God preserve your lordship many years.

To the INTENDANT OF THE ARMY, *Superintendent General of the two Floridas.*

G.

AFFIDAVITS.

Whereas, by the laws of the Territory of Florida, the judge of the circuit court is the only officer pointed out to issue a commission for taking depositions in suits not already commenced, and, as there is no such officer now in this circuit, the following depositions are, therefore, taken without said commission:

CITY OF ST. AUGUSTINE, *Territory of Florida:*

Personally appeared this twentieth day of January, 1823, before me, Waters Smith, mayor of the city of St. Augustine, Antonio Alvarez, who, being duly sworn, doth depose and say, that this deponent acted as chief clerk to Governor Coppinger, and was present at a talk held between the said Governor and some Indian chiefs shortly after the establishment made by Mr. Wanton on the Alachua; that the chiefs complained that white men had settled at the Alachua; the Governor replied that they were sent there by Mr. Arredondo, with his (Governor Coppinger's) permission, in consequence of Mr. Arredondo's having obtained a grant of the land from a person having more power, or a greater man than himself, meaning thereby, the superintendent of the island of Cuba and both Floridas. The Indian chiefs said, in substance, that they were satisfied, and would comply with the Governor's request, and not molest or disturb the white men.

And this deponent further saith, that this talk was carried on with the usual formalities observed on such occasions, the King's interpreter, Antonio Huertas, being present and interpreting. And this deponent further saith, that the Indians have abandoned the Alachua ever since the year one thousand eight hundred and thirteen, since that time having had no regular settlements on these lands. This information is obtained by means of the office of chief clerk to the Governor, and not from this deponent's having actually been on the lands.

ANTONIO ALVAREZ.

Sworn to before me the day and year first above written.

WATERS SMITH, *Mayor.*

H.

TERRITORY OF FLORIDA:

On the twentieth day of January, in the year of our Lord one thousand eight hundred and twenty-three, personally appeared before me, Waters Smith, mayor of the city of Augustine, Peter Miranda, who, being duly sworn, doth depose and say that, shortly after Mr. Arredondo had sent Mr. Wanton to settle in the Alachua, this deponent was present at a part of a talk held with the Indians by Governor Coppinger. The Governor directed the interpreter to tell the Indians not to disturb the white men who had settled at Alachua, as the land had been given to Mr. Arredondo by a man at Havana having more command than himself, and who had command also over him, (the Governor.) This deponent then left the talk, and cannot, from his personal knowledge, say what further took place; but Governor Coppinger afterwards informed this deponent that the Indians were perfectly satisfied that Mr. Arredondo's agent should remain.

PEDRO MIRANDA.

Sworn to before me the day and year first above written.

WATERS SMITH, *Mayor.*

F.

CITY OF ST. AUGUSTINE, *Territory of Florida:*

On the 25th day of July, 1823, personally came and appeared before me, Waters Smith, mayor of the city of St. Augustine, William T. Hall, who, being duly sworn, doth depose and say, that he is a subject of the King of Spain, and that, about the month of September, in the year one thousand eight hundred and twenty, this deponent entered into an agreement with Peter Mitchell, (who understood that said Mitchell, Arredondo, and others, were owners of a tract of land in Alachua,) to go himself, and employ others with him, to make settlements at Alachua on said lands; that this deponent, shortly after, proceeded to Alachua to view said lands, and, on his return, employed two men by the names of John Smith and Patrick Lannam to become settlers with deponent; that, on the seventh day of November, of the same year, the said party reached Alachua, and immediately proceeded to clear land and erect dwellings of the following dimensions: one of twenty by fifteen feet, for the two men and other settlers which deponent calculated to send on, and one other thirty by twenty feet for the dwelling of deponent, and for a store. While Smith and Lannam were at work, deponent returned to St. Augustine, having fallen sick, and continued indisposed for two and a half months. Early in January, of eighteen hundred and twenty-one, Smith came to town, and reported that the houses were finished, wanting only locks and hinges, which report being confirmed by Burges, a very intelligent half-breed Indian, deponent furnished Smith locks and hinges, and forty dollars in cash, for the use of himself and Lannam. That, on the recovery of deponent, he understanding that several other settlers, employed by said Mitchell and Arredondo, had made establishments at Alachua, on the aforesaid lands, some of which settlers being personally disagreeable to deponent, he abandoned the project and settlement. And this deponent further saith, that, during the time he was engaged in the above-mentioned settlement, he kept a diary of the occurrences, but which was destroyed by the rains and wet in swimming creeks: Therefore, in this deposition, he has not stated dates with precision, but to the best of his recollection. And deponent further saith, that the settlement made by himself, Smith, and Lannam, was about one and a half miles east of old Payne's town. And the deponent further saith, that he is not directly or indirectly interested in any lands or grants in the Alachua.

WM. T. HALL.

Subscribed and sworn to before me, this 25th day of July, 1823.

WATERS SMITH, *Mayor.*

J.

City of St. Augustine, *Territory of Florida:*

On the 7th day of August, 1823, personally came and appeared before me, Waters Smith, mayor of the city of St. Augustine, Thomas Brush, who, being duly sworn, doth depose and say, that he, with other settlers from New York, arrived at Alachua the beginning of January last for the purpose of settling; their expenses, as well as one year's maintenance, being borne by the Alachua Company. That the settlers or company have opened a road from Picolata, on the St. John's opposite Buena Vista, to Alachua, being a distance of about forty-five miles; they have erected eight bridges, and made the road passable for wheel carriages. That, on the arrival at Alachua of deponent and his party, they found the Alachua settlement at Micanopé consisting of thirteen houses, most of the houses about twenty by eighteen feet, two of which, however, were larger, one being forty-five by thirty, and one thirty-five by twenty-five feet. To the settlement have since been added twelve houses, and materials ready for ten more; and hands are now employed sawing timber, and arrangements making, and many of the materials ready, for erecting a water saw-mill. The settlement at present consists of the following persons, viz: This deponent, Edwards, Thomas Brush, Jr., George Downs, Sidney Haines, Ogden, John Smith Penny, Jacob Brandenburgh, Elisha Morris, Bonnell, Warburg, Chateauneuf, Moore, Levy, Edward Wanton, Elias Haines, Elihu Woodruff, William Wanton, and Dr. Kelly. The above persons, with their families, make in all forty-seven persons. There are three different plantations at the Alachua, and this present year there is planted, as near as this deponent can judge, about one hundred and fifty to one hundred and fifty-five acres. There are, in those three plantations, about three hundred acres of cleared land, and the settlers are about clearing land for twelve more plantations. That provisions from the seaboard to the Alachua, before the road above mentioned was opened, were transported at a very great expense; and deponent thinks that every bushel of corn must have cost, by the time it was delivered at the settlement, five dollars per bushel, and other provisions in proportion.

And further this deponent saith not.

THOMAS BRUSH.

Subscribed and sworn to before me the day and year first above written.

WATERS SMITH, *Mayor.*

I do hereby certify that the foregoing are true and correct copies of four depositions taken before me, having been this day compared by me with the originals.

In testimony whereof, I have hereunto set my hand and affixed the seal in the city of St. Augustine, at the [L. S.] said city, this eleventh day of August, in the year of our Lord one thousand eight hundred and twenty-three.

WATERS SMITH, *Mayor.*

City of St. Augustine, *Territory of Florida:*

On the 11th day of September, A. D. 1823, personally came and appeared before me, Waters Smith, mayor of the city of St. Augustine, Edward M. Wanton, who being duly sworn, doth depose and say, that, on the 16th day of December, 1820, he was applied to for the purpose of settling at Alachua; deponent then resided at Picolata, and on the same day started for *Volusia*, and there concluded an agreement with Horatio S. Dexter to go and settle on the Alachua lands; and as said Dexter had previously entered into terms with the Alachua Company to settle on said lands, this deponent agreed with said Dexter to go and settle there, and to participate in the agreement previously made between Dexter and the company; and, on the agreement being made with Dexter, deponent immediately began to make preparation for the settlement, and continued at Volusia perfecting his arrangements until the 8th day of April following, when he left Volusia, and, on the 16th day of the same month, arrived at Alachua, and has ever since continued to reside there with his family; also, deponent's son, with his family, and still resides there. And deponent further saith, that the Alachua Company still continue to carry on and support the settlement at very great expense and trouble; and the establishment has been progressing ever since deponent first became a settler, and at the present time consists of twenty-eight houses, and preparing to erect others; have dug several wells, and established three plantations, on which is about three hundred acres cleared land, and about one-half of the cleared land cultivated the present season. Preparations are making for eleven or twelve more plantations. The company have had a road cut from Buena Vista to Alachua, a distance of forty or forty-five miles. A number of bridges have been erected on this road, as near as deponent can now recollect, about eight or ten. A saw-mill is about to be erected, the materials being ready; the present population being about fifty. And deponent further saith, that, before the road was cut from Buena Vista to Alachua, it is his opinion that the cost and transportation of corn to the Alachua settlement would bring the price to five or six dollars per bushel, and every other article proportionally high.

EDWARD M. WANTON.

Subscribed and sworn to before me the 11th September, 1823.

WATERS SMITH, *Mayor.*

No. 11.

To the honorable the Commissioners appointed to ascertain claims and titles to lands in East Florida:

The petition of Moses E. Levy respectfully showeth: that your memorialist claims title to a tract of land, consisting of fourteen thousand five hundred acres, situated on the west bank of the St. John's river, at a place called Hope hill. The first line runs south 75° west, 176 chains, to an old path of the Chocochate Indians. The second line runs north 25° west, 520 chains, to a stake on a path of the Okelooka Indians, and is bounded as follows: on the north by the Indian path last mentioned, on the east by the river St. John's, and on all other sides by unseated lands; which title your memorialist derives from a grant made to Fernando M. Arredondo, senior, by Governor Coppinger, in virtue of the royal order of 29th March, 1815, who sold the same to your memorialist, and is the whole original grant. And your memorialist further showeth, that he is in actual possession of said lands; that he is a citizen of the United States, and resident of Meconopé, in East Florida.

Documents filed with this memorial.

1. Copy of title to F. M. Arrendondo, marked A.
2. Plat of survey, marked B.

Other documents relating to this claim will be found filed with a memorial of your petitioner, marked A. A. The papers alluded to are marked C, D, E, G.

Bill of sale.

Know ye, that I, Don Fernando de la Maza Arredondo, inhabitant and merchant of this town, do declare that I am owner and lawful proprietor of a tract of land containing fourteen thousand five hundred acres, situated in the province of East Florida; and that Don Fernando, of the same surname, my son, is owner of another tract containing thirty-eight thousand five hundred acres, situated in the same province; which two tracts of land are intended to be sold to the firm of Hernandez and Chauviteau, under the condition that, within the final termination of two months, there shall be presented to them the necessary authority for the portion belonging to my aforesaid son, as also his title of acquisition therein; and, as respects the land which is my own property, there having only been required to be produced the copy, (of the title,) attested by the notary, Don Juan de Entralgo, of the 9th of August, one thousand eight hundred and nineteen, it is presented to them, as also the map and explanation of the location and boundaries of both tracts. In which state the firm of Hernandez and Chauviteau agreed to my guarantee and security respecting my son, Don Fernando. There remained another difficulty to be got over somewhat greater, which was, to make it appear that no duties were to be paid thereon, for the reasons stated to the superintendent sub-delegate of the two Floridas, in a representation made to him on the 7th of July last; who, having taken all the necessary informations in the business, declared, by a decree of the 24th of the said month of July, that, in conformity to the proceedings, (as made out,) the matter should be sent back to the general administration, that a permit might be delivered as petitioned, with exemption from duties; and the only requisite that, on the delivery of the document, there should be a copy thereof given in to the Government and national bureau of Florida for the proper effect; upon view whereof, the administration aforesaid so determined yesterday, as will more particularly appear by the proceedings which are attached hereto upon nine sheets of paper, that the consequences which are just may ensue. And, in pursuance thereof, I declare for myself, and in the name of the said Don Fernando de la Maza, my son, on whose behalf, in the fullest manner, I give my voice and assurance, *derato et grato*, with an express denunciation of all laws upon the case, and which shall be cancelled upon a delivery of the power and title of ownership mentioned in the beginning, and upon these conditions I actually sell, and give in perpetual alienation to the firm of Hernandez and Chauviteau, inhabitants and merchants here, the aforesaid two tracts of land, the one, my property, containing fourteen thousand five hundred acres, and that of my son, thirty-eight thousand four hundred acres, both situated in the province of East Florida, having the bounds and courses appearing on the map attached to the proceedings, which are hereunto annexed, upon which also are found the titles of my property; and, as respects the thirty-eight thousand four hundred acres of my son, his title of ownership shall be produced at the end of two months, a little more or less, attached to the power, which is to be added with proper notification to this writing; which two tracts of land I transfer in favor of the aforesaid Hernandez and Chauviteau, according to, and in their present state, with all their inlets, outlets, uses, customs, and appurtenances, acquired and lawful, thereto belonging and appertaining, I and my son, Don Fernando, having possessed them free from all incumbrances, as I, the recorder of mortgages, do declare and certify hereafter, for the price and sum of twenty-five thousand dollars, out of which twenty thousand are appropriated for the land and sale of my son, and the remaining five thousand dollars for the land and sale of my own property; and of which two portions or amount of twenty-five thousand dollars, to which the price of both tracts amounts, as received in ready coin to my satisfaction, I renounce the proof, delivery, exception on account of pecuniary misreckoning, fraud, and other circumstances in the case, and do deliver, in the fullest manner, a formal receipt. Manifesting, as I do declare, that the price and just value of both lands is that already stated, and if they are worth any thing more, or may be valued above the contract, whatever it may be, I make of it to the purchasers a gift and donation, absolute, entire, perfect, and irrevocable, according to the right titles made out, with all recordings, clauses, entails, and requisites, for their better and necessary validity. In consideration whereof, I separate, quit, and transfer from myself and my legitimate son, Don Fernando, all title of property, voice, and appeal, useful possession, ownership, and other deeds, real, personal, lawful, direct, and indirect, which to the aforesaid two tracts of land we had and held in the part and portion which is set forth belonged to each: therefore, under the recited conditions and guarantee, I renounce and transfer them to the firm of Hernandez and Chauviteau, or to whomsoever may hold their power, that, as their own property, they may possess, enjoy, or alienate at their will by virtue of this writing, which I deliver them in testimony of an actual delivery, whereby is acknowledged their having acquired possession and holding the same without a necessity of other proof, from which I absolve them; and I bind myself to the security and validity of this sale with my present and future property, and by making a full guarantee for punctual fulfilment thereof, upon which I renounce all laws and privileges in my favor, which I moreover hereby bar. And we, the firm of Hernandez and Chauviteau, being present, do accept in our favor this writing, which is made to us of the aforesaid two tracts of land, for the sum, and in the manner which they are sold to us, and of which we acknowledge the delivery, with a renunciation of all the laws upon the case, and do deliver a formal receipt, dated in the ever faithful city of Havana, the 3d of August, in the year one thousand eight hundred and twenty.

I, the public notary, certify that I am acquainted with the parties conveying, who, moreover, ratified, delivered, and signed hereto, there being as witnesses, Don Rafael Garcia, Don Thomas Gomez, and Don Buenaventura Calvet, present, and residents.

　　　　　　　　　　　FERNANDO DE LA MAZA ARREDONDO.
　　　　　　　　　　　HERNANDEZ & CHAUVITEAU.

Before me:　CAYETANO PONTO.

Copy of the title of ownership in favor of Don Fernando de la Maza Arredondo, of fourteen thousand five hundred acres of land, situated to the west of St. John's river.

Don Joseph Coppinger, colonel in the royal army, civil and military Governor, and head of public finance in this city of St. Augustine, in Florida, and province, on behalf of his Majesty:

Whereas, by a royal order of the 29th of March, one thousand eight hundred and fifteen, his Majesty has deigned to approve the gifts and rewards proposed by my predecessor, Brigadier Don Sebastian Kindelan, for the officers and soldiers, not only regulars, but citizens and other individuals of this province, who united in the defence thereof in the time of rebellion. One of the said favors being a distribution of vacant lands, and in consideration of Don Fernando de la Maza having manifested to me the distinguished and extraordinary services which he has rendered in various employs, which he exercised with liberality and usefulness to the royal treasury, and in duty towards his King and country, as also in the defence of the said province when it was invaded in the year one thousand eight hundred and twelve, as appears more fully by the memorial which he has presented to me, dated the 21st of March, one thousand eight hundred and seventeen, in regard to which, and in consequence of the authority which I exercise, I have thought fit, by my decree of the 24th of the same month of March, to grant his request, whereby, as a remuneration of his said services, there should be awarded him a donation of thirty thousand acres of land, with titles of absolute property, which have been designated in three different places, and one of them consisting of fourteen thousand five hundred acres, is situated to the west of the river St. John's, commencing its measurement to the north by the old path of the Chocachati Indians, whose dimensions and boundaries are known in the following manner: The first line runs south seventy-five degrees to the west, measuring one hundred and seventy-six chains; the second line runs north twenty-five degrees to the west, measuring five hundred and twenty chains parallel to the river St. John's until it meets the road from the town of Okelawaca, which road from thence to the river forms the last line, and finishes on the same path of the Indians, as more fully appears by the plan made out by Mr. Andrew Burgevin, surveyor, dated the 5th of the present month, in pursuance of my decree of the 8th of June of the present year, authorizing him for that purpose, and by virtue of that which is granted by the aforesaid decree of concession of the 24th of March, one thousand eight hundred and seventeen; all which united proceeding remains in the archive of the present notary: Therefore, and in reference to the said worthy services, in compliance with the will of our sovereign, and of what is imposed by the laws for rewarding with distinction such as may be worthy, and in consideration of the said services, and of the persons who rendered them, I have determined to grant, and, in the name of his Majesty, and of the royal justice which I administer, do grant to the aforesaid Don Fernando de la Maza Arredondo the aforesaid fourteen thousand five hundred acres of land in the place designated, without prejudice to a third person, for himself, his heirs, and successors, in absolute property, and make out to him, as by these presents I do, the suitable title thereto, whereby I separate it from the royal exchequer, all right and dominion which it held to the said land, and do yield and transfer to the aforesaid Don Fernando de la Maza Arredondo, his heirs and successors, that, by virtue thereof, he may possess it as his own, use and enjoy the same, without any rent, with all its inlets, outlets, uses, customs, rights, and appurtenances, which it has held and holds, and of acquisition or in right thereto belonging, and may touch, and of his own free will, sell, cede, transfer, and alienate, as they may best think fit: to all which I give my judicial authority, as far as I can do, and of right ought, by virtue of what is set forth, and of the will of the sovereign.

Given under my hand, and countersigned by the underwritten notary of the Government and royal exchequer, in this said city of St. Augustine, in Florida, the 9th of August, 1819.

JOSEPH COPPINGER.

By order of His Excellency:

JUAN DE ENTRALGO,
Notary of Government and Royal Finance.

St. Augustine, Florida, *August* 9, 1819.

Conformable to the original remaining in the archives under my charge, to which I refer, and at the request of the party, do sign and subscribe this present copy on three sheets of common paper, stamps not being used.

JUAN DE ENTRALGO,
Notary of Government and Royal Finance.

Conformable to the originals remaining in the registry under my charge, to which I refer, and at the request of the party, I give these presents, at the ever faithful city of Havana, the 9th of August, 1820.

Correction.—" Los concessiones" testado is correct; " acordado" to be left out.

CAYETANO PONTON.

College of Notarial Scriveners of the Havana.

We, the subscribers, do certify that Don Cayetano Ponton, by whom this preceding copy appears attested, is also a public, faithful, legal, and confidential person, and to his acts there is and ought to be given all faith and credit in law and equity.

In witness whereof, we seal this with our national collegiate seal, in this ever faithful city of the Havana, on the day of the above date.

PHS. ALVAR,   (*Rubric.*)
JOSE NUNO DE CUETO,   (*Rubric.*)
MANUEL DE AYALA.   (*Rubric.*)

Faithfully translated from the originals in the Spanish language.   Certified at St. Augustine, East Florida, this 5th day of June, 1822, and the 46th year of the independence of the United States of America.

CHARLES VIGNOLES, *Public Translator.*

I certify the foregoing to be a true and correct translation from a document in the Spanish language.

F. J. FATIO, *S. B. L. C.*

St. Augustine, Florida, *March* 1, 1817.

Don Fernando de la Maza Arredondo, inhabitant of St. Augustine, and actually residing in the city of the Havana, through his son, of the same name, residing in this place, to your excellency, respectfully showeth:

That he has the honor of having served His Majesty in different employments and destinations, and particularly in the department of commissary of the Indians, without any salary, or any other emolument whatever, for more than twenty years, having discharged the duties of that office with the utmost exactitude, to the satisfaction of all the Governors of this place, contributing thereby to the peace and harmony which existed with those savages; with which commission, and that of the comptroller *pro tem.* of the royal military hospital of this town, which he likewise discharged for many years without any salary or emolument; which meritorious services have saved to the royal revenue many thousands of dollars, as is well known to your excellency, and to the public authorities of this place.

Latterly, after obtaining a discharge from these different employments, he separated himself from the service of His Majesty to attend to the discharge of his duty towards his family; he engaged himself in the fatiguing service of patrols, and aid-de-camp to the Governor de Estrada, in consequence of the invasion of this province, in the year 1812, and for want of officers for that service, in which he was occupied until the year 1813; when, having been elected by a majority of votes, with all the necessary solemnities on the occasion, elector of the parish and district of this said province, he was obliged to go to the city of Havana, and remain there as one of the deputies of the Provincial Junta.   To discharge the said duty he was under the necessity, as a loyal subject, to expend large sums, which he willingly did, in the service of his King and country, being well persuaded that he would be rewarded for it at a future period.

He has been informed that the royal order of His Majesty of the 29th March, 1815, directs that a remuneration of grants of land be given to all the individuals who were armed in the defence of their country during the insurrection which began in 1812; and as your petitioner is one of them, and is entitled, for this reason, to said gifts; as also being one of the oldest settlers, and having augmented his family and negroes ever since the cession of this province to His Majesty, and one of those whom the royal ordinances and laws recommend that they may be attended to, both in quality of first settlers, as also on account of his distinguished services, that he be preferred in the partition of lands; he therefore prays your excellency will be pleased to grant him, in absolute property, thirty thousand acres of land, to say, fifteen thousand acres to the southwest of the large lagoon known by the name of lake George, which survey may be so made that a creek of sweet water, situate in that place, may occupy the centre of the front thereof; and the remaining fifteen thousand acres, on the west side of the St. John's river, the measurement of which to commence from the old Indian Chucichatty path, opposite the site on which the firm of Panton & Leslie had their store established, known by the name of the Upper store, being at the south side of the great lagoon known by the name of lake George, and thence in line to run southerly until it completes the number of acres; and, as the actual circumstances of the province do not permit at present the measurement and chaining of said lands; and, at the same time, as the survey could not take place for want of surveyors, as Don George Clarke, named by this Government, has other occupations which give him no time to attend to it; he therefore hopes, from the justice of your excellency, that you will be pleased to suspend the acknowledgment of the titles of the property whilst the memorialist does not obtain the plats of said lands, in order that their situation and limits may be specified with exactness, for perfecting the location and situation of the same; and, in the mean time, the grant which your lordship may think fit to make him may serve as a title, under your decree, in continuation; for it is the wish of the memorialist that, when the same be given him, it may have all the requisites necessary; a favor which he hopes to receive from the justice of your excellency.

FERNANDO DE LA MAZA ARREDONDO.

To the GOVERNOR.

ST. AUGUSTINE, March 24, 1817.

In attention to the services which this party specifies, which are manifest and notorious, and making use of the power conferred on me by the laws and the royal will, I grant, in the name of His Majesty, and the royal justice which I administer, to Don Fernando de la Maza Arredondo, the senior, the thirty thousand acres of land he solicits, in absolute property, in the places he has designated, without prejudice to a third person; of which titles of dominion will be given as soon as the plats to be made by the surveyor be presented, serving, in the mean time, this decree, and an equivalent, in all its parts, which, with the foregoing petition, will be filed in the archives of the notary of Government and royal finance office, from whence the interested will be furnished with a certified copy of the proceedings, properly authenticated, and in due form, in order that this concession may be duly credited, and that he may be able to make use of said lands, and to dispose of them as he may think proper.

COPPINGER.

Before me,   JUAN DE ENTRALGO,
Notary of Government.

I hereby certify the foregoing to be a true and correct translation from a document in the Spanish language.
F. J. FATIO, S. B. L. C.

ST. AUGUSTINE, FLORIDA, June 8, 1819.

Don Fernando de la Maza Arredondo, Jun., inhabitant of this city, and in the name, and as attorney for his father, of the same name, now residing in the Havana, to your excellency respectfully showeth:

That, under decree of the 24th March, 1817, your excellency thought proper to grant to his said father, in absolute property, thirty thousand acres of land, in the two situations marked and designated in the certified copy which accompanies: And whereas, the unfortunate situation of this province have not permitted that said lands be measured and laid off by the Surveyor General, Don George Clarke, who had not time to attend to this survey, in consequence of his absence, having been and now actually occupied on other service for the Government in the northern part of this province; and as there is a favorable opportunity for your memorialist having the said survey made by Don Andres Burgevin, a person who, by special commission of this Government, supplies the place of said Clarke, and who has hitherto refused to travel to the above-mentioned place, fearing the hostile disposition of the Indians; all of which were the causes that hindered his said father from obtaining the titles of dominion and property which he is entitled to, ever since the above-mentioned date of the 24th of March, 1817: Therefore, your petitioner prays your excellency be pleased to authorize said Andres Burgevin, that he may proceed to the survey of said lands as is specified in said concession, separating from the second tract five hundred acres, which he will survey, commencing about one mile to the south of the old Indian path of Chocochate, in order that they may be made in three different surveys: that is to say, one, of fifteen thousand, the other, of fourteen thousand five hundred, and one, of the said five hundred acres; a favor which he hopes to obtain from the justice of your excellency.

FERNANDO DE LA MAZA ARREDONDO, JUN.

To the GOVERNOR.

ST. AUGUSTINE, June 8, 1819.

Let his request be granted accordingly; Don Andres Burgevin previously accepting the same, and taking the necessary oath, citing the parties to appear having lands adjoining.

COPPINGER.

Before me,   JUAN DE ENTRALGO,
Escrivano to the Government.

In St. Augustine, on the same day, month, and year, I notify the foregoing decree to Don Fernando de la Maza Arredondo.

I attest: ENTRALGO.

On said day I notified Don Andres Burgevin the appointment of surveyor made him, and, in consequence thereof, said he accepted the same; promising, under oath, according to law, to comply well and truly, and to the best of his abilities, said commission, and signed, of which I attest.

Before me,   JUAN DE ENTRALGO.

ANDRES BURGEVIN.

I certify the preceding to be a true and correct translation from a document in the Spanish language.
F. J. FATIO, S. B. L. C.

In the ever loyal city of Havana, on the 2d of November, 1820, before me, the notary, and witnesses, whose names will appear at foot, that the commercial firm of Hernandez & Chauviteau, inhabitants and merchants of this city, whom I know, and give full faith and credit, appeared before me and declared that they gave their full power, which by right is required and necessary, to Don Moses Elias Levy, inhabitant of this place; that, in the name of said grantors of said power of attorney to represent their persons, rights, and actions, may dispose, at the highest price which at the time of sale may be offered, fifty-two thousand nine hundred acres of land, the property of said grantors, which they purchased in two lots, comprising, the one of fourteen thousand five hundred acres, the other, of thirty-eight thousand four hundred acres, situated in the province of East Florida, under the limits and boundaries which the surveys set forth, attached to the documents and bill of sale which Don Fernando de la Maza Arredondo made in this office the 3d August, in this present year, and by which said attorney will be guided in giving the competent bill of sale of said fifty-two thousand nine hundred acres of land, under the clauses, renunciations, cessions, obligations, and requisites, which may be required for its validity and stability; all of which they now approve and ratify, as if they were personally present at its execution, disposing of the receipts thereof according to instructions, and, if necessary, requiring of Don Fernando de la Maza Arredondo the exact fulfilment of the condition pending in the said bill of sale, made to them on the 3d of August last past, without omitting the necessary judicial and extra-judicial proceedings or conciliatory steps which may be offered in the discharge of the duties which, by this power of attorney, are conferred on said Moses Elias Levy; being well understood that the omission of any precise clause or circumstance which, in this instrument, ought to be included, may not detain him from practising in all which may necessarily occur in all its incidents and occurrences which they confer on him, the said Levy, in the most ample and general form, without any limitation whatever, with ample power to judge, to take oath, to summon, to protest, to take exception, to appeal, to supplicate, to ask for terms, to abandon and separate, or to continue the same, as may best suit him; as also to substitute, to revoke substitutes, to name others, and exonerate them in due form; for the security of which they bind themselves, their properties, present or future, with an inserted clause of guarantee for its punctual fulfilment, upon which they renounce, from this time, when the occasion may offer, to realize the effects for which this power of attorney is given, all the laws and privileges in their favor and defence, and that which prohibits it.

In testimony whereof, the parties have signed this instrument before the witnesses, Rafael Garcia, Tomas Gomez, Buenaventura Calvet, present, and inhabitants.

HERNANDEZ & CHAUVITEAU.
MANUEL DE AYALA.

Before me,

Conformable to its original on file in the office of Don Cayetano Ponton, to which I refer, and in consequence of the indisposition of said officer, and at the request of the party, I give these presents, in the ever loyal city of Havana, this second day of November, 820.   MANUEL DE AYALA.

I certify the foregoing to be a true and correct translation from a document in the Spanish language.
F. J. FATIO, S. B. L. C.

This indenture made the 8th day of June, in the year of our Lord 1821, between Francisco Hernandez, of the city of Havana, in the island of Cuba, merchant, and John Joseph Chauviteau, of the same place, merchant, by Moses Elias Levy, of Philadelphia, in the Commonwealth of Pennsylvania, their attorney, duly qualified, constituted, authorized, and appointed by them for that purpose by a power of attorney, bearing date on the 12th day of November, 1820, of the one part, and Abraham M. Cohen, of the city of Philadelphia, merchant, of the other part, witnesseth: That the said parties of the first part, for, and in consideration of, the sum of $35,875 to them in hand, paid at or before the sealing and delivering of these presents, the receipt whereof they do hereby acknowledge, and themselves therewith fully satisfied, contented, and paid, have bargained, sold, aliened, transferred, conveyed, released, and confirmed, and, by these presents, do bargain, sell, alien, transfer, convey, release, and confirm, unto the said Abraham M. Cohen, his heirs and assigns, all that piece, parcel, or tract of land, situate, lying, and being in the Territory of East Florida, bounded as follows: situate on the west bank of the river San Juan, bounded on the north side by an old Indian path of the Chocochati Indians, and containing fourteen thousand five hundred acres of land, more or less, which said tract of land was surveyed by Andres Burgevin, surveyor, appointed by a decree of the Government of Florida, a copy of a draught of whose survey is hereunto annexed, marked A, reference being had thereunto, the boundaries, situation, and extent of the said tract will more fully appear; also, a certain other tract of land, situate, lying, and being in the said Territory of East Florida, situate on both sides of a creek called Alligator creek, beginning at seven miles west of an Indian town called Alligator town, (leaving the said distance of seven miles between the said Indian village and the now described tract,) being about twelve miles in length and five in breadth, that is to say, two and a half miles on each side of said river, containing thirty-eight thousand four hundred acres, a plan or draught of which last mentioned tract is hereunto annexed, marked B, by which the boundaries, situation, and extent of the said last mentioned tract will more fully appear, being the tracts conveyed by Don Fernando de la Maza Arredondo, on behalf of himself and son, to the said parties of the first part, by an instrument of writing, bearing date at Havana, the 3d day of August, 1820, and confirmed subsequently by Don Fernando, the son, together with all and singular the woods, under-woods, waters, water-courses, ways, houses, fences, improvements, rights, members, hereditaments, and appurtenances thereunto belonging, or in any wise appertaining; and the reversion and reversions, remainder and remainders, rents, issues, and profits thereof, and of every part and parcel thereof; and, also, all the estate, right, title, interest, benefit, property, claim, and demand whatsoever, in law or equity, of them, the said parties of the first part, and each of them, of, in, and to the same, and every part and parcel thereof, to have and to hold the said lands, tenements, and hereditaments, and all and singular the premises hereby granted, or intended so to be, with the appurtenances, unto the said Abraham M. Cohen, his heirs and assigns, to his own proper use and behoof forever; and the said Francisco Hernandez and John Joseph Chauviteau, for themselves, their heirs, executors, and administrators, separately and jointly, do covenant, promise, and agree to and with the said Abraham M. Cohen, his executors, administrators, and assigns, that they have not jointly done, committed, or suffered any act, matter, or thing whatsoever, whereby the title of the said parties of the first part to the premises, as above described, has been or can be impaired, weakened, destroyed, or encumbered, and that the said parties of the first part, each, against his own acts and deeds, and against his own heirs, and all person or persons claiming under him or his heirs, all and singular the premises, unto the said Abraham M. Cohen, his heirs and assigns, shall and will warrant, and at all times defend, by these presents.

In witness whereof, the parties to these presents have, interchangeably, hereunto set their hands and seals, the day and year first above written.
FRANCISCO HERNANDEZ,
J. JOSEPH CHAUVITEAU,
M. E. LEVY.

By their attorney,

The word " year" being first inserted in the second line.
Sealed and delivered in the presence of
A. A. BROWNE, and J. SIMON COHEN.

Received, on the day of the date of the above indenture, of the above named Abraham M. Cohen, the sum of $35,875, the consideration named.

M. E. LEVY.

Witness: J. SIMON COHEN.

UNITED STATES OF AMERICA:

Be it remembered, that, on the ninth day of June, Anno Domini one thousand eight hundred and twenty-one, before me, the Hon. Bushrod Washington, one of the associate justices of the Supreme Court of the United States, came Joseph Simon Cohen, of the city of Philadelphia, attorney at law, one of the subscribing witnesses to the above written indenture, who, being duly sworn, did depose and say that he was present, and saw Moses Elias Levy, therein named, sign, seal, and deliver the said indenture, as the attorney of Francisco Hernandez and John Joseph Chauviteau, for the uses and purposes therein mentioned; and this deponent, together with A. A. Browne, signed their names thereto, as witnesses thereof.

J. SIMON COHEN.

Witness my hand and seal the day and year last aforesaid.

BUSHROD WASHINGTON.

Recorded 18th January, 1822.   A true copy from the records in my office.
Attest: JAMES SCOTT TINGLE, C. C. C.

This indenture made the 8th day of June, in the year 1821, between Abraham M. Cohen, of the city of Philadelphia, within named, of the first part, and Moses E. Levy, of the said city, of the other part, witnesseth, that the said party of the first, for and in consideration of the sum of $35,875, to him in hand paid at or before the sealing and delivery of these presents, the receipt whereof is hereby acknowledged, have bargained, sold, aliened, and confirmed, and by these presents do bargain, sell, alien, assign, convey, release, and confirm unto the said Moses Elias Levy, his heirs and assigns, those two several tracts or pieces of land described and contained in the within deed, with all and singular the appurtenances and hereditaments belonging, or anywise appertaining, and the reversion and reversions, remainder and remainders, rents, issues, and profits thereof, and every part thereof, and the estate, right, title, interest, benefit, claim, and demand, whatsoever, in law and equity, of him, the said party of the first part, of, in, and to the same, and every part thereof, to have and to hold the same, and all and singular the premises hereby granted, or intended so to be, with the appurtenances, unto the said Moses Elias Levy, his heirs and assigns, to his own proper use and behoof forever; and the said Abraham M. Cohen, for himself, his heirs, executors, and administrators, doth covenant, promise, and agree to and with the said Moses Elias Levy, his executors and administrators, and assigns, that he has not done, committed, or suffered any act, matter, or thing, whatsoever, whereby the title of the said party of the first part, to the premises, as above described and conveyed, has been, or can be, weakened, impaired, destroyed, or encumbered; and that he, against his heirs, and all person or persons claiming under him or them, all and singular the premises unto the said Moses Elias Levy, his heirs and assigns, shall and will warrant and at all times defend by these presents.

In witness whereof, the said Abraham M. Cohen hath hereunto set his hand and seal the day and year first above written.

ABRAHAM MYERS COHEN.

Sealed and delivered in the presence of
A. A. BROWNE and J. SIMON COHEN.

Received, on the day of the date of the above indenture, of the above named Moses Elias Levy, the sum of $35,875, the consideration above named.

ABRAHAM MYERS COHEN

UNITED STATES OF AMERICA:

Be it remembered, that, on the 9th day of June, Anno Domini eighteen hundred and twenty-one, before me, the Hon. Bushrod Washington, one of the associate justices of the Supreme Court of the United States, came Joseph Simon Cohen, of the city of Philadelphia, attorney at law, one of the subscribing witnesses to the preceding indenture, who, being duly sworn, did depose and say that he was present, and saw Abraham M. Cohen, the grantor therein named, sign, seal, and deliver the said indenture as his own act and deed, for the use and purposes therein mentioned; and that this deponent, together with A. A. Browne, signed their names thereto, as witnesses thereof.

J. SIMON COHEN.

Witness my hand and seal the day and year last aforesaid.

BUSHROD WASHINGTON.

Recorded the 18th January, 1822.   A true copy from the records in my office.
Attest: JAMES SCOTT TINGLE, C. C. C.

Don Andres Burgevin, as surveyor, appointed by a decree of this Government, made the 8th of June of the present year, in favor of the interested:

I certify that I have measured and laid off to Don Fernando de la Maza Arredondo, Sen., a tract of land containing fourteen thousand five hundred acres, situated on the west bank of the river St. John's, beginning on its north side, by the old Indian road to Chocochati, and being conformable, in its other points, to the preceding plat. [See plate 7.]

In witness whereof, I give the present, which I sign in St. Augustine, Florida, the 5th August, 1819.

ANDRES BURGEVIN.

A copy of its original, to which I refer.

ANDRES BURGEVIN.

Dr.   *Messrs. Hernandez and Chauviteau, in account with Fernando de la Maza Arredondo.*   Cr.

1820, August 3. To a tract of land, consisting of thirty-eight thousand four hundred acres, in East Florida, on the margin of the creek known by the name of Alligator creek, belonging to my son, of the same name, as appears by the indenture and bill of sale in the office of Panton, the notary public, of this date, which expresses having been sold for $20,000, but in reality for - - - - -	$25,000	By M. E. Levy's order on said gentlemen, dated the 10th May, and paid by the said gentlemen, - - -	$5,000
To fourteen thousand five hundred acres of land, situated on the banks of the river St. John's, of said province, in the old Indian tract, or road of Chocochati, belonging to me, for the amount of $10,875, although, in the said sale, appears to have been sold but for $5,000 - - -	10,875	By do. of this day's date, - - -	5,000
		By 15,000 lbs. copper leaches or boilers, which I have received, - - -	15,000
		By M. E. Levy's note, payable in one and two years after the United States of America taking possession of said province, free of any responsibility of said Messrs. Hernandez and Chauviteau, - - -	10,875
	$35,875		$35,875

Havana, *August 3, 1820.*

(Duplicate.)   FERNANDO DE LA MAZA.

St. Augustine, *December 17, 1823.*

I certify the above to be a true translation of an account current in the Spanish language.

F. J. FATIO, *S. B. L. C.*

Moses E. Levy *vs.* United States.

Evidence of Thomas Murphy.

Question. How long have you been acquainted with the settlement of Alachua?

Answer. I have been on the land in 1821. I have been previously acquainted with the circumstances of the settlement in February of the same year, and was employed by Mr. Mitchell, one of the owners, and Mr. Dexter, agent, to keep the books relative to this settlement.

Question. Do you know when Mr. Dexter was engaged to promote that settlement?

Answer. The 1st of November, 1820, as far as I recollect, he was engaged by Mr. Mitchell to make a settlement at Alachua, but would be more certain by referring to his books.

Question. Were any other persons engaged at the same time?

Answer. Not in December, but in February Mr. Wanton was engaged by Mr. Dexter, on the part of Mr. Mitchell; and afterwards, and in March of the same year, by Mr. Arredondo, confirmed the said nomination.

Question. How do you know of such arrangements, and Mr. Arredondo's agreement to it?

Answer. I was present at Volusia when Mr. Dexter engaged Mr. Wanton. Mr. Arredondo's assent became acquainted with by correspondence from himself.

Question. Do you know what powers Mr. Mitchell gave Mr. Dexter?

Answer. I do not know whether he gave him any more powers than to effect a settlement at Alachua, with the consent of the Indians.

Question. Was it to induce others to go to the land?

Answer. I do not know, at that time; but subsequently, and ever since, that Mr. Mitchell approved of the employment of Mr. Dexter, of myself.

Question by Mr. Hamilton. How long did you stay at Alachua, and at what time did you go there?

Answer. I went in August, 1821; staid there until the spring of 1822. Have not been there since.

Question. Do you consider yourself a settler there? Answer. I do not.

Question. Were you, at the time, a Spanish subject? Did you make a settlement of yourself at the time?

Answer. I did not.

Question. Was there a settlement there the first time you went? Answer. There was.

Question. Describe it.

Answer. There were about eight buildings; one large log house, used as a lodging house, a trading store with the Indians, a corn house, a kitchen, and two negro cabins. The second time there were very little alterations, except some additional negro houses.

Question. Was Mr. Wanton a Spanish subject? Answer. He was.

Question. Had he any family?

Answer. He had a son the first time I was there, and in November following his —— came there as I was about leaving the settlement.

Question. Have they remained there since? Answer. I believe they have.

Question. Did Mr. Wanton go there to make a settlement, or trade with the Indians?

Answer. To make a settlement.

Question. Did Mr. Wanton do any thing but trade with the Indians?

Answer. He cleared and cultivated part of a field, and introduced stock there.

Question. Had he any negroes?

Answer. He had about seven or eight the first time; I found that he had cleared, when I went there in August, the field.

Question. Was any arrangement made by the Indians to permit Mr. Dexter and Mr. Wanton to make this settlement? What was the nature of the arrangement? Answer. As far as I know, to cultivate and establish.

Question. What was the establishment? Answer. Principally a trading establishment, and to cultivate the land.

Question. Who were the Indians?

Answer. One of King Hijah's sons, John Hicks, Osecke, Latake, and others that I do not recollect.

Question. Was Micanope or Jumper there? Answer. Neither.

Question. Did Micanope or Jumper ever approve of the settlement?

Answer. Does not recollect whether they approved of it. Has frequently heard them speak, and never heard them speak as regards the settlement.

Question. Was Mr. Dexter there the first time you went? Answer. Yes.

Question. Did you see Mr. Dexter the first time you went?

Answer. I did. He, Mr. Dexter, never lived there permanently.

Question. What did Mr. Dexter do?

Answer. I have seen him assist Mr. Wanton in the store, and also in making arrangements for the reception of the Indian agent, bringing up provisions from the river St. John's to the Alachua settlement.

Question. Did Mr. Dexter never build a house there? Answer. Never, to my knowledge.

Question. Where is the place of residence of Mr. Dexter? Answer. At Volusia, and occasionally in town.

Question. Are you certain Mr. Dexter was employed to make a settlement on account of the Alachua proprietors?

Answer. I am positive he did.

Question. Do you not know that he went there for the purpose of making the settlement, and, at the same time, had a trading house? Was the said store for himself, or the Alachua concern?

Answer. I conceive it was on account of the Alachua concern.

SATURDAY, *December* 20, 1823.

Mr. Murphy re-examined by Mr. Hamilton.

Question. Have you ever understood that Mr. Dexter had an Indian title to this land? Answer. I have.

Question. Have you seen it?

Answer. I have not. I have seen a copy of a relinquishment of the Indians of said lands in favor of Dexter, as agent of Arredondo & son.

Question. Who do you understand were the witnesses to said contract?

Answer. Edward Wanton, William M. Gibson, and William Wanton.

Question. Do you know whether these persons are interested in this grant?

Answer. Mr. E. Wanton is interested in the grant.

Question. Was there any difficulty in making this settlement?

Answer. It was considered dangerous at that time.

Question. After obtaining permission from the Indians, do you imagine it was dangerous?

Answer. I imagine not.

Question. Did you understand why the settlement was not commenced before? Answer. No.

Question. Was either of the Arredondos residents of this Territory at the time of the settlement?

Answer. Fernando Arredondo, Jun.

Question. Were any Spanish families introduced, antecedent to 1822, into this Territory, for this settlement?

Answer. I do not know; I never understood that there were.

Question. Are the Arredondos men of large property? Answer. I do not know.

Question. Did you understand that the Arredondos owned large grants, other than this?

Answer. Merely from general rumor.

Question. Did you understand that those grants were antecedent to this grant? Answer. I know nothing of it.

Question. Do you understand that Mr. Dexter makes an adverse claim to this grant? Answer. I have.

Question. When did you come to this province? Answer. In May or June, 1818.

Question. Were any attempts made to settle the Alachua at that time? Answer. None that I know of.

Question. Did you ever hear of the Alachua grant before you were engaged to settle it? Answer. No, never.

Question. Did you ever understand from Messrs. Dexter, Mitchell, and others, that it was necessary to commence the settlement in order to save the grant?

Answer. No; I did not.

Question. Was there not a great deal of anxiety expressed on the occasion?

Answer. Mr. Mitchell wrote to Mr. Dexter on the occasion.

Question. When did the settlement commence? Answer. In April, 1821.

Question by Mr. Lancaster. Might there not, as far as you know, have been improvements at Alachua previous to 1821?

Answer. There might.

Question. Do you know whether Mr. Dexter was a Spanish subject at the time he was employed to make this settlement?

Answer. He was.

Question. Do you know whether Mr. Dexter was to settle on the land by agreement with the proprietors?

Answer. I do not.

Testimony of Hipolite Chateauneuf.

Question by claimant. Are you established at Alachua? Answer. I am.

Question. How long have you been established? Answer. One year.

Question. From whence came you? Answer. From France.

Question. From what part of the United States? Answer. From Delaware county, State of New York.

Question. By whom were you engaged to come to this country? Answer. By Mr. Levy, now present.

Question. How long are you from France? Answer. Six years.

Question. Were you in this country all that time? Answer. No, in the United States.

Question. Did any other persons come with you from New York to Alachua?

Answer. Yes, twenty-seven or twenty-eight.

Question. For what purpose did you come to Alachua?

Answer. To cultivate the olive, vine, and other productions of the south of France.

Question. Who paid your expenses?

Answer. Mr. Levy paid my expenses from the north, as well as the persons who came with me.

Question. Do you know what were the expenses of yourself and other persons from New York to Alachua?

Answer. I do not, but imagine them to be very great.

Question. Were not you and the other settlers engaged as permanent settlers? Answer. We were.

Question. How have you all been supported at Alachua?

Answer. By provisions principally furnished by Mr. Levy.

Question. Has not the maintenance of the settlement been very expensive? Answer. Yes, very expensive.

Question. For what purpose do you leave the Territory?

Answer. For the purpose of bringing my family and two other French families.

Question. How many houses are there built at Alachua?

Answer. There are about twenty finished, and about as many not.

Question. How many persons are there at the establishment? Answer. About fifty odd, white and black.

Question. How many negroes are there? Answer. Seventeen or eighteen.

Question. Do you know that there are a great number of families in Europe engaged to come to Alachua?

Answer. I have understood it from Mr. Levy and a Mr. Warburg.

Question. Where is Mr. Warburg from? Answer. From Hamburg.

Question. When did Mr. Warburg arrive at the settlement? Answer. At the same time I did.

Question. Are the settlers now at Alachua engaged in clearing and making new settlements?

Answer. Yes, certainly.

Question. About what quantity of land is there cleared? Answer. About seven or eight hundred acres.

Question. How many acres of land have there been cultivated this year?

Answer. I cannot say, but believe about two hundred.

Question. How many acres have the settlers cleared? Answer. Mr. Levy has about one hundred and twenty.

MONDAY, *December* 22, 1823.

Testimony of Mr. Alvarez.

Question by claimant's attorney. Do you know the signature, now before you, of Juan Nepomuceno de Arrocha?

Answer. I am acquainted, as clerk, with the signature of *Arocha*, and, to the best of my knowledge, believe it to be the same.

Question. Were all the acts sent by him to this office sent enclosed with acts of the Intendant, or were they sometimes sent without them?

Answer. They were generally sent enclosed in official letters of the Intendant, and at others without.

Question. When they were sent without letters of the Intendant, were they regarded as evidence? Was it customary to receive a certificate without a seal of office? Answer. Yes; the secretary has no seal of office.

Question by Mr. Hamilton. Has the Intendant any seal of office?

Answer. I am not certain whether it was a public or private seal.

Question. Has the Intendant a seal he affixes to public papers? Answer. He does.

Question. Does he affix it to royal orders? Answer. No.

Question. To what does he affix the seal of office?

Answer. To patents, grants; and the secretary has no right to place the seal of the Intendant to any document.

Question. Whose duty was it to promulgate the royal orders to the Governor of Florida?

Answer. The secretary issued the royal orders, and the Intendant enclosed them to the Governors.

Mr. Alvarez states that, if the secretary had affixed the Intendant's seal to any certificate of his own, it would have been rejected.

Testimony of John Cavedo.

Question by attorney of claimant. When were you last in Havana?

Answer. About the month of February or March, 1823.

Question. Do you know the signature of the secretary of the Intendancy?

Answer. Yes; I have seen the signature both in the Havana and at St. Augustine; have seen his signature in the notary public's office and custom-house.

Question. Did you know Arrocha as secretary of the Intendancy? Answer. I did.

Question. Have you seen him at his office?

Answer. I have; I never spoke to him, and have seen him at his table writing; I have never seen any document, bearing his signature, in his office.

Question. Was it not a matter of public notoriety that he was the secretary of the Intendancy at Havana?

Answer. Yes.

Question. Was the Intendant in the office at the same time you were there?

Answer. No; he had a separate office.

Question. Did you understand that the secretary acted of his own will, or under the direction of the Intendant?

Answer. I never understood that he had powers separate from those of the Intendant.

Question. Those papers you have seen in the custom-house with Arrocha's signature, were they sent there by him or the Intendant?

Answer. In letters of the Intendant.

Mr. Gomez's testimony.

Question. Is that the signature of Mr. Arrocha? Answer. It is, to the best of my knowledge.

WEDNESDAY, *December* 24, 1823.

George J. F. Clarke, being introduced and sworn, was examined by claimant's counsel.

Question. What was the state of the Seminole nation, in the neighborhood of Alachua, in the years 1818, 1819, 1820; whether disturbed or not? and, if so, the causes of disturbance?

Answer. General Jackson's army broke up at Micasooky town, on the borders of Florida, in May, 1818; the army then progressed east of the town of Suwanee, lying northwest of the centre of Alachua about thirty miles, which they broke up. The Indians, in consequence of which, were dispersed in small parties, and were scattered over East Florida, as far as Indian river and the seaboard. With these circumstances I became acquainted from report. I am unacquainted with them myself. I am not certain with regard to the distance from Alachua to the *Suwanee*. The Indians were dispersed in small marauding parties, and it was considered dangerous to go among them. This was the state of affairs, more or less, until the late transfer of this country to the American Government.

Question. Did the unsettled state of affairs in Spain, in 1818, 1819, 1820, cause any degree of stagnation in the business generally in this Territory?

Answer. Florida has been upon the decline from the revolution in France, and at this period was at a very low ebb; so low, indeed, that it scarcely could have been worse.

Question. Was not the Government of this Territory jeopardized or enfeebled by the unsettled state of Spain?

Answer. The Government was almost destitute, at that period, of funds and military, and unable to protect those who were at a distance from the town.

Question. Were not the enterprise and exertions of the inhabitants of this Territory, at that time, very much cramped and paralyzed in consequence of these causes?

Answer. The efforts of the inhabitants were much enervated, in consequence of their political insecurity.

Question. Whether, from these causes, emigration from all quarters, and particularly from Spain, was not checked?

Answer. It was; and I believe from these causes. As for emigration from Europe, we seldom had much; but from the United States, from which we generally received emigrants.

Question. Was it not more difficult to get emigrants from Europe, under such a state of affairs, than if no disturbances or difficulties had existed?

Answer. It was.

Cross-examined.

Question. Do you think that this state of affairs would prevent emigration from Cuba to this country, even under the protection of some wealthy or powerful personage?

Answer. I really cannot say.

Question. Were the inhabitants of this Territory in the habit of travelling into the interior?

Answer. It was not customary; there was but little travelling.

Question. Why not?

Answer. Because, in the first place, they had no business to call them there, and there was danger, besides, apprehended.

Question. Was there any apprehension of the Indians by the inhabitants? Answer. There was.

Question. Were the inhabitants averse to making settlements upon the outskirts of the present settlement?—I do not mean insulated location among the Indians.

Answer. Yes. They were averse to being on the frontier, although there were some hardy few who formed a frontier, though none wished or was willing to go beyond them.

Question. What are the Spanish inhabitants in the Territory, emigrants of old Spain?

Answer. I do not know.

Question. Do you know whether they are few or many? Answer. I do not know.

Question. Do you know whether there are twenty or one hundred more or less, either one or the other?

Answer. I really do not know; I never made any inquiry.

Question. Have you ever resided in the city?

Answer. I have had occasion to be here frequently, but never for a long period at once since the year 1808.

Question. Have you not made it your study to gain an intimate acquaintance with the population and general resources of Florida?

Answer. I have, sir, until the change of Governments.

Question. Are you not the author of many pieces appearing in the Florida Herald, signed *A native Floridian?*

Answer. I am.

Question. Have you not published some pieces upon the subject of the Indians?

Answer. Some of my pieces have been published, but not by me.

Question. Have you known any emigration of Spanish subjects, not *Minorcans,* unconnected with Government?

Answer. Yes; from Cuba, who came upon a bounty paid by the Spanish Government.

Question. Did you know any of them?

Answer. I did; do not recollect the names at present; came here about 1800; their descendants have left this place.

Question. Do you recollect of any emigration from Old Spain direct, or from Europe, Spanish subjects?

Answer. I do not.

Question. Do you know whether it has been the subject of solicitude of the Spanish Government to increase the population of Cuba, Puerto Rico, and the Floridas?

Answer. It was. I have seen a proclamation in one of the publications of the United States, which was intended to induce persons to emigrate and settle in Cuba—did not obtain my knowledge of Puerto Rico from the same source.

Question. Was the Spanish Government jealous of the emigration of the citizens of the United States?

Answer. It was. At one time, about 1792, the Territory was open to all; afterwards a proclamation, about 1804 or 1805, prohibiting the emigration only of citizens of the United States.

Question. Was this order of prohibition enforced?

Answer. It was, until the cession, although there were occasional exceptions.

Question. Did not the revolution in 1817, under McGregor, increase the jealousy?

Answer. It did not.

Question. The incursion under McGregor was principally conducted by Americans, and principally conducted by them—was it not?

Answer. Yes.

Question. What was the conduct of the Spanish population at that time?

Answer. Generally in favor of the Government.

Question. Was the revolution in 1812 principally supported by the American population of this Territory, aided by the American army?

Answer. It was.

Question. Do you know of any American citizen who aided McGregor in his revolution?

Answer. I recollect but one only.

Question. In consequence of the revolution of 1812, were not bounties of lands given by orders of the King to such persons as remained faithful in their allegiance, and served the Government in some military capacity.

Answer. Yes.

Gabriel William Perpall, on part of the claimant.

Question by Mr. Lancaster. Will you state the situation of the Seminole Indians in the neighborhood of Alachua in 1818, 1819, 1820?

Answer. They were in a very disturbed and turbulent state. The Indian settlements having been broken up, and their towns destroyed by Jackson's army, they dispersed themselves over the country as far south as Indian river, and between that and Tampa, and on the coast.

Question. Were they considered as stationary? Answer. No; they were roving about.

Question. Was it not considered as dangerous, at that time, to go out to Alachua, for fear of meeting some of those roving parties of Indians?

Answer. It was; it was always necessary for the surveyors to take with them, as a safeguard, a *negro* to whom the Indians were known, and who was known by them.

Question by Col. Hamilton. What do you suppose is the number of the Spanish inhabitants, settlers, from Spain? Answer. I know of but three from Spain.

Question. Do you know of any settlers, Spanish subjects, from Spain, since the year 1800? Answer. No.

Question. Have the Spanish Government been jealous of the population from the United States latterly?

Answer. They were, I believe.

Question. What induces you to suppose so?

Answer. The Government could neither grant them lands, nor even allow them to take the oath of allegiance.

Question. What was the cause of this restriction?

Answer. The revolution of 1812 was one of the causes.

Question. Did the Government of this country entertain any doubts of its political security in 1812 or 1817?

Answer. I do not know.

Question. Did the inhabitants of this country, in the years 1817, 1818, 1819, from the insecure and unsettled state of the Government?

Answer. They did feel themselves insecure by reason of the incursions of these disturbers of the public tranquillity.

Question. Were the inhabitants of the country friendly to the Spanish Government in 1817, 1818, 1819?

Answer. Some were, and some were not.

Mr. Francis P. Sanchez examined by Mr. Lancaster, in behalf of claimant.

Question. Were you employed by Messrs. Mitchell and Arredondo for the purpose of furnishing supplies for the Alachua settlement?

Answer. I was employed in the last of 1820 or '21, by Messrs. Mitchell and Arredondo, to procure supplies for the Alachua settlement: I was busied, from the time of my engagement with Messrs. Mitchell and Arredondo, in furnishing supplies till the last of 1822, to the amount of four or five thousand dollars.

Question. What were the supplies which you furnished?

Answer. They were principally provisions; some few dry goods.

Question. Did you understand whether the supplies were for the purpose of making a settlement or entering into trade?

Answer. I understood that they were intended for a settlement.

Question. Are you aware of any other expenses incurred by the company than those in which you were concerned, and was the amount large or small?

Answer. As large or larger than those in which I was concerned.

Question. Were these expenses incurred during the time in which they were contracting their expenses with you?

Answer. They were.

Question. Who incurred them? Answer. Messrs. Arredondo and Mitchell.

Question. Do you know, of your own proper knowledge, that this settlement was made by Mr. Levy?

Answer. I know it only from my correspondence with Mr. Levy's agent. I had written to Mr. Wanton, Mr. Levy's agent, giving him directions concerning the erection of buildings, &c.: from Mr. Levy and from the agent I received letters, saying that the works and improvements had been attended to, and were progressing as fast as possible.

Question. How long were you employed by Mr. Levy to furnish him with supplies for his settlement?

Answer. From March or April, 1822, until some time in the beginning of 1823.

Question. What was about the amount of supplies furnished for Mr. Levy?

Answer. About fifteen or sixteen hundred dollars.

Question. Do you know of any other expenses incurred by Mr. Levy for this settlement?

Answer. I do: he has paid in my presence moneys to different persons for the settlement, besides not less than fourteen negroes, which I received from Mr. Levy for the settlement at Alachua.

Question. Can you form any estimate of what amount Mr. Levy expended upon the settlement?

Answer. I suppose he has expended from three to five thousand dollars, exclusive of his account with me, and the cost of the above fourteen negroes, besides stock sent there by Mr. Levy.

Anthony Rutant examined on part of claimant, by claimant's attorney.

Question. Did you go to Alachua last year to take charge of Mr. Levy's agricultural establishment there, and at what time? Answer. I did, on the 18th July, 1822.

Question. Was it your intention to establish yourself permanently there?

Answer. Yes, in concert with Mr. Levy.

Question. Be so good as to state whether, and if any, what articles you took there, and the amount?

Answer. As near as I can tell about seven hundred and ninety-nine dollars in value, of which two hundred dollars were in dry goods, six horses, and other articles of agriculture, made up the amount of about seven hundred and ninety-nine dollars, as per invoice, more or less.

Question. Will you state what was the state of the settlement when you arrived there?

Answer. There were about twenty-five acres cleared and planted in corn.

Question. How many negroes did you find there?

Answer. But one. Mr. Wanton, the agent, used occasionally to hire Indian negroes. There were two white persons employed there.

Question by Colonel Hamilton. How long did you remain there? Answer. Between two and three months.

Question. Are you a settler there now? I am not.

Question. Have you been there since? Answer. I have been there occasionally, but not as a settler.

Dr. William Simmons sworn, and examined by claimant's attorney.

Question. Will you be so good as to state generally what you know concerning the settlement at Alachua?

Answer. I think it was in February, 1822, I was there; there were then five, or six, or seven houses. Mr. Wanton was there, and established there, and I understood had been there upwards of a year. There were five or six negroes about the establishment. I remained there about a fortnight on my visit to that place. I observed, during my stay, several head of cattle belonging to the establishment. I was there again in the course of the last month; there were three additional houses; there was also an additional white family, a Mr. Brush, with whom was residing three white men, who, I understood, had come out as settlers. I was also at Mr. Levy's settlement, Pilgrimage, about three miles off. I do not recollect the number of persons there, but I should judge that there were thirty, about eight or nine of whom were whites. I observed five or six horses and three team of oxen, which were employed on the settlement. I did not see the rest of the stock. There was a range of tenements which would accommodate nearly all the persons there; besides which I observed a corn-house, stable, and an out-house, which served, I believe, as a negro house, besides a blacksmith's shop. There was a good crop of corn raised this year; quite sufficient, I should think, for the support of the whole establishment for a year.

Question. You travelled upon a road from Alachua to St. John's river, which road was made by the Alachua Company?

Answer. I did. The road must have been made at a considerable expense, as it extends for about fifty miles; the road being sufficiently wide for a carriage, and having on it nine bridges.

Question. From the information which you have been able to obtain, can you say what number of people there are settled at Alachua?

Answer. Upon the three settlements, Mr. Wanton, Colonel Haines, and Mr. Levy's, there were about fifty persons.

Question. Did there appear to be any preparations making for any other settlement?

Answer. There were two other settlements under way, having commenced clearing and cutting for the purpose of building: there was more than one family at each settlement. The largest portion of settlers is at Mr. Levy's, the next at Mr. Wanton's.

Question by Colonel Hamilton. What was your intention or motive for visiting that part of the country?

Answer. Merely from motives of curiosity, and having a desire to see the country.

Question. Had Mr. Wanton his family there in 1822? Answer. He had.

Question. Were there any families besides the one you have mentioned.

Answer. There were two negro families besides.

Question. What was Mr. Wanton's occupation?

Answer. He had the directions of the planting, and other concerns, and had a store for the purpose of trading with the Indians.

Question. Were there any other persons besides the negroes there?

Answer. The proprietors were expected, and had arrived, but merely to look after their concerns. I saw Mr. Murphy there?

Question. Do you think that Mr. Wanton was in Alachua for any other purpose than that of trading with the Indians?

Answer. I understood that Mr. Wanton was there rather for the purpose of becoming a settler under the conditions of the grant.

Question. Did you understand that Mr. Murphy was there for the same purpose?

Answer. No. I understood that he was employed by the concern as corresponding clerk. He was not established there; but, by engagement, he was to meet the proprietors at that time. At my first visit there was no other person established there but Mr. Wanton and some negroes.

Testimony of James Riz, examined by claimant's attorney.

Question. Were you not, some time ago, engaged to forward a settlement on the Alachua?

Answer. I was engaged by Mr. Peter Mitchell, of Savannah, in November, in 1820, to assist in promoting the settlement at Alachua, under the direction of Messrs. Arredondo and William T. Hall.

Question. When did you arrive there?

Answer. I arrived on the 5th of December, of the same year, at Picolata, and on the next day at St. Augustine; I brought a small schooner boat, of about five tons burden, laden with goods, for the settlement; said goods were shipped by Mr. Mitchell, and landed at Picolata under charge of Mr. Wanton, who was requested to take charge of them by Mr. Mitchell.

Question. Do you know the value of the goods?

Answer. I do not, but believe I have a copy of an invoice, or a bill of lading, at home. I have heard it said that the value of the goods might be about two thousand dollars. I know that some of the articles were sent to Alachua. I was engaged by Mr. Mitchell to assist in any way pointed out by Messrs. Arredondo and Hall. In January I became a Spanish subject. There was nothing actually done until the month of April, 1821; after which time, until the 17th July, I was engaged in forwarding supplies, consisting of corn, &c., from this place to Buffalo Bluff, and from thence to Alachua. I discontinued services on account of sickness.

Cross-examined by district attorney.

Question. Were the goods sent to Alachua not intended principally for the Indian trade?

Answer. They were not; the principal part corn, strouds, &c., a greater part of which was required for the persons employed at the settlement. Should application be made to Mr. Sanchez, he could give correct information upon the subject.

Question. Did you never hear the proprietors declare an intention of entering into trade with the Indians?

Answer. No.

Question. When you were first employed by the company, did they not state that they were anxious to have the settlement made as soon as possible, that the conditions of the grant might be fulfilled?

Answer. No. I understood that the settlement was made.

Examined by Colonel Hamilton.

Question. Did not Mr. Rattenbury engage you to come to this country?

Answer. He induced me to come, by giving me, in conjunction with nine others, five hundred acres of land.

Question. Was Mr. Rattenbury's grant a conditional one? Answer. Yes.

Question. Were you not engaged by Mr. Rattenbury to come to this country for the purpose of settling the land?

Answer. The conditions were, merely, that I should come to St. Augustine. I was induced to come to this country, and would have settled upon the lands of Mr. Rattenbury, could I have done so, but was prevented by the Indians, in consequence of which we purchased a lot of land on Picolata.

Question. Did your companions settle with you on Picolata? Answer. They did; there were six of us.

Question. Have you ever told any one that Mr. Rattenbury deceived you?

Answer. I think he did deceive me.　He told me that there were no instances of fever here, but my mother and father both died of it.

Question. You came on from Savannah in continuation of your original scheme from Liverpool?

Answer. Yes.　I came on in Mr. Mitchell's boat, and paid Mr. Mitchell ten dollars for my passage.　I understood that Mr. Alexander, Mr. Rattenbury's partner, or agent, had died a few months before in St. Augustine, which materially affected my affairs.

Question. Did you enter into any engagement with Mr. Mitchell in Savannah?　Answer. I did.

Question. What was the nature of that engagement?

Answer. That I should come on to St. Augustine, and assist in the settlement of Alachua.

Question. Did you consider yourself, from the time you left Savannah, as under the direction of Mr. Mitchell?

Answer. Yes; I was directed to apply to Messrs. Arredondo and William T. Hall.

Question. Did either of the Alachua concern repay you the money for your passage?　Answer. No.

Question. Were you ever on the Alachua tract?　Answer. No.

Question. Were you ever requested to go there?　Answer. Yes.

Question. To go as a settler?　Answer. Yes.

Question. By whom was this request made?

Answer. By Mr. Wanton, who wrote to me while at Buffalo bluff; but I was prevented from going from the nature of my engagements.

Question. Did either of your companions take part in the establishment at Alachua?　Answer. No.

Question. Were either of your companions included in your engagements with Mr. Mitchell, in Savannah? Answer. No.

Question. Do you not consider Mr. Rattenbury as bound in justice to repay the amount of your expenses?

Answer. I do not consider him bound, by our engagements, to pay them: for, should I obtain the lands, I shall consider him exonerated; but should I not, I shall consider him in honor bound to refund me the amount.

Examined by Judge Blair.

Question. Were you engaged by Mr. Mitchell, in Savannah, to come to this country for the purpose of facilitating the settlement of the Alachua tract?

Answer. I was.

Examined by Mr. Drysdale, for claimant.

Question. You understood that, upon your arrival here, Mr. Hall was sick?

Answer. I did; he was sick of the fever and ague.

Question. Did you not have occasion to pay the Indians in your intercourse with them?　Answer. I did.

Question. Did you pay them in money, or in corn, or other articles?

Answer. The payments were principally made in money; sometimes they were paid in corn, and other small articles.

Question. Were your engagements with Mr. Rattenbury such as to prevent your engaging in other employ-ments?　Answer. No, they were not.

Testimony of Andrew Burgevin—examined by Mr. Hamilton.

Question. Did you ever survey a tract of land for Mr. Arredondo on the St. John's.

Answer. I surveyed several; one of fifteen or sixteen thousand acres.　I am not certain as to the number of acres.　I measured the front alone with the chain.　The survey was not made according to the Government order, as Mr. Hamilton states it, one-third front and two-thirds back.

Mr. Cox, for claimant.

Question. Witness never was directed to survey the land in any particular manner?

Answer. I never heard that it was required that the land should be surveyed in any particular manner, except in case of Mosquito, by Governor White.　I, myself, never had any orders for a particular mode of survey.　I never saw any directions of survey.　My surveys have been always considered as correct by the Government, and titles given on them.

Question by Colonel Hamilton.　What proportion does the line upon the river bear to the back, or any reced-ing from the line upon the river?　Answer. Not quite two to one.

Testimony of George J. F. Clarke.

Question. Have you any written explanation of your orders of survey?

Answer. I have; and will present a fair copy on Monday.

Frederick S. Warburg's testimony.

Question. Do you know for what purpose Mr. Levy purchased this tract?

Answer. I do.　From a correspondence held by me with Mr. Levy since 1816, it was purchased for the pur-pose of settling it with certain families.

Question. Do you know whether Mr. Levy made any arrangements with those families to come to Florida?

Answer. I know that Mr. Levy did make such arrangements with some of them.

Question. Will you state at what time Mr. Levy first left his home for the purpose of purchasing or procuring lands for the families you speak of?

Answer. He left St. Thomas in 1816 to purchase lands for this purpose.　The lands were to be purchased in some part of the United States.

Question. At what time did Mr. Levy procure the land?

Answer. I think it was in 1820.　I procured this information from Mr. Delavente, in London, a correspondent of Mr. Levy, who had received letters from Mr. Levy; which letters I saw.

TERRITORY OF FLORIDA, *District of East Florida:*

Moses E. Levy vs. the United States.　Deposition of Warburg.

The examination of Frederick S. Warburg, on the part of the plaintiff, taken before Elias B. Gould, a justice of the peace for the county of St. John's, in said Territory, to be read in evidence before the honorable the land commissioners to adjudicate on the claims and titles to lands in said district of East Florida.

Frederick S. Warburg being sworn, says: In the fall of the year 1816, deponent saw Mr. Levy in London; that Mr. Levy informed deponent that it was his intention to settle a number of families in America.　In 1820

Mr. Levy informed deponent, through Mr. Delavente, that the families could now come out, as he had purchased lands in Florida; that Mr. Levy again sent to deponent in 1821, and engaged him to come out to this country. When deponent came out, he stayed for some time at the north to wait the arrival of several families who were also to come for the purpose of forming a part of the contemplated settlement; that, on the arrival of said families, deponent came with them to Florida; (say twenty-two persons, including colored people;) that the families who were principally relied on for the said settlement in Alachua still remained in Europe, with the exception of some who are now in the United States waiting for an opportunity to come. Deponent further states, that the number of persons now waiting in the United States and in Europe, who are expected to arrive at the settlement in Alachua to form a part of it, are from forty to fifty, and that engagements with them are of long standing; that, from 1821 to this period, deponent has been continually engaged in procuring settlers upon the lands of the said Levy in the Alachua, and is still in correspondence with individuals in Europe for that purpose; that deponent, from the knowledge he has of the original plan of Mr. Levy, further states that said settlement was to consist of about sixty families; that there are about five heads of families on Mr. Levy's settlement at the present time, and twenty-three souls, including fifteen slaves.

Upon the inquiry of the United States' attorney, deponent states that the reasons why the families have not arrived here before this, are the inconveniences of accommodation; for want of proper buildings, and other necessaries to render them comfortable. Deponent says that he has been acquainted with Mr. Levy since 1816; that he does not know whether he is a Spanish subject.

Being further interrogated by the plaintiff's counsel, deponent says that Mr. Levy has expended about eleven thousand dollars.

F. S. WARBURG.

Affirmed before me this 7th day of January, 1824.

E. B. GOULD, J. P.

On application of F. S. Warburg to correct an error in the deposition taken before E. B. Gould, Esq., the said Warburg being first duly sworn, says, that the twenty-two persons alluded to in the said deposition, were partly on account of Moses E. Levy, and partly on account of the Alachua proprietors in general; that the colored people joined deponent in the river St. John's.

F. S. WARBURG.

Sworn and subscribed before me:

W. FLOYD.

Francis J. Fatio, Esq., sworn, and swears to the hand-writing of Fernando de la Maza Arredondo, in an account current in the Spanish language.